Water for the Americas

The chapters in this volume are peer-reviewed editions of the papers presented at the seventh meeting of the Rosenberg International Forum on Water Policy, which was held in Buenos Aires, Argentina on November 15–17, 2010. The theme for Forum VII was Water for the Americas: Challenges and Opportunities.

This Forum was devoted to examine the water problems of the Americas and to identify water management experience in other parts of the world that might be useful in addressing the problems of the Americas. There was consensus among the participants about the need to work together to ensure that everyone has access to adequate quantities of healthy water supplies and to appropriate sanitation services.

This volume's approach is to identify different responses and policies that address common issues and learn from contrasts and experiences. The value and potential that this approach affords is that it provides critical judgments about what has worked well and what needs to be done to gain a better future for the Americas' water resources and society. Chief among the issues covered in the volume is serving the unserved. These issues are so pressing and urgent that any delays putting out new facilities in many rural areas of Central America may cost lives and reduce the outlook for children. Additionally, the volume makes clear that the outlook for the poorest and the future of hundreds of growing cities are threatened by climate change. This book looks into the future by analyzing present and relevant data, and gains insight from the different developmental stages of the hemisphere.

Alberto Garrido is a Professor of Agricultural and Natural Resource Economics at the Technical University of Madrid, Spain.

Mordechai Shechter is a Dean at the School of Sustainability, Interdisciplinary Centre (IDC), Herzilya, Israel.

Contributions from the Rosenberg International Forum on Water Policy
Edited by Henry J. Vaux Jr

Managing Water Resources in a Time of Global Change
Mountains, valleys and flood plains
Edited by Alberto Garrido and Ariel Dinar

Water for Food in a Changing World
Edited by Alberto Garrido and Helen Ingram

Water for the Americas
Challenges and opportunities
Edited by Alberto Garrido and Mordechai Schechter

Water for the Americas

Challenges and opportunities

Edited by Alberto Garrido and Mordechai Shechter

Routledge
Taylor & Francis Group
LONDON AND NEW YORK

First published 2014
by Routledge
2 Park Square, Milton Park, Abingdon, Oxon OX14 4RN

and by Routledge
711 Third Avenue, New York, NY 10017

Routledge is an imprint of the Taylor & Francis Group, an informa business

British Library Cataloguing in Publication Data
A catalogue record for this book is available from the British Library

Library of Congress Cataloging in Publication Data
Rosenberg International Forum on Water Policy (7th : 2010 : Buenos Aires, Argentina)
Water for the Americas : challenges and opportunities / edited by Alberto Garrido and Mordechai Shechter.
pages cm. — (Contributions from the rosenberg international forum on water policy)
1. Water-supply—America—Management—Congresses. 2. Water resources development—America—Congresses. 3. Water-supply—Management—Congresses. 4. Water resources development—Congresses. I. Garrido, Alberto. II. Shechter, Mordechai. III. Title.
HD1693.R67 2010
333.910097—dc23
2014001026

ISBN: 978-1-138-02584-4 (hbk)
ISBN: 978-1-315-77484-8 (ebk)

Typeset in Times New Roman
by FiSH Books Ltd, Enfield

Printed and bound in the United States of America by
Edwards Brothers Malloy on sustainably sourced paper

This volume is dedicated to the memory of
DAVID HARDING GETCHES (1942–2011)
teacher, lawyer, human being extraordinaire

At the time of his death David Getches was the Raphael J. Moses Professor of Natural Resources Law at the University of Colorado Law School. He served as Dean of the Law School for nearly a decade before stepping down to return to teaching and legal research. David was a superb teacher, and was internationally renowned as a legal scholar of both natural resources law and American Indian law. During his distinguished career he served for four years as executive director of the Department of Natural Resources of the State of Colorado and as special consultant to the US Secretary of the Interior. David founded and was the first director of the Native American Rights Fund in Boulder, Colorado, now the oldest and largest non-profit law firm in the USA dedicated to advancing the welfare of Native Americans and their institutions. David imparted wisdom, excellence, and a deep sense of humanity in everything that he touched. He was a regular participant in the Rosenberg Forum, beginning with Forum I, held in San Francisco in 1997, and was a keynote speaker at Forum VII in Buenos Aires in 2010. We will remember him fondly as a colleague and friend.

Contents

Illustrations

Figures

Tables

Contributors

Rosenberg International Forum on Water Policy

Henry J. Vaux Jr is Professor of Resource Economics, Emeritus at the University of California, Riverside. He is also Associate Vice President, Emeritus of the University of California System. He has served as the Chair of the Rosenberg International Forum on Water Policy since its founding in 1996.

Volume editors

Alberto Garrido is Professor of Agricultural and Natural Resource Economics at the Technical University of Madrid, Director of the Research Centre for the Management of Agricultural and Environmental Risks, Deputy Director of the Water Observatory of the Botín Foundation, and a Member of the Advisory Committee of the Rosenberg International Forum on Water Policy since its founding in 1996.

Mordechai Shechter is Dean of the School of Sustainability at the Interdisciplinary Center Herzlyia (IDC), Professor Emeritus of the Department of Economics and of the Department of Natural Resource and Environmental Management, at the University of Haifa, Israel, and the founder (1985) and Director (until 2010) of the Natural Resource and Environmental Research Center. He also served as Rector, Dean of Research, Head of the Economics, and the Natural Resource and Environmental Management Departments, and Chair of the Senior Faculty Association. In 2000–2005 he served as President of Tel-Hai Academic College in northern Israel. He headed Israel's National Parks and Nature Reserves Authority Council and the Israel Information Center for Climate Change Adaptation, holds a PhD in Agricultural Economics from Iowa State University (1968), and teaches and publishes in the areas of environmental and natural resource economics and management. He is a Member of the Advisory Committee of the Rosenberg International Forum on Water Policy.

Contributors

Patricia Ávila-García is a researcher in Political Ecology and Society in the Center for Ecosystem Research of the National Autonomous University of Mexico. She received a PhD in Social Sciences with speciality in Social Anthropology. She has received the National Award in Social Sciences from the National Academy of Sciences, and she has written and edited several papers and books on social–environmental issues.

David H. Getches was Dean and Raphael J. Moses Professor of Natural Resources Law at the University of Colorado School of Law in Boulder, Colorado. He taught and wrote on water law, public land law, environmental law, and Indian law. He received his BA from Occidental College and his JD degree from the University of Southern California Law School. From 1970 to 1976 he served as Executive Director of the Native American Rights Fund (NARF), a nonprofit law firm specializing in Native American issues. He joined the law faculty at the University of Colorado School of Law in 1979. He took two leaves of absence from the university, first in 1983–1987 to serve as the Executive Director of the Colorado Department of Natural Resources, during the administration of Governor Richard Lamm, and then in 1996, to serve as a special consultant to the United States Secretary of the Interior. In 2003, he was appointed to serve as dean of the law school. He died in July 2011, and this volume is dedicated to his memory (see page v).

Blanca Jiménez Cisneros is an Environmental Engineer from Mexico with a PhD in wastewater treatment and reuse. She is a full researcher at the Environmental Engineering Department of the Institute of Engineering of the National Autonomous University of Mexico (UNAM). She has authored more than 412 papers in scientific journals, books, and conferences. In 2009 she received the Mexican National Prize for Science. She was president of the Environmental Engineers' Association (1999–2000), and of the Mexican Federation of Sanitary Engineers and Environmental Science Association (2001–2002). She is the coordinating leading author for the Water Resources chapter for the 5th IPCC Assessment on Climate Change. In 2010 she was awarded the Global Water Award by the IWA.

Emilio J. Lentini is an economist, a Professor and Researcher at CETA (Center for Transdisciplinary Studies of Water), University of Buenos Aires (UBA), and a Member of the International Research Network (GDRI) "Water, Cities and Lands" (Wat-Cit-Ter) "Governance and access to water in the Americas" of the National Centre for Scientific Research (CNRS) of France and UBA.

Rob C. de Loë holds the University Research Chair in Water Policy and Governance at the University of Waterloo, and is Director of the multi-university Water Policy and Group (www.wpgg.ca). Previously he held the Canada Research Chair in Water Management at the University of Guelph. During the past two decades, he has written extensively about water security and related concerns such as source water protection, water allocation, transboundary water governance, and climate change adaptation.

Raúl A. Lopardo is a Hydraulic and Civil Engineer. Doctor, Mention Physical Sciences University of Toulouse, France. He is President of the National Water Institute of Argentina (INA), Professor of Basic Hydraulics at La Plata National University (Argentina), a Member of the National Academy of Engineering (Argentina), and a Member and Past Vice-President of the National Academy of Physical and Natural Sciences (Argentina).

Abel Mejía is a water consultant for international agencies and the private sector. Until October 2009, he was a Lead Water Engineer and Manager of water and environment at the World Bank. Mr Mejía is a Civil Engineer with graduate degrees from Stanford University, and advanced training from Cambridge, Harvard and ECLAC in Chile.

J. Michael Miltenberger is one of the longest-serving Members of the Legislative Assembly of the Northwest Territories of Canada. Mr Miltenberger was re-elected to his fifth consecutive term as the Member for Thebacha, representing the community of Fort Smith, on October 3, 2011. He currently serves as the Minister of Environment and Natural Resources, Minister of Finance, Chairman of the Financial Management Board and Government House Leader of the 17th Legislative Assembly.

Víctor Pochat is a Master of Science in Engineering, and International Consultant and Professor on Water Resources Planning and Management. He was formerly Coordinator of UNESCO International Hydrological Programme for Latin America and the Caribbean, and Coordinator of Case Studies on the La Plata Basin for the UN World Water Assessment Programme. In Argentina, he was Undersecretary and National Director for Water Resources, President of the Board of Directors of Hidronor S.A., and President of the National Institute for Water Science and Technology.

R. Maria Saleth is Director at Madras Institute of Development Studies (MIDS), Chennai, India. Earlier, he has been a Principal Researcher with the International Water Management Institute, Colombo, Sri Lanka. Professor Saleth works in the areas of water resource management, institutional reform, and agricultural development, and has published three books, five edited volumes, and several papers in journals and edited volumes related to these areas. He is also the editor of *Review of Development and Change*.

Robert W. Sandford is EPCOR Chair of the Canadian Partnership Initiative in the Support of the United Nations Water for Life Decade. Besides being involved in many initiatives across Canada, Bob is also a member of the Rosenberg International Forum on Water Policy and senior policy advisor for the Interaction Council, a forum of more than 30 former heads of state (including Jean Chretien, Bill Clinton, and Gro Brundtland) that in 2011 committed to addressing the growing global water crisis.

Tushaar Shah is an economist and public policy specialist, and a former director of the Institute of Rural Management at Anand in India. Over the past 30 years, Shah's main research interests have been in water institutions and policies in South Asia, a subject on which he has published extensively. His notable contributions have been in comparative analyses of groundwater governance in South Asia, China, and Mexico. More recently, his interests have been in comparative analyses of water institutions and policies across Asia, and between South Asia and Sub-Saharan Africa. Shah has also worked extensively on the energy–irrigation nexus in India. Shah was honored with the Outstanding Scientist award of the Consultative Group of International Agricultural Research (CGIAR) in 2002. His most recent publication is *Taming the Anarchy: Groundwater Governance in South Asia*, published by the Resources for the Future Press, Washington. Shah is a Fellow of the Colombo-based International Water Management Institute, and works out of Anand in western India.

Katherine Vammen is Deputy Director of the Nicaraguan Research Center for Aquatic Resources of the National Autonomous University of Nicaragua (CIRA/UNAN). She founded and coordinates the Regional Central American Master´s Programme in Sciences of Water. She is representative for Nicaragua in the InterAmerican Network of Academies of Sciences' Water Programme.

Preface

The chapters in this volume are peer-reviewed editions of the papers presented at the seventh meeting of the Rosenberg International Forum on Water Policy, which was held in Buenos Aires, Argentina on November 15–17, 2010. The theme for Forum VII was Water for the Americas: Challenges and Opportunities. This Forum was unique in examining the water problems of the Americas and identifying water management experience gleaned in other parts of the world that might be useful in addressing the problems of the Americas. The sessions illustrated how the water problems of the Americas are common problems, differing only in degree from basin to basin. There was unanimity among the participants about the need for all inhabitants of the Americas to work together to ensure that everyone has access to adequate quantities of healthy water supplies and to appropriate sanitation services.

Members of the Water Committee of the InterAmerican Network of Academies of Sciences (IANAS) were highly visible participants in the Forum. Representatives from Argentina, Mexico, Nicaragua, and Canada were among the paper presenters and chapter authors. All of the Academies of Science in the Western hemisphere were represented, and the Forum provided an excellent example of how scientists with differing backgrounds and from different countries can work together to fashion solutions to modern water problems.

The Rosenberg International Forum on Water Policy was created with an endowment gift to the University of California in honor of former Bank of America Chairman Richard Rosenberg on the occasion of his retirement. Chairman Rosenberg rallied the California business community to address the drought of 1987–1992 and has maintained an abiding interest in sound water policy and good management practices. The Bank of America had its origins in California and it was, for some nine decades, a historically important institution in California. The Rosenberg Forum is held every two years at different locales around the world. To date Forum venues have included San Francisco (USA), Barcelona (Spain), Canberra (Australia), Ankara (Turkey), Banff (Canada), Zaragoza (Spain), and Buenos Aires (Argentina).

Participation in each Forum is limited to 50 water scholars and senior water managers. Typically 25–30 countries are represented around the table. Participants are asked to read the papers in advance of the Forum and come prepared to engage in interactive discussions, which are at the heart of each Forum. Forum themes are identified by an Advisory Council, which provides programmatic advice and oversight. The editors of this volume, drawn from the membership of the Advisory Committee, were Dr Alberto Garrido from the Technical University of Madrid and Dr Mordechai Shecter from the University of Haifa. It is the hope of the editors and the Advisory Committee that the lessons emerging from these chapters will make a significant contribution to the resolution of some of our most difficult global issues.

Henry Vaux, Jr.
Chair, Rosenberg International Forum on Water Policy
Series Editor

Part I

Introduction

1 Introduction and overview

Alberto Garrido and Mordechai Shechter

Introduction

The Americas contain some of the world's sharpest contrasts in human development and economic wealth. Marked geophysical, climate, and hydrological differences are found not only between countries, but perhaps more markedly within each of the largest countries. With widely different historical and political backgrounds, all countries in the hemisphere face significant water challenges. Many of these are common, others are country-specific, and some are shared by two or more countries.

Shared interests have given rise to various international co-operative programs to address and diagnose water issues in the hemisphere (e.g. IANAS 2012). The Seventh Biennial Rosenberg Forum was held in Buenos Aires in November 2010 under the title "Water for the Americas: Challenges and Opportunities." The papers that were presented in the forum and make up the contributions of this volume provide the common themes and underlying processes that are ongoing, and reveal the coping capacity of social, economic, and environmental challenges in upcoming decades. This volume takes a different approach than other noteworthy and recent efforts to reach conclusions and inform the water policy agenda for the hemisphere. It sets out to address a limited number of issues and topics from America's Northern and Southern perspectives. Furthermore, considering the rapid and diverse institutional reforms that are occurring in virtually all 35 American countries, it has been considered instructive to add some of the views from another emerging continent in the world – Asia.

The volume's approach is to identify different responses and policies that address common issues and learn from contrasts and experiences. The value and potential that this approach affords is that it provides critical judgments about what has worked well and what needs to be done to gain a better future for the Americas' water resources and society. Some issues covered in the volume are so pressing and urgent, chief among them is serving the unserved, that days of delay in putting out new facilities in many rural areas of Central America may cost lives and reduce the outlook for children. Additionally, this volume makes clear that the outlook for the poorest and the future of hundreds of growing cities are threatened by climate change. The volume looks into the future by analyzing present and relevant data, and gains insight from the different developmental stages of the hemisphere.

The volume's main topics

The volume begins by asking whether and to what extent water scarcity is becoming an issue in the Americas. By all means, data seem to suggest that the Americas are endowed with abundant water resources on per capita terms. Abel Mejía (Chapter 3) reports that only Haiti, Barbados, and Antigua have less than 1,700 cubic meters per person, per year. And yet, it is difficult to find a country in the Americas that does not include regions and a significant percentage of the population whose water access is not threatened by climate change, environmental deterioration, or accelerated urbanization processes. Moreover, the region, especially Argentina and Brazil, is becoming a food basket of the world. The agricultural frontier is growing day by day in South America. The World Bank reckons that 28 percent of the world's land that is potentially arable and presently not cultivated (445 million hectares) is located in Latin America (Deininger and Byerlee 2010). But unlike Sub-Saharan Africa's 201 million hectares of available land, 53 percent of it is located more than six hours from the nearest market. In Latin America, only 24 percent of the available land is that far from the market. Irrigation is growing in Canada, Perú, Brazil, and Argentina, within regions where water resources are scarce, and the pressure to produce more will remain high with prospective high prices of the main commodities (OECD-FAO 2012). With adequate institutional conditions and sufficient financial resources, irrigation will likely grow in countries with abundant land and water resources (Central America, Colombia, Venezuela, Bolivia or Ecuador). FAO claims that irrigation could grow in South America by a factor 5 to 78 million hectares, 65 percent of which includes Brazil, Argentina, Mexico, and Perú.

The second underlying topic of the volume is the social problem of insufficient or inadequate access to safe drinking water and basic sanitation services. This is clearly the most marked difference among the countries in the Americas in terms of people's material well-being. In 2008, 20 percent of the population in Latin America and the Caribbean did not have an improved sanitation facility which guarantees that human excrement does not come in contact with people or that they need not defecate in the open air (IANAS 2012; see also Chapter 5 of this volume). Even in Argentina, with $17,376 of per-capita income (at PPP), only 47 percent of customers are connected to a sanitary network, and only 12 percent of the collected wastewater is treated before being returned to the natural source (see Chapter 4 of this volume; IANAS 2012).

The third cross-cutting issue of the volume looks at transboundary basins. The Americas have a number of the internationally shared largest watersheds in the world: Columbia, Rio Grande/Rio Bravo, Amazon, La Plata, and perhaps the largest internationally shared aquifer – the Guaraní. Significant progress has been made in sharing peacefully and cooperatively many of these transboundary basins. While issues and disagreements will always be there, even if they don't grow or exacerbate, most shared basins have international institutions that channel them to peaceful resolution. But transboundary issues also occur within nations, some with lasting and especially acrimonious developments. Two cases have been discussed extensively in the literature for their significance and sheer population repercussion: the megacities of Mexico D.F. (see Chapter 8) and the Los Angeles Metropolitan District. But a similar process is threatening the entire water supply system of the city of Sao Paulo, Brazil. These are three emblematic cases of mega conurbations that not only provide the living environment of tens of millions of people but hold some of the most competitive business and income-generating companies of their nations. Should water systems in the Americas' cities collapse or be threatened by a major catastrophe or hazard, the consequences would be unimaginable.

The fourth topic is idiosyncratic to the Americas: the issue of indigenous cultures and rights. In no other continent in the world has there been so much recognition and legal support to indigenous people's water rights. A lot has been written on the topic, especially in the United States and Canada, where Indian tribes and First Nations were granted water and land rights over significant areas of the territory (see Chapter 2). The topic is addressed in the volume by examining the role of indigenous knowledge. Greiner defines indigenous knowledge (IK) as:

> unique, traditional, local knowledge existing within and developed around the specific conditions of women and men indigenous to a particular geographic area. The development of IK systems, covering all aspects of life, including management of the natural environment, has been a matter of survival to the peoples who generated these systems. Such knowledge systems are cumulative, representing generations of experiences, careful observations, and trial-and-error experiments.
>
> (Grenier 1998: 12)

There is an obvious link between IK and the way and mode indigenous institutions are set up and operate. The volume provides space in two chapters for a reflection on the role in the Americas of traditional cultures and governance structures to manage water resources.

The last topic of the volume jumps to Asia to learn about institutional innovations. Asia's lessons are of significant value for the Americas, but especially for developing and emerging countries. It is much more densely populated, has grown more rapidly, has the largest irrigated surface in the world in absolute and relative terms, and has seen groundwater resource use expanding at a scale unknown in human history. Furthermore, the diversity of institutional responses to address water scarcity in both democratic and non-democratic regimes found in Asia provides a rich mosaic of experiences, each of which offers lessons to all countries experiencing rapid economic growth.

Structure and major themes

Following this introduction, forming Part I of the book, the volume is structured in five main parts (Parts II–VI), with a concluding chapter forming Part VII.

Part II, under the heading "Water Scarcity in the Americas," has two chapters. Chapter 2, by David H. Getches, looks at water scarcity issues in the Americas, from the Northern perspective. Because they are determinants of scarcity at local and regional levels and typically inextricably linked to one another, Getches identified and focused his chapter on issues of policy related to climate change, urbanization, groundwater, indigenous rights, and transboundary allocation as the most critical water problems in North America. Chapter 2 closely examines scarcity issues from the United States' perspective, describing the two principal allocation mechanisms prevailing in the states – riparian and prior appropriation – which have traditionally been applied in Eastern and Western states, respectively. And yet, increasingly important considerations of public interest standards are applied modifying the common law system (riparian), making the two canonical United States water law doctrines less distant than in the past. Getches claims that "all water problems are policy problems." Competing users, even if they share broad policy objectives, face conflicts because of unavailable resources to meet their demand, so regulatory mechanisms and economic incentives must complement self-restraint and conscientious users. Getches identifies six challenges for US water policy in the present day:

- climate change;
- urbanization;
- groundwater use;
- Indian tribes;
- environmental protection; and
- transboundary issues.

Getches takes on these six challenges to analyze the Colorado River. These six issues cut across the entire volume and receive close attention in subsequent chapters.

Chapter 3, by Abel Mejía, provides a comprehensive overview of water scarcity in Latin America and the Caribbean. One marked difference between the sub-region of Mexico, Central America and the Caribbean, and South America is that seasonality of precipitation is much strongest in the former than in the latter. Mejia distinguishes between water physical scarcity and economic scarcity, the latter being serious in all countries in the region, with the exception of Panama, Costa Rica, Ecuador, Surinam, and Uruguay. Many countries in the region have their largest share of population living in the most arid parts of the country (Perú, Mexico, or Venezuela). But the region's growth potential in irrigation and hydropower stands in contrast with very poor rates in waste water treatment, and water pollution, the vulnerability to serious floods in many areas, including Sao Paulo, Rio, and Buenos Aires. Prevalence of diarrhea in most of Latin America is comparable to that of less developed Africa and South Asia. Mejia claims that the actual drivers of scarcity are rapid urbanization and weak governance. The author finishes his chapter by identifying the most urgent policy reforms in Latin America and the Caribbean, and that includes bridging the gap in drinking water and sanitation services, and improving water governance. Numbers, according to Mejia, sustain a fallacy of water abundance and high-infrastructure coverage. Chapter 3 attempts to disprove serious misleading myths about water in the region.

Part III, under the title "Serving the Unserved," also contains two chapters. Chapter 4, by Raúl A. Lopardo and Emilio Lentini, first looks at global data on water and sanitation coverage, and then focuses on the case of Latin America and, more specifically, on Argentina. The authors provide a positive, though still far from complete, overview of the coverage rates in the region. They then discuss the organization and regulatory framework of services provision in Argentina which, as a federal country, is the competency of the province. As in many other countries, insufficient provision and extension of services hurt primarily the poorest households in Argentina – a problem that plagues the region and is also the focus of Chapter 5, by Katherine Vammen. In the last part of their chapter, Lopardo and Lentini analyze the problem of the rise of the groundwater table in the urban macro region of Buenos Aires.

Vammen, in Chapter 5, focuses on serving the unserved rural population. She reviews national data from 1990 to 2006, reporting on the progress made between these years. Improvements vary significantly – from coverage growths of 38 and 40 percent in Argentina and Mexico, to no improvement at all in Brazil (still with a 37 percent sanitation coverage in 2006). The consequences of insufficient sanitation coverage are numerous and especially flagrant in terms of mortality of children there. Vammen discusses the reasons for insufficient coverage, including, among others the poverty trap (low household income → inability to pay for the service → low investment in rural areas → prevalence disease → low work productivity → low household income); lack of good-quality governance and effective institutional frameworks; poor targeting of needed households, resulting on subsidies that are granted to not-too-poor households; and lack of technical skills of local authorities and communities. In the final sections of Chapter 5, Vammen lists a number of remedies and recommendations to improve coverage rates in the region.

Part IV is devoted to transboundary issues, and has three chapters. Chapter 6, by Víctor Pochat, provides a historical overview of the international cooperation in the La Plata River Basin, a huge catchment of 3.1 million km^3 with five sharing countries (Argentina with 29.7 percent of the area, Bolivia with 6.6 percent, Brazil with 45.7 percent, Paraguay with 13.2 percent, and Uruguay with 4.8 percent), and three main rivers: Paraná (4,300 km), Paraguay (2,500 km), and Uruguay (1,600 km). The La Plata case is a history of realized opportunities, and of a slow but incremental buildup of trust and cooperation architecture. It is instructive to learn that, even under very conducive conditions, achieving a close cooperation to the extent of having a permanent committee and secretariat took almost four decades (since the signature of La Plata Treaty in 1969), during which most of the progress was made in the form of bilateral and trilateral agreements and with specific projects.

In Chapter 7, Rob de Loë provides an overview of the Mackenzie River Basin (MRB) in northern Canada. With a catchment area of approximately 1.8 million km^2, it is shared by the provinces of British Columbia, Alberta, and Saskatchewan, and by two territories (the Yukon and Northwest Territories). Part of the catchment falls within the area covered by treaties and land claims that have been negotiated with Canada's Aboriginal peoples. Managed under a complex governance scheme, a board was created in 1997 by the MRB Transboundary Waters Master Agreement. Not only federal, provincial, and territories governments have specific roles, but also Aboriginal peoples, industries, and civil society have water-related functions. Water governance in the MRB is fragmented along jurisdictional and agency lines, but the signatory parties recognized the need of a coordinating approach to achieve common goals. De Loë shows how equity among unequal parties has been a founding element in moving from a narrow approach based on bilateral agreements among signatories of the agreement to more a cooperative environment, amidst tremendous industrial pressure to develop extractive industries in the basin, and uncertainty and ambiguity with respect to role of Aboriginal peoples. Despite the significant challenges faced by the MRB, the author is optimistic about finding ways to enhance the cooperation regimes, but he remarks that this requires the roles of the Aboriginal people to be clarified and elevated.

Blanca Jiménez Cisneros, in Chapter 8, looks at the case of Mexico City and the aquifers in the Tula Valley. It is well known that the water situation in the Mexican capital city (21 million inhabitants) has been a source of serious concern for decades. As the capital economy and population has been grown, contributing now to 20 percent of the Mexican GNP, its water supply system has faced two interrelated challenges: ensuring a reliable water supply to sustainably meet its increasing needs, and how to get rid of the waste water that the city's growing metabolism creates. Jiménez Cisneros provides a detailed overview of the specific challenges that the system must face, including finding alternative water supply options; averting the process of soil subsidence in Mexico City, which, because soil sinks differently, creates serious problems for buildings structures and creates faults in main water lines, sewers, and even oil pipelines; finding solutions to the loss of drainage capacity; and averting groundwater quality deterioration. Finally, the chapter describes the paradoxical situation of Mexico City of being in need to pump from the Tula Valley downstream the city's main waste water canals to be reused upstream by the city's customers. This will affect inhabitants in other cities of the state of Hidalgo. The chapter concludes with a number of substantive proposals for Mexico City's water supply system, of which the author reiteratively highlights the need to create a Metropolitan Water Authority to manage water in an integrative way, in which all levels of government can embark on short-term and long-term programs.

Part V contains two chapters devoted to the role of indigenous rights and cultures. Chapter 9, by Patricia Ávila-García, sets out to analyze the conflicting coexistence of collective rights and communitarian organizations, and of policy reforms that promote the reevaluation of water as an economic good and use efficiency. A clash of two antagonistic cosmogonies and definition of values, as the author frames it, is occurring in many regions and areas in Latin America. As Getches in Chapter 2 suggests, valid and legitimate values of different groups of people standing in contrast provides the milieu for political maneuvering and resolution. Very often communitarian cosmogonies have been incorporated and recognized as indigenous people's rights, normally attached to the territory that the communities control. Since natural resources are recognized as the public domain of the state or nation, modern laws are applied also on water resources that are underground or flow across territories under the control of indigenous groups. As Ávila-García claims, modern water codes exclude communitarian management in these territories. But a few initiatives have made significant advances recognizing water as a human right and including indigenous rights in their constitutions and laws (Mexico, Guatemala, and Bolivia). The chapter describes two specific conflicts with special relevance in the context of Latin America: the Mazahua people in Mexico, and the Maya people in Guatemala. The creation of the Latin American Water Tribunal in 2000 has been a bold initiative to reverse alleged violations of indigenous rights and protect human rights to water. In connection with Chapter 8, a ruling of the Tribunal of March 2006 declared that a water transfer to Mexico City from other basins was not a viable solution and violated the rights of the Mazahua people over their territory. The author delineates a number of recommendations for public policy to ensure that the human right to water in connection with the indigenous people's rights are adequately protected and harmonized with modern law's doctrines and approaches.

J. Michael Miltenberger, in Chapter 10, explores the state of traditional knowledge in northern Canada and considers in some detail the challenges associated with use and application of traditional knowledge, and the opportunities for its application to inform environmental management and decision making in water management. After millennia of Aboriginal peoples inhabiting the Northwest Territories of Canada (NWT), a significant and detailed knowledge about the land, animal behavior, climate, and ecological relationships has been accumulated. As de Loë indicated in Chapter 7, land claim agreements have been the materialization of the recognition of Aboriginal rights by Canadian courts. But the governance configuration and regulatory framework used to manage natural resources in the NWT are far from simple. In a context of ongoing and increasing pressures in the MRB, "Northeners" (as the author refers to) have concerns for visible contamination processes originating from mining and agricultural production, and climate change impacts in the hydrological regimes of important tributaries. Miltenberger describes the content and objectives of Northern Voices, Northern Waters: NWT Water Stewardship Strategy (made public in May 2010), an initiative of the NWT and Canadian governments, drafted in collaboration with the Aboriginal governments and other boards and organizations. The strategy recognized the role of traditional knowledge, and recommends that it should be put into practice to protect northern waters. A critical challenge to accomplish this is the fact that traditional or indigenous knowledge has been transmitted through oral narrative in a generations-long acquisition process totally juxtaposed over everyday life. Differences between IK and western science (in the author's words) are rooted in mutually professed distrust by advocators of each mode of knowledge. More recently, and based on a closer examination of how IK is processed, the contrasts have been dismissed as "artificial distinctions." The author elaborates on many examples and initiatives of the potential use and harmonization with western knowledge of IK, and lists a number of recommendations to ensure that it is put into practice. Among them, Miltenberger recommends that IK be decomposed in its parts so that databases can be created and historical and ongoing community-based monitoring can be added to them, accordingly with more precise definitions and standards, to ensure that data can be compared and contrasted.

Part VI looks at institutional innovations, and the lessons from Asia. R. Maria Saleth, in Chapter 11, provides a theoretical framework for characterizing different forms of water governance, identifying broad typologies as they are found across countries, and setting up to evaluate their relative efficiency. Saleth starts by claiming that a concise definition of institutional typologies, be there six or any other number, represents only discreet points within a continuum ranging from open-access to market-centric arrangements. To evaluate efficiency, the structural features and the external environment (socio, demographic, economic, political, and cultural factors) have to be included in the analysis. Chapter 11 applies the framework of six governance priorities to the urban and the agricultural sectors, and then discusses different approaches to evaluate their relative efficiencies, including qualitative (subjective) and quantitative (objective) research elements. Based on nine indicators, Saleth concludes that governance structures involving state bodies fails on most counts in urban supply systems, while the contrary is found in the agricultural sector. He then elaborates on these two relevant conclusions and takes on the discussion about institutional reform and change. In the final section, Saleth reaches some conclusions focusing on water governance and institutions as applied in the Americas, indicating some markedly differential elements with Europe, Asia and Africa, but claiming that multiple and poly-centric governance configurations are needed to ensure efficient adaptation to meet different regional and sectoral requirements.

Chapter 12, by Tushaar Shah, sets out to provide an overview of global groundwater economy and its use in agriculture in four different parts of the world, namely, the NEMA region, the industrialized world, Sub-Saharan Africa, and in monsoon Asia. Shah provides astonishing data of the expansion of groundwater use in agriculture in the MENA, industrialized countries, and South Asia and China. It is in Asia, in which more than 70 percent of global annual groundwater is accounted, where the worst consequences of overdraft are visible. Millions of private tube well owners operating under little or no control confront resource management challenge. Shah defines four types of socio-ecologies: arid agrarian systems, industrial agricultural systems, groundwater-supported extensive pastoralism, and smallholder intensive farming systems. Neither groundwater use nor these four socio-ecology types are relevant in Latin America presently, with the exception of Mexico. But the sheer scale of the groundwater governance challenge in Asia may somewhat anticipate similar phenomena in the future in Latin America. Next, Shah discusses various groundwater governance instruments, including administrative regulation, economic instruments, tradable water rights, community aquifer management, and crowding out tube wells through supply augmentation. The last topic of the chapter addresses groundwater innovations in India. Shah reviews both demand- and supply-side options, each illustrated with case studies that are eloquent of misfired and unanticipated outcomes. The diversity of experiences and contexts make India the showcase of groundwater governance innovation around, and the state of Gujarat, the most illustrative example of the potential of both supply- and demand-side instruments, coupled by leadership, collective work and wise government. Shah claims that the groundwater boom "is rewriting India's irrigation and water management rule book."

In the seventh and final part of the volume, R. W. Sandford (Chapter 13) draws an interpretative summary of the main challenges for Americas' water resources. He emphasizes the impact of climate change, population growth and urbanization as the main threatening drivers to sustainable water management in the hemisphere. Sandford makes an urgent call for the international community to think seriously about the implications of non-stationary climatic patterns for all aspects of resource conservation, use, and management. With equal eloquence, he identifies the lack or insufficiency of water and sanitary services for poor households in the Americas as a solvable and crucial challenge that good governance and political determination could easily face. Paying for water use and treatment is also an indispensable condition for meeting future water needs in all middle- to high-income people in the Americas.

References

Deininger, K. and Byerlee, D. (2010) *Rising Global Interest in Farmland: Can it Yield Sustainable and Equitable Benefits?* Washington, DC: The World Bank.

Grenier, L. (1998) *Working With Indigenous Knowledge: A Guide for Researchers*. Ottawa: International Development Research Centre.

IANAS (2012) *Diagnóstico del agua en las Américas*. Coordinated by B. Jiménez Cisneros and J. G. Tundisi. Tlalpan: InterAmerican Network of National Academies of Sciences. Available at www.ianas.org/water/book/diagnostico_del_agua_en_las_americas.pdf (accessed February 28, 2014).

OECD-FAO (2012) *Agricultural Outlook 2012*. Available at http://dx.doi.org/10.1787/agr_outlook-2012-en (accessed February 28, 2014).

Part II

Water scarcity in the Americas

2 Water scarcity in the Americas

Common challenges – a Northern perspective

David H. Getches

Introduction: common problems, common solutions?

Mission for conference: a mutual learning experience

In many respects, the water problems of the world are shared by all, and scarcity is at the core. The wisdom of several Rosenberg Conferences in convening experts to study and debate problems lies in the commonality of problems and the potential for sharing solutions. Focusing on the Americas increases the potential for exchanging lessons learned and transferring knowledge. For North America, the scarcity problem is less likely to be about survival than it is about economic growth and environmental concerns. This is not to diminish the reality of entire communities being without potable water, at least temporarily, even in some places in the developed and developing countries of the northern hemisphere. It is true that north and south differ in the extent of scarcity for the most fundamental need for water – drinking and other domestic uses. But even that difference is less pronounced between the northern and southern hemispheres of the Americas than it is, say, between Europe and Africa.

Issues of policy related to climate change, urbanization, groundwater, indigenous rights, and transboundary allocation are the most critical water problems in North America. They are the determinants of scarcity at local and regional levels, and they are typically inextricably linked to one another. This chapter explains each of these policy issues as they occur in the United States of America. It then goes on to illustrate how they are interrelated, using the case study of the Colorado River. While each of the issues varies in relative seriousness as between the Northern and Southern Hemisphere – and even within the Northern Hemisphere – they are pervasive throughout the continents as driving forces in water scarcity, and they are surely among the greatest water policy issues of our time. It is likely that the experiences of one region – mistakes and struggles, as well as successes– will be useful in enhancing the capacity of experts to address these challenges as they arise in another. At a minimum, the chapter should illustrate the complex policy nexus of water problems and the need for integrated consideration of major issues rather than attempting to solve water scarcity problems in isolation as simply supply and delivery issues.

US allocation and administration systems

To set the backdrop necessary for explaining the future challenges for water policy it is helpful to understand the basic elements of the legal and institutional context. Recognizing that there are substantial differences among the several systems of North America, this chapter focuses on the United States of America – which itself has multiple systems. The challenges identified are not the result of the allocation and administration systems in the United States. Rather, the ways in which challenges have been addressed – or not – has been affected by the assumptions and practices that have grown up under these systems.

Two historically different water allocation systems converge

The United States has multiple water allocation systems, with each of the fifty states setting the rules for allocating and administering available water supplies. Generally, those legal systems emanate from two distinct approaches – riparian rights and prior appropriation. Although the historical roots are different, and each state maintains its particular nuances, almost all the states now have permit systems that operate with more similarities than differences.

In its simplest terms, "riparian rights" to water are held by those whose land borders watercourses. Thus, water rights are linked to land ownership. Although in its purest form the doctrine did not allow water to be used on non-riparian land (land not contiguous to a stream), that impractical rule was overtaken by exceptions.

Eventually most riparian jurisdictions adopted permit statutes that require applications to be submitted to an administrative agency that grants rights to use particular quantities of water to individuals, cities, companies, and others. The agency applies criteria found in statutes to determine how to prioritize rights among water users. One of the criteria may be one's location near to a stream – a riparian value. But the criteria may also include consideration of historical use of water – a value that is fundamental to the appropriation doctrine discussed next (Getches 2009: 103–7).

The "prior appropriation" system is the source of water laws in most of the western United States. It was based on the simple justice of the West's early miners who, in absence of a formal legal system, were making claims on minerals based on who found them first. The "first-in-time, first-in-right" idea applied to water so that anyone could begin taking water and putting it to use for mining, farming, or any other "beneficial use" and thereby get a "water right" to continue using the amount originally put to use. The right was then good against anyone else who later claimed a water right, and was subordinate to rights claimed earlier. This system operated to enable full use of one's rights so long as there was enough water in the stream and the use did not interfere with uses by any other water rights holder. One of the great positive features of the system is that it allowed rights to be transferred to others.

The system could be criticized as protecting old uses that were highly inefficient and for eschewing sharing when water supplies were short. Indeed, it is anomalous to see flood irrigation being used on western farms today when other, more efficient methods are available. And it seems inequitable to see a flooded field of an irrigator with senior rights next to a dry and barren field of a farmer with junior water rights. Moreover, the system historically paid no respect to arguments that there should be enough water in a stream to maintain flows for fish and wildlife and recreation (Wilkinson 1992: 231–5).

Today, prior appropriation has been modified by statutes recognizing the public's interest in instream flows, establishing recreation as a beneficial use, and allowing appropriations of water without diverting it from the stream in order to use it to maintain fish and wildlife habitat. Indeed, like the riparian states, most prior appropriation states now have permit systems. Those systems generally require new water uses to be in the "public interest." Although most water in the streams of the generally arid West is already appropriated and subject to existing rights, the public interest requirements apply also to changes to new uses when rights are transferred.

The permit systems that prevail in the prior appropriation states do, indeed, defer to the priority of existing water users in granting or administering water rights. But so do the permit systems in the riparian states. A variety of other considerations, including expansive and often discretionary public interest standards, are applied and substantially modify the common law system that developed in the nineteenth-century American West (Wilkinson 1992: 282–4).

Federal system: state allocation, federal regulation

Although the state systems are surely dominant in terms of most issues of allocation and administration, the federal government also has a role. Under the United States Constitution, federal legislation is supreme, preempting the operation of state law to the extent that it might interfere with fulfillment of a federal purpose. For instance, federal law – the Clean Water Act – demands the achievement of certain water quality standards for streams. A state law that makes water quality goals subordinate to the ability of water users to exercise their water rights could apply to state water quality laws but would be preempted if the exercise of water rights resulted in degrading water quality contrary to federal law. Similarly, the federal Endangered Species Act (ESA) prevents water users from diverting or damming a stream – even if they hold a state water right to do so – if it would imperil a species of fish protected under the ESA (*Riverside Irrigation Dist. v. Andrews*, 1985).

Another way in which federal laws and policies impact state water laws is through congressional designations of uses for federal lands. About a third of all lands in the United States are owned by the federal government. If federal law "reserves" lands for specific federal purposes that require water, the government effectively has reserved a right to sufficient water for that purpose. Thus, state-created water rights may not interfere with the purposes of setting aside those federal lands. Similarly, if national legislation creates a Wild and Scenic River, a person holding water rights under state law cannot use water from the river to defeat the federal purpose (*Potlatch Corp. v. United States* 2000).

The protection of federal purposes for reserving federal lands from conflicting water uses is called the reserved rights doctrine. It was created by the United States Supreme Court as a means of reserving sufficient water to fulfill the purpose of creating Indian reservations. Often reservations were created to ensure that tribes had a territory where they could subsist, usually by farming. In other cases tribes needed enough water to keep streams flowing through their reservations to preserve habitat for fish, to allow them to exercise traditional fishing rights. The tribes are considered to have reserved water rights to sufficient water to fulfill such purposes. State-granted water rights are subordinate to reserved rights and cannot be exercised if they interfere with the fulfillment of the reservation purposes. The realities of this system of reserved water rights do not always match their potential, as discussed below (Tarlock *et al.* 2009: 861–2).

All water problems are policy problems

Water issues are typically discussed as physical problems: finding and managing a natural supply and the need to construct delivery systems, dams, and purification systems. But essentially all water problems have a policy nexus. It is rare that a water problem cannot be solved if public policy can be harnessed and directed effectively. And the problems are far more expansive than matters of supply and delivery. If water problems were ever that simple, finding sustainable solutions today requires far wider consideration.

Characterizing water problems as competition between individuals or competition among or within sectors – cities versus farmers, cities versus cities – oversimplifies the issue. The self-interest that drives competition often inhibits making the "wisest" choices. Water is cheap; I will use all I want. If our city gets the water first and puts it fully to use, we will get the tax base from faster growth. And so on. Often these problems of competition can be privately resolved by payments from one party to another. But public policy must intervene if water is to serve more and varied interests inasmuch as water is a public good.

"Wise" choices are also inhibited, even in public decision making, unless broad-based values are represented in the process. How do we resolve conflicts among different types of water uses, all of which are rational and important but more or less so in the minds of different people (e.g., agriculture versus municipal or industrial uses)? The problem is complicated because people or entities can share broad policy objectives that cannot all be served – where all objectives are desirable but honoring one trumps the other. For instance, we may want enough water for a vibrant community and still want a viable, flowing stream for fishing, but the fishing stream will be depleted if the stream is developed for municipal growth.

Choices continually have to be made among reasonable goals. Sometimes society can count on individual values and ethics to restrain water uses that cause damage to others or long-term deterioration of natural conditions. But, in the end, behaviors must be guided not by self-restraint alone, but also by a combination of regulation and market forces. Public policy governing water allocation, development, use, and conservation therefore must utilize regulatory mechanisms and market incentives as well as providing information to help people make wise and ethical choices.

Challenges for water policy today

Climate change

Experts in the once-uncertain field of climate change research are reaching agreement on certain principles that portend serious concern for water planners and suppliers. Although there is a wide range of estimates of the average temperature changes that will be experienced due to climate change, and the various climate models differ on localized impacts, most scientists have now reached a consensus that changing global climate patterns will impact the timing and quantities of water supplies. Temperatures generally are rising, at least in part, because of concentration of greenhouse gases in the atmosphere.

The 2007 report of the Intergovernmental Panel on Climate Change (IPCC) provides estimates about the probable distribution of impacts in North America based on the most widely accepted climate change models. According to the report, over the last 60 years streamflow has decreased by about 2 percent per decade in the central Rocky Mountain Region while showing increases in the eastern United States (Field *et al.* 2007). Overall, the fraction of precipitation falling as rain instead of snow increased in the western mountains of the United States and Canada. Glaciers throughout North America are melting.

Much of the discussion of global climate change is about how to stem the human causes, and that sets off a debate about the extent to which human activity is responsible for the phenomenon. From the perspective of water experts, this debate is largely moot. The only action within the grasp of water managers is how to cope with the effects. Any mitigation through reduction in the emission of greenhouse gases will take decades to achieve. Indeed, the IPCC stated that adaptation "will be necessary to address impacts resulting from the warming which is already unavoidable due to past emissions" (Parry *et al.* 2007: 25).

Adaptation begins with planning that incorporates the most reliable and current estimates of climate change impacts on water supplies. Planners must anticipate drier, warmer conditions and differently timed precipitation patterns. Variations in climate may be more pronounced; floods and droughts may be more frequent and more severe. One of the most troubling consequences of changing climate is that the systems of water collection, storage, and distribution were designed based on precipitation patterns and resulting river flows derived from data collected in the late nineteenth and early twentieth centuries. The IPCC concluded that current water management practices are "very likely" to be inadequate in reducing the negative impacts of climate change on "water supply reliability, flood risk, health, energy, and aquatic ecosystems" (Bates *et al.* 2008: 127). It called for greater incorporation of climate variability into water management. This means that water managers must reconsider the hydrological assumptions on which their predecessors premised the locations, sizes, and operating regimes for reservoir systems. It also means that managers and political leaders must take action to reduce water demand. Moreover, the legal systems for allocating water and for controlling water quality may have to be examined. Until recently, few states required any consideration of climate change in water resources planning. One of the exceptions is in California where the legislature adopted the sweeping Global Warming Solutions Act, which includes a Water-Energy subgroup (CDWR 2008: 8). In 2007, the California legislature passed Assembly Bill 662, which specifically addressed water conservation in the face of climate change.

Urbanization

Much of the American West suffers from a scarcity in natural water supplies. Yet it is the part of the country that has experienced the greatest population growth over the past half century. The western United States is characterized by open spaces – forests, mountains, and deserts. Remarkably, however, the West is the most urbanized area in the nation. That is, most of the population is concentrated in urban areas (National Research Council 2007: 17). And therefore the fastest growing demand for water is for municipal supply.

Western states experienced a 20 percent population growth in the 1990s, compared with a national average of 13 percent (Travis 2007: 51–5). Nevada, Arizona, Colorado, Utah, and Idaho grew at 37 percent during the same period. Projections are that the West will add 28 million people by 2030. Rarely is the cost of water a significant factor in locating housing and so urban and suburban growth has followed lifestyle preferences and employment opportunities without regard to the difficulty of acquiring or transporting water.

Urban areas are confronted with the reality that nearly all water in the West is allocated under prevailing systems of water rights. Even in the eastern United States, shortages are occurring with greater frequency because of growth and undependable supplies. And in both regions meeting municipal water demands is the greatest concern.

Urban water demand is typically in tension with agricultural uses. Historically, the earliest demands for water in the West were for agriculture, which uses large quantities of water, especially in arid or semi-arid areas. Thus, the annual flows in most of the West's relatively meager surface streams were legally allocated to agricultural use. Today, agriculture uses about 62 percent of all surface water withdrawn (Kenny *et al.* 2009).

To meet the growing demand for urban water with an essentially static supply requires reallocation from existing uses to accommodate population expansion. Water has greater economic value in urban uses than for almost any agricultural purpose. Thus, market forces attract water away from farms and to the cities. Economic forces promote the movement of water to cities causing the decline of some rural communities whose economies were fueled by agriculture.

The United States has not yet faced the issue of how loss of agricultural production can be reconciled with a growing population. Transfers of water to cities from farms may nevertheless be politically unpopular, causing some cities to seek alternatives to drying up agriculture to secure a water source. There are methods for mitigating the impact on agriculture, however, while firming or expanding urban supplies. For instance, a city can enter into a dry year lease allowing for water to be removed from irrigated lands in a drought but leaving irrigation water to be used on the farm in other years (National Research Council 1992: 30–4).

By reducing demand, cities can also avoid the expense and political opposition that sometimes come with importing new supplies at the expense of agriculture and rural economies. Mandatory conservation measures can be highly effective. Today, most newly constructed buildings must have low water demand toilets and showers. But because most urban demand comes from outdoor uses, the type and extent of outdoor planting such as grass lawns must also be limited. Some cities limit lawn size and planting, but the most effective way to reduce outdoor usage is to limit lot size. This requires consideration of water demand in urban planning. Measures to control the size of subdivisions also help to prevent sprawl. Nevertheless, it is rare for local government or state-mandated land use plans to require water conservation measures such as limiting lot size or even requiring that developers secure long-term water supply (Hirt *et al.* 2008). There are exceptions such as Arizona, which requires a 100-year assured supply of water before approval of any new subdivisions (ARS 45-576). Similarly, in California, two bills (SB 221 and SB 610) required developers to prove the presence of adequate water supplies before major subdivisions, commercial developments, or large-scale residential developments are built.

Cities are challenged by a lack of capital to install and maintain water systems. For new growth, some charge substantial "tap fees" that help to meet the costs of expanding systems. As new consumers are added to systems they eventually outstrip the capacity of water supplies and of water treatment facilities. The amounts charged for tap fees are often kept below the actual expense of expanding or maintaining infrastructure by political opposition to raising government revenues and by decision makers in local governments hoping to attract growth to a community. A dearth of financial resources for constructing and maintaining these systems results in existing consumers paying higher rates to support new growth even as existing facilities deteriorate.

The infrastructure problem is serious for cities. The funding once provided by the federal government for water treatment plants has dwindled because of growing government deficits and because politicians refuse to raise taxes. Although the United States, like most of the developed world, could once boast the absence of problems of inadequate potable water for its citizens, in recent years there have been several reports of failing municipal water systems causing health threats to local consumers. The US Environmental Protection Agency refers to "the nation's water systems having entered a 'rehabilitation and replacement' era in which much of water utilities' existing infrastructure has reached or is approaching the end of its useful life" (USEPA 2009: 3). Some experts estimate that the number of waterborne diseases in the US exceeds 19 million annually (Reynolds *et al.* 2008).

Groundwater use

Groundwater is a primary source for agricultural or urban water supply in many areas of the country, accounting for about 20 percent of all water withdrawn in the United States, with 67 percent of that amount being used for agriculture (Kenny *et al.* 2009). Groundwater is used to supply much of the nation's urban growth with half the population now drinking groundwater. With the waters of the West's rivers at or near their full capacity under water rights allocation systems, and their use facilitated by publically financed water projects, groundwater becomes a very attractive alternative. Relying on water supplied from aquifers also has the benefit of not being subject to evaporation and not fluctuating with precipitation.

Experts have concluded that states generally do a poor job of managing groundwater (Leshy 2008). It has long been well accepted that groundwater and surface water should be used conjunctively, but state legal institutions have been slow to respond.

The varieties of groundwater laws often have little to do with the geology that produces the resources. State laws governing groundwater allocation treat water pumped from wells as if it comes from an entirely different source than surface water. Much groundwater is hydrologically connected to a river (i.e., "tributary" water). Laws concerning use of this water may or may not (more often not) respect the use rights of surface water users.

Other aquifers are all or largely non-renewable resources. They are not replenished by precipitation or the flows of connected streams. A variety of widely differing laws governs non-tributary water. Some states embrace the quaint notion that the overlying landowner "owns" the water beneath the land area. That raises questions of just how much the owner is entitled to pump without injuring the rights of other overlying owners. The ownership idea has been tempered by a "reasonable use" rule in most states. In other places competing pumpers may sue one another over interference with their presumed rights – such as when it becomes impossible or more expensive for one person to pump because another person's pumping depletes the water table.

A few courts apply prior appropriation principles to protect earlier users from injury by the pumping of junior users – but only to protect a "reasonable" pumping level. The meaning of "reasonable" under rules using the term may depend on economic factors. In most jurisdictions groundwater is considered a public resource so that states are not inhibited in its regulation through legislation.

Other kinds of regulation include permit systems that take account of impacts on others and, like permit systems for use of surface water, consider public interest factors. Some states create special districts to deal with the management of depleting aquifers. Some allow a certain amount of water to be "mined" each year, effectively amortizing the resource. Property rights, torts, and public policy form the basis for the extensive variations of these rules (Getches 2009: 267–84).

Today, aquifers in many parts of the country are being depleted to the point of crisis. Some states have allowed excessive use because of political pressure not to curtail economic activity, or because the aquifer underlies another state and the water would be pumped in the second state if it were not allowed in the first state. Of all areas of water law and policy, groundwater rules are the most incongruous with the physical nature of the resource and its importance to society.

Indian rights

Indian tribes in the United States – like indigenous peoples elsewhere in the world – have cultures that depend on water use. Many are able to sustain their residence and subsistence in territories that have been limited in scope by dispossession of tribal lands by treaties, agreements, and federal legislation and the resulting encroachment of non-Indian communities into traditional areas. Many tribes living on reservations that are vestiges of their former territories now depend on agriculture that requires irrigation. Some depend on fishing and hunting which requires streamflows and habitats to be maintained.

Recognizing the necessity of water to sustain Indian life on lands that were reserved to the tribes, the United States Supreme Court ruled that tribes have rights to water sufficient to fulfill the purposes of their reservations. In a 1908 case, *United States v. Winters*, non-Indian settlers had moved to areas formerly occupied by Indians and the tribes confined to a reservation. In that case, the non-Indians began irrigating and depleted the river that ran along the border of the Fort Belknap Reservation. Although the non-Indians argued that they had begun taking water out of the river before some of the Indian irrigation began, thus entitling them to water rights under the prior appropriation doctrine, the Court found that the tribe had "reserved rights." Instead of tying tribes' water rights to the date of their first use, the Court said that, in creating Fort Belknap Reservation, Congress had also manifested an intention to reserve sufficient water to fulfill the purposes for setting aside the land. That purpose included agriculture. The Court said this was a "necessary implication" to avoid injustice to the Indians.

In the century since the decision, non-Indians – even if they obtain water rights under state law – should be on notice that their uses of water sources proximate to Indian reservations are subject to being preempted by new Indian uses. This reality has been offensive to states who believe they have primacy in matters of water allocation, notwithstanding the supremacy of federal law as discussed above. And the uncertainty caused by the possibility of Indians asserting water rights after non-Indians have begun using water portends practical problems, including frustration of investment in farms and irrigation systems.

Historically, however, the practical consequences have not been serious. The non-Indians have expanded their water uses and most Indian tribes have had inadequate resources to develop their own irrigation systems and farms. The federal government has provided some funds for Indian reservation irrigation systems, but more typically the government has subsidized systems for non-Indians that use the waters of the same streams needed by the tribes, leaving less water for Indian uses (DeCoteau 2006). The reserved rights doctrine, though its benefits in practice have fallen short of the apparent promise of prior and paramount water rights, has allowed many tribes to develop farms and some to ensure streamflows for fisheries.

It is difficult to quantify a tribe's reserved rights that are simply defined in case law as being in amounts "sufficient to fulfill the purpose" of the reservation. The "formula" for determining how much water is required to fulfill the purpose of an Indian reservation requires looking first for the purposes revealed in the documents creating the reservation and next using experts to calculate how much water that will take. One major case announced that the water needed for reservations established for agriculture would be set based on the water needed for irrigation of all "practicably irrigable acreage" (*Arizona v. California*, 1963). In that case and others, litigation was pursued to establish the relative priority dates and quantities of reserved rights that pertain to a particular reservation. Because of the costliness of litigation, the states and non-Indian users, as well as the tribes, have resorted to negotiated settlements to quantify and resolve tribal water rights.

Over the past 25 years, the rights of more than 30 reservations have been decided through negotiation, typically followed by an Act of Congress ratifying the terms. This approach is generally considered less burdensome than litigation and can create incentives for non-Indians to cooperate in the process. Still, a negotiated settlement can take many years and requires the involvement of divergent interests along with their lawyers and experts, making the process cumbersome and costly.

Although each reserved rights settlement is distinct, there are common features. Nearly all have guaranteed a quantity of water to the tribe and most have provided funds in trust to be used for water development or generally for economic development. The funds are usually federal, with some state contributions. Most settlements have allowed the tribes to lease or sell water to be used by non-Indians on, and sometimes off, the reservation. Because public funding is involved and so many different interests have to be satisfied, there are political barriers. Today, almost as many settlements are in various stages of negotiation as have been concluded (Tarlock *et al.* 2009: 925–7).

Quantifying and implementing an Indian reserved water rights settlement is difficult and time consuming, but it does start from the premise that tribes have significant water rights. Moreover, quantification – after the expenditure of time and money – has produced substantial benefits for several tribes. The reserved rights doctrine itself appears here to stay, although in some modern cases, the Supreme Court has seized the opportunity to narrow the doctrine, for instance, by limiting the reservation purposes to "primary" purposes (*United States v. New Mexico*, 1978). Compared to legal treatment of water rights for indigenous peoples in other countries, however, the reserved rights doctrine appears to be relatively advantageous.

Environmental protection

Before the 1970s, water was developed and used without much concern for impacts on the environment. Dams were built and streams were depleted with sometimes damaging consequences for fisheries and habitat, and streams were degraded by depletion and pollution. Since then, far-reaching federal legislation has been enacted to protect stream water quality, drinking water, wetlands, endangered species, and other environmental values. Today, the greatest concern for water suppliers attempting to develop new sources is complying with environmental laws. It is very difficult to divert and transport water from any source to the place of use without encountering major legal obstacles designed to protect the environment.

Nearly all water use and development affects water quality; even the extraction of water from a stream leaves less water flowing in the stream to dilute pollutants added by others. There are more dramatic impacts as streams are dried up, obstructed, and polluted by the return of water to the stream after it has been polluted by municipal, irrigation, or industrial uses.

In the United States, the most protective environmental laws are federal. Because water rights are created under state laws that grant rights without regard to the environmental consequences of diminished water quality, there are conflicts between the two sets of laws that set off federalism debates. In fact, some states actually have laws saying that water quality protection laws must yield if they would inhibit the development of water under state water rights.

The ideal of federal deference to state water law is often recited, but in practice it is more myth than reality (Getches 2000: 6–18). Invariably, potential conflicts are resolved in favor of federal law, which is supreme under the Supremacy Clause of the Constitution so long as Congress was clear about its objectives when it passed legislation. The federalism conflict after all derives from the historical response of the national government to public demand for better environmental quality as state laws proved too weak even to provide protection of human health.

Today, the most formidable federal environmental laws confronting water development are a wetlands protection law prohibiting the placement of any structure in waters of the United States without a federal permit and the Endangered Species Act prohibiting actions that would "jeopardize the continued existence" of a threatened or endangered species (Doremus 2001).

The most significant state environmental laws potentially in conflict with water development provide for instream flow protection. These laws take several forms, but generally attempt to sustain fisheries with sufficient water flows in streams, or levels in lakes. One type of law allows the state to prevent depletion of a stream below a certain flow rate. Another model lets the state appropriate water for instream uses – fish or recreation. The latter type of law treats the instream flow right as just another water right that can prevent junior water rights holders from interfering with the flow needed for the right, but which can be defeated by the exercise of senior rights held by others. But because these instream flow laws were passed in the late twentieth century, the rights appropriated under them are usually junior to most rights in a stream, still allowing for the exercise of senior rights to dry up the entire stream. It is possible for junior rights to impede a water development project that acquires senior rights if the project requires approval for a change of use which, under state law, is not allowed if it will harm even junior uses. Such instances are rare (Amos 2006).

Transboundary issues

The ability of each state to allocate waters running through its territory creates the possibility of conflict when a stream flows through or along the border of more than one state. What happens when all or nearly all the water of a river that crosses a state line is allocated for use in an upstream state? Or if a downstream state on such a river allocates water to water users before there is demand in a slower developing upstream state? These problems have arisen many times in the United States and have been addressed in a number of ways.

The first method used to resolve such problems is litigation. Although an individual in one state who wants to challenge the use by an individual in another can sue the user in the other state, this is rarely done (*Bean v. Morris*, 1911). This approach may be effective where the differences in laws between the two states are not great and where the parties all can agree to submit the case to the jurisdiction of one state.

More typically, a state acting for the benefit of its citizens will sue another state to protect against an interference with the amounts of water the first state is entitled to allocate for its citizens to use within its boundaries. Such cases are within the "original jurisdiction" of the United States Supreme Court, meaning that the case starts there. Fourteen rivers of the United States have been the subject of such interstate litigation. The Supreme Court is not equipped to try cases, hear evidence, and find facts, so the Court assigns the case to a special master who writes a report that the Court reviews and accepts all or parts of the report within its decision.

Interstate litigation over the rights to use water has produced a set of legal principles that the Supreme Court applies. The first is that the Supreme Court will not decide the case unless the complaining state can show the existence or likelihood of present harm. The general principle for deciding such cases is known as equitable apportionment where fair allocation, rather than fulfilling expectations of the parties or following the law of a particular state, is the standard. Thus, the Court will look at factors such as climate and other physical conditions, present consumption of water from the river, established uses and economies, availability of water storage, wasteful uses, and damage to upstream areas compared to downstream areas if upstream uses are curtailed (Tarlock *et al.* 2009: 437).

Another approach to interstate disputes over the waters of a stream claimed by one or more states is by negotiating a compact. This is essentially a contractual arrangement, which, under the Constitution, requires congressional ratification. Compacts have been used many times and deal not only with allocating quantities of water but also with water quality, navigation, and other matters of common interest. Some of them call for the creation of compact commissions that have authority to interpret compact provisions and to administer water allocation between compacting parties. Although the terms of some compacts were based on mistaken facts or have inherent ambiguities that cause difficulties, and in some cases litigation has commenced anyway, they still provide an orderly, more predictable, and less costly alternative to litigating rights to interstate rivers (Wolf 2005: 138–40).

There are a few rivers in North America that cross international borders, raising issues similar to those raised by interstate rivers in the United States. The international law for allocation of the waters and resolving other river disputes is strikingly similar to the US law concerning interstate rivers. In the few cases in which disagreements have reached international forums, they have essentially applied equitable apportionment principles.

As rivers within one state or nation are subjected to greater demands, transboundary disputes become inevitable. Tempering provincial concerns and narrow self-interest are chronic problem. Individual jurisdictions and water users within them continue to insist on using as much water as possible and pressing their individual interests. These disputes can be managed by interstate or international bodies if the doctrine of equitable apportionment is applied fairly – or if the parties are willing to negotiate in good faith toward such equitable ends. The equitable apportionment doctrine is not unlike the public interest considerations used in some states in issuing water rights permits.

A North American case study: the Colorado River

The six challenges posited by this chapter as the greatest concerns for North American water policy are brilliantly exemplified by the Colorado River. This case study is offered as an illustration of how each of the challenges has arisen and been dealt with – though not necessarily as a model for addressing them. The six challenges intertwine in a century of history of the Colorado River, and each of them remains a challenge today.

The Colorado is an interstate, international river. As Figure 2.1 shows, it is shared by seven states and between the United States of America and the Republic of Mexico. Early in the twentieth century it became apparent that the growing economies of the states along the river would need its water to sustain their growth. Most notably, California was growing rapidly in population, especially in the Los Angeles area. The city first used copious artesian wells but exhausted their capacity. It extended its boundaries to capture the economic benefits of a larger tax base and to respond to the pressures of powerful development interests. Clandestinely, the city's water department bought farmland far north of the city in Owens Valley in order to transport the water that was being used to irrigate farms there to support development in the city (Reisner 1993: ch. 2).

Soon more water was needed for growth. The city turned to the Colorado River. By the first decade of the twentieth century large amounts of water were already being diverted into California's hot but fertile Imperial Valley for large farms. Politicians and business people in California beseeched the federal government to provide funding for dams and canals to deliver more Colorado River water to the state and to generate electricity for its use. They also cited the need

Figure 2.1 Map of the Colorado River System

for an "all-American" canal to the Imperial Valley that did not pass through a foreign country – Mexico (Reisner 1993: 124–5).

Perceiving the thirst of California for what the Colorado River could produce, some of the upstream states became concerned. A young Colorado lawyer named Delph Carpenter was concerned that the growing city of Denver and other places outside California would not have any water to use from the river if the principles of prior appropriation applied as among water users in different states. So with the support of his state, he rallied other interests and by 1922 a meeting of commissioners appointed to represent each of the seven Colorado River basin states was convened under the direction of a federal chairman. The states decided to divide the river into two "basins" – upper and lower – and to divide the presumed flow of the river so that the states of each basin collectively got half the water produced on average each year.

It was then up to the state legislatures to ratify the agreement of the seven states' commissioners – an interstate compact. But Arizona refused to join the six other states in ratifying the compact. Ultimately, Congress passed the Boulder Canyon Project Act in 1928, which ratified the 1922 Compact and deemed it to be effective without Arizona's action. This legislation authorized federal construction of Hoover Dam and other facilities – a huge benefit to California (National Research Council 2007: 31–4).

Fearing that California's use of the facilities would allow it to dominate use of the river, Arizona brought several original actions in the United States Supreme Court to try to stop the development and protect its right to future use. It even called out the state militia and tried to use force to interfere with construction in a comical but tragic episode. In one of the lawsuits the Supreme Court rejected Arizona's claim that the legislation was unconstitutional. Arizona lost the other suits as well, including an action seeking equitable apportionment of the river. The latter suit was dismissed because the United States was an indispensable party that, as a sovereign, could not be sued without its consent (Getches 1985).

Arizona, wracked by a multi-year drought and experiencing growth of its own, eventually ratified the compact in 1935 as its only means of getting water from the vast federal water project that would otherwise be monopolized by California. Ratification opened the way to a federal contract for water, but Arizona had no facilities to deliver the water. The enormous Central Arizona Project (CAP) to be built for that purpose took decades for Congress to authorize – over vehement political objections by California. It was finally authorized in 1968 on the condition that Arizona's water rights would be subordinate to California's. Another condition was that Arizona either had to begin responsible management of groundwater or not be eligible for federal contracts for water under the long-awaited project. Arizona had been overdrafting groundwater at a grossly unsustainable rate – withdrawing 4.8 million acre-feet annually from aquifers with annual recharge of only 2.6 million acre-feet (Larson *et al.* 2005).

Eventually and reluctantly Arizona complied by enacting a groundwater management act (GMA). It was an agonized process that pitted mining and municipal interests against agriculture. The law gave strong control of groundwater to the state and mandated the creation of "active management areas." Growing cities were required to demonstrate a 100-year guaranteed supply of water for new development. Surprisingly, this has not constrained development. Developers immediately pressed for legislative reform and in 1993, the Central Arizona Groundwater Replenishment District (CAGRD) was formed. The CAGRD allowed developers to purchase surplus CAP water and inject it into the aquifer to create an assured supply. This effectively undermined the purpose of the GMA of reducing groundwater demand. Moreover, CAGRD acknowledges that by 2015 it will have to seek new water supplies to fulfill its obligations (Hirt *et al.* 2008).

Some cities like Tucson have imposed commendably rigorous conservation requirements, controlling the growth of water demand for outdoor watering. But urbanization of this desert state continued apace, at least until the economic downturn of 2008 and 2009.

Instead of shifting water use primarily to Colorado River water delivered by the CAP, Arizona cities have continued to stake their growth on groundwater pumping and farmers have continued to pump groundwater for irrigation. Groundwater still provides more than 50 percent of water for irrigation and 35 percent of the municipal water supply in the state (CAST 2009). The cities were disappointed with CAP water quality as discolored water came out of taps, and some cities have reverted to using wells. Although CAP was conceived as a project for agricultural supply, the water proved to be too expensive for many farmers and so much of the state's Colorado River entitlement remained unused and groundwater was still the source of choice.

When Arizona continued not to use its Compact allocation, California was able to take the unused portion. Arizona's responded by creating a "bank" for underground storage of its unused entitlement so it could keep water from being used across the border in California and hold it so that future entitlements might be sold later. This was indirectly a subsidy to the farmers who would continue taking groundwater – now supplemented by CAP water injected at state expense – instead of buying the CAP water directly. It also was provided a means for Arizona to sell some of its Colorado River water to Nevada (Megdal 2007).

In Arizona, even in the most urbanized active management areas, there is no agreement on how to achieve safe annual yield and groundwater overdraft in Arizona continues. The Arizona Department of Water Resources predicts that if no new water efficiencies are created, groundwater overdraft in the Phoenix AMA alone will increase to 471,000 acre-feet by 2025, an increase of over 30 percent from 1995 (ADWR 1999: ch. 11). The state seems to lack the will to curtail this overdraft as the economic force of urbanization and sympathy for farmers allow easily accessible groundwater to be mined.

Urbanization has continued apace in arid Southern California and Nevada as well. Like these areas depend entirely on imported water for growth. Growth in these areas has not been constrained by the lack of natural water supplies. Typically, people move to an area without considering the reliability of future water supply and, because the cost of domestic water is such a small factor in the cost of housing, they assume that investments will be made by someone else, and that water will be provided. It always has been.

Southern California depends on importing Northern California water through a state water project bringing water from the north as well as importing Colorado River water. But the safety valve for new growth has been the Colorado River, which it has tapped for quantities well beyond its legal entitlement to Colorado River water. California's share of water from the river, like the shares of Arizona and Nevada, was set in the 1928 Boulder Canyon Act. Congress, in authorizing dams and facilities and ratifying the 1922 Colorado River Compact carved up the share of water that was supposed to be used in the lower basin states according to that Compact. The idea was that the federal dams would be built to store this water and the federal government would deliver it under contracts with water users in the various states. But the assumption under these laws was that if one state, or one basin, did not use all the water allocated to it, others could use it until the states that were not using their shares had demand for it (Reisner 1993: 124–5).

So, California as the fastest growing state could soak up the water not needed by the slower growing upper basin states and which could not be used in Arizona because of its lack of delivery facilities, at least until the CAP was built. By the end of the twentieth century, California was using 5 million acre-feet, about 15 percent more than its legal entitlement of 4.4 million acre-feet. During years of negotiation the seven states of the Colorado River hammered out complex plans for how California would begin to reduce demands on the river, reining in slowly, the overuse of water that has slaked the thirst of growing cities in Southern California. Some adjustments were made in how water would be used – and shared among states – in drought, effectively modifying the apparent hard edges of the Compact. Part of California's "soft landing" instead of a forced curtailment of Colorado River use was tied to conservation measures that allowed huge agricultural districts to sell saved water to growing urban areas of Southern California.

A 2003 Quantification Settlement Agreement (QSA) was intended to resolve long-standing tensions among agricultural and municipal suppliers as well as to curtail overall use of Colorado River water in Southern California. The irrigation districts' use was to be reduced by modernizing their irrigation systems and cutting back on irrigation of the least productive lands. One feature was the lining of two vast canals that take river water through desert sands to irrigated district lands (Erie 2006: 140–3).

The QSA took many years to negotiate and will require billions of public dollars to implement. It has not really quelled some of the hostilities among users and its practical effectiveness has not been tested. At a minimum, the approach illustrates the difficulty of reducing the dependence of an urban area on a water supply to which it has become accustomed. Moreover, its fate is complicated by the fact at, as of this writing, the QSA has been invalidated by a 2010 California trial court decision that is being appealed.

The quest to reduce California's overuse of the river illustrates the persistence of transboundary competition for water notwithstanding the existence of a compact, multiple legislative acts, the investment of billions of federal dollars, and extensive interstate litigation. The upper basin states of Colorado, Utah, Wyoming, and New Mexico have struggled to force California to reduce its use so that if and when those states collectively are able to put their share of Colorado River water to use, it will be available.

The Colorado River, of course, is shared by Mexico through which it passes before reaching the Gulf of California (also known as the Sea of Cortez). The Colorado River Compact allocated no water to Mexico, saying only that if it were later determined that Mexico was entitled to water from the river the obligation to deliver it would be shared equally by the upper and the lower basin states. By the 1930s, Mexico had registered its strong views that it needed validation of a right to water from the river. Finally, in 1944 the United States and Mexico signed a treaty assuring Mexico of 1.5 million acre-feet per year. This marked a shift in the United States' longstanding position that under the doctrine of absolute territorial sovereignty it owed Mexico nothing and could use the river to extinction within the United States. The change of position coincided with increasing anxiety over maintaining friendly relations with Mexico, a neighbor with an extensive shared border, during World War II (Mumme 2000).

The Colorado River basin's first major environmental problem to cause legal issues – though not the last – was salinity. It was manifested as another international transboundary problem, and it arose under ambiguities left in the 1944 Treaty. Following the building of Hoover Dam and associated facilities the other basin states campaigned relentlessly for federal investment in projects to benefit them. Many were authorized by Congress and by the 1960s some had been built. The most significant was Glen Canyon Dam. With a capacity of 27 million acre-feet, it is about the same size as Hoover Dam. Together they could store about four years' annual flow of the river. During the many years it took the reservoir behind Glen Canyon Dam (called Lake Powell) to fill, only the bare minimum flows required under the treaty reached Mexico. By the time the water left the United States, much of it had been many times diverted, used, and returned to the river increasingly laden with salts picked up from the irrigated soils.

Mexico protested, arguing that the water left over for Mexico's farmers was too salty to use – such that it actually killed some crops. This was alleged to be a violation of the Treaty with Mexico. Again, the US was firm with Mexico in its resistance, at least at first. It simply replied that the treaty guaranteed delivery of water, not water of a particular quality. Eventually the two countries worked out an amendment to the treaty, Minute 242, requiring that salt concentrations in the water delivered to Mexico be similar to salt levels in the water being diverted for irrigation in the United States. The agreement with oil-rich Mexico was reached during the 1970s energy crisis in the United States (Mumme 2000).

Implementing the reduction in salinity proved very costly. It involved lining the Coachella Canal, protective pumping, interception of salt seeps, and other measures. The largest source of salts was a single, large irrigation project in southwest Arizona at the mouth of the Gila River. The Wellton-Mohawk Irrigation Project facilities had been built by the federal government. Taking water from the Colorado River through these facilities, the district applied them to lands with saline soils. The irrigated area became increasingly saturated and drainage was needed. Wells then pumped the salty water to a tributary of the Colorado, causing noticeable increases in the river's salinity and sparking an outcry from Mexico. Taking the area out of irrigation to solve the salinity problem was not seriously considered (US Bureau of Reclamation 2005).

One of the most ambitious plans for enabling the US to produce water of a sufficient quality to satisfy the agreement with Mexico was construction of the Yuma desalination plant, which would remove salts from the Wellton-Mohawk irrigation return flows so that this water could be mixed with the saltier river water destined for Mexico. While the plant is being constructed, however, the briny waste would go through the canal built to deliver it to the plant and then continue through an extension of the canal to an area near the delta of the Colorado River. Once the plant became operational and could process the salty water this was to stop. The expensive desalination plant was completed in 1992, but did not operate for the next eighteen years, and so the brine continued passing to this delta area known as the Santa Clara Slough (National Research Council 2007: 46–7).

The most recent environmental issue that has engaged the United States and Mexico involves the delta area where the river terminates in the Sea of Cortez. Many thousands of acres of rich wetlands in Mexico for centuries sustained vast populations of birds and fish. A vibrant fishing industry thrived there and indigenous people lived comfortably using local resources. When the flows to Mexico dwindled to the minimum required under the treaty, and nearly all of it was taken for use on Mexican farms, the delta area dried up. Then a vestige of these wetlands was revived and sustained by the highly saline water that was being disposed in the Santa Clara Slough – a supposedly temporary measure until the desalination plant was built.

Then, in the 1990s, during a few high-flow years, the reservoirs on the Colorado in the US exceeded their capacity and "surplus" water flowed to Mexico. The delta area was revitalized, and scientists and environmentalists began an effort to secure sufficient flows to make permanent this accidental restoration. That ten-year effort continues with multi-party collaboration in trying to secure the relatively small annual flows, plus occasional large surges, that are needed to make the restoration of the delta sustainable (Pitt 2001). The interest of US water interests and state and federal governments and the Mexican farmers and governmental entities has been aroused by the prospect for linking environmental restoration with projects for water and sewage treatment and activating the long-moribund desalination plant. The border cities are especially in need of support for such facilities.

Of all the environmental impacts of the dams on the Colorado the greatest attention has been given to another issue. It concerns a few, nearly extinct species of fish indigenous to the river. Although scientists had been aware of the problem for a long time, the long-neglected issue gained poignancy because of a powerful federal law. In the 1980s, the United States Fish and Wildlife Service announced that no more water development could take place on the Colorado or its tributaries without assurance that it would not cause harm to the continued existence of the several threatened and endangered fish species. The Endangered Species Act was to become the primary barrier to water development in the basin as scientists agreed that a primary cause of the demise of the fish was damming and depletion of the river. A process initiated in 1984 among the upper basin states engaged state and federal officials, water developers, and environmentalists to find a way to comply with the ESA without thwarting all water development. After four years, a recovery program was agreed upon, and since then more that $120 million in public money has been spent to implement it. The expenditures were for restoring habitat destroyed by water project development. Unfortunately, it appears that fewer fish survive today than when the program began (Rosner 2010). A similar program was initiated in the San Juan River basin, a tributary to the Colorado. And in the lower basin there is a large, Lower Basin Multi-Species Conservation Program. Tens of millions of dollars have been spent on these programs as well.

A relatively recent, transboundary issue with Mexico involves groundwater. Early in the twentieth century, in addressing the interstate issues discussed above, the US Congress agreed to build federal water facilities. One of the projects undertaken after the passage of the 1928 Boulder Canyon Project Act was the construction of the All-American Canal. At the time, a rich agricultural industry had grown up in the hot and fertile, but otherwise dry Imperial Valley based on Colorado River water. The water had been taken through the Alamo Canal constructed in Mexico in 1901 to fields north of the border in California. The canal broke during flood years causing damage and interrupting irrigation. To forestall further disasters and to allay concerns that Mexico would lay claim to the water passing through the canal in its territory and thereby disrupt the valley's lucrative enterprise, California and local interests championed a canal entirely within the United States. The All-American Canal was completed in 1940, diverting 3 million acre-feet of water per year at Imperial Dam and delivering it to irrigation districts just north of the border.

This huge canal not only delivered vast amounts of water to US farmers, but it leaked large quantities of water – about 67,000 acre-feet per year. At first, this caused flooding of Mexican communities, but local farmers and others began pumping and using the water, and became dependent on it. The seepage also had environmental benefits, feeding wetlands and terrestrial habitat.

In 1988, the United States Congress authorized a canal lining project to capture the seepage so the water could be used in the United States. This was seen partly as a means of providing water to satisfy the commitment made to provide water to the San Luis Rey Indian tribes in Southern California as part of a settlement of their water rights claims on a river having no connection to the Colorado. But the lining would also make more secure quantities of water from the Colorado for growing urban areas of Southern California (San Luis Rey Indian Water Rights Settlement Act, 1988). Congress did not provide federal funds for the project because it assumed that the cities benefiting from the canal lining would pay for the project (US Bureau of Reclamation 2006: 1.1–1.2).

The failure to consult with Mexico or local water users before the United States unilaterally assumed that the seepage water belonged to it created international tensions and Mexico protested. Few discussions were held between the two countries. Canal lining remained a threat to Mexico, but was not moving ahead because of a lack of funding. California eventually said it would pay for the project as part of the Quantification Settlement Agreement discussed above. Thus, it became an element in the complicated arrangement for resolving interstate differences and helping California reduce its overuse of Colorado River water.

Opposition to the canal lining project was not confined to Mexico, but included interests in the United States. This led to a federal lawsuit focusing on the environmental impacts by varied interests, which ranged from community groups in Mexico, to a US city, to environmental organizations in both countries. The action was eventually dismissed with the United States Court of Appeals for the Ninth Circuit holding that the environmental claims were moot because, while the appeal of a lower court dismissal was being considered in 2006, Congress passed legislation saying that the only law governing construction of the canal was the 1944 Treaty with Mexico. This effectively left the court nothing to decide under the National Environmental Policy Act, the Endangered Species Act, the Migratory Bird Treaty Act, and other laws cited by the plaintiffs (*Consejo de Desarrollo Economico de Mexicali v. United States*, 2007). The canal construction could – and did – proceed (Cortez-Lara *et al.* 2008).

Tribal rights to water are another critical issue on the Colorado. Thirty-four Indian reservations are located within the Colorado River Basin and though not all have land contiguous to the river or its tributaries (Pontius 1997: 69). No reliable estimates exist for the potential water rights claims of these tribes but one extreme estimate for the Navajo Nation alone was as high as 2 million acre-feet per year (Back and Taylor 1980: 74).

The case of *Arizona v. California* decided by the Supreme Court in 1963 included the reserved water rights claims of five Indian reservations along the mainstream of the Colorado. The practicably irrigable acreage formula adopted by the Court for quantifying such rights resulted in findings that the tribes were entitled to use more than 1.3 million acre-feet per year. At this point, only a small fraction of these rights is being used. On a river where others now use more than the total average annual flow, the assertion of these rights would be profoundly disruptive. Meanwhile, many other tribes in the basin are seeking adjudication of the quantities of water to which they are entitled. For the last thirty years, the Navajo Nation has engaged in a series of negotiations with the various Colorado River Basin states to claim its outstanding water rights. These efforts resulted in enactment of the Navajo Indian Irrigation Project and securing a share of the Gila River Indian Community Settlement. Notably, the Navajo Nation's long-standing water rights claims with the state of New Mexico were recently resolved and embodied in federal legislation, the Omnibus Public Lands Management Act of 2009. The Act secured the use of 600,000 acre-feet per year to the Navajo Nation as well as allocating \$870 million for water delivery infrastructure. The Navajo Nation has significant outstanding water rights in both Utah and Arizona as well, which some believe could amount to an additional 450,000 acre-feet per year (Jenkins 2008).

Several Arizona tribes on tributaries to the Colorado have had their rights quantified and – given the other pressures on scarce water supplies – Congress has declared that the water for those tribes is to come from the CAP and from reclaimed sewage. As discussed earlier, CAP water has proven uneconomical for many users in Arizona, so this arrangement provides not only a way to furnish water to the tribes but puts the federal government itself in the position of assuming the cost – which is otherwise repayable to the federal government by users of CAP. Moreover, the tribes may sell the water on a limited basis. Because they need not pay for the water because it is part of their entitlement they can effectively sell CAP water at less than the usual cost to irrigators and cities. Negotiations are underway for the settlement of water claims of as many as 13 tribes in the Colorado River basin states (Weldon and McKnight 2007).

All of the issues discussed – transboundary competition, growth in urban demand, environmental pressures, tribal rights, groundwater availability – are compounded in times of water shortage. And for the states whose water uses depend on the Colorado shortages are an unavoidable reality. First, the transboundary allocation arrangements beginning with the 1922 Compact were erroneously predicated on average flows being 16.5 million acre-feet, which then seemed reasonable based on the short period of record available. The idea was to build enough reservoirs at the right places to distribute that quantity of water, on average, each year. But the Colorado River basin, like many others in the West, experiences highly variable flows and droughts as part of the natural scheme. Flows in the Colorado have varied from a high of 22.2 million acre feet per year in 1984 to a low of 3.8 million acre-feet per year in 2002 (USGS 2004). In addition, new data based on studies of tree rings going back several centuries reveal a troubling reality: the average flow appears to be only about 13.5 million acre-feet (Woodhouse *et al.* 2006).

The cyclical variations in stream flows exacerbated by multi-year droughts, and the over-allocation of the water produced by the river, are now further complicated by climate change impacts, some of which are being felt already, and other graver impacts are being projected by modeling that has gained increasing consensus among scientists. A study based on the IPCC data predicts that in the Colorado River basin runoff may decrease 30 percent during the twenty-first century and that the requirements of the Compact may be only met 60–75 percent of the time by 2025 (Bates *et al.* 2008). A recent study that has combined multiple climate models makes more modest findings, still projecting supply being reduced below current demand (Christensen and Lettenmaier 2007). Projecting growth in demand, including allowing the upper basin states, which are not using their full apportionment, creates an even more troubling scenario.

Conclusion

The multiple and intersecting water policy challenges facing the Colorado River illustrate the confounding complexity of modern water problems. Although not all regions experience as elaborately the six challenges discussed in that case study, several of those scarcity-inducing challenges exist in some measure throughout the Americas. Coping with these challenges by forming policies that take account of the forces inherent in each, rather than assuming that "water problems" are simply about finding and delivering a water supply, is the work of water experts and water managers, as well as the work of community and national leaders.

References

ADWR (1999) *Third Management Plan for Phoenix Active Management Area 2000–2010.* Phoenix, AZ: Arizona Department of Water Resources.

Amos, A. (2006) "The Use of State Instream Flow Laws for Federal Lands: Respecting State Control while Meeting Federal Purposes." *Environmental Law* 36: 1237.

Back, W. and Taylor, J. (1980) "Navajo Water Rights: Pulling the Plug on the Colorado River." *Natural Resources Journal* 20: 71.

Bates, B. C., Kundzewicz, Z. W., Wu, S. and Palutikof, J. P. (eds) (2008) *Climate Change and Water.* Technical Paper of the Intergovernmental Panel on Climate Change. Geneva: IPCC Secretariat.

CAST (2009) *Water, People, and the Future: Water Availability for Agriculture in the United States.* Issue Paper 44. Ames, IA: Council for Agricultural Science and Technology.

CDWR (2008) *Managing an Uncertain Future, Climate Change Adaptation Strategies for California's Water.* Sacramento, CA: California Department of Water Resources. Available at www.water.ca.gov/climatechange/docs/ClimateChangeWhitePaper.pdf (accessed February 28, 2014).

Christensen, N. S. and Lettenmaier, D. P. (2007) "A Multimodel Ensemble Approach to Assessment of Climate Change Impacts on the Hydrology and Water Resources of the Colorado River Basin." *Hydrology and Earth System Sciences* 11: 1417–34.

Cortez-Lara, A., Donovan, M. K., and Whiteford, S. (2009) "The All-American Canal Lining Dispute: An American Resolution over Mexican Groundwater Rights?" *Frontera Norte* 21(41): 127–50.

DeCoteau, J. (2006) "Effects of Non-Indian Development on Indian Water Rights." In J. E. Thorson, S. Briton, and B. G. Colby (eds), *Tribal Water Rights: Essays in Contemporary Law, Policy, and Economics*, pp. 115–28. Tucson, AZ: University of Arizona Press.

Doremus, H. (2001) "Water, Population Growth, and Endangered Species in the West." *University of Colorado Law Review* 72: 361.

Erie, S. P. (2006). *Beyond Chinatown: the Metropolitan Water District, Growth, and the environment in Southern California*. Stanford, CA: Stanford University Press.

Field, C. B., Mortsch, L. D., Brklacich, M., Forbes, D. L. Kovacs, P., Patz, J. A., Running, S. W., and Scott, M. J. (2007) "North America." In M. L. Parry, O. F. Canziani, J. P. Palutikof, P. J. van der Linden, and C. E. Hanson (eds), *Climate Change 2007: Impacts, Adaptation and Vulnerability. Contribution of Working Group II to the Fourth Assessment Report of the Intergovernmental Panel on Climate Change*, pp. 617–52. Cambridge: Cambridge University Press.

Getches, D. H. (1985) "Competing Demands for the Colorado River." *University of Colorado Law Review* 56: 413.

—— (2000) "Metamorphosis of Western Water Policy." *Stanford Environmental Law Review* 20: 1.

—— (2009) *Water Law in a Nutshell*, 4th edn. St Paul, MN: Thomson/West.

Hirt, P., Gustafson, A., and Larson, K. L. (2008) "The Mirage in the Valley of the Sun." *Environmental History* 13: 482–514.

Jenkins, M. (2008) "Seeking the Water Jackpot." *High Country News* (March 17): 10–16.

Kenny, J. F., Barber, N. L., Hutson, S. S., Linsey, K. S., Lovelace, J. K., and Maupin, M. A. (2009) *Estimated Use of Water in the United States in 2005*. Circular 1344. Reston, VA: US Geological Survey. Available at http://pubs.usgs.gov/circ/1344/pdf/c1344.pdf (accessed February 28, 2014).

Larson, E. K., Grimm, N. B., Gober, P., and Redman, C. L. (2005) "The Paradoxical Ecology and Management of Water in the Phoenix, USA Metropolitan Area." *Journal of Ecohydrology and Hydrobiology* 5(4): 287–96.

Leshy, J. D. (2008) "The Federal Role in Managing the Nation's Groundwater." *Hastings West-Northwest Journal of Environmental Law and Policy* 14: 1323.

Megdal, S. B. (2007) "Arizona's Recharge and Recovery Programs." In B. G. Colby and K. L. Jacobs (eds), *Arizona Water Policy: Management Innovations in an Urbanizing, Arid Region*, pp. 188–203. Washington, DC: RFF Press.

Mumme, S. P. (2000) "Minute 242 and Beyond: Challenges and Opportunities for Managing Transboundary Groundwater on the Mexico-US Border." *Natural Resources Journal* 40: 341.

National Research Council (1992) *Water Transfers in the West: Efficiency, Equity, and the Environment*. Washington, DC: National Academies Press.

—— (2007) *Colorado River Basin Management: Evaluating and Adjusting to Hydroclimatic Variability*. Washington, DC: National Academies Press.

Parry, M. L., Canziani, O. F., and Palutikof, J. P. (2007) "Technical Summary." In M. L. Parry, O. F. Canziani, J. P. Palutikof, P. J. van der Linden, and C. E. Hanson (eds), *Climate Change 2007: Impacts, Adaptation and Vulnerability. Contribution of Working Group II to the Fourth Assessment Report of the Intergovernmental Panel on Climate Change*, pp. 23–78. Cambridge: Cambridge University Press.

Pitt, J. (2001) "Can We Restore the Colorado River Delta?" *Journal of Arid Environments* 49(1): 211–20.

Pontius, D. (1997) *Colorado River Basin Study*. Final Report to the Western Water Policy Review Advisory Commission.

Reisner, M. (1993) *Cadillac Desert: The American West and its Disappearing Water*, revised edn. New York: Penguin Books.

Reynolds, K. A., Mena, K. D., and Gerba, C. P. (2008) "Risk of Waterborne Illness Via Drinking Water in the United States." *Reviews of Environmental Contamination and Toxicology* 192: 117–58.

Rosner, H. (2010) "One Tough Sucker." *High Country News* (June 7): 12–19.

Tarlock, A. D., Corbridge, J. N., Getches, D. H., and Benson, R. (2009) *Water Resource Management: A Casebook in Law and Public Policy*, 6th edn. New York: Foundation Press.

Travis, W. (2007) *New Geographies of the American West*. Washington, DC: Island Press.

US Bureau of Reclamation (2005) *Quality of Water, Colorado River Basin*. Progress Report 22. Available at http://www.usbr.gov/uc/progact/salinity/pdfs/PR22.pdf (accessed February 28, 2014).

US Bureau of Reclamation (2006) *All-American Canal Lining Project Supplemental Information Report*. Available at www.usbr.gov/lc/region/programs/AAC/SIR_1-12-06.pdf (accessed February 28, 2014).

USEPA (2009) *Drinking Water Infrastructure Needs Survey and Assessment: Fourth Report to Congress*. EPA 816-R-09-001. Washington, DC: Office of Water, US Environmental Protection Agency.

USGS (2004) *Climatic Fluctuations, Drought, and Flow in the Colorado River Basin*. Fact Sheet 2004-3062, version 2. Reston, VA: US Geological Survey.

Weldon, J. B. and McKnight, L. M. (2007) "Future Indian Water Settlements in Arizona: The Race to the Bottom of the Waterhole". *Arizona Law Review* 49: 441.

Wilkinson, C. F. (1992) *Crossing the Next Meridian: Land, Water, and the Future of the West*. Washington, DC: Island Press.

Wolf, A. (2005) "Transboundary Water Conflicts and Cooperation." In D. Kenney (ed.), *In Search of Sustainable Water Management*, pp. 131–54. Northampton, MA: Edward Elgar Publishing.

Woodhouse, C. A., Gray, S., and Meko, D. (2006) "Updated Streamflow Reconstructions for the Upper Colorado River Basin." *Water Resources Research* 42(5): W05415 (doi:10.1029/2005WR004455).

Cases and documents

Arizona v. California, 373 US 546 (1963).

Bean v. Morris, 221 US 485 (1911).

Consejo de Desarrollo Economico de Mexicali v. United States, 482 F.3d 1157 (9th Cir. 2007).

Potlatch Corp. v. United States, 12 P. 3d 1256 (Idaho 2000).

Riverside Irrigation Dist. v. Andrews, 758 F.2d 508 (10th Cir. 1985).

San Luis Rey Indian Water Rights Settlement Act, Pub. L. No. 100-675, title I, 102 Stat. 4000 (1988).

United States v. New Mexico, 438 US 696 (1978).

United States v. Winters, 207 US 564 (1908).

3 Water scarcity in Latin America and the Caribbean

Myths and reality

Abel Mejía

Why water scarcity matters

The main purpose of this chapter is to discuss some underlying issues that drive water scarcity in the Latin America and Caribbean (LAC) region. It argues that rapid urbanization over the past 50 years, lack of infrastructure (including rehabilitation of existing facilities), and weak governance are crucial factors to explain scarcity in an apparently water-rich region.

With a population of 554 million in 2008, over a territory of 20,136,000 km^2, LAC is a mosaic of 34 countries within a very diverse climatic and geographical setting. While these countries enjoy a relative abundance of water on a per-capita basis and high coverage of water supply services, there is ample evidence that water scarcity is affecting the daily life of millions.

There is also a growing perception that scarcity is mostly driven by climate change and El Niño/La Niña cycles. Moreover, the expectations are that water investments should be done at no cost to the population. As a consequence, water policy and infrastructure investments have become a focus of attention of civil society organizations and the news media to achieve universal access to potable water and sanitation services, reduce pollution, and protect people and economic activities from devastating floods.

This chapter suggests that water scarcity in the LAC region should be seen beyond the traditional framework of the water supply, sanitation, and irrigation sectors. Therefore, the analysis is expanded to include the unmet demand for water infrastructure services that reduce pollution, and improve flood and ecosystems management. It is not fortuitous that these are also high development priorities for the LAC region to help reduce poverty, and support sustainable economic development.

Facts and indicators about water scarcity

With 30 percent of rainfall and 33 percent of the world's water resources, water is relatively abundant in LAC – about 28,000 m^3 per inhabitant per year (FAO 2009; Table 3.1). However, surface water availability is highly seasonal and unevenly distributed in space. For instance, in the sub-region of Mexico, Central

Table 3.1 Distribution of water resources in the Latin America and Caribbean region

Sub-region	*Area*	*Precipitation*		*Water resources*	*Per capita water*	*Water withdrawals*
	km²	*mm*	*km³*	*km³*	*m³/hab*	*km³*
Mexico	1,958,200	772	1,512	409	4,338	78
Central America	521,598	2,395	1,194	6,889	20,370	12
Greater Antilles	198,330	1,451	288	82	2,804	15
Lesser Antilles	8,460	1,141	17	4		
Guyana sub-region	378,240	1,421	897	329	191,422	2
Andean sub-region	4,718,320	1,991	9,394	5,186	49,902	50
Brazil	8,547,400	1,758	15,026	5,418	33,097	55
Southern sub-region	4,121,190	846	3,488	1,313	22,389	50
LAC region	20,451,190	1,556	31,816	13,429	27,673	263
World	133,870,200		110,000	41,022	6,984	3,253
LAC/world (%)	15.27		29	33		8.1

Source: UNESCO (1999)

America, and the Caribbean, 49.3 percent of the stream flow takes place between August and October, but only 7.3 percent from February to April. In South America the ratio between the wettest and driest three months of the year are less skewed – 34.6 percent of stream flow between May and July, and 17 percent between November and January (UNESCO 1999).

The Falkenmark indicator is a common and widely used metric of water scarcity (Falkenmark 1989). It proposes a threshold of 1,700 m³ of renewable water resources per capita per year to characterize water stress at the country level. This threshold is based on estimates of water requirements in the residential, agricultural, and energy sectors, as well as environmental needs. Countries that fall below 1,000 m³ are under water scarcity, and below 500 m³ are under absolute water scarcity. Only Haiti, Barbados, and Antigua are below the 1,700 m³ threshold. The rest of the countries are well above this limit with the exception of El Salvador, the Dominican Republic, and Trinidad and Tobago. These latter countries are getting closer to the 1,700 m³ thresholds.

The water vulnerability index proposed by Professor Shiklomanov is often quoted and frequently used in global and regional analysis of water scarcity. It deals with water scarcity by considering both supply and demand. This index estimates the total annual withdrawals as a percentage of available water resource for each country, and aggregates information for 26 economic regions in the world.

The index suggests that a country is water scarce if annual withdrawals are between 20 and 40 percent of annual supply, and severely water scarce if this figure exceeds 40 percent. In the case of the LAC region, only Cuba with 21 percent barely falls in the range of water scarce. Mexico with 19.1 percent, the Dominican Republic with 16.1 percent, and Argentina with 10.1 percent is in the range of 10 to 20 percent – the rest of the countries have a very low water vulnerability ratio.

These indexes have been useful for aggregated analyses that identify trends and priorities that are important inputs for global policy discussions. However, its usefulness for water scarcity analysis at the country level, including policy analysis and investment planning, is limited since they do not capture seasonal and geographical distribution of water availability, and because of the implicit limitations of the estimates of cumulative water withdrawals.

More recently, the International Water Management Institute (IWMI) has proposed to take into account a more detailed estimation of water demand by calculating the share of the renewable water resources available for human needs, accounting for existing water infrastructure (IWMI 2004). Its analysis of demand is based on consumptive use (evapotranspiration), and the remainder of water withdrawn is accounted for as return flows. IWMI estimated water demands in 2025, including an assessment of potential infrastructure development and increased efficiency in irrigation through improved water management policies (IWMI 2007).

In IWMI's approach, countries are called "physically water scarce" when they are not able to meet water demand in 2025, even after accounting for future adaptive capacity. On the other hand, countries that have sufficient renewable water resources, but not infrastructure to make these resources available to satisfy demand, are defined as "economically water scarce."

According to this approach to scarcity, with the exception of Panama, Costa Rica, Ecuador, Surinam, and Uruguay, the rest of the countries in the LAC region will be economically water scarce by 2025.

The concept of economic water scarcity is particularly useful for the LAC region because it facilitates a deeper understanding of scarcity beyond simply per capita water availability. However, for meaningful policy analysis and decision-making in the water sector, a broader approach to demand for water services would be considered.

A suggestion for further analysis is to split the economic water scarcity index in two components: one that reflects the deficit of infrastructure to deliver water services (infrastructure water scarcity), and another that considers the institutional and policy capacity to deliver water services at the desired performance level (governance water scarcity).

The basic insight behind this suggestion is that insufficiency of water in the LAC region, is primarily driven by inefficient supply of services rather that by water shortages. The World Water Assessment Programme has explicitly addressed this important recommendation by recognizing that the lack of basic services for water supply and sanitation is often due to mismanagement, corruption, lack of appropriate institutions, and bureaucratic inertia (WWAP 2006).

Plenty of water, but...

Asymmetries between water resources availability and population at the country level are large. Water resources are mostly located in the inland of the continent, while urbanization and land development followed the path of decisions made in colonial times. Cities and economic activity in the colonies was concentrated either near the coast to facilitate exports to Spain and Portugal, or on the hinterland of the main cities of the Aztec and Inca empires to take advantage of free and abundant labor.

In the case of Mexico, 77 percent of the population, 84 percent of the economic activity, and 82 percent of the irrigated area is located in the central and northern plateau and above the 1,000-meter elevation. In contrast, 72 percent of water availability is in the south and below that altitude.

Peru, with a per capita water availability of 58,000 m^3 per year, has 70 percent of the country's population of 29 million, and 90 percent of the economic output is located along the Pacific Coast, with only 1 percent of the country's water availability. This asymmetry, makes the most economically dynamic region of Peru severely water stressed.

In Venezuela, 90 percent of population and economic activity is located in the north of the country with less than 10 percent of water availability. Most of the water availability is found south of the Orinoco River, away from the northern coast.

Over the past 50 years, the LAC region has witnessed a large expansion of water and sanitation infrastructure, irrigated area, and hydropower generation (Table 3.2). Coverage of water supply services in urban areas has increased from about 40 percent in 1950 to 92 percent in 2005. This indicator is particularly impressive because, at the same time, with the exception of the smaller islands in the Caribbean and Guyana, the LAC region had experienced accelerated demographic growth and rapid urbanization – in the case of Guyana, urban population has decreased 0.1 percent per year since 1990. With 85 percent of population in urban areas, as a consequence of an annual urban growth of about 2 to 3 percent over the period 1990–2005, the LAC region is today the most urbanized of the developing world.

However, in spite of high network coverage levels of water supply and sanitation services, their quality is still low. Continuity of water services, 24 hours and seven days a week, adequate pressure in the pipes, and meeting the Pan American Health Organization drinking water standards at the point of use, are challenging for many cities of LAC. The high level of unaccounted-for water (UFW) within 35 to 50 percent in many utilities of the LAC region, portraits well the paradox of water abundance, high coverage levels of network infrastructure, and low quality of water services (Table 3.3).

Reducing unaccounted for water is not only about repairing leaking pipes, replacing water meters, and reducing wastage, but more importantly they are related to the effective implementation of governance policies to enhance institutional accountability, charge water tariffs that are reflective of costs and implement transparent policies to address affordability issues.

The irrigated area in the LAC region has increased from 8 million to about 18 million hectares from 1960 to 2000 (FAO 2009). However, the actual irrigated area should be significantly lower when considering the existing problems in operation, maintenance, and rehabilitation of irrigation systems (public and

Table 3.2 Water indicators by country within the Latin America and Caribbean region

Country	*GNI/cap*	*Area*	*Population*	*Urban pop*	*Urban growth annual %*	*Ag land*	*Ag land*	*Hydropower*	*Freshwater*	*Water withdrawal*	*Water supply urban coverage*	*Water supply rural coverage*	*Sanitation urban coverage*	*Sanitation rural coverage*	*Under-5 mortality*	*Diarrhea prevalence*
	US$	*Thousand km²*	*Thousands*	*%*	*1990–2005*	*%*	*Million Ha*	*%*	*m³/cap*	*%*	*%*	*%*	*%*	*%*	*1000 births*	*% under 5*
Mexico	7,310	1,908.70	103.10	70.00	1.70	56	106.89	11.20	3,967	19.10	100	87	91	41	27	9.70
Guatemala	2,400	108.40	12.60	47.20	3.20	43	4.66	34.70	8,667	1.80	99	92	90	82	43	13.30
Belize	3,570	22.80	0.29	48.30	3.00	7	0.16		54,832	0.90	100	82	71	25	17	11.00
Honduras	1,120	111.90	7.20	46.50	3.60	26	2.91	48.10	13,311	0.90	95	81	87	54	40	19.30
Nicaragua	950	121.40	5.10	59.00	2.50	58	7.04	11.40	36,840	0.70	90	63	56	34	37	14.00
El Salvador	2,450	20.70	6.90	59.80	3.30	82	1.70	31.20	2,587	7.20	94	70	77	39	27	19.80
Costa Rica	4,700	51.10	4.30	61.70	3.60	56	2.86	79.00	25,975	2.40	100	92	89	97	12	
Panama	4,630	74.40	3.20	70.80	2.00	30	2.23	65.60	45,613	0.60	99	79	89	51	24	12.60
Cuba		109.80	11.30	75.50	0.60	61	6.70	0.60	3,361	21.50	95	78	99	95	7	
Jamaica	3,390	10.80	2.70	53.10	1.20	47	0.51	1.90	3,540	4.40	98	88	91	69	20	
Puerto Rico	10,950	8.90	3.90	97.60	2.70	25	0.22		1,815							
Dominican Republic	2,460	48.40	8.90	66.80	2.80	76	3.68	11.50	2,361	16.10	97	91	81	73	31	20.10
Haiti	450	27.60	8.50	38.80	3.30	58	1.60	47.50	1,524	7.60	52	56	57	14	120	25.70

Table 3.2 continued

Country	*GNI/cap*	*Area*	*Population*	*Urban pop*	*Urban growth annual %*	*Ag land*	*Ag land*	*Hydropower*	*Freshwater*	*Water withdrawal*	*Water supply urban coverage*	*Water supply rural coverage*	*Sanitation urban coverage*	*Sanitation rural coverage*	*Under-5 mortality*	*Diarrhea prevalence*
	US$	*Thousand km²*	*Thousands*	*%*	*1990–2005*	*%*	*Million Ha*	*%*	*m³/cap*	*%*	*%*	*%*	*%*	*%*	*1000 births*	*% under 5*
Trinidad and Tobago	10,300	5.10	1.30	12.20	2.90	26	0.13		2,911	8.20	92	88	100	100	19	
Barbados		0.40	0.27	52.70	1.40	44	0.02		371	90.00	100	100	99	100	12	
Antigua and Barbuda	10,500	0.40	0.08	39.10	2.50	32	0.01		1,208		95	89	98	94	12	
Dominica	3,800	0.80	0.07	72.90	0.50	31	0.02				84	100	86	75	15	
Grenada	3,860	0.30	0.11	30.60	0.50	38	0.01				97	93	96	97	21	
Saint Kitts and Nevis	7,840	0.40	0.05	32.20	0.40	28	0.01				99	99	99	99	20	
Santa Lucia	4,580	0.60	0.16	27.60	1.00	33	0.02				98	98	89	89	14	
San Vincent and the Granadines	3,530	0.40	0.12	45.90	1.40	41	0.02				93	93	96	96	20	
Curacao																
Aruba																
Bonaire																
Martinique and Guadalupe																

Table 3.2 continued

Country	*GNI/cap*	*Area*	*Population*	*Urban pop*	*Urban growth annual %*	*Ag land*	*Ag land*	*Hydropower*	*Freshwater*	*Water withdrawal*	*Water supply urban coverage*	*Water supply rural coverage*	*Sanitation urban coverage*	*Sanitation rural coverage*	*Under-5 mortality*	*Diarrhea prevalence*
	US$	*Thousand km²*	*Thousands*	*%*	*1990–2005*	*%*	*Million Ha*	*%*	*m³/cap*	*%*	*%*	*%*	*%*	*%*	*1000 births*	*% under 5*
Suriname	2,540	156.00	0.45	73.90	1.30	1	0.16		195,887	0.80	98	73	99	76	39	14.80
Guyana	1,020	196.90	0.75	28.20	-0.10	9	1.77		320,812	0.70	83	83	86	60	63	
French Guyana																
Venezuela	4,820	882.10	26.60	93.40	2.70	25	22.05	71.00	27,185	1.20	85	70	71	48		21.00
Colombia	2,290	1,109.50	45.60	72.70	2.10	38	42.16	79.80	46,316	0.50	99	71	96	54	21	13.90
Ecuador	2,620	276.80	13.20	62.80	2.60	27	7.47	58.90	32,657	3.90	97	89	94	82	25	19.90
Peru	2,650	1,280.00	28.00	72.60	2.00	17	21.76	72.30	57,780	1.20	89	65	74	32	27	15.40
Bolivia	1,010	1,084.40	9.20	64.20	3.10	34	36.87	49.00	33,054	0.50	95	68	60	22	65	24.80
Brazil	3,550	8,459.40	186.40	84.20	2.30	31	262.24	82.80	29,066	1.10	96	57	83	37	33	13.10
Argentina	4,470	2,736.70	38.70	90.10	1.40	47	128.62	30.40	7,123	10.60	98	80	92	83	18	
Chile	5,870	748.80	16.30	87.60	1.80	20	14.98	45.40	54,249	1.40	100	58	95	62	10	
Paraguay	1,040	397.30	5.90	58.50	3.50	63	25.03	100.00	15,936	0.50	99	68	94	61	23	16.10
Uruguay	4,360	175.00	3.50	92.00	0.90	85	14.88	81.00	17,036	5.30	100	100	100	99	15	
Total		20,136.20	554.76				719.40									

Sources: World Bank; FAO Aquastat; World Resources Institute

Table 3.3 Performance of water utilities in selected countries within the Latin America and Caribbean region

Country	*Year*	*Water coverage (%)*	*Sewerage coverage (%)*	*Non-revenue water (%)*	*Metering coverage (%)*	*Operational cost (US$/m³ sold)*	*Collection period (days)*	*Operating cost ratio (%)*
Brazil	2004	80	26	46	82	0.79	135	1.00
	2008	81	43	39	76	1.04	112	1.49
Chile	2002	100	98	28		0.23		2.84
	2006	100	99	33	98	0.62	88	1.39
Colombia	2003	88	82	45	86	0.48	241	1.43
	2004	89	83	44	92	0.53	220	1.51
Costa Rica	2002	94	38					1.02
	2004	97	31	50	23	0.17	40	3.27
Ecuador	2003	63	28	73	59	0.29	148	2.44
	2005	68	34	71	80	0.70	151	1.04
El Salvador	2006	73	39	34	65	0.03	93	1.17
Bolivia	2002	99	78	33		0.52	192	0.57
	2006	88	66	35	92	0.26	72	1.56
Argentina	2002	88	63	31	11	0.13	124	1.71
	2006	85	63	31	33	0.16	61	1.49
Mexico	2005	100	84	32	82	0.66	108	1.14
	2006	100	64	28	62	0.63	65	1.16
Nicaragua	2002	73		50				
	2005	94	34		69	0.38	151	1.11
Panama	2002	99	55	69		0.13	298	2.24
	2006	100	48	39	43	0.18	112	1.44

Table 3.3 continued

Country	*Year*	*Water coverage (%)*	*Sewerage coverage (%)*	*Non-revenue water (%)*	*Metering coverage (%)*	*Operational cost (US$/m³ sold)*	*Collection period (days)*	*Operating cost ratio (%)*
Paraguay	2002	75	43	45		0.14		
	2005	72	32	44	91	0.17	170	
Peru	2004	84	76	61.9	63	0.44	149	1.01
	2008	86	78	42	63	0.58	67	1.18
Uruguay	2001	96	15	51	96	0.89	71	1.55
	2006	94	22	54	97	0.82	45	1.66
Venezuela	2006	90	74	62	38	0.26	416	0.95

Source: van den Berg and Danilenko (2011)

private) and inconsistencies in reporting irrigated and rain-fed areas. For instance, available information on irrigated crops of 8.5 million hectares is only about 50 percent of the total irrigated land.

While there are large statistical inconsistencies in the data sources, there is convergence in the estimation of the agriculture land, which is vast – 719 million hectares, or about 35 percent of total available land. According to FAO, the irrigation potential is estimated at 77.8 million hectares, of which 65 percent is located in Brazil, Argentina, Mexico, and Peru. While LAC's share of the global irrigated area is less than 7 percent, over the past decades it became a large world exporter of rain-fed agriculture.

An increase of irrigated areas is foreseen for the less-humid regions where irrigation constitutes a production support, but in many countries it has reached a limit due to scarcity and mismanagement. In tropical and other humid climate areas: the Pampa in Argentina, Lesser Antilles, Central America, Colombia, Amazon basin and Andean countries, programs are being carried out for supplementary irrigation on high-yielding crops with the objective of stabilizing production during dry periods. At the same time, there is a trend towards a better integration of surface water and groundwater in countries like Argentina, Ecuador, Peru, Mexico, and the Dominican Republic.

In Mexico, 2.8 million hectares of irrigation districts, and 2.4 million hectares of supplemental irrigation (*distritos de temporal tecnificado*), constitute the largest area with drainage infrastructure of the LAC region. However, there are increasing problems related to excess water in areas that are susceptible to water logging, and salinization. For instance, water-logging valleys (*varzeas*) in Brazil cover approximately 1.2 million hectares. Salinization induced by irrigation is also a serious concern in Argentina, Cuba, Mexico, and Peru, and northeastern Brazil.

Water pollution is related to infrastructure and governance deficits in the water sector. Only 20 percent of wastewater is effectively treated in LAC, but there is infrastructure to treat about 35 percent. While large investments in wastewater treatment have been planned for Buenos Aires, Mexico City, Bogota, Lima, and Sao Paulo, they have been delayed for many years because of the lack of strong institutions and policy frameworks that are hindering effective actions.

In 2009–2010, Sao Paulo, Rio, and Buenos Aires suffered from devastating floods with a balance of casualties and large economic losses. Urban floods are linked to a more intense hydrologic cycle but, more importantly, they are the consequence of increases in imperviousness cover that reduces runoff concentration time and increases peak flows; fragmented decision making of metropolitan authorities; and lack of adequate planning and construction of regulating and trunk infrastructure to manage floods in urban watersheds.

In rural areas, floods are typically related to recurrent climatic events in large alluvial valleys and in foothill areas (flash floods). In the case of Argentina, a significant portion of the population and economic activity is located in the flood plain of the Parana River system, which has suffered a major flood event with a recurrence of about once every 10 years. Since the early 1990s, the Argentinean federal government has undertaken a major effort to build infrastructure and implement non-structural measures to protect urban and rural areas. However, it needs strong coordination between the government authorities of the provinces and the federal levels, and substantial budgetary allocations to operate and maintain the extensive flood-management infrastructure in place.

Since the early 1960s, construction of dams and hydropower generation facilities has been impressive. A sustained financial effort to expand hydropower makes the LAC region the world leader in production of renewable energy as a proportion of total generation capacity. In most of the countries in South America, as well as in Panama and Honduras, hydropower represents more than 50 percent of the installed capacity for electricity generation (Table 3.2).

The potential for hydropower development in the LAC region has been estimated in excess of 200 GW, and governments are eagerly interested in new projects. Expansion of hydropower capacity is taking place in sensitive ecosystems: the Amazon (Madeira, Tocantins, and Xingu), the eastern slope of the Andes (Peru), the Caroni River in Venezuela, and in southern Chile. All these new developments are facing formidable opposition because of their social impacts, issues linked to indigenous rights, and multiple environmental concerns (environmental flows, and protection of biodiversity hotspots).

Water scarcity is also affecting urban and rural areas that are supplied from groundwater. In Mexico, about two million hectares (33 percent of irrigated area) depend on groundwater resources, and approximately 75 million people (about three-fourths of Mexico's population) as well as a large part of the industries depend on groundwater. As a consequence of wrong policy choices, including over-allocation of water rights and large electricity subsidies in rural areas, over-exploitation has increased: from 20 aquifers in 1970, to 103 in 2003. They supply 14 km^3 per year – about half of the total groundwater abstraction consisting of 9 km^3 from annual recharge and about 5 km^3 from storage accumulated during thousands of years (World Bank 2005).

What drives scarcity?

This chapter makes the argument that the main driving force behind scarcity in the LAC region is the combination of rapid urbanization and weak governance. It also claims that a main consequence of urbanization and weak governance is the formation of slums – 27 percent of the urban population of the LAC region lives in slums (UN-Habitat 2008). While not all living in slums have the same level of deprivation, most are affected by poor water and sanitation services (economic water scarcity), and some, typically the poorest segment, are further affected by the lack of security of tenure, insufficient living area, and houses of non-durable materials.

Empirical evidence shows that cities are integral to development and economic success, in spite of slums and other negative consequences like environmental degradation. While the rush to cities in developing countries seems chaotic, there is strong evidence that it is unavoidable and even necessary. The challenge is that countries must manage the rapid growth of cities when they still have low income and nascent institutions, as once happened in today's most developed cities (Paris, New York, Dublin, and Tokyo).

Historical data demonstrate that urbanization for developing countries over the period 1985–2005 is remarkably similar to the average for European and North American countries between 1880 and 1900 (World Bank 2009). It takes several decades to absorb informal settlements into more organized city structures – the development challenge is to speed up this process in the most efficient and equitable way.

This simplified conceptual framework of urban growth in developing countries allows for a deeper understanding about the dynamics of city growth and poverty. Such a framework is also needed to design policies and set development priorities that address supply and demand gaps for urban water services over several decades, taking into account that the relative abundance of water and the existence of network infrastructure are frequently misleading.

The proposition is that development priorities should be set to support governance and infrastructure investments that raise the performance of water services provided to the poorest segments of the population. Governance requires public policy reforms that enhance accountability and support efficiency incentives. Water investments should include a major component of rehabilitation of poor-performing infrastructure that has suffered from inefficient operational practices and maintenance neglect.

This strategic development priority is strongly supported by recent evaluations of the cost of environmental degradation in the LAC countries that have shown that the hidden economic cost of poor quality of water and sanitation services could be in the range of 1–2 percent of GDP. In the case of Colombia, a country with one of the highest coverage levels in the region, the economic cost of poor quality of water supply and sanitation was estimated in 1.04 percent of GDP (World Bank 2007a). This cost is associated to high-morbidity rates of water-borne diseases and to about 1,500 premature deaths per year. It represents a high cost to the economy due to life losses, costs of medical treatment and coping strategies, and losses in labor productivity due to illness.

By a simplistic inference, the cost of environmental degradation associated to the lack of adequate water and sanitation services should be much higher in other countries of LAC that have worse health indicators than Colombia, which has an average under-five mortality rate per thousand births of 21. This is the case of Haiti with 120, Bolivia with 65, Guyana with 63, and Guatemala with 43. This cost is even higher when considering the high morbidity related to diarrhea prevalence.

Unfortunately, the data show that prevalence of diarrhea in most LAC countries is comparable with less-developed countries of Africa and South Asia, which have lower coverage of water and sanitation services and a more limited stock of water infrastructure. Most countries in the LAC region are in the range of 13–25 percent for diarrhea prevalence (Table 3.2), which is similar to countries like India (19.2 percent), Tanzania (12.6 percent), Uganda (19.2 percent), Kenya (17.1 percent), and Egypt (18.4 percent).

In addition, these average country indexes also hide large distributional disparities across income levels. This observation is particularly relevant for the LAC region, which is considered the most unequal of the world as measured by the Gini coefficient. Sao Paulo, Belo Horizonte, Fortaleza, and Bogota have Gini coefficients above 0.6, which is considered extremely high. Quito, Buenos Aires, Santiago, and Mexico City are in the range of 0.5 and 0.59, which reveal high levels of inequality. Montevideo, Asuncion, Caracas and Guatemala City are between 0.4 and 0.49, which are dangerously high levels (UN-Habitat 2009).

The analysis done in several countries of the LAC region prove that environmental degradation and low quality of water supply and sanitation services are not only highly correlated, but also the fact that they disproportionately affect the well-being of the poorest and most vulnerable population – children, elderly, and women. In Colombia, the health impact of environmental degradation is three times higher in the poor population and ten times higher when it is weighted per unit of income. In other areas and countries of the region: Central America, Peru, and Ecuador, where these studies have been made, health impacts of environmental degradation on the poorest segments of society are similar.

However, while urbanization and governance are the main drivers of scarcity, they are not the only ones. The comparative advantage of the LAC region to compete in the global market (water and land) is also a major driver to expand the agriculture frontier – mainly for exports of soybeans, sugar, and meat. As global trade is rapidly transforming the regional landscape, it is also increasing water demand in rural areas at the river basin scale.

This is particularly relevant for Argentina, Paraguay, Bolivia, and especially Brazil that have developed world-class agriculture technologies and cropping practices that support high yields – even in hot and humid climates. As a consequence, a substantial volume of water is exported in trade of food commodities (virtual water). Worldwide, virtual water trade of crops has been estimated to be approximately between 500 and 900 km^3 per year. An additional 130–150 km^3 is traded in livestock products. The virtual water exported by the LAC region is projected at about 190 km^3, or about 20 percent of the world estimate (Hassan *et al.* 2005).

These are major drivers that are influencing quantity and quality of water availability at the river basin scale with changes in land-use intensity and land-cover change. Land-use changes affect evapotranspiration, infiltration rates and runoff quantity and timing. It is particularly relevant to consider the reduction on the overall quantity of available runoff associated with different types of land-cover change and how this can be transferred downstream through river networks.

Lastly, climate change is another important driver of water scarcity in the medium to long term. Most global circulation models show that climate variability, intensification of extreme events and more frequent water-related natural disasters are enormously important for the LAC region. Projections derived from global circulation models point to changing precipitation patterns across the region, with increased winter rainfall in Tierra del Fuego, higher summer precipitation in southeastern South America, and drier conditions in Central America and the southern Andes (World Bank 2010).

The most relevant climate-driven effects in the region are expected to be wholesale coral bleaching in the Caribbean, rapid retreat of tropical glaciers in the Andes, loss of density in the Amazon rainforest, coastal flooding, and increased frequency and intensity of hurricanes. For instance, the IPCC assessment and research from climate scientists have concluded that Mexico may experience significant decreases in runoffs of the order of minus 10 to 20 percent nationally (Milly 2005). Ongoing studies show that a temperature increase of 4 degrees centigrade might lead to a collapse of the Amazon's rainforest ecosystem (Levy 2004). Water supply to cities will be affected – in the case of Quito, new sources of water to substitute a glacier east of the city will increase productions costs by 30 percent.

Conclusions and policy implications

An attempt has been made by the author to summarize myths and realities about water scarcity issues from the perspective of politicians and water policy makers (Table 3.4). As described elsewhere, there is the fallacy of water abundance and high-infrastructure coverage when in reality water cannot be consumed directly from the tap, and the poor have to pay several times more than the rich to cope with the poor quality of water services.

Table 3.4 Water scarcity: myths and reality

Water scarcity indicator	*Myths of politicians about water*	*Reality for water policy-makers*
Availability of water	Plenty	Asymmetry between population and economic activity and water
Water supply	High coverage, meet the MDGs	Low quality of services, high cost to the poor
Sanitation	More pipes	High incidence of water-borne diseases, lack of hygiene, service in slums
Irrigation	More dams and channels	Focus on rainfed and sustainable use of groundwater. Improve drainage and reduce salinity; eliminate electricity subsidies
Floods	Remove water from flooded areas as quick as possible	Non-structural measures manage water within their basins, reduce peak flows
Pollution	Contract wastewater treatment plants	Existing capacity is not fully utilized
Hydropower	Develop new projects	Large social and environmental tradeoffs

Perceptions about water policies have been summarized, taking into account findings of an independent review of about 1,800 water projects financed by the World Bank in the period 1997–2007, and the experience gained by the author in the policy and strategic dialog about water in many countries of the LAC region. It tries to capture different perspectives about water policies, and it is expected that it will be a practical contribution to focus the discussions about policies and the political economy of water scarcity.

Using the broader definition of scarcity suggested in this chapter, priorities should account for deficits of water services that go beyond water availability, and include lack of infrastructure (infrastructure water scarcity) and inadequate governance systems (governance water scarcity). Based on the analysis of data, regional reports and experience in development assistance, it is proposed that the priority water scarcity issue in the LAC region is in urban areas, in particular to improve governance of water utilities.

Improving the accountability framework of utilities and implementing demand management policies and investments are the main priorities for water utilities in the LAC region. While the region has powerful utilities and technical capacity, and generally cover their operational cost with the exception of Bolivia and Venezuela (Table 3.3), they are still highly inefficient because public utilities generally lack strong performance incentives and accountability frameworks that are linked to efficiency objectives.

Modernizing utilities requires reforms to clarify the role of governments, strengthen regulatory institutions, and build stronger performance incentives for managing utilities. A first generation of reforms has been implemented to address these issues, but they have only been partially successful. However, there are also some clear successes over the past 20 years. Important progress has been made in advancing regulatory reform to reach coverage of about 75 percent of the region's urban population, and these are pushing utilities to be more transparent in reporting performance and in achieving a stronger focus on efficiency (World Bank 2010).

Demand management to reduce unaccounted for water, control wastage, and adjust consumption to efficient levels have been identified as the most effective investment to address the supply/demand gap (McKinsey 2009). Water use in the industrial sector is expected to increase from current levels of 10–15 percent of total withdrawals, in the most advanced countries, to 20–25 percent that might even surpass domestic consumption. It will also require careful attention to establish incentive and enforcement instruments to reduce water consumption in the energy sector (cooling of power plants) and increase reuse.

However, in spite of the potential increase of water supply to cities by simply reducing water losses, and rehabilitating and updating existing water facilities, water transfers have become one crucial investment for water-starved cities of the region. Some of the largest cities of the region are already transferring important volumes of water from neighboring river basins: Mexico City from the Cutzamala system; Lima from the Mantaro River, which belongs to the Amazon River basin; Sao Paulo from the Cantareiras system and Rio de Janeiro from the Paraiba do

Sul River, which are part of the Parana River basin; and Caracas from the Camatagua River in the Orinoco River basin.

These are examples of massive investments that have been made over the past 40 years. There are more to come in Sao Paulo, Bogota, Lima, Quito, La Paz, and Tegucigalpa as a consequence of increasing population and economic growth, and because of reduced rainfall and increased variability of runoff related to the long-term impacts of climate change.

Another option for increasing supply is desalination, which is already in use in small Caribbean islands and by high-end tourist developments. Furthermore, Trinidad, Curacao, cities in the gulf of California, and Northern Chile are also considering large investments in desalination, since energy intensity has been reduced to less than five kilowatts per cubic meter, and production cost, including capital costs, are becoming more competitive (GWI 2010).

Managing water in urban areas is complex, and it goes beyond utility management. It should support economic growth and poverty reduction in the most efficient way by ensuring that demand for water services is met where and when needed, at the required quality and performance levels, including cost-effective management of extreme events (droughts and floods).

To achieve this goal, there is a need for integrated approaches to the provision of urban water services that consider urban development (including services to slums) and sustainable use of environmental resources. Unfortunately, management of water resources (surface and groundwater) and water services in urban areas is very fragmented and political decisions for integrated water management in cities remains a big challenge.

Other important priorities to address scarcity are: improved efficiency in irrigated areas and in rain-fed agriculture, managed groundwater resources sustainably, reduced impacts of urban and rural floods, increased efficiency of pollution control, and the need to investigate emerging issues and conflicts of water allocation.

Rehabilitation of irrigation systems, addressing salinization and water logging issues, and sustainable management of aquifers are development priorities for the LAC region in order to optimize the use of existing irrigation infrastructure, and improve water productivity, as well as to increase income and reduce poverty in rural areas. At the same time, reforms in the governance framework of irrigation systems, such as the transfer of infrastructure operation responsibilities to user's association, provides a proven approach that has been implemented in Mexico, Argentina, and northeastern Brazil – they provide a pool of good regional practices and models that should be more widely disseminated.

However, such institutional improvements require transparent rules and policies for allocating water rights. Chile's Water Code has been successful in enhancing investment in irrigation and increasing water productivity through a system of water rights that facilitate the transfer of water to higher value crops. Following the experience of Chile, irrigation systems in the Pacific Coast of Peru have proven that stable macroeconomic conditions, more transparent allocation of water rights, and dissemination of technologies (like drip irrigation) have large impacts in improving water productivity, and in fostering innovation and entrepreneurship.

The 2008 World Development Report (World Bank 2007b) emphasized that in order for agriculture to meet future demand, water productivity improvements need to be achieved, not only in irrigated but also in rain-fed areas. However, improvements in rain-fed areas might also imply large increases in evapotranspiration, which has impacts on runoff, in downstream flow of rivers and in groundwater recharge.

The potential for expansion of rain-fed agriculture and supplemental irrigation in LAC is large, and it requires sustained financial and institutional support for research and development (R&D) and for the generation and dissemination of agro-climatic information that can be used by farmers (World Bank 2010). While institutions like EMBRAPA in Brazil and others in Mexico and Peru, including CGIAR Centers, are world leaders in R&D in the agriculture sector, the institutional framework for production and dissemination of agro-climatic information is not yet at the same level.

Wastewater use for urban and peri-urban agriculture is an emerging priority for LAC countries. It can reduce water scarcity and provide a reliable source of water, improve agriculture productivity, reduce pollution, and create livelihood opportunities for urban households (World Bank 2010).

However, there are tradeoffs that need to be managed, including risks to human health, and to the environment. Wastewater use in agriculture is growing steadily around most of the large cities of the LAC region, and their contribution to local markets of vegetables, fruits, poultry, and dairy is significant. In Mexico alone, about 25 percent of municipal wastewater is reused in agriculture to irrigate about 300,000 hectares (Jiménez 2001).

To address these types of issues, there is broad consensus in the LAC region about the need of integrated approaches to optimize policy and investment decisions, as well as having well-functioning basin-wide water institutions. However, in spite of multiple efforts made over the past 50 years to create river basin agencies, their impact in improving water management is disappointing.

Sustainable management of groundwater resources is another priority for LAC countries. Mexico, Central America, Brazil, Paraguay, Argentina, and Peru have substantial groundwater issues of overexploitation and contamination. Mexico is the country with the most severe set of groundwater issues of the region, and it has attempted multiple approaches to improve management of its overexploited aquifers.

Results to date of these attempts are mixed, including efforts to collect and analyze information, planning, and modeling tools, and policy-oriented programs to reduce the over-allocation of water rights and eliminate perverse electricity subsidies to rural electricity. The design and balance of successes and failures in implementing these options offer a wealth of information that should be analyzed and disseminated.

In August 2010, devastating floods in Pakistan, India, and China took the center stage of the media with staggering videos of human suffering, deaths and loss of livelihoods of the poorest people of those countries. The LAC region is not different; over the past months, Rio de Janeiro, Sao Paulo, and Buenos Aires have also suffered from major urban floods and mud slides with a large balance of fatalities and economic losses.

These flood events are linked to large transformations of land use at river basin scales, urbanization characterized by uncontrolled expansion of impervious areas and lagging drainage infrastructure, and to the intensification of extreme weather conditions that are related to changes of the hydrologic cycle that cannot be explained by traditional projections of historical records. Moreover, since floods travel across spatial scales and administrative jurisdictions, their management requires a strong coordination of water agencies across and within countries.

At the same time, flood management infrastructure, such as dams, engineered channels, levees, and other facilities that keep rivers from entering the floodplains are generally considered public goods that require large investments and substantial budget allocations to cover recurrent costs of operation and maintenance.

Unfortunately, the disparate combination of large demands for investment and budgets with weak, fragmented, and uncoordinated institutions to provide flood-mitigation services has not delivered, and it has led to a major public policy failure in LAC countries, which is not different from other developing countries of the world – most notably India.

This situation is often aggravated in developing countries due to deficiencies of solid-waste collection and disposal, and poor management practices for erosion and sedimentation control. Furthermore, poor management of solid waste and erosion issues is often combined to cause clogging of existing (and generally insufficient) drainage infrastructure.

Fortunately, there are also a few successful initiatives to address flood and drainage issues more systematically, which can provide good lessons and practices that would be useful across the region. Specifically, there are urban flood-management projects in Curitiba, Belo Horizonte, and Porto Alegre in Brazil, and in the Maldonado and Matanza-Riachuelo urban river basins in Buenos Aires, that offer useful policy and implementation lessons to address urban floods with a balance of structural and non-structural measures.

Similarly, the emergency, rehabilitation, and prevention programs for alluvial floods from the Parana River in Argentina also offer valuable lessons on how to design and implement a large program of investments, regulation of land use, reallocation of population, and coordination of federal, provincial, and local governments' jurisdictions.

Cities, particularly in the high-end, middle-income countries of the region, are demanding increasing priority to eliminate pollution from their urban rivers. In Sao Paulo, Buenos Aires, Bogota, and Caracas, urban rivers have pollution levels that are similar to open sewers, with negative impacts on the quality of life and degradation of potentially high-value urban land and property.

There are multiple initiatives, and large investments to reduce pollution but results to date are below expectations, even after a large portion of the contaminant load is removed. While there is not a single explanation to the limited impact of current initiatives, it can be speculated that they are related to uncontrolled discharges from informal areas (slums), illegal connections to the storm-water network, and the contribution of non-point sources of pollution, among others.

At the same time, there is also an expectation to reach a high level of pollution control in a relatively short period of time from 20 to 30 years, while countries in Europe with more resources and higher income levels have managed to control pollution of their rivers in a much longer timeframe – as in the Thames and Seine rivers.

In some cases, following the logic of a stylized Kuznets environmental curve, water pollution might deteriorate even further while average income continues rising. It might be argued that it will be enormously difficult and expensive to achieve very high levels of removal of pollutants if a large part of the city is informal, and if there is not an explicit strategy to build individual connections and trunk infrastructure that it is adapted to high-density and irregular patterns of urbanization.

There are, however, several useful experiences to manage quality and control pollution in large cities of the LAC region. For instance, the experience of Sao Paulo investing billions of US dollars to build treatment plants along the Tiete River, and develop the US$500 million Guarapiranga Water Quality and Pollution Control project that included sewerage connections, slum upgrading of 200,000 poor urban dwellers, and wastewater treatment to protect one main source of drinking water for the city, have provided a wealth of lessons that can be useful to other cities in the LAC region.

Currently, there are other large wastewater treatment investment programs in Mexico City, Caracas, Bogota, Lima, Buenos Aires, and Santiago that can gain much by learning from each other and from the analysis of their collective experience. Some of these initiatives to clean rivers from pollution and restore degraded urban areas have been taken under strong pressure from the public opinion and the judiciary.

This is the case of numerous pollution-reduction projects in municipalities in Brazil that are responding to judicial pressure of legal suits presented by the Public Prosecutor (Ministerio Publico). A similar approach is taking place in Buenos Aires by the High Court (Corte Suprema) that has mandated the Federal Government, the City and the Province of Buenos Aires to proceed with the cleanup project of the Matanza-Riachuelo River.

Water conflicts between countries in the LAC region are not major when compared with the situation in the Middle East and in South Asia. In these regions, water conflicts are considered a threat to national security, as it is in the Nile, Indus, and Euphrates Rivers, which have become an important concern for the international community. In the case of the LAC region, while the level of international water conflicts is relatively low from a broader international perspective, there are increasing areas of dispute and conflict at the country level.

These country conflicts are generally associated with scarcity and the distribution of decision-making power about water allocation among federal, state, and local levels of government, and between river agencies. Generally, potential water disputes arise due to uncertainty about future allocation of water and the discretionary power that can be exercised through administrative permits and concessions. In LAC countries, water is allocated at the federal level with the exemption of Argentina, which follows provincial legislation, and Chile, which is the only country with a system of private water rights.

However, the fact that the current level of international water conflicts is low does not mean that the LAC region is problem-free when taking into consideration that most of the surface water in the LAC region is shared by several countries. In South America, more than 90 percent of the surface water is in the Amazon, Parana, and Orinoco river basins.

In Central America, about 60 percent of the surface water is also shared, including the sensitive Lempa River basin, which is essential for El Salvador, and is shared with Honduras, and Guatemala. Similarly, the Guarani aquifer, which is claimed as one of the largest reserves of fresh water in the world, is shared by four countries, and there are several other groundwater reserves in South and Central America that are shared by two countries.

The long history of LAC region with international water treaties has been instrumental to address international water development issues. For instance, there are about 100 years of experience of multilateral and bilateral negotiations of international agreements in the Parana-La Plata river basin that have provided a legal framework for development of multiple binational hydropower projects, support inland navigation, and facilitate a fluid exchange of relevant river basin data. In the case of the Amazon basin, there is a successful agreement among eight countries, with a permanent secretariat in Brasilia, and sector programs covering science and technology, environment, health, tourism, transport, communication and infrastructure, education and indigenous affairs.

The key to these agreements has been the implicit recognition of the complementarities across countries, and the needs of joint development to expand the benefits of river basin development. This culture of water negotiations has been ratified again just recently with the decision taken by Brazil, Argentina, Paraguay, and Uruguay to continue their joint efforts to evaluate and monitor the Guarani aquifer, following the recommendations of a highly successful GEF international waters project that was managed by the four countries with assistance of the OAS and the World Bank.

Finally, water scarcity issues in LAC have been seen from a country perspective and less from a regional viewpoint; therefore, the untapped potential for enhanced collaboration is large. A higher level of collaboration is expected to facilitate a more-effective and better-informed approach to water problems, specifically, by learning from systematic evaluations of successes and failures in managing water resources and delivering water services within the LAC region and elsewhere. However, to be successful, such efforts need much stronger regional networks, more effective relationships with international agencies, and a closer interaction with water agencies and research institutions outside LAC.

References

Falkenmark, M., Lundqvist, J. and Widstrand, C. (1989) "Macro-scale Water Scarcity Requires Micro-scale Approaches: Aspects of Vulnerability in Semi-Arid Development." *Natural Resources Forum* 13(4): 258–67.

FAO (2009) "AQUASTAT." Available at www.fao.org/nr/water/aquastat/main/index.stm.

GWI (2010) *Water Technology Market*. Oxford: Global Water Intelligence.

IWMI (2004) *Water Scarcity: Fact or Fiction?* Battaramulla: International Water Management Institute.

—— (2007) *A Comprehensive Assessment of Water Management in Agriculture*. Battaramulla: International Water Management Institute.

Jiménez, B. E. (2001) *La Contaminación Ambiental en México*. Mexico City: Editorial Limusa.

Levy, E. A. (2004) "Modelling the Impact of Future Changes in Climate Change, CO_2 Concentration, and Land Use on Natural Ecosystems and Terrestrial Carbon Sink." *Global Environmental Change* 14: 21–30.

McKinsey (2009) *Charting Our Water Future*. New York: McKinsey & Co. Available at www.mckinsey.com/client_service/sustainability/latest_thinking/charting_our_water_future.

Hassan, R., Scholes, R., and Ash, N. (eds) (2005) *Ecosystems and Human Well-Being: Current State and Trends*. Findings of the Condition and Trends Working Group. Millennium Ecosystem Assessment Series. Washington, DC: Island Press.

Milly, P. E. (2005) "Global Pattern of Trends in Streamflow and Water Availability in a Changing Climate." *Nature* 438: 347–50.

UNESCO (1999) *World Water Resources at the Beginning of the 21st Century*. Paris: UNESCO.

UN-Habitat (2008) *State of the World's Cities 2008/2009*. Nairobi: UN-Habitat.

—— (2009) *Global Urban Observatory*. Nairobi: UN-Habitat.

van den Berg, C. and Danilenko, A. (2011) *The IBNET Water Supply and Sanitation Performance Blue Book: The International Benchmarking Network for Water and Sanitation Utilities Databook*. Washington, DC: World Bank.

World Bank (2005) *Water Rights Program for Mexico*. Washington, DC: World Bank.

—— (2007a) *Environmental Priorities to Reduce Poverty in Colombia*. Washington, DC: World Bank.

—— (2007b) *World Development Report 2008: Agriculture for Development*. Washington, DC: World Bank.

—— (2009) *World Development Report 2009: Reshaping Economic Geography*. Washington, DC: World Bank.

—— (2010a) *Improving Wastewater Use in Agriculture: An Emerging Priority*. Washington, DC: World Bank. Available at http://elibrary.worldbank.org/doi/book/10.1596/1813-9450-5412.

—— (2010b) *Improving Water Management in Rain-Fed Agriculture: Issues and Options in Water-Constrained Production Systems*. Washington, DC: World Bank.

—— (2010c) *Low-Carbon Development: Latin America Responses to Climate Change*. Washington, DC: World Bank.

WWAP (2006) *Water: A Shared Responsibility*. United Nations World Water Development Report 2. Perugia: World Water Assessment Programme.

Part III

Serving the unserved

4 Supply and sanitation

Serving the urban unserved in Latin America, with a special focus on Argentina

Raúl A. Lopardo and Emilio J. Lentini

Introduction

During the last century, water consumption has increased at a rate more than twice the rate of population growth. It is estimated that 884 million people, 14 percent of the world's population, currently lack access to improved drinking water, and 2,500 million people, 38 percent of the world's population, do not have adequate sanitation facilities (WHO/UNICEF 2008).

By 2020, 60 percent of the world population will be urban, a concentration that makes the development of infrastructure for water supply in cities an extremely urgent issue. These factors, which influence the world's water resources, are all interrelated and cannot be treated separately, which further complicates analysis of the situation (UNESCO 2003a). It is estimated that by 2030, two-thirds of the population will live in towns and cities, which will cause a dramatic increase in water demand in urban areas. An estimated 2 billion people live in squatter settlements and slums. This segment of the urban population suffers from lack of clean water and sanitation facilities (United Nations 2006).

Daily water consumption varies between 200 and 300 liters per person in most European countries, and is around 575 liters in the United States. By contrast, the average use in countries such as Mozambique is less than 10 liters. People who lack access to piped water in developing countries consume less water, in part because they have to travel long distances carrying it, and water is heavy. The international standards set by organizations like the World Health Organization (WHO) and the United Nations Fund for Children (UNICEF) suggest a minimum consumption of 20 liters a day from a source within one kilometer of home. This is enough for drinking and basic personal hygiene. People who are unable to gain access to this amount of water are limited in their ability to maintain physical well-being and dignity that cleanliness provides. If water needs for bathing and washing are considered, the amount per person increases to about 50 liters per day. Much of the world's population is well below the minimum thresholds for basic water needs. There are approximately 1,100 million people who live within a mile of a water source and use less than five liters of water daily that is not safe (UNDP 2006).

A report on Latin America by ADERASA (2007) with data from 2006 for 32 companies that provide drinking water to the region, found that the average sold or consumed water was 171 liters per capita per day, with a maximum of around 400 liters per capita per day (Buenos Aires and Panama) and a minimum of 104 liters per capita per day (Bogotá). It should be noted that such use does not take into account the net loss of water released (on average 44 percent). Hence, the average daily per capita output is 305 liters.

In Argentina, the national average production per capita water provided is estimated at 380 liters per capita per day, with a wide range of variation between different provinces, from a maximum of 654 liters per capita per day in the Province of San Juan and a minimum of 168 liters/capita/day in the Province of La Pampa. The level of unaccounted-for water is one of the main problems of efficiency in water services. It is estimated that 40 percent of the water produced is lost in the network and through illegal connections. The average water consumption in Argentina is in the order of 230 liters per capita per day. Moreover, it is estimated that the real average consumption, based on the results of operating systems with micro measurement, is on the order of 180 liters per capita per day (WHO 1999).

The objectives of this chapter are aimed at exposing relevant aspects of the issue of water and sanitation in urban centers, with special emphasis on Latin America and particularly Argentina, in order to provide a summary of basic information, such as contribution to generate ideas and suggestions for actions to discuss and set priorities to meet the current and future challenges in the field. To reach these goals, the authors analyze the water and sanitation coverage, as a main aspect, but include also information about the organization of the provision, urban service quality, network losses, access to services of drinking water and sanitation, water and health, and levels of investment in water and sanitation. A summary of the impacts of the rise of groundwater in Buenos Aires metropolitan zone is also included.

Water and sanitation coverage

It was estimated in 2006 that 87 percent of the world's population used improved drinking water sources, 54 percent with a pipe connection in the home, plot or yard, and 33 percent with other drinking water sources (UNDP 2006; WHO/UNICEF 2008). This means that 5.7 billion people worldwide were using an improved source of drinking water, an increase of 1.6 billion since 1990. Approximately 3.6 billion people use a pipe connection that provides running water in their homes or nearby (UNDP 2006; WHO/UNICEF 2008).

With regard to sanitation, an estimated 62 percent of the world's population had access to improved sanitation (i.e., a hygienic manner ensuring no contact between people and human excrement). Eight percent share an improved sanitation installation with one or more houses, and another 12 percent use unimproved sanitation facilities (i.e., does not guarantee avoiding contact between people and human excrement). The remaining 18 percent of the world's population practice indiscriminate defecation ('*air libre*'). This value indicates that the coverage of sanitation in the developing world increased from 41 percent in 1990 to 53 percent in 2006. About 1.1 billion people in developing nations have incorporated improved sanitation facilities in that period (UNDP 2006; WHO/UNICEF 2008). Many studies have identified the crisis in water and sanitation as a crisis of poverty. More than two-thirds of people without access to clean water survive on less than two dollars a day – and one in three on less than one dollar a day. More than 660 million people without adequate sanitation live on less than two dollars per day and less than 385 million live on less than a dollar a day. This clearly shows the serious problems in funding improvements in water and sanitation services (UNESCO 2009).

Table 4.1 shows the percentage of population covered with water and sanitation services by region. Africa has the least urban household water supply, followed by South Asia. Urban sanitation is similar.

The lack of potable water supply and sanitation has grown and continues to be the international agenda in recent years. In September 2000 at the Millennium Summit of the United Nations, under Objective no. 7, "Ensure environmental sustainability", the goal was stated to be to "reduce by half the proportion of people without sustainable access to safe drinking water by 2015." In the Johannesburg Summit (August 26 to September 4, 2002), this commitment was reaffirmed by adding a line to the previous goal: "halving by the same year the proportion of people without access to sanitation."

To achieve the 2015 target only in Africa, Asia, Latin America, and the Caribbean, 2.2 billion people will need access to sanitation and 1.5 billion will need access to water before that date. In practice, this would have meant providing water supply services to 280,000 people and sanitation to 384,000 people every day for 15 years (WHO/UNICEF 2008).

Financial resources for water are stagnating. In recent years, the average total official development assistance (ODA) for the water sector was around 3 billion dollars annually, to which was added an additional 1.5 billion dollars in the form of non-concessional loans, supplied mainly by the World Bank. However, only a

Table 4.1 Percentage of population adequately supplied with water and sanitation by region

Region	*Urban household water supply*	*Urban sanitation*	*Urban water*
East Asia	70%	92%	71%
South Asia	53%	93%	64%
Sub-Saharan Africa	39%	82%	55%
Middle East and North Africa	92%	96%	90%
Western Europe and Central Asia	98%	98%	90%
Latin America	95%	96%	84%
OECD	100%	100%	100%

Source: WHO (2004)

very small proportion of that money (12 percent) goes to the interests of the needy, and only 10 percent goes to finance the development of policies, plans, and programs relating to water. Additionally, private investment in the services of water supply and sanitation has declined (United Nations 2006).

In Latin America, according to estimates at the regional level, 96 percent of the urban population had access to a potable water supply in 2006 (92 percent in 1990) and 79 percent to sanitation (77 percent in 1990). Of the rural population, only 78 percent (56 percent in 1990) had services available for water supply and 49 percent (39 percent in 1990) for sanitation services (WHO/UNICEF 2008). During that period, 926 million urban dwellers gained access to improved drinking water sources. At the same time, the urban population without improved drinking water sources increased from 107 million to 137 million. Most of these increases occurred in urban areas in the developing world, including several Latin American countries. Note that of the population with access to drinking water, two-thirds are connected to water main service within the home, while the remaining one-third used other sources outside the home (e.g., public tap) and are not in contact with pollution.

Rapid population growth in urban areas represents a growing problem: the number of urban dwellers using improved sanitation has increased by 779 million since 1990, but has not kept pace with urban population growth of 956 million. According to WHO/UNICEF (2008), in developing countries in 2006, 4 of 25 people lack access to clean water, and 13 did not have adequate sanitation.

The challenge posed by the current situation is even greater when one considers that by 2010, due to rapid population growth, the deficit in coverage was projected to increase by about 77 million people – almost all in urban areas (CEPAL/CELADE 1999). It should be noted that "improved sanitation" facilities to ensure hygienic separation of excreta includes not only the connection to the sewerage system but also septic tanks, and latrines.

Figure 4.1 shows data from the urban coverage of piped water through household connections for each of the countries of the region for the years 1990 and 2004, according to statistics released by WHO/UNICEF (2008). This coverage is defined as the percentage of the total urban population that has water service inside the house or on the property. But improved sanitation information was not broken down as a percentage of population with household connections. Therefore no comparison can be made consistent with the 1990 data (note that WHO warns of this problem in the document).

According to the information provided by the World Health Organization, the statistics are based on various international surveys and national censuses. The methodologies used in the censuses of different countries may vary, generating heterogeneity among data.

By 2004, the average coverage of water per connection in Latin America increased to 90.2 percent. Countries exceeding that level were Brazil (91 percent), Colombia (96 percent), Costa Rica (99 percent), Chile (99 percent), Dominican Republic (92 percent), Honduras (91 percent), Mexico (96 percent), Panama (96 percent), and Uruguay (97 percent). This increase in the coverage of

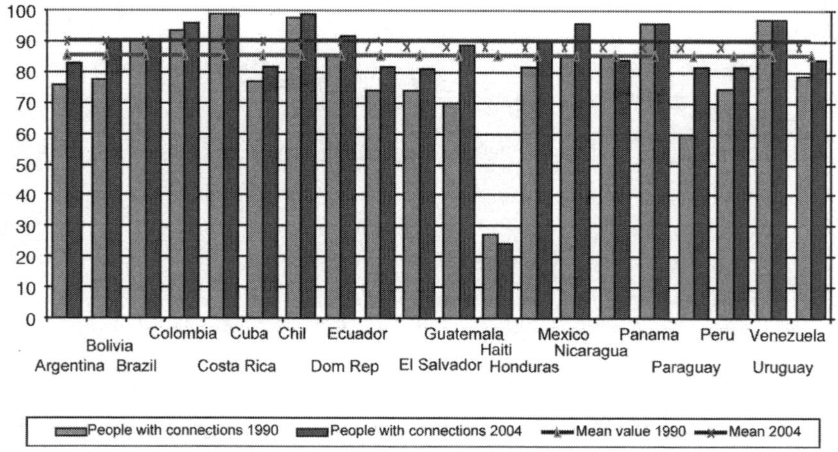

Figure 4.1 Evolution of the percentage of population with access to drinking water through household connections between 1990 and 2004

Source: WHO/UNICEF (2008)

water service connection means that 4.7 percent more people accessed service in that period. Other countries that increased their coverage, albeit by lesser amounts, were Paraguay, Guatemala, Bolivia, and Mexico.

With regard to sewer service, Figure 4.2 shows the percentage of urban population with access to sewer service through a household connection. Around 1990,

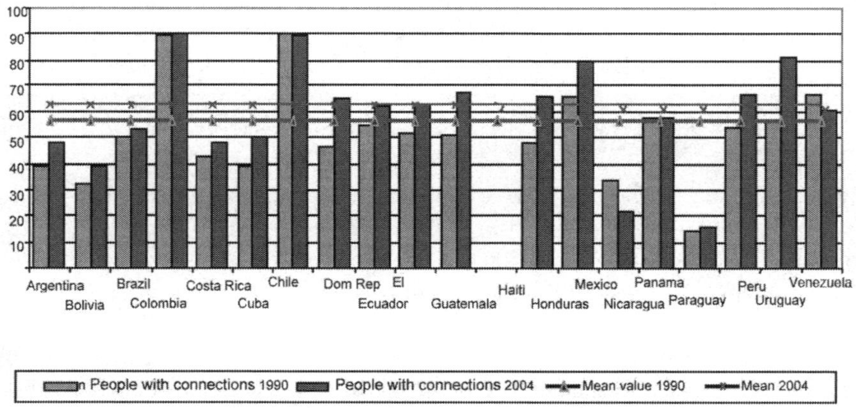

Figure 4.2 Evolution of the percentage of population with sewerage services through household connections between 1990 and 2004.

Source: WHO/UNICEF (2008)

the weighted average of the urban population connected to the sewerage system was 57 percent. Of the countries surveyed, six were over the average: Colombia (89 percent), Chile (90 percent), Mexico (66 percent), Panama (58 percent), Uruguay (57 percent) and Venezuela (67 percent).

For 2004, the average coverage of all countries is 63 percent, a 6 percent increase over 1990. In terms of population, this represents the incorporation of nearly 89 million people to the sewer service. Countries that are above average: Colombia (90 percent), Chile (89 percent), Dominican Republic (65 percent), Guatemala (68 percent), Honduras (66 percent), Mexico (80 percent), Peru (67 percent) and Uruguay (81 percent).

The experience of most companies in the region indicates that the high levels of unaccounted-for water arise from deficiencies in business management, primarily billing issues, collection of payments and inadequate policies on overdue accounts, and a high percentage of leakage losses in distribution systems. The population covered with adequate monitoring systems and quality control for drinking water is very limited in urban areas: only 24 percent of the urban population in the region has effective systems for monitoring the quality of drinking water. It is estimated that in large cities in the region, 94 percent of the drinking water is disinfected effectively, but almost 18 percent of the samples violated national standards with regard to their microbiological, chemical, physical, and aesthetic properties. The lack of coverage and poor quality of service is further complicated by increasing water pollution that has reached alarming levels in many water bodies, mainly due to the widespread lack of wastewater treatment. It is estimated that only 14 percent of the wastewater collected by sewerage systems in 2001 received some degree of treatment (Jouravlev 2004). By 2004, an estimated 28 percent of collected wastewater in the region, on average, was treated (Lentini 2009). In Latin America, the highest rate of coverage is for drinking water service, then sewerage services, and finally treatment of effluents. This suggests an evolutionary process whereby industry first extends coverage of potable water and sewage. Then, finally, it advances in the treatment of effluents.

While the degree of coverage is an indicator of service performance in a given region, it is not the only one. In the case of sewer service, a very important determinant of its development is the treatment of wastewater collected (Lentini 2009).

In Argentina, both the levels of potable water and sanitation show large regional and provincial disparities between urban and rural areas. The tables presented below show the evolution of coverage in water supply and sanitation in Argentina for the period 1990–2004. Figures for potable water service coverage show that house connections increased 10 percent in the last 15 years. This increased coverage partially reflects other types of household connections. In the case of sewer service, it is noted that coverage through household connections has remained stable over the past 15 years. This implies that the coverage has been growing with the population, while the population without coverage has dropped for other types of connections. According to INDEC (National Statistic Center of Argentina), in the last quarter of 2006 the coverage of the 32 urban agglomerates

Table 4.2 Coverage of urban drinking water in Argentina

Region	*Drinking water*	*Sanitation*
Argentina (total country)	96%	68%
Gran Buenos Aires	73%	52%
Córdoba	96%	35%
Rosario	99%	61%
Mendoza	96%	80%
La Plata	92%	68%

Source: INDEC (2006)

(70 percent of the national urban population) had an average 96 percent network access to drinking water. Sanitation coverage reached 68 percent of the population.

Historically, the provision of sanitation has been lower than coverage for the drinking water network. This gap between potable water and sanitation has been varied and emerges in a comparison of the districts. The way to measure this is through the ratio of water users for each user of sanitation services, where the most expresses the greatest asymmetry.

Marginal urban areas present difficulties associated with the expansion of potable water, collection and disposal of effluents, as well as the improvement of intermittent supplies and disinfection. Rural areas require the extension of coverage and implementation of measures and technologies for water disinfection (PAHO 1998).

Regarding the wastewater treatment, it is estimated that Argentina processes only about 12 percent of the total liquid collected. In a set of 10 provinces between 50 percent and 85 percent of total wastewater is treated. In the country's largest cities, treatment is usually limited to no more than 10 percent.

Organization of the provision in Argentina

The current distribution of water and sewer service is similar in structure to that of the country – each province sets its own jurisdictional rules. Consequently, each province makes its own institutional decisions in the areas of water and wastewater. Each has its own regulatory framework, typically structured in a regulatory agency, and a private operator or the state providing local urban services in the provinces. In several cases with small suppliers, usually in small towns, the structure of the organization is by the state.

The facilities for drinking water in Argentina emerged as a preventive action by the state to address the cholera epidemics that ravaged the city of Buenos Aires in the late nineteenth century. Over three quarters of a century, the company Obras Sanitarias de la Nación (OSN) was the sole body responsible for the operation, design, and construction of these facilities. Since the early twentieth century, the evolution of water and sewer service in Argentina can be distinguished by four stages.

During the first phase, from 1912 to 1980, investment and service delivery were the responsibility of the federal government through OSN. In 1964 a new organization, Servicio Nacional de Agua Potable (SNAP), was created to finance and facilitate the expansion of services in rural areas. This was the beginning of a series of programs funded by the Inter-American Development Bank that provided financial support for the nation and the provinces. It also laid the groundwork for the formation of 1,500 cooperatives to take charge of the service in small and medium towns.

The second stage began in 1980 when the National Government Services OSN became decentralized and transferred to the provinces. The assets were transferred free of debt or charges, but with the obligation for companies to find a new economic formula to cover operating expenses and for investments in renovation and service expansion.

The third stage began with the state reform program in 1989–1990 and was characterized by widespread transformation in the organization of public services. This was based on the incorporation of private companies in the administration of services, mainly in large cities, which until then were operated by companies and public institutions. The organizational structure was completed with the formulation of standards established in a regulatory framework and the creation of specialized agencies and autonomous regulation and control over the provision of services. Moreover, the government established the National Board of Water and Sanitation Works (ENHOSA), which has jurisdiction throughout the country and whose mission is to organize, manage, and implement infrastructure programs resulting from national policies and water sector basic sanitation.

The first grant to a private company was in the province of Corrientes in 1991, when services were delegated to Aguas Corrientes SA. However, the concession was signed with a higher profile in 1993 for the Buenos Aires metropolitan area with the consortium called Aguas Argentinas SA, led by the French firm Lyonnaise des Eaux–Suez. During the period from 1991 to 2000, about 20 services were privatized in Argentina, including major cities, such as Santa Fe and Rosario (Santa Fe Provincial Water SA), Cordoba (Cordoba SA Water), La Plata and Bahía Blanca (Azurix SA), Tucumán (Aguas del Aconquija SA), Salta and Corrientes. This model showed its first crisis with some failed processes. Concession contracts were terminated in 1997 in Tucumán, and during 2002 in the Province of Buenos Aires. In both cases services were returned to the state.

The fourth stage, characterized by the nationalization of services, occurred after a macroeconomic crisis and the devaluation of 2002 brought a widespread process of renegotiating contracts. Later, contracts were terminated with Aguas de Santa Fe Provincial (2005), Aguas Argentinas SA, Buenos Aires (2006), Aguas de Buenos Aires SA–Suburbs of the City of Buenos Aires (2006) and Aguas de Catamarca (2008). Thus, private water companies in Argentina went from having a stake of about 70 percent of the users connected to the drinking water network in the mid-1990s to 30 percent today. It is important to note that participation was only 13 percent before privatization, mainly due to the presence of cooperatives and neighborhood associations. It is estimated that currently there are 1,830

Table 4.3 Providers of urban drinking water in Argentina

Type of provider	*National level*	*Provincial*	*Municipal*	*Total*
State society	1	8	0	9
State society	0	3	2	5
Autarkic entity	0	1	10	11
Centralized entity	0	4	377	381
SA private	0	7	10	17
Cooperative	0	0	639	639
Neighborhood association	0	0	768	768
Total	1	23	1806	1830

Source: Lentini (2009)

providers of water services, of which 365 provide sewer services. Table 4.3 shows the classification by legal nature of the provider and the level of decision or jurisdiction.

Urban service quality

In many countries of the region, levels of service coverage are not sufficient to assess the true state of development of sanitation. The level of service coverage is measured by the amount of network connection or access to any benefit. However, in the case of water, service may be continuous yet only provides several hours a day, or rationing may occur for some time during the year. The quality of the water supply also may not meet minimum parameters required by health standards or the food code (such as color, taste, or smell, and chemical, biological or, in a few cases, radioactive contaminants). There are also problems of continuity and network losses. Water quality conditions are usually met at the exit of plants or wells, but deteriorate in transport and distribution, and therefore, the domestic supply is inadequate. In the case of sewerage services, the networks also may lack devices/means to prevent blockages or overflows.

For this reason, it is important to know through some indicators the quality of provision in order to determine the population's degree of satisfaction with services provided. Potable water services in many countries of the region suffer from a lack of continuity. At the beginning of this century, it is estimated that more than 200 million people, about 60 percent of the population served through house connections to water, were served by systems with intermittent problems (PAHO 2001a). And there were countries in which more than 95 percent of the supply systems were discontinuous (PAHO 2001b).

Many countries in the region are deficient in drinking water quality control systems. At the turn of the century, it was estimated that only 24 percent of the urban population of the region had effective control systems for drinking water quality (PAHO 2001b). In large cities in the region, 94 percent of the drinking water is disinfected effectively, but almost 18 percent of the samples violated national standards (WHO/UNICEF 2000).

Continuity is an important factor to take into account when determining the status of a service due to low values of this indicator. Some customers are induced to use alternative sources or use household drinking water reserves. Metering performed by the operator needs a continuous flow for the proper functioning of meters. Therefore, an area served can have 100 percent coverage, but programmed cuts to ensure a minimum of pressure to parts of the area reduce the quality of service.

This is especially relevant for continuity in Peru, where the average was 17 hours a day by 2004. Thirty-seven percent of service companies (EPS) provide a continuum of less than 12 hours, 37 percent between 12 and 20 hours, and 26 percent more than 20 hours. That is, 74 percent of EPS presented problems of continuity in the provision of water service, some of which offered the service on average four hours per day (Ministry for Housing, Construction and Sanitation 2006).

In Colombia, according to World Bank (2004), the national inventory did not report information on the continuity of service, but advance work in 1996 by the Comptroller General Republic showed a continuity of less than 12 hours a day in four of 21 departmental capitals.

As an alternative way to approximate the continuity of service, the Association of Regulators of the Americas (ADERASA 2007) developed an indicator called "density of water service cuts." This is the percentage of water connections that have been affected by water cuts of more than six hours in a period of one year. For a sample of 13 companies, ADERASA (2007) finds that the density of cuts is between 1 percent, in the case of COMPESA (Brazil), and 248 percent for the case of ESSAL (Chile). Three other companies have values higher than 100 percent. The latter value implies that the number of connections affected within one year of service cuts is equal to the number of total connections. On average, each connection was cut more than six hours in a year.

Information on the level of quality of drinking water supplied and sewage collected is contained in the benchmarking of companies from countries in the region made by ADERASA (2007). While this study does not provide complete information to perform a comparable analysis by country, some trends can be seen in the most important companies providing various countries. The information excerpted from that report refers to the following indicators:

- overall implementation of drinking water analysis;
- implementation of wastewater analysis;
- overall compliance with drinking water analysis;
- general conformity with the analysis of wastewater; and
- density of total claims.

"Overall implementation of drinking water analysis" is defined as the amount of potable water analysis carried out in an annual period, compared to the amount required by applicable law. On a sample of 22 companies, it is noted that 20 of them meet at least 100 percent of the tests required by the applicable rules, while two companies do not. This indicator needs to be interpreted with caution as an over-compliance to the requirements may mean that water quality is bad and this creates the need for increased controls, or that water quality is good but the penalties for finding values below the standard is high, or that the monitoring plan is inadequate. The same also happens in the sewer service for the indicator of "Running wastewater analysis." For this last indicator on a sample of 17 companies, only two do not meet 100 percent of the tests required by applicable law. For this reason, both indicators should be interpreted in conjunction with the indicators of "general conformity analysis" (i.e., those whose results meet the required standards).

"General conformity analysis of drinking water quality" is the total amount of drinking water testing results in relation to all the tests carried out in the annual period considered. About 22 observations for the year 2006 found that 13 of the companies provided 100 percent satisfaction with the required standard, while the remaining three were below 95 percent. As was the case for drinking water, ADERASA (2007) produced an index of "general conformity analysis of sewage" (defined similarly). Sixteen companies out of 22 show that only two met 100 percent compliance with current regulations, while another 10 were above 80 percent and three were below this last number. Both potable water and sewage can be an indicator of quality in service provision. However, nothing guarantees that the policy will be uniform throughout the region. This means that a country with lower-quality standards can satisfy those standards with higher probability.

Finally, a way of measuring the quality of service can be made by users' perception through the many claims made. In this sense, ADERASA developed an index of "density of total claims," which computes all claims received by a provider during the annual period and is reported as a percentage of total accounts for water and wastewater. The average for the sample of 31 observations by ADERASA (2007) was 15 percent, with a maximum of 42 percent. The latter value implies that on average the company involved has received two claims for every five users per year. There are six enterprises with indicators above 30 percent that show some deficiency. Importantly, this indicator not only reflects the perception of quality of service but also the efficiency in resolving claims. More precisely, low levels of claims may occur because there is a perception that the service is of good quality or the service may be poor but as the claims are not resolved people do not make them.

As for Argentina, the system of drinking water supply of Greater Buenos Aires is a low-pressure system and usually has storage buildings, ensuring that almost all the population has continuous drinking water service. However, during privatization, investments in production capacity for rehabilitation and renovation of infrastructure were not enough to improve water production volumes and levels of loss, as planned originally. This inefficiency resulted in low-pressure problems in almost 70 percent of the potable water network and in sewage system overflows. Sometimes this fact affected the quality of water supplied in some areas of the conurbation, as during peak-demand summer months. To maintain pressure levels required for the continuity of service, supplemental flows from groundwater were used by pumping from wells that have high levels of nitrates. This created events that exceeded the allowed limit of nitrate content.

Network losses

The availability of drinking water is clearly affected by network losses. That is, not all the water produced is marketed because some of it fails to reach its destination. In a sample of 32 companies in Latin America, ADERASA (2007) found average net losses around 44 percent. It reports estimates in the larger companies in Chile of 30.9 percent for Andean Water SA (Gran Santiago and others); 39.2 percent ESSBIO (Concepción, Rancagua, others); and 41.5 percent for ESVAL (Valparaiso and other) (SISS 2008). In the case of Greater Buenos Aires, because it only measures 12 percent of water consumed, the determination of the volume of water losses in the network is unreliable. But AySA (Agua y Saneamientos Argentinos SA, formerly Aguas Argentinas SA) estimated service is currently about 35 percent of produced water.

The absence of metering in many countries results in consumption that is considerably higher than normal values. Given the existing problems of coverage in Latin America, the use of gauges could collaborate with the rationalization of consumption and free allocations of water for people without access.

ADERASA (2007) estimated the coverage of metering by the total number of household meters to total operating water connections for a sample of 36 companies in Latin America. There was wide variation in the values recorded for 2006 covered services from 100 percent micro-measured micro-measurement services with less than 10 percent and with a sample mean of 72 percent.

Levels of investment in water and sanitation

While the governments of Latin American countries have made efforts to expand coverage of potable water and sanitation, deficits are widespread in the countries of the region. Historical investment levels have been below the minimum requirements to address the replacement of existing assets and population growth, the achievement of universal coverage, and compliance with higher standards of environmental quality.

There are difficulties in obtaining data about the levels of investment in the sector. Even in the cases that are available, there are problems of consistency or referred to partial scope. Specifically, the main reasons why such information is scarce, incomplete or not available are:

- in some countries investments to state enterprises are broken down into administrative levels with a multiplicity of actors that complicates the aggregation of figures and is aggravated by different accounting policies to record investment;
- different procedures or criteria for allocating investment accounting (e.g.,

there is a very thin dividing line between the concept of renewal and rehabilitation, which is an expense, and the concept of improvement and maintenance, which is an investment);

- the specificity of the investments cannot be compared between countries, even between regions within a country; and
- finally, international comparisons generally do not accurately reflect the magnitude of the investment because of periods of high inflation endured in the region in the last 35 years and because of the use of different currencies.

Data from some countries about the participation of sectoral investment in Gross Domestic Product (GDP) show a comparison of the efforts in this area. Notwithstanding the caveats mentioned above, with overall figures of reference one can size the level of sectoral investment and make some comparisons. In this regard, it is estimated that in the period 1990/2000 in the countries of Latin America and the Caribbean, investments were made in the amount of US$24 billion (Chama 2005). It is estimated that in 2000 the countries of Latin America (excluding Cuba and Paraguay) invested about US$ 3.7 billion. This represented 0.2 percent of GDP of this group of countries and 1 percent of total investment.

In Argentina, in 1970–1980, the national government and the provinces spent an average of US$308 million and the next period from 1981 to 1991 (i.e., from decentralization to privatization), the average annual investment dropped US$160 million. The downward trend has been deepening sectoral investments since 1989, primarily as a result of worsening macroeconomic conditions in the country.

In the period 1970–1980, the annual investment in the sector represented on average 0.17 percent of GDP and 0.70 percent of Gross Domestic Fixed Investment (GDFI). In the period 1981–1991, these percentages fell to 0.08 percent of GDP and 0.46 percent of the GDFI. While the decline in sector investment coincides with a similar trend in total public investment, the process of decentralization of the provision deepened this fall, as the impact of that policy was not offset by provincial resources. Tariff levels by provincial lenders were not adapted to the real needs for improvement and expansion of services, so the operation became highly deficient and dependent upon the provincial budget resources, including for recurrent expenditures. With these financial conditions, investment had to depend almost exclusively on provincial budgetary resources, and to a lesser extent on domestic funds or loans from multilateral agencies. Consequently, the sector investment levels were low, even to maintain and replace existing facilities.

In the period 1993–2001, characterized by significant private sector participation in providing services, there was a growing level of investment in the sector. Since the economic crisis of 2001 onwards, however, the annual investment amounts were reduced dramatically. But there are plans in the works that would involve a significant increase in sectoral investments in the coming years, based on the contributions of the state budget financing and loans from multilateral banks.

AySA launched a greater Buenos Aires master plan for 2007–2020 to meet the needs of drinking water and sewers within the entire area of its concession, which involves an investment of about US$6 billion. This includes a water treatment plant in Tigre, servicing two million, the expansion of water treatment facilities, scrubbers and pumping stations, and a program of renovation and rehabilitation of existing networks and facilities. At launching stage is the construction of a sewage treatment plant in Berazategui for four million people and a sewage system Matanza-Riachuelo, which involves the construction of two interceptor-collecting ducts that allows flexible operation of the drainage sewer for future expansion, and the construction of a pretreatment plant and outfall for River Plate. These investments will reasonably meet the millennium goals, reaching 90 percent of drinking water coverage.

Access to services of drinking water and sanitation

The investment needs identified in the previous section not only have a benefit in increasing and improving the infrastructure but also involve a redistribution of income towards low-income people. The 2006 Human Development Report developed by UNDP emphasizes that almost two in three people lacking access to clean water survive on less than US$2 a day, and one in three live on less than UD$1 a day. More than 660 million people without sanitation live on US$2 a day and more than 385 million on less than US$1 a day. These facts have important policy implications, because they clearly indicate the limited capacity of the unserved population for adequate access to water and sanitation financed by private spending.

While it is possible to argue that the private sector can have a role to play in providing public funding, it is the key to overcoming deficits in water and sanitation. In many countries, the distribution of adequate access to water and sanitation go hand in hand with the distribution of wealth. The average number of households with access to piped water is about 85 percent to 20 percent of countries with greater resources, compared with 25 percent in 20 percent of the least developed countries. The inequality goes beyond access. A perverse principle that exists in many developing countries is that the poor not only have access to less water and less clean water, but also pay higher prices because the distance from the public supply raises prices. As water passes through intermediaries and each one adds the marketing and transport costs, prices increase. The population living in slums pay five to ten times more per liter than people with more resources in the same city.

The pricing policy of public utilities is an additional problem. Currently, most utilities implement tariff schemes by block. The aim is to combine equity with efficiency by raising the price of the volume of water used. In practice, the effect is usually that the poorest households are covered by the higher prices because the intermediaries who supply water to poor households buy water in bulk at the highest rates.

Recent studies suggest that the coverage of potable water services is greater, four to 16 times, in families with higher income than those with lower income (PAHO 2001b). A study by the IADB (2004) elaborated on the basis of household surveys for the countries of Latin America, indicated that 50 million people are without access to drinking water (70 percent correspond to the two lowest income quintiles) while 125 million people are without sanitation services (84 percent correspond to the two lowest income quintiles). Similar results were found in a recent study by UNICEF/WHO (2008). It notes that the richest quintile of each country has an average coverage of sanitation services three times that of the poorest quintile.

In urban areas, the proportion of spending for water among the poorest families is two to four times higher than among the richest families. The population has no access to adequate drinking water supply and sanitation, and thus adopts alternative solutions. In the case of drinking water, these include public sources, individual wells, tankers, illegal connections to the network of public system or water-catchment rivers, lakes, or other water bodies without treatment. Many such solutions do not guarantee the quality of water obtained and have a high cost to the user. On the other hand, the widespread use of septic tanks and latrines has caused groundwater pollution in some cities.

There have been no adequate studies on the place of water in the budgets of poor households. What is clear is that for millions of households, the high price of water overloads the already insufficient resources. In the evidence collected in Latin America for the 2006 Human Development Report developed by UNDP, it was found that 20 percent of the poorest households in Argentina, El Salvador, Jamaica and Nicaragua, the costs of water represented 10 percent of expenses.

About half of these households live on less than US$1 a day, the extreme poverty line (Gasparini and Tornarolli 2006). A positive relationship is noted between the rate of coverage compared to GDP per capita, with a correlation coefficient (r) of 0.62. Variance in the coverage rate should be compared to variations in the GDP per capita.

The development of sanitation services is a process of major investment over a long period. The intensity and regularity of this process of investment is conditional on the macroeconomic context. Growth and economic stability within the framework of rational and consistent policies are conducive to good public finances, improving the ability to pay the population and providing the context for public and private investment. For this reason, it is understood that the policies and the country's macroeconomic conditions have decisive impact on the development of health-sector performance under both private and public provision.

Just as important as the growth of the economy is to achieve the necessary conditions for investment in health infrastructure, this condition alone is not sufficient. In fact, stable and sustained growth matters because it determines the degree of predictability of the economy and the environment for both private and public investment (Lentini 2009).

Water and health

The distribution of wealth generated from the universalization of potable water and sanitation not only improves the income of poor through reductions in costs associated with these services, but also improves the health and welfare of lower-income people. It is estimated that in the developing world, 80 percent of illnesses are due to the consumption of unsafe water and poor sanitary conditions (UNESCO 2003b).

Almost one-tenth of the diseases could be prevented from an improvement in the conditions of water supply, sanitation, hygiene, and water resource management. Such improvements reduce child mortality and improve health and nutrition levels steadily. These improvements yield multiple benefits from the standpoint of economic and social well-being, and indirectly by increasing the access of individuals to health-related services. Improvements in water supply and sanitation services could also improve education and allow more women to attend school instead of wasting time fetching water (UNDP 2006).

Poor water quality is a major cause of poor living conditions and health problems in the world. In 2002, diarrheal diseases and malaria took the lives of approximately 3,100,000 people. Ninety percent of the deaths were children under 5 years old. It has been estimated that each year the lives of 1,600,000 people could be saved if they were offered the possibility to access drinking water supplies, sanitation, and hygiene (United Nations 2006).

In the urban household sector, special emphasis is on the lack of access to adequate quantities of safe water and adequate sanitation and hygiene promotion. Water-related diseases are a human tragedy that every year kills more than five million people. Approximately 2.3 billion people suffer from water-related diseases. About 60 percent of global child mortality is caused by infectious and parasitic diseases, mostly related to water. In particular, the map below outlines by region the number of deaths associated with diarrhea problems worldwide. Sites that stand out as most vulnerable are regions of Sub-Saharan Africa and southern Asia.

The problem of diarrhea especially affects children. About 1.4 million children die each year from preventable diseases related to diarrhea. Diarrhea is one of the main factors of death among diseases related to water, sanitation and hygiene, contributing 43 percent of deaths in the region of Sub-Saharan Africa and South Asia.

For Latin America, the World Health Organization developed an index called WSH (water, sanitation and hygiene), which counts the number of deaths or illnesses by unsafe water, inadequate sanitation and poor hygiene. Measurement units of this index can be two: the first is the number of deaths, and the second is the DALY (disability-adjusted life years) index, which is determined using the years of delay or number of years lost to an early death from disease.

DALY is a measure that weights the deaths and illness from the years lost to the disease contracted. WHO defines it as a measure of the health gap that extends the concept of potential years of life lost due to premature death (years of potential life lost, or YPLL) to include equivalent years of "healthy" life without disease or disability. This unit of measurement combines a measure of time lived with illness or disability and time lost due to premature death. One DALY can be thought of as a year of "good health" lost, and the burden of disease as a measure of the gap between current health status and the ideal state in which the individual lives into adulthood free of disease or disability (for further references, see the WHO's web page at www.who.int/healthinfo/boddaly/en).

In 2008 the World Health Organization (Prüss-Üstün *et al.* 2008) estimated that the percentage of diseases related to WSH for the world was 9.1 percent (measured in DALYs), with 10 percent for the least developed countries and 0.9 percent for developed countries. In Latin America, the percentage of diseases related to WSH is 3.8 percent.

Figure 4.3 represents the indicators reported by the World Health Organization for Latin American countries in 2002, compared to the values of the coverage comparison index. The function index drawn coverage regressed against the ASH index (the Spanish denomination for WSH) has coefficient of determination (R^2) of 0.51.

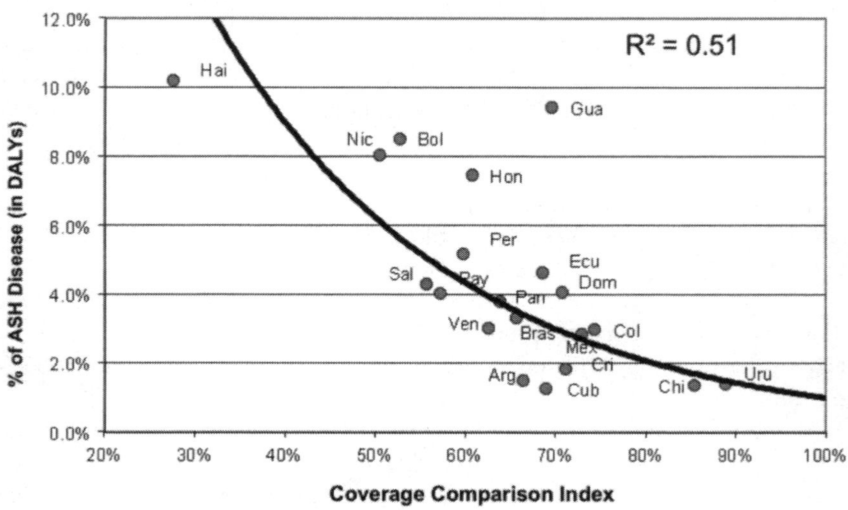

Figure 4.3 Relationship between the percentage of water, sanitation and hygiene disease (ASH; in disability-adjusted life years) and coverage comparison index

Source: WHO/UNICEF (2008)

Impacts of the rise of groundwater in Buenos Aires

Over the last century, the urban macro region of Buenos Aires, Argentina (including the Buenos Aires city itself and 19 districts), suffered an intensive demographic growth process and a concentration of economic activity, becoming one of the more dense urban areas in the world. This metropolitan zone has 4000 km^2 and more than 12 million inhabitants, one-third of the total population of the whole country, and approximate one-half of the Argentinean economic activities. It includes also the seat of the national government.

Many localities of the Greater Buenos Aires urban area suffer the consequences of a disagreeable invasion of liquid coming up from the subsoil. The rise of the groundwater table is a big problem, and it requires the attention of the local authorities and research institutions. The origins of this progressive elevation of the groundwater level are under discussion, connected with the responsibilities of different sectors. According to some preliminary explanations, the process can be associated with an increment of the rainfall in the region due to climate factors, the water importation from sources placed out of the basin, the deficiency of wastewater networks, the systematic decline of the public water supply by wells from a complex aquifer named "Puelches," and the strong decline of the domestic and industrial water wells from the unconfined aquifer.

In addition, water coming from the subsoil has severe pollution conditions. Briefly, the problems associated with the uncontrolled rise of groundwater level would be: inundation of cellars (even in highlands), structural foundation problems, water outcrop in lowlands with inundated fields, cave-in of cesspools, polluted water in human contact, pavement destruction in streets and, finally, a severe deterioration of the quality of life.

According to some preliminary explanations, the process can be associated with an increment of the rainfall in the region due to climate factors or associated with anthropogenic actions. These include the water importation from sources placed out of the basin, the deficiency of wastewater networks, the systematic decline of the public water supply by wells from the Puelches aquifer, and the strong decline of the domestic and industrial water wells from the unconfined aquifer. The first objective (Bianchi and Lopardo 2003) was to identify the real factors causing the groundwater level variations in order to calculate the percentage of responsibility of each variable, determine the areas subjected to the groundwater rise problems, produce actions on the correct information to raise the awareness of the population on the subject, and propose immediate remediation activities.

For the evaluation of the actual conditions in critical zones and mitigation actions, diverse activities were developed: evaluation of existing data, diagnosis of the existing wells network action on the groundwater level, hydrological and meteorological characterization groundwater studies, mathematical modeling of the physical process, groundwater quality determinations, surface urban drainage evaluation, land type and use, sanitary risk zones identification, and environmental characterization.

For the institutional coordination, the following activities were programmed: contact with public institutions of different levels and private sectors, institutional capacities identification, financial capacities identification, development of an institutional strategy, proposal of responsibilities and coordination officers, and the formulation of an integrated plan.

In order to reach the general and specific outcomes the following critical actions were considered:

- data analysis for the general diagnosis and the integration in a GIS, to have rainfall data, evaporation, public water supply networks, wastewater networks, land use, location of water supply wells, water quality data, social and economic data, groundwater levels and piezometric levels;
- evaluation of the hydrological and hydraulic processes to enable the description of the physical behavior of the water resources in the whole region;
- modeling of the surface water and groundwater interaction;
- preparation of regional risk maps to identify the critical regional distribution of the problem; and
- environmental and economic analysis of the diverse water management alternatives, including groundwater level control, external water supply, water transfer from groundwater to surface drainage, management of water excess, protection of urban areas and environmental impact assessment.

As a study case of this general program, a specific research was developed. The chosen municipality was Lomas de Zamora (Figure 4.4), a zone considered by the government as being in "hydrological emergency" during 2001–2002. The municipality of Lomas de Zamora, located in the southern region of the Greater Buenos Aires, has a surface area of 88 km^2. Its population has grown from 574,330 inhabitants in 1991 to 613,192 in 2010 (INDEC 2010).

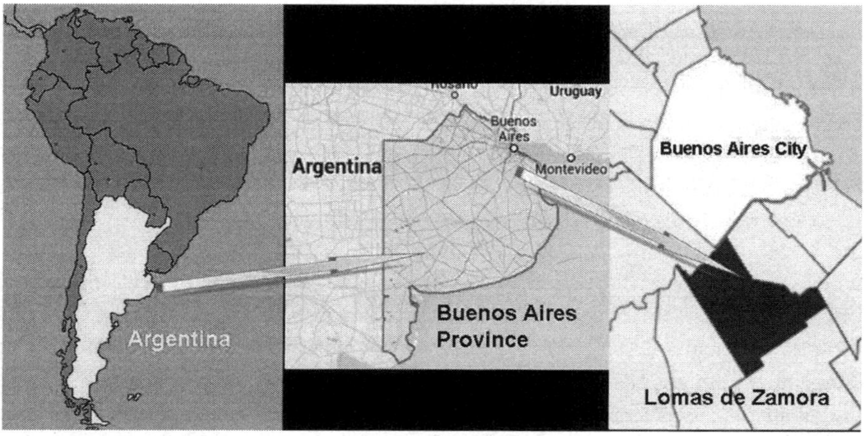

Figure 4.4 Location of Lomas de Zamora within Argentina

Physiographically, Lomas de Zamora is located in the lower area of the Matanza River Basin, with inefficient natural surface drainage characteristics towards the Matanza-Riachuelo system. This aspect gives to Lomas de Zamora more vulnerability than other regions of the Buenos Aires metropolitan urban area, located at average or higher territories. The maximum level of the district is located in the south, with 25 m over the sea level, and one-third of the territory is below the 5 m level. The groundwater source is the Puelches referred to earlier, containing a semi-confined aquifer. A layer called "Epipuelches," made up of silts with some sand layers, contains two interconnected aquifers: the lower one semi-confined (previously mentioned), and the free groundwater level.

The high population growth in the past decades was not followed by a simultaneous growth of the wastewater network infrastructure. Natural and anthropogenic factors have caused changes in that period. In 1991, the public water supply network (coming from the Puelches aquifer) connected a 69.9 percent of the population in the municipality of Lomas de Zamora, while the wastewater network connected only 22.7 percent of the population. Ten years later, the public water supply connected more than 90 percent of the population, but now the source is surface water, imported to the district by big aqueducts from the La Plata River, as a consequence of the privatization of the water supply system for the metropolitan urban area of Buenos Aires five years ago. On the other hand, the wastewater network was delayed in the timetable of the concession contract, and less than 50 percent of the population of the district was connected in 2001.

Other anthropogenic factors can be also considered in the analysis of this municipality, as the deforestation in the scarce rural sectors, the sharp drop in industrial activities, with less groundwater requirements from wells, and the cited change of the public water supply source. This aspect has two different impacts, both negative for the groundwater table rise: the abandonment of big wells from the aquifer generates a growth of its piezometric levels and, at the same time, external water imported without the corresponding wastewater network and pluvial drainage infrastructure increases the soil incorporation of water.

Even if the causes of groundwater level variations are conceptually identified, the goal of the project was the evaluation of their impact. This requires a particularly detailed analysis of each variable to allow its integration in a water balance and the calculation of the incidence of each variable in the general behavior of the system. The difference between the input water (precipitation and importation from external sources) and outputs (surface drainage and evapotranspiration) of the system is, in terms of water balance, the possible volume for infiltration, which can increase the groundwater level. The magnitude of the volumetric imbalance and its effect on groundwater levels depend on the surface and underground physical characteristics of the local basin. Taking into account this conceptual framework, a specific methodology was used to reach a quantitative diagnosis in a short time (with existing data) and a mean time analysis, including new data incorporated during the project. This methodology is considered a useful tool for the emergency measures proposal, the analysis of the actual operations, and the optimization of structural and nonstructural actions to identify the final solution of the problem.

In the territory of the Lomas de Zamora district, three different homogeneous zones were identified, taking into account topographic aspects, urbanization degree, existing infrastructure, and water supply source before the service private concession.

The unconfined groundwater level variation comparison between 1992 and 2000 showed firstly that a progressive rise of the groundwater level was produced along the last decade, and secondly that this rise was not uniform in all the territory of Lomas de Zamora. Even though the "Central Zone" and the "NE Zone" are the highest topographic areas of the district. With higher impermeability coefficients, surface flow and drainage infrastructure, they have the greatest rise in unconfined groundwater levels. Due to this fact, a well network system to decrease the groundwater level was installed by the government. The third region of the district, "Low-Land Zone," near the Matanza River, where the lower-income population lives, does not have any significant variation of groundwater levels.

Due to the topographic characteristics of the Greater Buenos Aires territory, where very low slopes are present, the vertical process of recharge and discharge of the unconfined aquifer are extremely predominant over the horizontal flows, particularly in the Central Zone and the NE Zone. This conceptual hypothesis was determinant for the quantification of the diverse processes affected by natural and anthropogenic factors causing groundwater rise.

From the total water volume coming to the unconfined aquifer during the analyzed period (1991–2001) around 50 percent has anthropogenic origin. Considering the natural factors, a decrease of 5 percent of the water infiltration in the soil was detected for the period 1995–2001 (120.2 Hm^3) relative to the period 1991–1995 (126.2 Hm^3). Despite the fact that precipitation increased in the Buenos Aires region during the period of the study, the decrease in infiltration over the same period balanced the system (Figure 4.5).

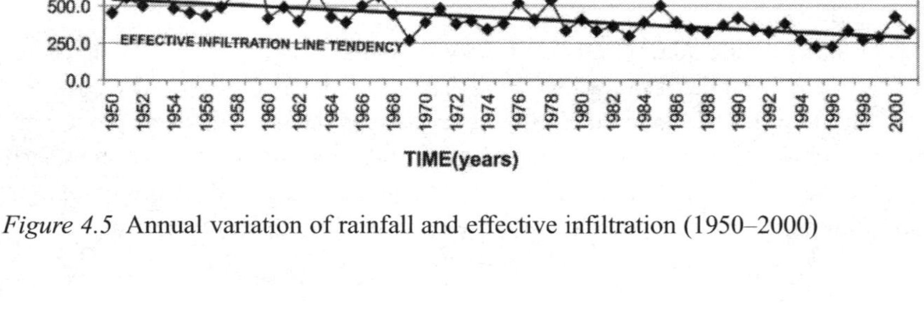

Figure 4.5 Annual variation of rainfall and effective infiltration (1950–2000)

The anthropogenic water inputs were substantially higher during the period 1996–2000 than the water inputs during the period 1991–1995, increasing around 35 percent. The rise of water inputs due to anthropogenic factors is more important in the NE Zone (56 percent) than the Central Zone (35 percent) and the Low-Land Zone (20 percent). This anomaly can be explained because the NE Zone has the maximum increase of the public water supply network (271 percent in that period). In the three zones, for both periods, the anthropogenic factor with the greatest impact is the polluted input from cesspools.

It is possible that the evapotranspiration effect can have some variation during the period of analysis due to the population growth, but the order of magnitude detected on this subject is not important for the present study. The natural surface flow to the rivers, with particular interest for the Low-Land Zone, towards the Matanza River, and for the NE Zone, towards the Las Perdices Stream, were also analyzed, but they did not have any significant changes during the period of study either. Therefore, their influence on the groundwater level variation in Lomas de Zamora can be neglected. In short, variations of the water table had different causes and degree of impact, depending on their geographical location.

At the same time, the behavior of the water table within those locations is distinguished by different patterns of performance, influenced by topographic characteristics, degree of urbanization, drilling (for both drinking water and for industry), importation of water, development and age of potable water networks, sewage, and rain water. These features led to the creation of a new concept. It enabled orderly treatment of the problem, which was defined as homogeneous areas. The aim is the identification of areas or areas where vertical movements (recharge or discharge) of the water table are made from the domination of one specific factor, whether natural or anthropogenic. On the lower slopes where the metropolitan area is developed, the vertical movements are dominant over the horizontal flows.

Conclusions and recommendations

The countries of Latin America in general, and Argentina in particular, show a remarkable concentration of population in urban areas. The poorest live in the outlying areas of large cities, with very little or no land-use planning. This leads to a high vulnerability to water risk factors, both excess water (floods), defect (lack of provision of safe water), or poor quality (pollution of surface and underground water courses). The costs of providing increases as connections are made longer. And there are problems of competency in jurisdictions (nation, province, municipality).

To ensure service quality, it is necessary to make rigorous checks on an ongoing basis and throughout the water cycle. These quality controls should cover all stages of the process. It should start with raw water, continue through processing steps and output of water treatment facilities, and continue throughout the distribution system. The cycle must be completed by controlling the liquid waste to sewer dumps, as well as the effluent at treatment plants before discharge.

It should focus on the needs of those who still have no service and are in socio-economic difficulties through the development of flexible forms, the search for innovation, and adaptation of management. Therefore, people in the urban centers must help and promote cooperatives, which have proven to be efficient providers of water service and sewage in several cities in Argentina.

On the other hand, it is important to note that AySA has had considerable success doing specific work with lower-income sectors, through the methods of "participatory models of governance" and the "water and work plan" (*Plan agua más trabajo*), and to a lesser extent to a "sanitation and work plan," which is reflected by joint action with neighborhood communities, municipalities, government agencies, and social organizations. This is a strategy based on joint work-sharing and community sites to serve the municipalities and the company involved that is aimed at improving access of water and wastewater services to the population living in slums. The company performs most of the financing of projects and provides technical supervision and social support of the work. Neighbors help with labor, receive technical training, participate in workshops on proper use, and receive a discount on their bills. For its part, the municipality sets project priorities, provides equipment and machinery, and is responsible for the technical direction of work. It should be noted that the water and work plan was awarded the Latin American and Caribbean Prize for Water, Plate Business 2008 by the Center for the Humid Tropics of Latin America and the Caribbean in partnership with CARE USA, UNICEF, UNEP, and other institutions. In 2008, among works completed, service is running around 700,000, with more than 1,500 km of installed networks. It should take into account the possible impacts that a water supply from a source outside the basin may have on groundwater levels, and anticipate any risks of contaminated water upgrades on the quality life of the inhabitants.

References

ADERASA (2007) *Informe anual de benchmarking: Base de datos e indicadores de desempeño para agua potable y alcantarillado Ejercicio anual de evaluación comparativa de desempeño*. Asociación de Entes Reguladores de Agua Potable y Saneamiento de las Américas. Available at www.asep.gob.pa/agua/estudios/est_06.pdf.

AySA (2007) *Annual Report 2007*. Buenos Aires: AySA.

Bianchi, H. and Lopardo, R. A. (2003) "Diagnosis and Mitigation of Groundwater Level Rise in a Highly Populated Urban System." In *XXX IAHR Congress*, Thessaloniki, Greece, 2003, vol. B, pp. 629–36.

CEPAL/CELADE (1999) *Distribución Espacial y Urbanización de la Población en América Latina y el Caribe*. Santiago de Chile: CEPAL/CELADE.

Chama, R. (2005) *Water and the Millennium Development Goals: Investment Needs in Latin America and the Caribbean*. Washington, DC: Inter-American Development Bank.

Gasparini, L. and Tornarolli, L. (2006) *Disparities in Water Pricing in Latin America and the Caribbean*. HDOCPA-2006-22. New York: Human Development Report Office (HDRO), United Nations Development Programme.

IADB (2004) *Initiative for Water Supply and Sanitation*. Washington, DC: Inter-American Development Bank.
INDEC (2006) "Estatísticas de población y hogares" (Population and housing statistics), IV Trimestre, Buenos Aires: Instituto Nacional de Estadística y Censos.
—— (2010) "Provisory Data of Censo 2010."
Jouravlev, A. (2004) *Los servicios de agua potable y saneamiento en el umbral del siglo XXI*. Serie Recursos Naturales e Infraestructura no. 74. Santiago de Chile: CEPAL.
Komives, S. R., Longerbeam, S. D., Owen, J. E., Mainella, F. C., and Osteen, L. (2006) "A Leadership Identity Development Model: Applications from a Grounded Theory." *Journal of College Student Development* 47: 401–18.
Lentini, E. (2009) *Drinking Water and Sanitation: Lessons from Relevant Experience*. Santiago de Chile: ECLAC/CEPAL.
Ministry for Housing, Construction and Sanitation (2006) *National Plans of Housing and Sanitation from 2006 to 2015*. March. Lima: Ministerio de Vivienda, Construcción y Saneamiento.
PAHO (1998) *La salud en las Américas: Edición de 1998*, vol. I. Washington, DC: Pan American Health Organization.
—— (2001a) *Informe regional sobre la evaluación 2000 en la región de las Américas: agua potable y saneamiento, estado actual y perspectivas*. Washington, DC: Pan American Health Organization.
—— (2001b) *Salud, agua potable y saneamiento en el desarrollo humano sostenible*. 35a Sesión del Subcomité del Comité Ejecutivo de Planificación y Programación. Washington, DC: Pan American Health Organization.
Prüss-Üstün, A., Bos, R., Gore, F., and Bartram, J. (2008) *Safer Water, Better Health: Costs, Benefits and Sustainability of Interventions to Protect and Promote Health*. Geneva: World Health Organization.
SISS (2008) *Report on Health Sector Management 2007*. Santiago de Chile: SISS.
UNDP (2006) *Beyond Scarcity: Power, Poverty and the Global Water Crisis*. Human Development Report 2006. New York: UNDP.
UNESCO (2003a) *Water for the Future: What are the Trends?* Paris: UNESCO.
—— (2003b) *The International Year of Freshwater*. Paris: UNESCO.
—— (2009) *United Nations World Water Development Report 3: Water in a Changing World*. London: Earthscan.
United Nations (2006) *Water, a Shared Responsibility*. Second United Nations Report on the Development of Water Resources in the World. New York: United Nations.
WHO (1999) *Food Safety: An Essential Public Health Issue for the New Millennium*. WHO/SDE/PHE/FOS/99.4. Geneva: World Health Organization.
—— (2004) *Guidelines for Drinking-Water Quality*, 3rd edn. Geneva: World Health Organization.
WHO/UNICEF (2000) *Global Water Supply and Sanitation Assessment 2000 Report*. WHO/UNICEF Joint Monitoring Programme for Water Supply and Sanitation. Geneva: World Health Organization/New York: UNICEF.
—— (2008) *Progress on Drinking Water and Sanitation: Special Focus on Sanitation*. WHO/UNICEF Joint Monitoring Programme for Water Supply and Sanitation. Geneva: World Health Organization/New York: UNICEF.
World Bank (2004) *Recent Economic Development in Infrastructure (REDI) in Colombia*. Washington, DC: World Bank.

5 Supply and sanitation

How are the unserved to be served?

Katherine Vammen

Introduction

Water management involves the protection of resources in order to secure safe water for consumption and continued use by the world population. It is especially urgent to secure access to quality drinking water for human consumption and improved sanitation services to reduce waterborne diseases and promote economic and social development. Therefore, this chapter is directed to those who are not served with water supplies or basic sanitation services. Global Millennium Development Goals (MDGs), established by the United Nations, have been set to provide rural unserved people with sustainable access to safe drinking water and basic sanitation services by 2015 (JMP 2000). In most developing countries, rural populations are migrating to urban areas: from 2007 onwards, the world urban population will be greater than the rural population (DESA 2004). Even taking this into consideration, the World Health Organization (WHO)/United Nations Children's Fund (UNICEF) Joint Monitoring Programme for Water Supply and Sanitation (JMP) predicts that in 2015 the number of unserved rural dwellers (1.7 billion) will continue to be more than twice the number of unserved urban residents (7 million). At the current rate of growth, only 49 percent of the rural population will have sanitation services by 2015 (JMP 2008). Therefore, the number of unserved people in rural populations needs special attention in order to reach higher coverage with a healthful water supply and sanitation services. This is a special challenge in order to secure good water management in the Americas and contribute to improving safe water for consumption and sanitation in the developing countries of this hemisphere.

The unserved in rural areas in the Americas

According to the report *Progress on Drinking Water and Sanitation, Special Focus on Sanitation* from JMP (2008), the Latin American and Caribbean regions are advancing in their efforts to increase coverage of improved drinking water sources. From 1990 to 2006, the region has increased coverage in 8 percentage points, reaching 92 percent. As a comparison, it is notable that the global coverage in 2006 for developing countries is 84 percent and the world percentage is 87 percent. The numbers tell another story when the urban–rural disparity is taken into account, in which Latin America and the Caribbean have the highest differences between urban and rural coverage. The water supply coverage for urban areas is 97 percent and rural is only 73 percent. As a reference, the world coverage is 96 percent for urban areas and 78 percent in rural areas. As observed in Figure 5.1, large areas of Central America and South America have been found to have rural drinking water coverage of between 50 and 75 percent of the population. Rural access to improved drinking water sources remains low in the majority of countries of Latin America (Table 5.1).

The Joint Monitoring Programme has found that of the 53 million people in the Americas who do not have drinking water coverage, the majority (more than 68 percent) live in rural zones (JMP 2008). In most countries, access to water is unequal between rural and urban areas but also according to income groups. An example of two Latin American countries, Brazil and Peru, shows lower accessibility to drinking water in rural zones and in lower-income groups (Figure 5.2). In Latin America, the income share spent by the poorest quintile is more or less twice the income share spent by the richest quintile (Komives *et al.* 2005). If expenditures for non-piped services (water vendors and tanker trucks) are included, the income share for the poorest quintile increases even more. Global estimates indicate that the richest quintile of the income distribution is twice as likely to use improved water services as the poorest quintile. For sanitation services the estimates are four times more likely for the richest quintile than the poorest quintile.

Some countries have made considerable progress. In 2006, three Central American countries have rural drinking water coverage of more than 80 percent: Guatemala, Costa Rica, and Panama. In South America, four have more than 80 percent: Ecuador, Guyana, Uruguay, and Argentina. Among the Caribbean, five countries have more than 80 percent: Barbados, Jamaica, Dominican Republic, San Kitts and Nevis, and Trinidad and Tobago (Table 5.2).

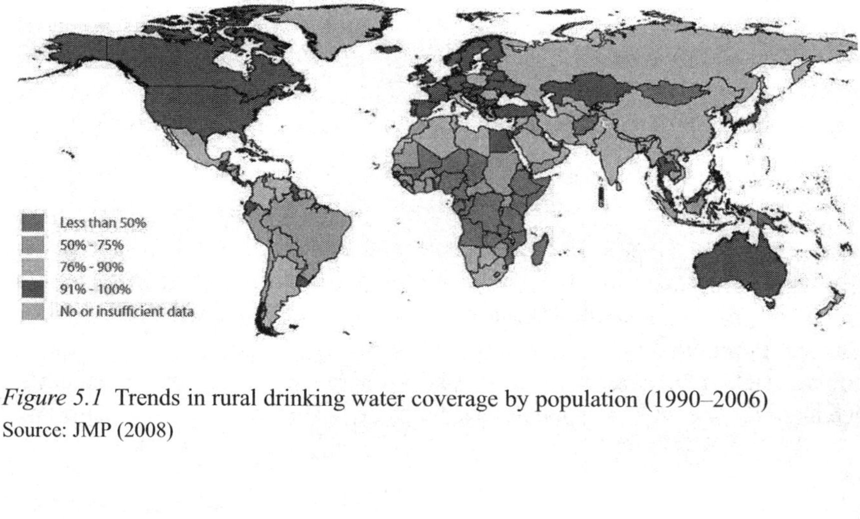

Figure 5.1 Trends in rural drinking water coverage by population (1990–2006)
Source: JMP (2008)

Table 5.1 Drinking water and sanitation coverage for Mexico, countries of Central America, South America, and the Caribbean for rural areas and total

Country, area or territory	*Year*	*Rural (%)*	*Drinking water Rural*		*Total*				*Sanitation Rural*				*Total*			
			Improved	*Piped into dwelling, yard or plot*	*Improved*	*Piped into dwelling, yard or plot*	*Other improved*	*Unimproved*	*Improved*	*Shared*	*Unimproved*	*Open defecation*	*Improved*	*Shared*	*Unimproved*	*Open defecation*
Mexico	2006	24	85	73	95	91	4	5	48	0	45	7	81	1	16	2
Central America																
Guatemala	2006	52	94	67	96	78	18	4	79	6	6	9	84	6	4	6
Belize	2006	52	–	–	–	–	–	–	–	–	–	–	–	–	–	–
Honduras	2006	53	74	67	84	79	5	16	55	5	12	28	66	8	10	16
El Salvador	2006	40	68	38	84	62	22	16	80	8	3	9	86	9	1	4
Nicaragua	2006	41	63	27	79	61	18	21	34	7	32	27	48	9	29	14
Costa Rica	2006	38	96	95	98	97	1	2	95	3	2	0	96	2	1	1
Panama	2006	28	81	79	92	89	3	8	63	6	31	0	74	10	16	0
South America																
Total	2006	27	77	63	93	87	6	7	58	7	15	20	78	11	5	6
Venezuela	2006	6	–	–	–	–	–	–	–	–	–	–	–	–	–	–
Ecuador	2006	37	91	65	95	81	14	5	72	4	12	12	84	3	7	6
Guyana	2006	72	91	61	93	67	26	7	80	8	11	1	81	0	9	1
Surinam	2006	36	79	46	92	71	21	8	60	10	9	21	82	9	4	5
Peru	2006	27	63	44	84	77	7	16	36	1	28	35	72	5	13	10
Bolivia	2006	35	69	45	86	75	11	14	22	3	21	54	43	15	16	26
Brazil	2006	15	58	17	91	77	14	9	37	–	23	40	77	–	14	9

Table 5.1 continued

Country, area or territory	Year	Rural (%)	Drinking water Rural		Total				Sanitation Rural				Total			
			Improved	*Piped into dwelling, yard or plot*	*Improved*	*Piped into dwelling, yard or plot*	*Other improved*	*Unimproved*	*Improved*	*Shared*	*Unimproved*	*Open defecation*	*Improved*	*Shared*	*Unimproved*	*Open defecation*
Paraguay	2006	41	52	29	77	62	15	23	42	1	57	0	70	3	27	0
Uruguay	2006	8	100	84	100	96	4	0	99	1	0	0	100	0	0	0
Chile	2006	12	72	46	95	92	3	5	74	–	25	1	94	–	5	1
Argentina	2006	10	80	45	96	79	17	4	83	–	17	–	91	–	9	–
Caribbean																
Antigua & Barbuda	2006	61	–	–	–	–	–	–	–	–	–	–	–	–	–	–
Bahamas	2006	9	–	–	–	–	–	–	100	–	0	0	100	–	0	0
Barbados	2006	47	100	–	100	–	–	0	100	–	0	0	99	–	1	–
Cuba	2006	25	78	49	91	74	17	9	95	–	5	–	98	–	2	–
Dominica	2006	28	–	–	–	–	–	–	–	–	–	–	–	–	–	–
Grenada	2006	69	–	–	–	–	–	–	97	–	3	–	97	–	3	–
Haiti	2006	61	51	4	58	11	47	42	12	6	31	51	19	13	34	34
Jamaica	2006	47	88	47	93	70	23	7	84	12	3	1	83	14	3	0
Dominican Republic	2006	32	91	62	95	82	12	5	74	15	3	8	79	15	2	4
San Kitts & Nevis	2006	68	99	–	99	–	–	1	96	–	4	–	96	–	4	–
San Vicente	2006	54	–	–	–	–	–	–	96	–	4	–	–	–	–	–
Santa Lucia	2006	72		–	–	–	–	2	–	–	–	–	–	–	–	–
Trinidad & Tobago	2006	87	93	72	94	74	20	6	92	7	1	0	92	7	1	0

Source: Data taken from JMP (2008)

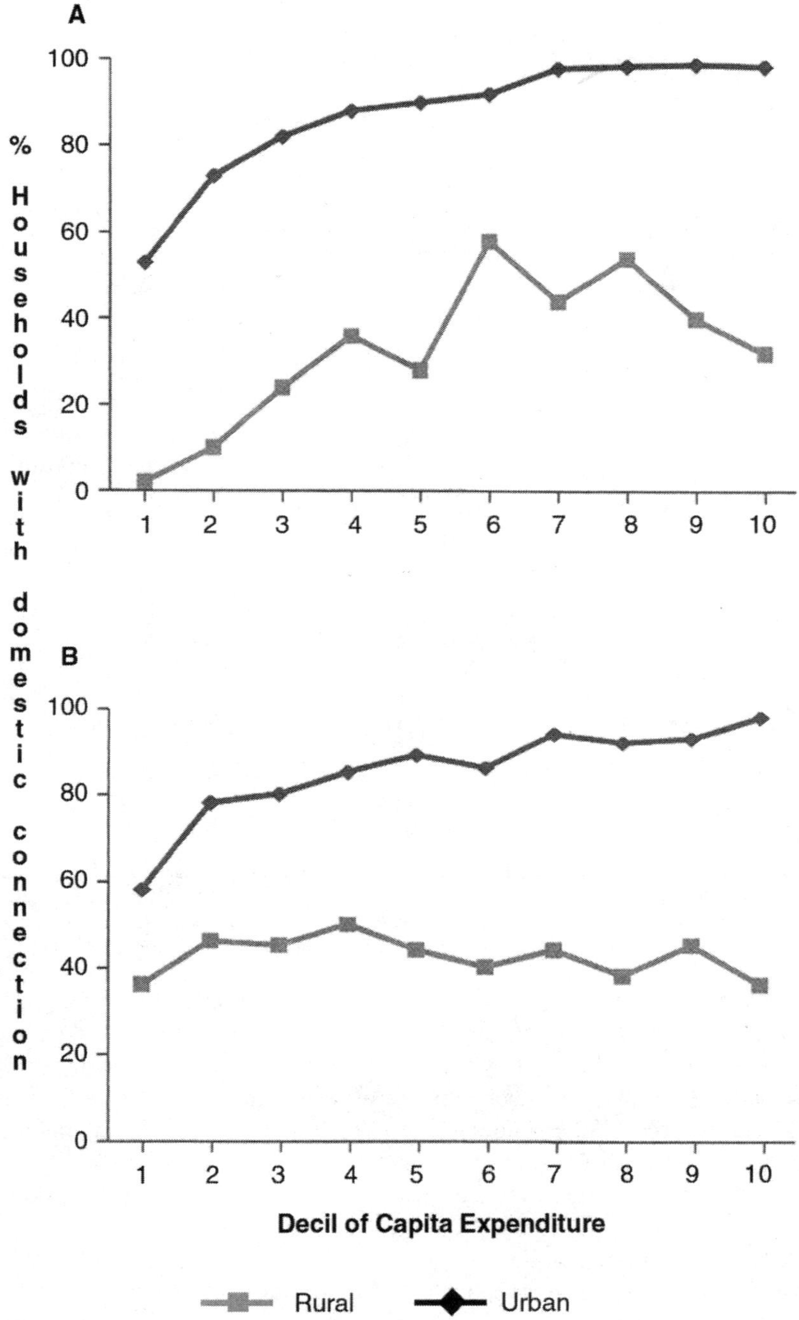

Figure 5.2 Drinking water coverage in rural and urban zones in (a) Brazil and (b) Peru in relation to spending

Source: OPS (2007a)

Table 5.2 Coverage of improved drinking water and sanitation for 2006 in Mexico, Central America, South America and the Caribbean

Region	*Rural population*	*Rural improved drinking water in the region*	*Countries above 80%*	*Rural improved sanitation in the region*	*Countries above 80%*	*Countries with a high open defecation in the population*
Mexico	24%	85%	Mexico	48%		
Central America	28–53%	63–94%	Guatemala, Costa Rica, Panama	34–95%	El Salvador (80%), Costa Rica	Honduras (28%), Nicaragua (27%)
South America	6–72%	52–100%	Ecuador, Guyana, Uruguay, Argentina (80%)	22–95%	Guyana (80%), Uruguay, Argentina	Colombia (20%), Surinam (21%), Peru (35%), Brazil (40%), Bolivia (54%)
Caribbean	9–87%	51–100%	Barbados, Jamaica, Dominican Republic, San Kitts & Nevis, Trinidad & Tobago	12–100%	Bahamas, Barbados, Cuba, Grenada, Jamaica, San Kitts & Nevis, Trinidad & Tobago	Haiti (51%)

Source: JMP (2008)

Another indicator of improving drinking water conditions is the progress that has been made in the use of "piped drinking water on premises." It has been observed that this is the best system to secure the improvement of health in a population (JMP 2008). Globally, the use of piped drinking water has increased by 6 percent since 1990 and now has reached 54 percent. But, again, this represents progress for urban populations, in which 90 percent of urban dwellers have piped water in Latin America and the Caribbean, but the rural areas have only 48 percent coverage.

Although basic sanitation has the lowest utility coverage ratios in the Americas, the proportion of the population without access to drinking water is six times higher in the rural zone as the urban zones, and the ratio for basic sanitation is three-and-a-half times higher in rural areas (OPS 2007b).

The number of unserved population with basic sanitation services is overwhelming on a global scale. The number of people who still do not have access to improved sanitation is extremely high, and this impacts health, which in turn affects earnings and keeps people living in poverty.

In 2006, the world's population was almost equally divided between urban and rural dwellers. Nevertheless, more than seven out of ten people without improved sanitation were rural inhabitants. Better sanitation is the most important improvement that can guarantee better health in a population. It "offers us the opportunity to save the lives of 1.5 million children a year who would otherwise succumb to diarrheal diseases and to protect the health of many more" (JMP 2008). Better sanitation has also been recognized as a basic requirement for human dignity and promotes economic development and supports financial progress in education and health. The actual status is that only "62 percent of the world's population has access to improved sanitation" (JMP 2008), which means sanitation measures that guarantee separation of human excreta from human contact.

The urban sanitation coverage in Latin America and the Caribbean has reached 86 percent, which is above the world coverage of 79 percent. But rural coverage has been incredibly neglected, demonstrating only 52 percent, which shows one of the highest disparities between urban and rural coverage in the world (Figure 5.3).

In 2006, only two countries of Central America (El Salvador and Costa Rica) had 80 percent or more in coverage of improved sanitation in rural areas. In South America, only three countries (Guyana, Uruguay, and Argentina) had more than

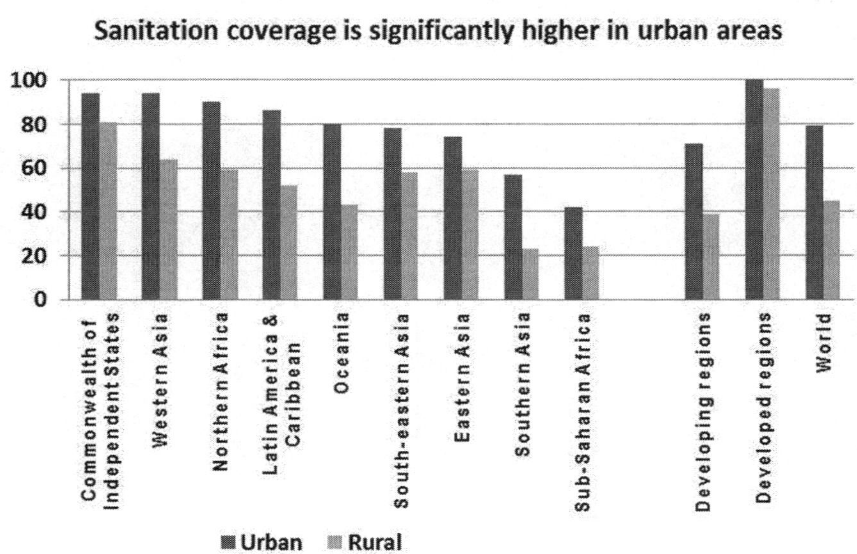

Figure 5.3 Urban and rural sanitation coverage (2006)

Source: JMP (2008)

80 percent coverage in rural areas. In the Caribbean, rural areas of the Bahamas, Barbados, Cuba, Grenada, Jamaica, San Kitts & Nevis, and Trinidad & Tobago had more than 80 percent coverage (Table 5.3).

High open defecation of the population causes contamination of water resources and, therefore, greatly impacts human health. In Central America, both

Table 5.3 Increase in coverage of sanitation in rural areas from 1990 to 2006 in Mexico, Central America, South America, and the Caribbean

Region	*1990*	*2006*	*Progress in % coverage*
Mexico	8	48	40
Central America			
Guatemala	58	79	21
Belize	–	–	
Honduras	29	55	26
El Salvador	59	80	21
Nicaragua	23	34	11
Costa Rica	92	95	3
Panama	–	63	
South America			
Colombia	39	58	19
Venezuela	47	–	
Ecuador	50	72	22
Guyana	–	80	
Suriname	–	60	
Peru	15	36	21
Bolivia	15	22	7
Brazil	37	37	0
Paraguay	34	42	8
Uruguay	99	99	0
Chile	48	74	26
Argentina	45	83	38
Caribbean			
Antigua and Barbuda	–	–	
Bahamas	100	100	0
Barbados	100	100	0
Cuba	95	95	0
Dominica	–	–	
Grenada	97	97	0
Haiti	20	12	–8
Jamaica	83	84	1
Dominican Republic	57	74	17
San Kitts and Nevis	96	96	0
San Vicente	96	96	0
Santa Lucia	–	–	–
Trinidad and Tobago	93	92	–1

Source: JMP (2008)

Honduras and Nicaragua have problems with the continuing practice of open defecation in rural areas, registering respectively 28 percent and 27 percent of the population. In South America, five countries still show a population practicing open defecation above 20 percent in rural regions: Colombia (20 percent), Surinam (21 percent), Peru (35 percent), Brazil (40 percent), and Bolivia (54 percent). In the Caribbean, Haiti has the highest defecation rate of 51 percent (Table 5.2).

Progress has been made in sanitation for rural areas in the Americas from 1990 to 2006. Mexico has improved from 8 to 48 percent. In Central America, Honduras, Guatemala, and El Salvador have made more than 20 percent progress in securing sanitation in rural zones of their countries. Peru has advanced in coverage by 21 percent, Ecuador by 22 percent, Chile by 26 percent, and Argentina by 38 percent. The countries of the Caribbean mostly had high coverage rates in rural areas, but it is to be noted that the Dominican Republic has improved by 17 percent, and Haiti has reduced coverage in the 16 years by 8 percent (Table 5.3).

The lack of coverage of sanitary infrastructure, the discharge of domestic wastewater without treatment into surface water, and deficient functioning sanitation systems (septic tanks and latrines) contaminate groundwater, which can create major health problems in populations. The risks of wastewaters have been associated with transmission of enteric illnesses, such as cholera and typhoid fever. Those most vulnerable to health hazards, above all children, are most likely to be affected by one of the several water-related diseases (e.g., diarrhea, intestinal helminthes, schistosomiasis, and trypanosomiasis). In an evaluation of drinking water and sanitation in the Americas, it was estimated in 2000 that the average production of wastewater reached 600 m^3 per second, of which only 14 percent received treatment and, in reality, only 6 percent received adequate treatment (OPS 2007b). Recent estimates show that improved water (sanitation) services reduce diarrhea morbidity on the average of 25 percent (JMP 2006). The lack of sanitation coverage has direct impacts on health. Figure 5.4 shows the reciprocal relationship between mortality in children under 5 years of age and coverage of sanitation in the countries of the region.

Results of the evaluation of costs and benefits of water and sanitation improvements in Latin America and the Caribbean countries have shown that meeting MDG10 of 50 percent reduction of the deficit of access to water and sanitation would have an annual benefit of US$9,635 million, versus a cost of US$788 million. The benefits include savings on health costs but the major benefit is saving time, which could be invested in other sectors, such as education, agriculture, industry, and tourism (Hutton and Heller 2004).

The quality and sustainability of water and sanitation services is a problem in rural areas. The majority of countries report discontinuity in services that risks public health and results in inefficient use of infrastructure. Deficiencies in the operation and maintenance of installations can mean affecting the quality of water, failures in disinfection, and loss of water in the distribution system. Keeping track of water usage and billing is usually very poorly developed in rural

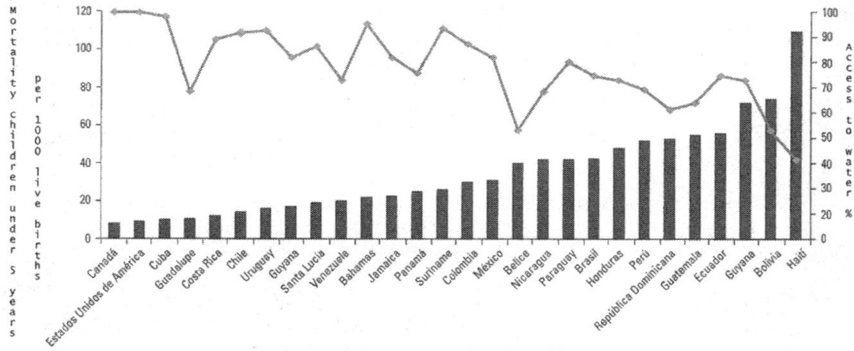

Figure 5.4 Comparison of rate of infantile mortality and population with access to sanitation infrastructure in the countries of the Americas

Source: adapted from Otterstetter *et al.* (2004)

areas, and there are enormous deficiencies and absence of disinfection of water, especially in rural areas (OPS 2007b).

One factor that is of utmost importance to secure good-quality water is the development of monitoring capacity for existing distribution systems and sources of drinking water. Monitoring systems do exist, but sometimes do not include rural areas. Good laboratory analytical services are essential, including basic chemical and physical analysis, determination of metal and organic compounds (hydrocarbons and pesticides), and analysis for bacteriological quality of water in the distribution system, as well as in surface and groundwater, which serve as present and future sources for potable water. Only laboratories with well-established quality control systems can provide valid and precise data for evaluation of good water quality.

Based on data reported by the provincial and district health authorities of Colombia (SSPD 2006), in 2005 64 percent of the districts for which information was available reported that the delivered water did not meet the legal standards defined in Decreto no. 475 (Ministerio de Salud de Colombia 1998).

Is it important to note that in meetings of ministers of environment and health of Latin-American and Caribbean countries in Ottawa in 2002 and in Mar del Plata in 2005, declarations emphasized a great need to promote integrated management of water resources. The deficient management of watersheds to protect water resources, combined with the discharge of wastewater without treatment and limitations in infrastructure to secure efficient treatment, are factors that cause deterioration of the quality of water distributed to consumers.

The protection of water resources (both surface and groundwater) is one of the first and largest problems in securing good-quality water for human consumption. In order to secure sustainable water sources, it is essential to impede the contamination of these water bodies. In rural areas, the contamination is dominated by pesticides used in agriculture, nitrates from sources of domestic and community wastes, and bacterial sources from poor-quality sanitation and open defecation, which is more frequently practiced in rural areas. Eutrophication of surface waters is due to changing of soil use, deforestation, and an increase in agricultural and pasture lands in the watersheds, which bring erosion and contamination with agrochemicals. This results in higher treatment costs and deterioration of drinking water quality due to high concentrations of organic substances which, on contact with chlorine, can be a risk to health. In a regional study by the Centro Panamericano de Ingeniería Sanitaria y Ciencias del Ambiente (Panamerican Center for Sanitary Engineering and Environmental Sciences, or CEPIS), more than 75 percent of the lakes and dams evaluated in the Latin American and Caribbean countries (Argentina, Brazil, Colombia, Cuba, Ecuador, El Salvador, Guatemala, Honduras, México, Nicaragua, Paraguay, Peru, Puerto Rico, Dominican Republic, and Venezuela) were classified as eutrophic or in the process of eutrophication (OPS 2007b).

Due to climate change, the demand for water will increase in just 20 years by 40 percent, and by more than 50 percent in the most rapidly developing countries. Supply expansion and improvements in efficiency will not be able to close the gap. Rural areas will be affected stronger in areas of low coverage, where irrigated agriculture dominates, and in semi-arid and arid zones. These factors will slow down economic development, and result in more hungry villages and degraded environments (Water Resources Group 2009).

On July 28, 2010, the United Nations adopted a resolution proposed by Bolivia with the support of several Latin American and Caribbean countries which declared the "right to safe and clean drinking water and sanitation as a human right that is essential for the full enjoyment of life and all human rights" (United Nations General Assembly 2010). The declaration called upon states and international organizations to "provide financial resources, capacity building and technology transfer, through international assistance and co-operation, in particular to developing countries, in order to scale up efforts to provide safe, clean, accessible and affordable drinking water and sanitation for all." The World Health Organization and the United Nations' High Commissioner for Human Rights published a document in 2003, the International Year of Freshwater, titled *The Right to Water*, in which the responsibility of governments were recommended to defend the right to water with the following practices:

- legislative implementation;
- adopting a national water strategy and plan of action to realize this right;
- ensuring that water is affordable for everyone; and
- facilitating improved and sustainable access to water, particularly in rural and deprived urban areas (WHO 2003).

These are new initiatives to emphasize a human rights-based approach to water that should guarantee a social and cultural value to the resource instead of dominantly economic. This should also mean that the unserved or "least served" are given priority in policies and management for the access of water.

Causes for the lack of service in rural areas

Why are water and sanitation services so far behind in coverage and quality in rural areas? Why are the numbers of unserved in rural areas the highest in the Americas?

Rural areas tend to have less economic activity, high poverty rates and usually lower population density. The lack of water and sanitation services in rural areas increases the risk of disease, which in turn means less productivity and economic possibilities of the household. Productivity is also extremely reduced, due to time spent in obtaining safe water from wells far away or from extremely expensive sources such as vendors. It can be said that lacking access to adequate water and sanitation services reduces personal opportunities to economic, social, and political dimensions of well-being.

It is obvious that the average income of the country, the availability of freshwater resources in both ground and surface waters conditioned by quantity and quality of water and also the spatial distribution and social–cultural aspects of the population affect the demand and supply and therefore the organizational forms of services in rural areas. Private service providers are usually not interested in serving rural areas due to the high atomization of the service needs and especially the low perspective of tariffs.

But, the causes for the lack of services in rural areas are multiple and have their essential source in the organization of society and decision-making, which neglects or has a lack of understanding and capacity in taking on challenges for improving equity of these services in rural areas.

The lack of quality governance and effective institutional frameworks that shape policy-making and public decision-making for rural areas are one of the principle reasons for the low coverage of water and sanitation services. Due to the low political representation in the government and the absence of special policies for securing safe water for all populations with emphasis on the unserved, the inhabitants of rural areas suffer from deficient performance of water services. Policies have not been developed to promote investments to benefit those who lack access, which are almost always prevalent in urban areas.

One of the results of good governance is the restructuring of economic policies to promote the increase in coverage of water and sanitation services in rural areas. In *The Political Economy of Water and Sanitation* (Krause 2009), it has been emphasized that "both improvements in allocative efficiency and improvements in equity are considered valid arguments for justifying welfare-enhancing in water and sanitation policies." In other words, adopting economic policies that make good usage of resources and that promote their best use for benefiting the unserved; that is evading urban bias in economic policies and putting priorities on rural areas. Most governments in the Americas give very little priority to rural water and sanitation, and prefer to invest in large-scale projects for urban populations that are able to pay for higher levels of service at full cost-recovery water rates. Evidence has been found that low-quality governance of sub-national governments compromises a more widespread access to services (Krause 2009). It is to be emphasized that a changing of priorities is needed both at central and local community government levels.

Sometimes rural communities are forced to pay for investment in basic services by taking loans. In most urban areas' water supply systems, infrastructure, electricity, sewerage, drainage, education, and health are all subsidized by the state. Some subsidy systems have reached only households that are connected to an established service provider, and it has been observed that "half of the households that are subsidized have an income that lies above the national poverty line" (Krause 2009).

In analyzing the reasons for low coverage within a country, it is necessary to examine the governance factors that influence collective decision-making and implementation of economic policies within the state. It is essential to evaluate the institutional framework and which components are responsible for rural areas and know how they are being politically represented. Who are the institutional actors that play a role in providing water and sanitation services?

Global estimations for developing countries indicate that 75 to 85 percent of the financing for the water and sanitation sector originated from public sources in the 1990s (65 to 70 percent from public domestic sources and 10 to 15 percent from international donors); at present, just about 3 percent of the population is served by providers that are fully or partially privately owned (Krause 2009). This means that it is vital to have cooperation of governments, civil society and private sector for investment, and the management of water and sanitation services in rural areas needs to be independent of the source of funding and involve cooperation of the different stakeholders involved.

It is sometimes found that public funds destined for the water and sanitation sector are not used sufficiently to expand services to the unserved in rural areas. Some of the factors that are responsible for this lack of investment for expansion are:

- the lack of capacity for and absence of territorial planning of districts in rural areas;
- the lack of civic participation in the planning process;
- lack of coordination between investments plans of service providers and public or district investment plans; and
- lack of supervision and transparency in the awarding of construction contracts.

There is evidence that private service providers can contribute to improvements in the internal efficiency of water and sanitation services but they have not been able to promote coverage expansion or improvements in better social distribution of services on a long-term basis (Krause 2009). These factors depend on the quality of governance.

Most analysis of water and sanitation services note that an effective institutional framework to accomplish a functional economy should include structures for three components: policy making, regulation, and service delivery. The design of the structure of these components varies. It has been recommended that citizens or users be incorporated into these structures to guarantee effectiveness for those benefitting from the service or in the user's interest.

As in other services that involve large investments in infrastructure, one requirement is considerable investments in long-lived assets. For this reason, reliability of water and sanitation policies is essential even in decentralized systems.

In rural areas, these institutional framework components are somewhat different but of utmost importance because the services are usually decentralized and imply highly atomized production units that require good cooperation at local and regional levels.

Here user participation is essential in all three – policy, regulation and service delivery – in order to guarantee good-quality service adapted to the characteristics of the specific rural areas in question. There are also good examples in Latin America of user cooperatives that are both owners and carry out the management of the service provider.

One of the causes that influence the coverage of services to rural areas and is observed in the practice throughout the Americas is clientalism, in which politicians deliver benefits according to political and economic support from different groups of the population. As poor rural areas usually have less potential to support candidates due to lack of economic means and reduced voter quantities, this phenomena has been observed to affect service coverage. This also affects the accumulation of capacity due to frequent technical and management staff rotation. This, combined with tendencies of corruption, affects policy making which turn back from equity policies and turn toward "private-regardedness rather than public-regardedness" (Krause 2009).

As has been emphasized before, controlling the quality of water being provided to the consumer is one of the main factors in assuring good water services with safe water, which should be monitored in the process of regulation according to legal norms. Due to lack of knowledge and information, the importance of the quality of water in rural areas has been neglected. It should be noted that in rural communities, even where the availability of water resources is secured, people suffer from water-related diseases due to the use of poor-quality water drawn from unprotected shallow wells or other sources. For this reason, the term access to safe drinking water or the availability of good-quality water systems is the real challenge. In many countries of Latin America, rural water resources are affected by natural arsenic contamination (Argentina, Nicaragua, Honduras, and others).

Lack of capacity of local authorities and communities required to manage water supply and sanitation service delivery is very prominent in rural areas. This means not only technical capacity but also the need for competence in mobilizing financial sources for investment in water and sanitation projects in rural areas and in the organization of the institutional framework of management and delivery of services. Regional and local authorities need to improve their capacity in organizing systems in outlying areas, logistical organization, and getting finance and materials required for the delivery of water and sanitation services. There is a lack of knowledge of small-scale technological solutions adequate for use in rural areas.

Wastewater services and sanitation needs special attention in rural areas because the coverage percentages are the lowest, as observed by the JMP mentioned above. The willingness to pay for sanitation is typically lower than for water, and the awareness among users of the benefits from sanitation services is lower. The demand for sanitation is also lower in rural areas because it depends on the level of hygiene education. This is partly due to a misconception of sanitation and lack of consciousness in the population about their necessity in rural areas:

> In many villages, the same source is used for all water purposes: drinking water, and washing cattle, clothes, and people. During the rainy season, the number of sanitation-related diseases increases because run-off water washes feces into the ponds.
>
> (Keirns 2008)

The common concept of sanitation systems involves only the toilet, but the system involves "more than just the user interface but includes the excreta collection unit: a method of transport from the site, the treatment process and, finally, the end use or disposal" (Van Vliet *et al.* 2010). Sanitation systems must also include not only physical infrastructure but also the users and management frameworks for the operation and maintenance of the whole treatment process. The entire system needs human interaction as individual user and communal group users. The development and design of systems especially for rural areas must take into consideration culture and the organization of the civil society in the specific area. In 2007 the Sustainable Sanitation Alliance defined sustainable sanitation as systems that:

> primarily protect and promote human health by providing a clean environment and breaking the cycle of disease, and that sustainable sanitation systems must not only be economically viable, socially acceptable, and technically and institutionally appropriate, but should also protect the environment and the natural resource base.
>
> (SuSanA 2008)

It should be noted that in many cases, the installation of the different systems of latrines have not solved the problem of sanitation, rather, in many cases, have even caused fecal contamination of drinking water sources. Awareness of the great need of sanitation services and solutions to problems involving appropriate design of sanitation systems adapted to community characteristics can only be achieved through education in hygiene in rural areas. This is achieved best through intensive community education campaigns in schools and wide public information activities.

It is also very important to emphasize that investing in sanitation infrastructure involves a long project cycle and, if the MDG sanitation target is to be achieved, innovative approaches need to be developed to reduce the time span from policy-making to services delivery.

The increased introduction of wastewater treatment and sanitation is of special importance as they increasingly have an impact on surface and groundwater sources due to deficiency or absence of systems in rural areas. Of course this, in turn, can affect the quality of drinking water sources. It is also a principal of good water management to secure good-quality "upstream" water resources and adequate wastewater services and sanitation as a precondition for solving other water issues, such as those of clean water supply in municipal and rural systems, downstream.

There are many conflicts of use for land and water in rural areas, especially between agriculture and domestic use, which impact drinking water accessibility and influence wastewater sanitation. This is, of course, driven by economic growth in this sector as an essential industry for food production: "Agriculture accounts for approximately 3,100 billion m^3 or 71 percent of global water withdrawals today, and without efficiency gains will increase to 4,500 billion m^3 by 2030 (a slight decline to 65 percent of global water withdrawals)" (Water Resources Group 2009).

Climate change also affects water availability, especially in rural areas with dry climate conditions. Climate change impacts due to dry events such as El Niño leads to scarcity of water resources in specific rural areas usually located in semi-arid and arid regions. Extreme climate events such as hurricanes and tropical storms cause flooding that leads to contamination of water resources by landslides and also in individual domestic wells that commonly lack protection in rural areas.

Remedies available for lack of service for low-income rural populations

Remedies for the lack of access to water and sanitation services in rural areas must involve the use of innovative technology, but innovation is also needed in creating good governance, which means institutional and financial mechanisms. Resolving problems of equity and good quality of services is key to all recommendations for remedies. Due to the conditions of population dispersion in rural areas that call for systems of large atomization of service units, the most appropriate solutions will be low-cost decentralized systems that are completely different from modern sanitation systems.

Sanitation in rural areas deserves special remedies. Some rural settlements probably will never have centralized sewage systems. Dry toilets, urine-diversion toilets, vacuum toilets, on-site composting, or anaerobic digestion are all potential means to keep places clean and hygienic, while making the need for sewage systems redundant. It is necessary to guarantee that these remedies are widely adapted to the specific area, which assures their acceptance and widespread use. It is essential to develop rural sanitation with a mix of scales, strategies, technologies, payment systems, and decision-making structures that better fit the physical and human systems for which they are designed (Van Vliet *et al.* 2010).

Martijn and Hubers (2001) have suggested several components for the technical design of treatment systems with effluent use. These would include types of post-treatment, effluent supply, irrigation method and technology, and crops and farming practices. Irrigated agriculture could therefore receive and use different qualities of water. Farmers could be inserted into the end point of the sanitation system that economizes nutrient uses; although it has been pointed out that it is hard to accomplish both hygiene and food safety along with the reuse of excreta. Special monitoring capacities and mechanisms for handling excreta are needed. The protection of water quality must be guaranteed, which means controlling runoff to local water resources. It has also been suggested that the introduction of simple sewage systems on a condominium level could be adapted to rural areas (WSP 2008).

One of the preconditions for these improvements is that governmental institutions or NGO's have to provide technical assistance and capacity strengthening on different levels from general hygiene education of the population up to the technical and institutional management of the water and sanitation systems. Also, local government authorities need capacities in order to coordinate activities and negotiations, as well as developing monitoring and regulation for decentralized systems.

Most economic studies have shown that there exists a bias towards big systems while completely neglecting on-site options and semi-collective solutions adapted to local spaces (Van Vliet *et al.* 2010). Therefore, it is necessary to develop alternative ways for financing the development and functioning of the decentralized systems. It has been suggested funding at the local level. Microcredit schemes have proven to increase the debt of poor households. Another proposal is for government authorities to develop a general system of subsidies on sanitation facilities. Sources of indirect financing could be from drinking water tariffs or funds (e.g., from abstraction of raw water or discharge of wastewater). Local businesses could be involved in the process. A system of subsidies for infrastructure expansion or new connections could lower the burden of investment costs for new users and promote wider use of sanitation (Krause 2009), and subsidies could be included for low-income households if the current tariff level is higher than the affordable limit for households living below the poverty line. These must be special subsidy systems that guarantee the priority of the poorest households. As mentioned before, subsidies often result in lack of sustainability adopting sanitation measures and even to partial use by the population; also they tend to create a culture of dependence on subsidies. It is therefore essential to first develop behavioral changes in approaching the introduction of sanitation improvements. There has been experience with social marketing or demand creation in different countries that have had very positive results in improving sanitation and hygienic habits (Well Fact Sheet 2005). One of these is Community Led Total Sanitation (CLTS), which used the methodology of "investing in community mobilization instead of hardware, and shifting the focus from toilet construction for individual households to the creation of "open defecation-free" villages (Chambers 2009). The CLTS emphasizes the community's desire for change, which stimulates their actions; this promotes community innovation to reach its own local solutions which of course leads to greater ownership and sustainability.

Better governance that prioritizes rural areas must involve forming special policies, measures of regulation and promote equity in service delivery for the water and sanitation sector. Institutions that promote democratic participation should look for systematic effects on policy making. Accountability of public officials to the population as a whole needs to be guaranteed through a system of checks and balances. It is important to reinforce user participation at all levels "in order to make regulators and service providers responsive to the interests and needs of users" (Krause 2009). In rural areas, it is especially important to emphasize the importance of the quality of local governance, because user participation and the availability of transparent information can prevent clientelism from affecting equity in the provision of services.

Some countries (for example, South Africa) have provided a special legislative framework for the responsibility for water supply and sanitation devolved from the national level to local governments in order to secure better access in both urban and rural areas.

Good planning of water and sanitation projects is vital, which means attacking the issue both at the local and national level. Institutional, financial, social, technical and environmental sustainability must be taken into consideration in all planning processes to guarantee that a long-term economic improvement can be reached. Participation and coordination among the different stakeholders is part of the planning strategy. The development of facilities that meet the needs and cultural preferences of the beneficiaries is key to the planning strategy in order to guarantee that they take ownership, are willing and have the capacity to maintain the system over a long period of time. Provisions must be taken into consideration to guarantee that the system remains functional and a system of tariffs that could lead to self-funding. It has been observed in many community projects that it is favorable to use local materials and labor in the construction process and it is of special importance to promote capacity building to guarantee good maintenance of the facilities by local people.

Communities should evolve their own systems of monitoring or be linked to a system for the periodic control of quality of water. It is now essential to introduce water harvesting in watersheds and groundwater recharge promotion to improve availability of water resources for the communities, especially in semi-arid and arid areas affected by climate change. A fundamental part of improving availability is the promotion of measures to increase the efficiency of water application and the net water gains through crop yield enhancement (Water Resources Group 2009). Stakeholders in water-deficient watersheds will have to eventually make decisions for water resource security, which could involve water-saving techniques for farmers.

There are many examples of community-based water and sanitation projects in Latin America. The Comitees para Agua Potable y Saneamiento (Comities of Potable Water and Sanitation, or CAPS) is a good example of how water services have been improved in rural areas where private and state companies have not reached. The comities have been formed in the majority of the watersheds of Nicaragua – from semi-arid to regions with high precipitation. Presently 1,200,000 Nicaraguans have water administrated by CAPS. Their functions are to solicit with municipal authorities construction works for drinking water and

Figure 5.5 Activities of comities of potable water and sanitation in rural areas of Nicaragua

sanitation; orientate, direct, and organize the construction; assure the care and maintenance of the works; and support initiatives for health campaigns, reforestation, and conservation of the environment. They also are distributing special filters to remove arsenic from contaminated wells in rural areas. They are planning a monitoring system for all water sources in coordination with the Nicaraguan Research Center for Water Resources of the National Autonomic University of Nicaragua. In 2010, a Special Law for CAPS was approved by the National Assembly of Nicaragua (Ley no. 722; La Gaceta/Diario Oficial 2010). The objective of this law is to institutionalize, regulate, support, and facilitate legal and administrative processes necessary for the community projects of existing CAPS, and to normalize the establishment of new CAPS.

Recommendations to reach a sharp reduction of unserved in rural areas in the coming decades

The challenge to sharply reduce the number of unserved in rural areas in both water supply and sanitation in the Americas is a big task, considering the existing gap of coverage. However, it is possible at a reasonable cost if all countries together with all stakeholders develop concerted efforts to bring a turnaround in the approach in adopting a total resource view in which water is seen as a key, cross-sectoral input for development and growth. It needs to fund water sector reforms and initiate high-intensity activities in poor rural areas. This turnaround implies changes in the governance of water focused on the unserved in rural areas. Society must be prepared to adapt policies that guarantee the expansion of water and sanitation services to rural areas that lack access. This means introducing programs to subsidize those households and communities in which the expenses are unaffordable, along with stimulating and introducing support and ownership of water supply and sanitation in different forms of community user participation and management. The countries should set up good water governance with a well-functioning system of checks and balances that includes an accountable regulatory system to prevent tendencies toward clientelism. They should also secure a good and transparent management of water services to improve the application of water policies that guarantee an equitable distribution of water and sanitation access. User participation and democratic accountability can make a difference in securing the just representation of rural areas.

A concentrated divulgation campaign and implementation of educational mobilization programs in rural areas is needed to increase social awareness of water issues and to raise consciousness of the importance of hygiene and water sanitation. Water projects in rural areas have been found to waste too much time from policy-making to delivery and, therefore, it is necessary to introduce special intensive programs designed to reduce this time span. It is important that governments, in cooperation with the civil society and private sector partners, promote the innovation of water and sanitation technologies and service levels that are technically, socially, environmentally, and financially appropriate for rural areas. The development of rural sanitation must be undertaken with a mix of scales, strategies, technologies, payment systems, and decision-making structures that better fit the physical and human systems in the specific rural areas. The introduction of technical sanitation infrastructure involving different management compartments that rely on human interaction in both individual and communal contexts should be closely related to specific cultural and economic aspects of the rural community. Watershed management to secure long-lasting availability of good-quality water resources for the communities is essential. Measures for water harvesting in watersheds and groundwater recharge promotion can improve availability in semi-arid and arid rural areas. The difference in the impacts from climate change should be taken into consideration for the management of different watersheds. Efficiency in the use of water for agriculture needs special attention in rural areas.

References

Chambers, R. (2009) "Going to Scale with Community-Led Total Sanitation: Reflections on Experience, Issues and Ways Forward." Available at www.communityledtotalsanitation.org/resource/going-scale-community-led-total-sanitation-reflections-experience-issues-and-ways-forward (accessed January 2012).

DESA (2004) *World Population Prospects: The 2004 Revision and World Urbanization Prospects*. New York: Department of Economic and Social Affairs of the United Nations Secretariat, United Nations. Available at www.un.org/esa/population/publications/WPP2004/wpp2004.htm (accessed December 11, 2011).

Hutton, G. and Heller, L. (2004) *Evaluation of the Costs and Benefits of Water and Sanitation Improvements at Global Level*. Geneva: World Health Organization. Available at www.who.int/water_sanitation_health/wsh0404/en (accessed December 11, 2011).

JMP (2000) *Global Water Supply and Sanitation Assessment 2000 Report*. New York: WHO/UNICEF Joint Monitoring Programme for Water Supply and Sanitation. Available at http://www.who.int/docstore/water_sanitation_health/Globassessment/GlobalTOC.htm (accessed December 11, 2011).

JMP (2006) *Meeting the MDG Drinking Water and Sanitation Target: The Urban and Rural Challenge of the Decade*. New York: WHO/UNICEF Joint Monitoring Programme for Water Supply and Sanitation. Available at http://www.who.int/water_sanitation_health/monitoring/jmpfinal.pdf (accessed December 11, 2011).

—— (2008) *Progress on Drinking Water and Sanitation: Special Focus on Sanitation*. New York: WHO/UNICEF Joint Monitoring Programme for Water Supply and Sanitation. Available at http://www.who.int/water_sanitation_health/monitoring/jmp2008/en/index.html (accessed December 11, 2011).

Keirns, P. (2008) *Water Supply and Sanitation Services for the Rural Poor: The Gram Vikas Experience*. Rugby: Practical Action Publishing.

Komives, K., Foster,V., Halpern, J., and Wodon, Q. (2005) *Water, Electricity, and the Poor: Who Benefits from Utility Subsidies?* Washington, DC: World Bank. Available at http://siteresources.worldbank.org/INTWSS/Resources/Figures.pdf (accessed December 11, 2011).

Krause, M. (2009). *The Political Economy of Water and Sanitation*. London: Routledge.

La Gaceta/Diario Oficial (2010) "Ley Especial de Comités de Agua Potable y

Saneamiento." Ley no. 722. Managua: La Gaceta/Diario Oficial 14/06/10. Available at http://legislacion.asamblea.gob.ni/SILEG/Gacetas.nsf/5eea6480fc3d3d90062576e300504635/132b7185bd44c353062577440050fab0/$FILE/Ley%20No.%20722,%20Ley%20especial%20de%20Comit%C3%A9s%20de%20Agua%20Potable%20y%20Saneamiento.pdf (accessed December 11, 2011).

Martijn, R. J. and Huibers, F. P. (2001) *Use of Treated Wastewater in Irrigated Agriculture: A Design Framework*. Working document WP4/3. Wageningen: Coretech Project.

Ministerio de Salud de Colombia (1998) "Por el cual se expiden normas técnicas de calidad del agua potable." Decreto no. 475, Diario Oficial 4329, March 16. Bogotá: Ministerio de Salud de Colombia.

OPS (2007a) *Desigualdades en el acceso, uso y gasto del agua potable en América Latina y el Caribe*. Serie de informestécnicos no. 2 and no. 11. Washington, DC: Organización Panamericana de la Salud en las Américas (Pan American Health Organization).

—— (2007b) *Salud en las Américas 2007: Volumen I – Regional*. Publicación Científica y Técnica No. 622. Washington, DC: Organización Panamericana de la Salud en las Américas (Pan American Health Organization).

Otterstetter, H., Galvão, L., Witt, V., Toft, P., Caporali, S., Pinto, P. C., Soares, L., and Cuneo, C. (2004) *Health Equity in Relation to Safe Drinking Water Supply*. New York: Pan American Health Organization. Available at www.paho.org/english/dbi/Op08/OP08_10.pdf (accessed December 11, 2011).

SSPD (2006) *Estudio sectorial servicios públicos de acueducto y alcantarillado 2002–2005*. Bogotá: Superintendencia de Servicios Públicos Domiciliarios.

SuSanA (2008) *Towards More Sustainable Sanitation Solutions*. Version 1.2, February. Available at www.susana.org/docs_ccbk/susana_download/2-267-en-susana-statement-version-1-2-february-2008.pdf (accessed March 3, 2014).

United Nations General Assembly (2010) "Resolution of the Right to Safe and Clean Drinking Water and Sanitation as a Human Right." A/64/L.63/Rev.1, July 26. New York: United Nations.

Van Vliet, B., Spaargaren, G., and Oosterveer, P. (eds) (2010) *Social Perspectives on the Sanitation Challenge*. Heidelberg: Springer.

Water Resources Group (2009) *Charting our Water Future: Economic Frameworks to Inform Decision-Making*. New York: McKinsey & Company. Available at www.mckinsey.com/clientservice/water/charting_our_water_future.aspx (accessed December 11, 2011).

Well Fact Sheet (2005) "Social Marketing: A Consumer-Based Approach to Promoting Safe Hygiene Behaviors." Available at www.lboro.ac.uk/well/resources/fact-sheets/fact-sheets-htm/Social%20marketing.htm (accessed January 2012).

WSP (2008) *El Estado del Saneamiento en Nicaragua, Resultados de unaevaluación en comunidadesrurales, pequeñaslocalidades y zonasperiurbanas*. Managua: Banco Mundial. Available at https://www.wsp.org/wsp/sites/wsp.org/files/publications/521200850008_Saneamiento_Nicaragua_final.pdf (accessed December 11, 2011).

WHO (2003) *The Right to Water*. Health and Human Rights publication series no. 3. Geneva: World Health Organization.

Part IV

Transboundary issues

6 The La Plata River Basin

Víctor Pochat

Introduction

La Plata River Basin extends across more than 3.1 million km², comprising the Paraná, Paraguay, and Uruguay systems, and includes important parts of Argentina, Bolivia, Brazil, Uruguay, and the whole territory of Paraguay. Thirty-seven large cities, more than 100 million inhabitants (nearly 60 percent of the total population), about 70 percent of the GDP of those countries, and 75 large dams demonstrate the social and economic importance of the basin.

The economies of Argentina, Brazil, and Uruguay show a significant production of industrial goods and services, while those of Bolivia and Paraguay remain more broadly based on agricultural production. Potential hydropower in La Plata Basin has been estimated as 92,000 MW, about 60 percent of which has either already been achieved or is in process of being realized. The waterways of the drainage system provide an important transportation artery linking the five countries.

Population growth and the expansion of the agricultural frontier have contributed to alter the environment and create ongoing problems, such as erosion of productive land, silting of waterways and reservoirs, soil and water pollution, and loss of habitat for fish and wildlife.

In February 1967 the Ministers of Foreign Affairs for countries of the La Plata Basin decided to create the Comité Intergubernamental Coordinador de los Países de la Cuenca del Plata (Intergovernmental Coordinating Committee of La Plata Basin Countries, or CIC). On April 23, 1969, they signed the Treaty of La Plata Basin, agreeing to join efforts with the objective of promoting its harmonious development and the physical integration. The treaty is broadly comprehensive in regard to its competence on plans and programs, but it is not an exclusive option for riparian states. In 1973, a push toward the realization of joint projects began, bi- and tri-laterally, through the creation of a diversity of institutions. At the time of writing in 2010, the CIC has a new "Program of Action" and is carrying out a project, with the support of GEF (Global Environment Facility), through UNEP (United Nations Environment Programme) and OAS (Organization of American States), whose general objective is to strengthen the efforts of the five countries to implement their shared vision for the environmentally and socially sustainable economic development of La Plata Basin, specifically in the areas of the protection and integrated management of its water resources, and adaptation to climatic change and variability.

Characteristics of the La Plata River Basin

Geographical, hydrological, and climatological characteristics

The La Plata River Basin is one of the greatest river systems of the world. Draining approximately one-fifth of the South American continent, extending more than 3.1 million km^2, and conveying waters from central portions of the continent to the southwest Atlantic Ocean, the La Plata River system rivals the better-known Amazon River system in terms of its biological and habitat diversity. It also far exceeds that system in economic importance to southern and central South America (UNEP-GEF 2003).

The La Plata Basin includes almost all of the southern part of Brazil, the southeast portion of Bolivia, a large part of Uruguay, the whole country of Paraguay, and an extensive part of northern Argentina (Figure 6.1).

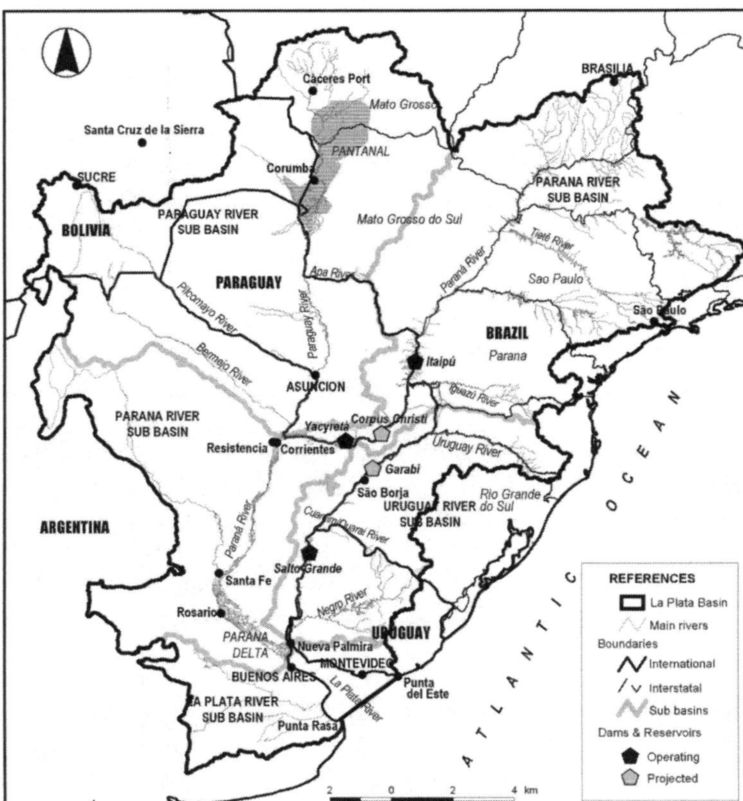

Figure 6.1 Map of La Plata River Basin

The basin embraces three large river systems – the Paraguay, and the Paraná, and Uruguay rivers, which join the La Plata River – the last and estuarine stretch of the river system. Table 6.1 shows the respective lengths of the main watercourses and drainage areas, divided by countries and totals. In addition, water that infiltrates into the groundwater system from within the basin provides recharge for the Guarani Aquifer – one of the largest continental groundwater reservoirs in the world.

In terms of discharge, the Paraná River is the most important in the basin, with a mean annual flow of about 17,700 m^3 per second. The Upper Paraná River lies entirely within Brazil and, downstream, the river forms the frontier between Brazil and Paraguay, and later, between Argentina and Paraguay. After joining the Paraguay River, the Paraná River remains within Argentinean territory.

After rising in Brazil, the Paraguay River feeds the Pantanal, the world's largest wetland, which extends more than 700 km in length with an area of 140,000 km^2 within the Paraguay Upper Basin. Further downstream of the Pantanal, the Paraguay River receives flows from the Pilcomayo and Bermejo rivers. Most of the Paraguay River Sub-basin is an immense alluvial plain with very low gradients, and subject to extensive seasonal flooding. Mean annual flow is about 3,800 m^3 per second.

Table 6.1 Lengths of main watercourses and approximate division of areas of the three sub-basins of the Paraná, Paraguay, and Uruguay rivers between the five countries of La Plata River Basin

Region	*Paraná*	*Paraguay*	*Uruguay*	*La Plata*	*Total by country*
Argentina	565 37.42%	165 15.07%	60 16.44%		790 25.48%
Bolivia		205 18.72%			205 6.61%
Brazil	890 58.94%	370 33.79%	155 42.46%		1,415 45.65%
Paraguay	55 3.64%	355 32.42%			410 13.23%
Uruguay			150 41.10%		150 4.84%
Argentina and Uruguay[a]				130 100.00%	130 4.19%
Total sub-basin area (10^3 km^2)	1,510	1,095	365	130	3,100
% of La Plata Basin	48.71%	35.32%	11.77%	4.19%	
Length of main watercourse (km)	4,300	2,500	1,600	250	

Note: [a]Total area in this row includes the area of the La Plata River Sub-basin itself (130,000 km^2) divided between Argentina and Uruguay.

Source: adapted from UNEP-GEF (2003)

The Uruguay River rises in Brazil. The Negro River is its larger tributary, joining the Uruguay River not far from the headwaters of La Plata River. After its confluence with the Negro River, the Uruguay River becomes wider, effectively forming an extension of the La Plata River. Its mean annual flow is about 4,300 m^3 per second.

The Paraná River delta width varies from about 18 km to more than 60 km, and its area exceeds 14,000 km^2. The delta is formed by the enormous volumes of sediment transported from the Paraguay River to the Paraná River, primarily through tributaries like the Bermejo River, and by the hydrological effects of the Uruguay River, and tidal influences in the La Plata River.

The La Plata River extends for 250 km from the Paraná River delta up to its mouth in the southwest Atlantic Ocean Large Marine Ecosystem. This mouth is defined by a line, about 230 km long, between a point near Punta del Este in Uruguay to a point near Punta Rasa in Argentina. The river is shared between Argentina and Uruguay.

Rainfall within the sub-basins varies from less than 700 mm per year in the western region to more than 1,800 mm per year in the Brazilian coastal ranges in the east. Rainfall is seasonal, and varies with location within the basin and altitude. In the northern portions of La Plata River Basin, rainfall regimes are essentially tropical, with rainfall confined to an approximately two-month period during the summer (December–January). In the southern portions of the basin, rainfall is more evenly distributed throughout the year.

Mean annual temperatures within the basin also vary from less than 10°C in the southern and western portions of the basin to greater than 30°C in the northern portions. Evaporation rates are high, ranging from between 600 and 800 mm per year in the extreme eastern portions of the basin to between 1,400 and 2,000 mm in the remainder of the basin.

The history of the Paraná River shows many occurrences of low-flows followed by floods. Recent research has detected a fluctuation with return periods of about 10 years. In addition, some climate studies (INA 2003) show evidence that stream flows are correlated with "El Niño" events. For example, in the middle reaches of the Paraná River, the four largest discharges on record followed the four "El Niño" events of 1905, 1982–1983, 1992, and 1998.

Besides fluctuations in climate, there is also some evidence of trends in climate. Over a large part of the La Plata Basin, annual minimum temperatures are increasing by about one degree per century; in some parts, there is evidence of positive trends in monthly and annual rainfall after the second half of the 1970s (UNEP 2004).

Social and economic characteristics

The economic heartland of Latin America is superimposed upon this geographic basin and its unique natural resources. Seventy-five large dams and 57 large cities – each with a population exceeding 100,000 inhabitants, including Buenos Aires, Sucre, Brasilia, Asunción and Montevideo, the respective capital cities of

Argentina, Bolivia, Brazil, Paraguay and Uruguay – are found within this basin. Nearly 60 percent of the total population of the five countries lives there. Its total population has grown from 61 million in 1968 to more than 100 million in 2000 (UNEP-GEF 2003; UNEP 2004; WWAP 2009).

Population density averages about 24 persons per km^2, but vary widely across the basin, with the majority of the population concentrated in the non-mountainous areas of eastern Argentina, Brazil, and Uruguay. Paraguay and the mountainous areas of Bolivia have much lower population densities, reported to be about six to seven persons per km^2. The urban population in La Plata Basin increased from an average of 45 percent at the beginning of the 1960s to an estimated present average of 86.6 percent. The state of São Paulo, Brazil, for example, has a population of 36 million, of which about 92 percent lives in urbanized areas.

These urban concentrations need water for domestic use, while incomplete treatment of urban wastewater affects both water quantity and water quality in the basin. In addition, poor people from rural areas are attracted to the urban centers by the possibility of a better life in cities, only to find that there is nowhere to live except along river margins. Thus, the likelihood of flooding and public health degradation is increased (UNEP-GEF 2003).

In 2007, the per capita gross domestic product (GDP) at constant market prices of the five countries, reported by the United Nations Economic Commission for Latin America and the Caribbean (ECLAC 2009), was about US$9,400 in Argentina, US$1,100 in Bolivia, US$4,200 in Brazil, US$1,500 in Paraguay, and US$7,250 in Uruguay. About 70 percent of the GDP of the five countries is generated within this drainage area (UNEP 2004).

The relative levels of industrialization vary among the countries. The economies of Argentina, Brazil, and Uruguay show relatively more significant production of industrial goods and services, while the economy of Bolivia and Paraguay remains more broadly based on agricultural production.

Cereals, soybeans and oleaginous plants are the main crops grown in the Argentinean plains; soybeans and sugar cane in southern Brazil; soybeans and maize in Bolivia; soybeans, cotton, and grains in Paraguay; and cereals and forage in Uruguay. Presently, soybeans are the most important crop, representing around 50 percent of the total harvested area in Argentina and Paraguay, almost 30 percent in Bolivia, and 26 percent in Brazil. In several areas of Argentina, Brazil, and Uruguay, farming is complemented with cattle raising (UNEP 2004).

Potential hydropower in the La Plata Basin has been estimated at 92,000 MW, about 60 percent of which has either already been materialized or is in the process of being so. Hydropower use is expected to increase as national demands for energy grow. More than 90 percent of the energy used by Brazil comes from hydropower, with the greater part of it being generated by impoundments on the Paraná River and its tributaries. The binational installations currently producing hydro-electricity are: Itaipú on the Paraná River (its production being shared between Brazil and Paraguay), Yacyretá on the Paraná River (shared between Argentina and Paraguay), and Salto Grande on the Uruguay River (shared between Argentina and Uruguay). On the international bordering reach of the Paraná River, between Argentina and Paraguay, downstream from Itaipú, a dam – known as Corpus Christi – is planned to be built. Another development is being planned at Garabí on the Uruguay River (between Argentina and Brazil).

The waterways of the La Plata River drainage system provide an important transportation artery, linking the five basin countries and forming a continuum across which the full range of the human condition is displayed. The Paraguay and Paraná Rivers – natural transport corridor running north–south from the heart of South America to the Atlantic Ocean, through the La Plata River – were navigated from the sixteenth century onwards by the Spanish fleet, and the city of Asunción on the Paraguay River bank was a center for expedition departures in colonial times since 1537. To a smaller extent, the Uruguay River has also provided a transportation route (UNEP-GEF 2003).

Nevertheless, only in 1988, encouraged by agricultural expansion in the Brazilian states of Mato Grosso (upper Paraguay river basin), together with the mining development in Brazil and Bolivia, and economic growth in Paraguay, did interest in improving the conditions of the waterways reappear. The required improvements would imply ensuring a whole year's minimum depth, structuring difficult stretches and buoying the waterway with day and night signals. The main navigable reaches include:

- The Paraguay-Paraná Rivers waterway (known as "Hidrovía Paraguay-Paraná," or simply "Hidrovía") from Cáceres Port, in Mato Grosso, to Nueva Palmira Port in Uruguay, covering a distance of 3,600 km. There are plans to improve navigation along portions of this waterway by, among other works, deepening the channel. However, environmental concerns over this development, particularly with respect to the Pantanal, have limited the whole implementation of the "Hidrovía" to date.
- The Tietê-Paraná River waterway, enabling products to be transported between São Paulo, Brazil, and the Itaipú reservoir. It passes through a highly industrialized region of Brazil which produces 35 percent of the Brazilian GDP.
- The Uruguay River waterway, downstream of the dam at Salto Grande. There is a navigable reach of the Uruguay River shared by Uruguay and Argentina. In addition, the river upstream of Salto Grande is navigable to São Borja in the Brazilian State of Rio Grande do Sul.

Environmental problems

Population growth and the expansion of the agricultural frontier are some of the main factors that have contributed during the last decades to alter La Plata Basin environment and create ongoing problems, such as erosion of productive land, silting of waterways and reservoirs, soil and water pollution, and loss of habitat for fish and wildlife (Cordeiro 1999).

Population growth

Population growth and an increase in social mobility resulting from migration from the countryside and the more impoverished areas to the urban areas have given rise to new metropolis, and several mid-sized cities. In the rapidly growing industrialized cities of the La Plata Basin, many urban centers lack basic economic and social infrastructure. Furthermore, damage to water resources and risks to human populations can also result from industrial wastewater and toxic spills in intensively industrialized areas.

Erosion and sedimentation

There are some areas of high sediment production in the Paraná and Paraguay basins. Some of the most severe erosion occurs in the upper basin of the Bermejo River, in the Andean region of Argentina and Bolivia. Another area of high erosion and sedimentation is the Upper Pilcomayo River Basin, in which 90 million metric tons of sediment is annually deposited on the wide flood plain of the Chaco, producing an extensive inland delta. In the Upper Paraguay River Basin in Brazil, most of the sediment from the headwaters is deposited in the Pantanal. In the Paraná River Basin, the largest volumes of sediment are eroded from sedimentary rock, mainly sandstone.

The expansion of the agricultural frontier is one of most severe cases of erosion in the region, induced by human activities. Deforestation in the basin has left some areas with only a small percentage of the original forest cover. In the Brazilian state of São Paulo, the area under primary forest has fallen from 58 percent at the beginning of the twentieth century to about 8 percent at its end. In the state of Paraná, forest cover fell from 83 percent in 1890 to 5 percent in 1990. In 1945, 55 percent of the eastern part of Paraguay was forested; however, by 1990, only 15 percent was under forest cover (Cordeiro 1999).

Because of the intensification of agricultural and industrial production, many areas formerly planted with coffee and food crops were converted to soybeans for export, and sugarcane for the production of bioethanol. The extent of lands used for cereal production has widened to include areas that are marginal for that type of crops, where intensive production has increased the risk of soil degradation. This is of great concern as soil organic content has fallen by 50 percent from its value at the start of the twentieth century, reducing the capacity of the soil to hold water. Direct seeding with minimum cultivation is now leading to some reduction in soil loss.

The impacts of erosion are evidenced primarily by the sedimentation of existing reservoirs and certain reaches of the river system. There has also been loss of productivity of croplands and pastures, and the destruction of land suitable for reforestation. Increased sedimentation in the main rivers and secondary basins has increased the cost of dredging in the La Plata River.

Pollution

Water pollution is caused primarily by the great increase in crops and industrial production, and by population growth. A large part of fertilizers and pesticides used in farming is carried by runoff into watercourses. This toxic pollution is not only creating risks for populations that depend on the rivers' productivity for their livelihoods but threatens the biodiversity of the maritime front of the La Plata River (Cordeiro 1999).

Natural hazards

Severe flooding, with loss of life and extensive damage to infrastructure and economic production, is a frequent occurrence, especially in the Paraná and Uruguay sub-basins. The Paraná River and its tributaries – including the Iguazú River, for example – have many riverside towns that are frequently flooded. That is the case of the Argentinean cities of Resistencia, Corrientes, Rosario, and Santa Fe, which suffer severely from flooding. During the "El Niño" event of 1982 and 1983, more than 40,000 people were affected in more than 70 towns along the reach of the Uruguay River within the Brazilian state of Rio Grande do Sul. In the La Plata Basin as a whole, losses associated with that "El Niño" event were estimated to amount to more than US$1 billion (UNEP-GEF 2003).

Fish and wildlife

The Pantanal serves as an example of critical areas for sustainable development activities. Due to its location at the center of South America, it is a bio-geographical meeting point of several endemic floral and faunal units. The Pantanal is the habitat for a unique and extremely rich array of wildlife: more than 230 species of fishes, 80 species of mammals, 50 species of reptiles, and more than 650 classified species of aquatic birds (Cordeiro 1999).

The principal factors causing environmental problems in this region are soil erosion, caused mainly by the large-scale, mechanized production of soybeans and rice, and water pollution caused by the intensive use of agrochemicals. This problem is exacerbated by the compaction of the soil by heavy farm machinery and the resulting lack of percolation of storm water. The Pantanal is also being affected by land clearing in the areas of inflow and along riverbanks, by pollution from ever-growing agribusiness, and by uncontrolled urban and industrial discharges into the river system. Throughout the basin, fish are threatened by overfishing and, most recently, by the dumping of hazardous chemicals, especially large quantities of mercury used in gold mining.

Associated with these existing problems are the potential effects of specific development projects, including the "Hidrovía," in which it is necessary to quantify possible negative influences caused by the rectification and dredging of river stretches in specific areas.

Institutional framework

The La Plata Basin Treaty system

At the standpoint of La Plata Basin structure, 40 years ago, each of the five countries of the region had contrasting approaches to regional development, emerging from each country's different historical, geographical, social, and political background. Nonetheless, this did not exclude the existence of common goals. At that time, the main issues were the utilization of water channel slopes for hydroelectric power generation, subsidiary attention to navigation, and little concern for water quality and other topics (del Castillo Laborde 1999).

The first meeting of the Ministers of Foreign Affairs from the five countries comprising La Plata Basin was held in Buenos Aires in February 1967. As a result of that meeting, the ministers issued a declaration that stated: "it is a decision of our governments to carry out the joint and integral study of La Plata Basin, with a view to the realization of a program of multinational, bilateral and national works, useful to the progress of the region."

As a first step, the CIC was created, with the aim of drawing up a statute for its definitive constitution. Further, the declaration ruled that to achieve the objective of the integral development of the basin, the referred study should take into account – in what concerns water resources – the main following subjects: facilities and assistance to navigation; establishment of new fluvial ports and improvement to existing ones; hydroelectric studies with a view to energy integration of the basin; installation of water services for domestic, sanitary, and industrial uses, and for irrigation; control of floods or inundations and erosion; and the conservation of animal and vegetal life.

During the second meeting of ministers, held in Santa Cruz de la Sierra in May 1968, the statute of CIC was approved and that body was entrusted to draw up a treaty in order to enforce the institutionalization of the basin's shared approach. At the same time, it was agreed to carry out preliminary studies in relation to concrete projects presented by the member countries. Among the projects shared by the five member countries, the following are of great importance (Pochat 1999):

A-1 Construction of a port in Bolivian territory on the Paraguay River and its connection to the railroad network (Bush port).
A-2 Hydrometeorology and future establishment and performance of the regional network of hydro-meteorological stations.
A-3 Inventory and analysis of basic information on the basin's natural resources and related subjects.
A-4 Study of problems to be solved and projects of measures to be taken (dredging, obstacle removal, signaling, buoyage, etc.) in order to allow permanent navigation and to secure its maintenance in the Paraguay, Paraná, Uruguay and La Plata rivers. [...]
A-7 Assessment of the ichthyologic resources of the basin.

On April 23, 1969, during their first extraordinary meeting held in Brasilia, the ministers signed the Treaty of La Plata Basin, which states (Article I): "The Contracting Parties agree to unite efforts with the objective of promoting the harmonious development and the physical integration of La Plata Basin and of its area with direct and considered influence." With that purpose, they will promote, within the ambit of the basin, the identification of areas of common interest and the promotion of research, programs and works, as well as the formulation of operative agreements or juridical instruments they consider necessary and that tend to:

(a) give facilitation and assistance as regards navigation;
(b) promote reasonable utilization of water resources, especially by means of the regulation of watercourses and their multiple and equitable development;
(c) achieve the preservation and the improvement of animal and vegetal life;[1]
[...]
(h) promote other projects of common interest and especially those that have relation to the inventory, assessment and development of the natural resources of the area;
(i) integral knowledge of La Plata Basin.

The basic organization was then constituted by the Conference of Foreign Affairs Ministers, the CIC, and a Secretariat. The Conference resolutions do not have mandatory character regarding member states, but they are applicable only in reference to the functioning of La Plata basin bodies. Among other things, they are compulsory when approving the budget, amending statutes, or incorporating new organs.

Asunción Declaration on the uses of international rivers

In the meetings of CIC during 1970, Argentina and Brazil expressed their different interpretations of the Basin Treaty. Argentina wished to draw up a set of general rules applicable to the basin water resources. Brazil requested the acceptance of its own technical judgment as enough guarantee for other riparians in relation to existing and planned hydroelectric power plants. It maintained that a country possessing the sources of a drainage basin could not willingly limit itself on the uses of the waters, and the only acceptable restraints could be those arising from technical reasons and its principles of legal responsibilities. It should be highlighted that this position is incorporated in Article V of the Basin Treaty, which states that "any joint activities undertaken by the Contracting Parties shall be carried out without prejudice to such projects and undertakings as they may decide to execute within their respective territories, in accordance with respect for international law and fair practice among neighboring friendly nations" (del Castillo Laborde 1999).

There were understandable arguments for these claims. Long reaches of the Paraná River sub-basin, situated in Brazilian, Argentinean, and Paraguayan territories, have relevant conditions for hydroelectricity, such as appropriate channel slope, large flow, basaltic soil, and embanked stretches. Since 1960, Brazil has launched the construction of numerous dams in the basin, in a restless building effort that is still currently effective and shall extend into the future. Paraguay and Argentina, lower riparians, planned also to construct two important dams in their shared stretch in the same period (the 1970s).

As Uruguay is not a riparian state of the Paraná River and Paraguay adopted a waiting role, Argentina held its isolated position versus Brazil as regards the Paraná River and pressed the incorporation of general international law rules applicable to the uses of international water resources as suitable rules for La Plata Basin (del Castillo Laborde 1999).

In a conciliatory success, the Ministers of Foreign Affairs established the following basic principles for water management applicable to La Plata Basin riparian states in the "Asunción Declaration on the Uses of International Rivers," approved in June 1971:

(a) In contiguous rivers, as riparians share their sovereignty, every use of the watercourse should be preceded by bilateral agreement of riparian states;
(b) In successive international rivers, where riparians do not share their sovereignty, each state is able to use the watercourse according to its needs provided the uses thereof do not cause appreciable harm to another basin state:
(c) Riparian states agree to exchange hydrological and meteorological data and cartographic results from field measurements;
(d) There is an emphasis on the improvement of river navigability and a warning that future works should not hamper navigation;
(e) States are required to take into consideration the living resources of basin waters in works planning.

Whereas the Asunción principles upheld the sovereignty of the riparian states, they brought about objective standards and from that circumstance many other agreements became possible for water undertakings in the basin (adapted from del Castillo Laborde 1999).

Though not a treaty, the Asunción Declaration expressly set on behalf of riparian states the rule of not causing "appreciable harm" in the utilization of international water resources. This, however, was not the only rule that downstream riparian states, mainly Argentina, wished to incorporate as mandatory principles for basin undertakings. It maintained that the principle of equitable and reasonable use of freshwater resources and the rule of previous consultation were also applicable as general international law rules regulating the use of international basins. The other riparians, especially Brazil, were prepared to only allow those restrictions incorporated in a treaty for each particular use.

These different positions became an issue at the Stockholm Conference of the

United Nations on the Environment, held in 1972,[2] and the general principles on international shared resources were incorporated as United Nations General Assembly Resolutions 2995 (XXVII) and 2996 (XXVII) of that year, and were followed up by Resolutions 3129 (XXVIII) and 3281 (XXIX),[3] whose Article 3 recognized the rule of previous consultation (del Castillo Laborde 1999).

Corpus-Itaipú Agreement

A particularly significant fact was the signature, on October 19, 1979, by the governments of Argentina, Brazil, and Paraguay of the Tripartite Agreement on Corpus and Itaipú hydroelectric infrastructures, with the purpose of establishing rules in order to harmonize the Brazilian-Paraguayan development of Itaipú with the Argentinean-Paraguayan of Corpus (afterwards called Corpus Christi), both on the Paraná River. This agreement was the result of a negotiation process, during the period 1977–1979, on firm technical grounds, prepared by the delegations of the three countries involved. On its terms, the operating elevation of Corpus reservoir should not exceed 105 m above sea level, and Itaipú power plant would operate with 18 turbines for a maximum water flow of 12,600 m^3 per second. According to the treaty, the operation of Itaipú should not cause fluctuations in the water level of the Paraná River greater than 0.50 m per hour and 2.00 m per day, and the surface velocity should not exceed 2m per second in the confluence of the Paraná and Iguazú rivers, where Argentina, Paraguay, and Brazil meet.

It can be said that the Corpus-Itaipú agreement has a significant historical value since it put an end to the controversy concerned with the Paraná River energy utilization (COMIP 1992; Pochat 1999).

Satellite organizations

In fact, the La Plata Basin Treaty is broadly comprehensive in regard its competence on plans, projects, works, and programs in the catchment's area. Nevertheless, it is not proposed as an exclusive option for the riparian states, but as a framework agreement that could add special benefits to its global scheme. Accordingly, Article VI states that "The provisions of this Treaty shall not prevent the Contracting Parties from concluding specific or partial bilateral or multilateral agreements designed to achieve the general objectives of the development of the Basin." Some examples of that follow.

In 1973 there was a push toward the realization of joint projects, bi- and trilaterally. Thus, on April 26, 1973, Brazil and Paraguay subscribed to the treaty in which Itaipú Binacional (Itaipú Binational) was created with the purpose of constructing Itaipú development. On November 19, 1973, Argentina and Uruguay signed the Tratado del Río de la Plata y su Frente Marítimo (Treaty on the La Plata River and its Maritime Front). This treaty settled the controversial situation about the exercise of jurisdiction over that vast river's waters. Apart from jurisdictional issues, the treaty deals with navigation, fishing, bed and subsoil, pollution prevention, pilotage, works, scientific research, and rescue operations, among other aspects of the river system. It also set up two permanent commissions: the Comisión Administradora del Río de la Plata (Administrative Commission for the La Plata River, or CARP) and the Comisión Técnica Mixta del Frente Marítimo (Joint Technical Commission for the Maritime Front, or CTMFM) for the adjacent maritime zone and the overlapping common fishing zone.

On December 3, 1973, the Entidad Binacional Yacyretá (Yacyretá Binational Entity) was created, by agreement between Argentina and Paraguay, with the purpose of constructing Yacyretá development. Subsequently, on February 26, 1975, Argentina and Uruguay agreed on the establishment of a special body for their shared stretch of the Uruguay River. The regulation of water uses, namely navigation, works, pilotage, bed and subsoil resources, fishing, pollution prevention, jurisdiction and settlement of dispute procedures are expressly dealt with. The administrative commission set up under this agreement is known as Comisión Administradora del Río Uruguay (Administrative Commission for the Uruguay River, or CARU) (del Castillo Laborde 1999).

The Corpus-Itaipú Agreement followed, in 1979, as previously referred. In 1980, Brazil and Argentina agreed upon the use of their shared stretch of the Uruguay River and decided to build the Garabí dam as a joint project.

It should be added to this system of binational commissions and entities those established before 1973: the Comisión Técnica Mixta de Salto Grande (Joint Technical Commission of Salto Grande, or CTM), created by Uruguay and Argentina in 1946 to carry out a joint hydraulic project, Salto Grande dam; and, in 1971, the Comisión Mixta Argentino–Paraguaya del Río Paraná (Argentinean–Paraguayan Joint Commission of the Paraná River, or COMIP), in charge of the administration of the stretch shared by both countries and of the development of Corpus Christi multiple-purpose project (Barberis 1990).

A repetition of the activity pattern of the 1970s focusing on the river basin can subsequently be seen in the creation of the Comisión Mixta Uruguayo–Brasileña para el Desarrollo de la Cuenca del Río Cuareim/Quaraí (Joint Uruguayan–Brazilian Commission for the Development of the Cuareim/Quaraí River Basin, or CRC), in March 1991; the Comisión Binacional Administradora de la Cuenca Inferior del Río Pilcomayo (Administrative Binational Commission of the Lower Basin of the Pilcomayo River), by Argentina and Paraguay, in September 1993; the Comisión Trinacional para el Desarrollo de la Cuenca del Río Pilcomayo (Trinational Commission for the Development of the Pilcomayo River Basin), by Argentina, Bolivia, and Paraguay, in February 1995; and the Comisión Binacional para el Desarrollo de la Alta Cuenca de los ríos Bermejo y Grande de Tarija (Binational Commission for the Development of the Upper Basin of the Bermejo and Grande de Tarija Rivers, or COBINABE), by Argentina and Bolivia, in June 1995 (Pochat 1999); and, more recently, in 2006, the creation of the Comisión Mixta Brasileña-Paraguaya para el Desarrollo Sustentable de la Cuenca del Río Apa (Joint Brazilian–Paraguayan Commission for the Sustainable Development of the Apa River Basin).

In the navigation field, the Comité Intergubernamental de la Hidrovía Paraguay-Paraná Puerto de Cáceres-Puerto de Nueva Palmira (Intergovernmental Committee for the Paraguay-Paraná Waterway Cáceres Port-Nueva Palmira Port, or CIH) was created in 1992. In this case, it is interesting to note that the Waterway Program was incorporated into the System of the Treaty of La Plata Basin in October 1991, although keeping the structure of the CIH. One of the most important achievements of this committee was to produce the Waterway Transport Agreement, approved by member states in 1992 and was enforced on February 13, 1995. The Transport Agreement, with eight protocols, is a common navigation code for waterway users applicable to the five riparian states.

In the financial field, it should be noted that the Fondo Financiero para el Desarrollo de la Cuenca del Plata (Financial Fund for the Development of the La Plata Basin, or FONPLATA) was created during 1976 within the framework of the treaty to lend financial support to the activities envisioned in the treaty.

While the diversity of institutions highlights the interest in resolving shared problems when they affect two or more countries, it also highlights the fragmentation and segmentation that prevails, often to the detriment of the "basin vision" that led to the treaty. Few of these institutions communicate either directly, or through the CIC, which should coordinate the activities of all those bodies; the reality is that they act autonomously. There is an important task to fulfill here, in order to bring together the pieces of this complex system.

In that regard, and related to groundwater, it is important to highlight that, on August 2, 2010, Argentina, Brazil, Paraguay, and Uruguay signed the Guarani Aquifer Agreement. Following an integrated hydrological approach, the states concerned have explicitly concluded this agreement within the framework of the La Plata Basin Treaty. The treaty reaffirms the sovereignty of the four states over the Guarani aquifer and includes the norms of general international law that regulate the use of shared natural resources, the obligation not to cause appreciable harm, the equitable and reasonable use, and the obligation to notify the other states sharing the same resource of any project that is likely to affect that aquifer system.

The treaty also creates a commission composed of the four states concerned with the aim of coordinating the cooperation among them for the accomplishment of the principles and objectives of the agreement. And although it has not been defined yet how the creation of that commission is going to be implemented in practice, the idea is that its functioning needs to be somehow connected to the management of surface waters, working together with CIC through a macro approach in water management (Querol 2010).

Mercado Común del Sur (Southern Common Market)

The signature of the Treaty of Asunción in 1991, creating the Mercado Común del Sur (Southern Common Market, or MERCOSUR/MERCOSUL), put into question the continuity of the CIC. However, the Conference of Foreign Affairs Ministers of the La Plata Basin, held in Montevideo in December 2001, reaffirmed the CIC and created the office of Secretary General (revolving among the countries). This conference also created a [Technical] Projects Unit "under Article I of the treaty... to revitalize the operating system of the organism, including the creation of linkages with other technical and financial institutions within La Plata Basin" (UNEP-GEF 2003).

Group of experts and technical counterparts

The efforts of experts in the different disciplines related to water resources, responding to the challenge of a basin with the complexity of La Plata, trying to solve fundamental issues in the search of sound knowledge about the behavior of its rivers, in normal and extraordinary situations, the most adequate way to utilize them, and the concern for preserving the basin's quality should be emphasized. To describe the constitution and example to exemplify the activities carried out by the technical experts within La Plata Basin organization, the following facts have been selected (Pochat 1999).

The initial Declaration of the Foreign Affairs Ministers in 1967 had proposed that each country would appoint their own technical advisers, since the CIC was an organization run by diplomats. In 1969, the ministers recommended to the CIC that they should constitute a Group of Experts in order to "consider extensively the subject of water resource" and establish "that the respective group of experts should present its report as soon as possible, by considering the importance and complexity of the issue." The corresponding meetings dealt with a combination of technical issues and their possible diplomatic consequences.

Subsequently, in December 1984, the ministers subscribed the "Declaration of Punta del Este," by which they convened an extraordinary meeting of undersecretaries or special representatives of the ministers, with the aim of analyzing and evaluating the institutional political state of the system of La Plata Basin. That meeting, held on November 1985, agreed with the necessity of cooperation on the basis of a pragmatic approach that gave it greater operating agility, allowing the concentration of efforts in four important subjects, among others: "Water Resources and other Natural Resources," "Navigation," "Fluvial and Terrestrial Transport," and "Border Cooperation."

The second extraordinary meeting of ministers, held in Buenos Aires in April 1986, established, among other issues, the concentration of the joint cooperation efforts of the member countries in those priority subjects, as well as the generation of technical cooperation by means of direct understanding among the national organisms competent in specific subjects. For that purpose the governments would nominate the responsible "Technical Counterparts" in selected areas. These "counterparts" developed a productive activity, particularly related to hydrological warning and water quality.

The effort has been rewarded with very positive results, such as the uninterrupted performance during more than two decades of the Hydrological Warning System, always kept active through a daily response in addition to the occurrence of particular phenomena, as well as the tasks carried out jointly to prepare the

Methodological Guide for the Operation and Evaluation of La Plata Basin Water Quality Network (Pochat 1999).

Nevertheless, it must be admitted that many difficulties have come up, and these difficulties have prevented the implementation of many very interesting proposals and projects, with some partial completions. Certain limitations arose from the way the institutional system of the basin was organized. As Barberis (1990) has noted, the system constituted on three levels (Conference of Ministers of Foreign Affairs, Intergovernmental Coordinating Committee, Groups of Experts or Technical Counterparts) did not work satisfactorily. One of its fundamental problems was due to the lack of a permanent technical organization. The CIC was a body composed of diplomats, whose training sometimes did not allow them to deeply consider the multiple subjects submitted to their consideration and decision. This circumstance has been the cause of the need to have a body that can provide technical knowledge for the CIC in order to adopt a political decision suitable to each case. The former Groups of Experts and Technical Counterparts were not able to make up for that failing. It frequently occurred that groups were not integrated by experts only, but diplomats participated as well. This often gave discussions on each subject the characteristics of a negotiation, thus moving away from its technical approach.

Another problem in the system was the fact that the resolutions of the meetings of ministers and of the CIC, addressed to the member states have, in general, the character of mere recommendations and, consequently, they lack a legal obligatory force (Barberis 1990). To that it should be added that when the resolutions concern subjects foreign to the usual competence of the Ministers of Foreign Affairs, the technical bodies of each government generally do not pay much heed to their recommendations.

Another problem was the lack of specific funds for the financing of the programmed activities. The results obtained were only possible because of the economic contributions of the organizations that the intervening experts came from and, generally, they were not included in a budget specially assigned to those activities. Nor could the promised financing from international agencies be obtained owing to the absence of concrete projects with an adequate level of development. This was also a consequence of the fact that the experts were only able to dedicate a small amount of time to the tasks agreed in the respective meetings.

The development of La Plata Basin established by the Treaty has lost a great part of its original vigor, and the works presently carried out in the basin are mainly the fruit of the activities of the bilateral or multilateral commissions or entities. In order to revitalize the basin's comprehensive approach in carrying out the original objectives conceived by the ministers at their first meetings, it is necessary to look for solutions to the obstacles stated above.

Present challenges

For La Plata Basin institutional system, the present circumstances offer a good possibility for improvement. The governing document of the CIC, approved at the meeting of foreign ministers during December 2001, established that the CIC would include two regular representatives and two alternates from each basin country. One of these representatives is political, invested by their government with plenipotentiary authority, and the other representative is technical, being a project specialist. The technical representatives constitute the Projects Unit created also by then, as mentioned before.

Program of Action of CIC

Following the new structure, the CIC approved its "Program of Action," selecting those initiatives that help strengthen its capacity for the integrated management of La Plata Basin. To this end, and with the goal in mind of improving the quality of life of the Basin's inhabitants, priority would be given to implementing the following activities within the timescales periodically determined by the CIC (UNEP-GEF 2003):

> Action 1: Enhance knowledge of water resources and their management to reduce vulnerability to floods and droughts, and to mitigate their impact on communications, transportation, production, and trade in the region;
> Action 2: Promote integrated management of water and soils to improve the quality of life of the inhabitants, preserve the health of the population, and maximize production in the region while preserving the quality of its waters, among institutional stakeholders and civil society in the member countries;
> Action 3: Promote integration within the region;
> Action 4: Harmonize and coordinate data and information gathering related to the region and dissemination of that information through the General Secretariat;
> Action 5: Promote environmental preservation;
> Action 6: Enhance harmonization of policies;
> Action 7: Promote training.

A framework for sustainable water resources management

In September 2001, a process was initiated by the countries of the La Plata Basin, beginning with a technical meeting convened by the CIC, in order to seek support for the idea of formulating a strategy for water resources management within the basin. The representatives of the five countries agreed to request to the GEF, through UNEP, some funding to identify and formulate an appropriate project to achieve that goal. Subsequently, in June 2002, as an outcome of the initial financial assistance of GEF, they instructed the Secretary General of the CIC to elaborate a proposal to develop a Framework for Sustainable Management of the Water Resources of La Plata Basin (UNEP-GEF 2003).

GEF initiatives within La Plata Basin have been implemented within the Bermejo River sub-basin, the Upper Paraguay River sub-basin, the La Plata River and its maritime front and the Guarani Aquifer. While each of these interventions, separately, has addressed key environmental and developmental issues within the basin, the range of projects so executed ignores the connectivity of the La Plata Basin as a hydrological entity. The CIC project, therefore, has been designed to provide a framework to better integrate and more widely disseminate the outputs and results of the projects currently being executed in the sub-basins comprised in this larger hydrologic unit. At the same time, this project is consistent with the Program of Action agreed by the countries within the framework of the CIC.

CIC project general objective

The general objective of the CIC project is:

> to strengthen the efforts of the governments of Argentina, Bolivia, Brazil, Paraguay, and Uruguay to implement their shared vision for the environmentally and socially sustainable economic development of La Plata Basin, specifically in the areas of the protection and integrated management of its water resources and adaptation to climatic change and variability.
>
> (UNEP-GEF 2003)

Coordinated and locally executed by the CIC, the project will harmonize and prepare for further implementation, in co-operation with the basin countries, a program of strategic actions for the sustainable management of La Plata Basin.

Project short-term and intermediate objectives

The CIC project has been designed to:

- Strengthen the technical capacity of the CIC in planning and coordinating the integrated and sustainable development and management of the environment of La Plata Basin.
- Advance the practice of integrated water resources management and adaptation to climate change, by increasing the knowledge and decision-making capacity of the country-based institutions and technicians responsible for the scientific analysis and prediction of climate change phenomena and their social, economic and environmental impacts.
- Implement a common strategic vision of the basin as a basis for planning, sustainable development, and integrated management of water resources in the basin as the basis for an agreed Mega-Transboundary Diagnostic Analysis (Mega-TDA) that identifies the root causes of the principal environmental problems of La Plata Basin in order to characterize, quantify, and define the strategic actions necessary for their resolution.
- Formulate agreed and integrated watershed management programs, based upon the Mega-TDA, a shared Framework Strategic Action Program (FSAP), and a common vision of the basin, that will advance the definition of, and agreement on, high-priority actions needed to formulate and

implement policies, develop capacities and management instruments, and channel investments that not only protect the shared resources but also allow efforts to advance the economic and social development of the basin in sustainable form.

- Identify the water resources that are at the greatest environmental risk (i.e., to identify critical areas and issues, and so-called "hot spots"), and define and prioritize projects for execution aimed at the restoration and protection of critical transboundary waters, taking into account both scientific information, and information on cost and feasibility of remedial measures generated by the Bermejo, Upper Paraguay-Pantanal, Guarani, and Maritime Front Global Environmental Facility – International Waters (GEF-IW) projects.
- Integrate the work of groups, and facilitate the participation of responsible institutions, interested organizations, and stakeholders in each country, to prepare and execute the recommended actions in a sustainable and coordinated manner.

Conclusions

By considering the facts and ideas discussed in this chapter, it can be seen that La Plata system has a sound institutional background and a long performance that provides valuable experiences and lessons in order to strengthen its organization and improve its future development. The present circumstances are also favorable to meet these goals. The current structure of the CIC, approved in December 2001 by the Conference of Foreign Affairs Ministers of La Plata Basin – creating the office of Secretary General and the [Technical] Projects Unit "to revitalize the operating system of the organism" – is in the process of consolidation. The existence of a comprehensive Program of Action, with numerous different initiatives, will help to increase its capacity for the integrated management of La Plata Basin. The availability of products of the preparation phase of the project devoted to develop a Framework for Sustainable Management of the Water Resources of La Plata Basin – carried out with the financial support of GEF – will also contribute to the idea of formulating a strategy for water resources management within the basin.

Those favorable conditions should be accompanied by the reinforcement of the office of the Secretary General, improving its present technical capacity with the establishment of a permanent technical team, integrated by a small but qualified group of experts in the main disciplines the CIC has to deal with. This permanent team will provide the technical support to the Secretary General in carrying out all the actions that the CIC should commit itself as the structure that "promotes, coordinates, and monitors the progress of multinational activities to develop the resources of La Plata Basin so as to promote the harmonious and balanced development of the region," as contemplated by the respective Program of Action.

The challenges to be faced are very wide. All the positive actions that have enabled countries making up the basin to speak the same "water" language should be supported. But it is necessary to go further, to be more ambitious, for strengthening the concept of the basin as a unit that led to the 1969 treaty and facing its future sustainable development by working together in an integrated way.

Some lessons learned

The existence of a broadly comprehensive river basin treaty, such as the Treaty of La Plata Basin, and the establishment of a coordinating committee, such as the CIC, have shown to be an adequate general framework for promoting the harmonious development and physical integration of a basin of the size and complexity of La Plata. On the other hand, a treaty of this kind is not an exclusive option. There exists the possibility of creating bi-, tri- or multi-lateral organizations, within that general framework, for dealing with specific matters. This approach has allowed the implementation of a diversity of joint projects. In order to improve the performance of such an institutional system, it would be necessary to strengthen the capacity of the CIC for coordinating the activities and fostering synergies among of all those organizations, by constituting a permanent technical team and ensuring adequate financial support.

Acknowledgements

This chapter has been prepared on the basis of the references detailed below, among which the works of L. del Castillo Laborde (1999) and N. Cordeiro (1999), and the concept document prepared for the project (UNEP-GEF 2003), deserve special mention.

Notes

1 The inclusion of this purpose in the Treaty of La Plata Basin, three years before the UN Conference on the Human Environment, held in Stockholm in 1972, shows an advanced concern of the La Plata Basin countries for environmental issues. However, that concern only started to be reflected in concrete actions since November 1985, when, in an extraordinary meeting, the Undersecretaries or Special Representatives of the Foreign Affairs Ministers agreed to concentrate efforts in several important subjects, including "Water Resources and Other Natural Resources", as will be discussed below.

2 The United Nations Conference on the Human Environment (Stockholm, June 5–16, 1972) established – among other principles – that "States have . . . the sovereign right to exploit their own resources pursuant to their own environmental policies, and the responsibility to ensure that activities within their jurisdiction or control do not cause damage to the environment of other States or of areas beyond the limits of national jurisdiction" (United Nations 1972a) and recommended "Nations agree that when major water resource activities are contemplated that may have a significant environmental effect on another country, the other country should be notified well in advance of the activity envisaged" and "The net benefits of hydrologic regions common to more than one national jurisdiction are to be shared equitably by the nations affected" (United Nations 1972b).

3 Available at www.un.org/documents/resga.htm.

References

Barberis, J. A. (1990) "La Plata River Basin." In *River and Lake Basin Development. Proceedings of UN Interregional Meeting on River and Lake Basin Development with Emphasis on the Africa Region. Addis Ababa, 10–15 October 1988*. New York: United Nations.

COMIP (1992) *Aprovechamiento Energético del Río Paraná*. Buenos Aires: Comisión Mixta Argentino-Paraguaya del Río Paraná.

Cordeiro, N. V. (1999) "Environmental Management Issues in the Plata Basin." In A. K. Biswas, N. V. Cordeiro, B. P. F. Braga, and C. Tortajada (eds), *Management of Latin American River Basins: Amazon, Plata and São Francisco*, ch. 6. Tokyo: United Nations University Press. Available at www.greenstone.org/greenstone3/nzdl?a=d&c=envl&d=HASH9ddacf08e066ad1baf1235.5.3&sib=1&p.a=b&p.sa=&p.s=ClassifierBrowse&p.c=envl (accessed March 4, 2014).

del Castillo Laborde, L. (1999) "The Plata Basin Institutional Framework." In A. K. Biswas, N. V. Cordeiro, B. P. F. Braga, and C. Tortajada (eds), *Management of Latin American River Basins: Amazon, Plata and São Francisco*, ch. 7. Tokyo: United Nations University Press. Available at www.greenstone.org/greenstone3/nzdl;jsessionid=B9B1BA118D08024643DEB92DCF19B7C1?a=d&c=envl&d=HASH9ddacf08e066ad1baf1235.5.4&sib=1&p.a=b&p.sa=&p.s=ClassifierBrowse&p.c=envl (accessed March 4, 2014).

ECLAC (2009) *Statistical Yearbook for Latin America and the Caribbean 2008*. Santiago: Economic Commission for Latin America and the Caribbean. Available at www.eclac.org/cgi-bin/getProd.asp?xml=/publicaciones/xml/7/35437/P35437.xml&xsl=/deype/tpl-i/p9f.xsl&base=/tpl-i/top-bottom.xslt (accessed March 4, 2014).

INA (2003) *Vinculación entre el caudal del río Paraná y el fenómeno de El Niño*. Protección Ambiental del Río de La Plata y su Frente Marítimo: Prevención y Control de la Contaminación y Restauración de Hábitats project, PNUD/GEF RLA/99/G31, P. R. Jaime and Á. N. Menéndez (eds). Ezeiza: Instituto Nacional del Agua. Available at http://laboratorios.fi.uba.ar/lmm/informes/it_parana_ni%F1o_feb03.pdf (accessed March 4, 2014).

Pochat, V. (1999) "Water-Resources Management of the Plata Basin." In A. K. Biswas, N. V. Cordeiro, B. P. F. Braga, and C. Tortajada (eds), *Management of Latin American River Basins: Amazon, Plata and São Francisco*, ch. 5. Tokyo: United Nations University Press. Available at www.greenstone.org/greenstone3/nzdl?a=d&c=envl&d=HASH9ddacf08e066ad1baf1235.5.2&sib=1&p.a=b&p.sa=&p.s=ClassifierBrowse&p.c=envl (accessed March 4, 2014).

Querol, M. (2010) "The Guarani Aquifer and the Plata Basin Treaty." Presentation at the Seminar Transboundary Aquifers and International Law: The Experience of the Guarani Aquifer System, University of Surrey, Guildford, August 31.

UNEP (2004) *Patagonian Shelf*. GIWA Regional Assessment 38. A. Mugetti, C. Brieva, S. Giangiobbe, E. Gallicchio, F. Pacheco, A. Pagani, A. Calcagno, S. González, O. Natale, M. Faure, S. Rafaelli, C. Magnani, M. C. Moyano, R. Seoane, and I. Enríquez (authors). Kalmar: University of Kalmar, Sweden. Available at www.unep.org/dewa/giwa/areas/reports/r38/giwa_regional_assessment_38.pdf (accessed March 4, 2014).

UNEP-GEF (2003) *Concept Document for Sustainable Water Resources Management in the La Plata River Basin*. Prepared by the Intergovernmental Coordinating Committee of La Plata River Basin Countries (CIC) and the General Secretariat of the Organization of American States (GS/OAS). Nairobi: United Nations Environment Programme/Washington, DC: Global Environment Facility.

United Nations (1972a) "Declaration of the UN Conference on the Human Environment." Available at www.unep.org/Documents.Multilingual/Default.asp?DocumentID=97&ArticleID=1503&l=en (accessed March 4, 2014).

—— (1972b) "Recommendations for Action at the International Level." Available at www.unep.org/Documents.Multilingual/Default.asp?DocumentID=97&ArticleID=1506&l=en (accessed March 4, 2014).

WWAP (2009) "Argentina, Bolivia, Brazil, Paraguay, and Uruguay: La Plata River Basin." In World Water Assessment Programme (ed.), *Facing the Challenges: The United Nations World Water Development Report 3 – Case Studies Volume*, pp. 66–71. London: Earthscan. Available at http://unesdoc.unesco.org/images/0018/001819/181993e.pdf#page=419 (accessed March 4, 2014).

7 Transboundary water governance in the Mackenzie River Basin, Canada

Rob C. de Loë

Introduction

In an increasingly interconnected world, the management of transboundary water resources has emerged as a critical challenge. It is estimated that 145 countries currently share 263 international water courses that cover approximately half of the Earth's land surface. Generating around 60 percent of the global flow of fresh water, these basins are home to roughly 40 percent of the world's population (Loures *et al.* 2008).

Shared international basins have been a focus for both disputes and cooperation for millennia. In 1984 the United Nations Food and Agriculture Organization (FAO) identified more than 3,600 treaties that were created between the years 805 and 1894, most focused on resolving issues relating to navigation (Food and Agriculture Organization of the United Nations 1984). Modern agreements address a broader range of concerns, and reflect a trend towards normalization of basic principles for water transboundary water governance. To illustrate, the 1997 United Nations Convention on the Law of the Non-Navigational Uses of International Watercourses (the "UN Water Convention") is based on a broad consensus regarding how water resources that cross international boundaries should be shared (McCaffrey 2008). Chief among the principles espoused by the Convention are the following:

- equitable and reasonable utilization and participation;
- not causing significant harm to other watercourse states;
- cooperating with other watercourse states to achieve optimal utilization; and protection of international watercourses;
- regular exchanges of data and information; and
- equality among types of uses.

The UN Water Convention reflects a growing global consensus that international transboundary watercourses must be managed cooperatively to maximize joint benefits, rather than unilaterally and competitively (Grey and Sadoff 2003; Phillips *et al.* 2008; Tarlock and Wouters 2007). Importantly, however, the need for cooperative management of transboundary watercourses within countries can be just as strong (Box 7.1). This is especially true in federations that are divided into jurisdictions that have some degree of sovereignty over water resources. Examples include Australia, the United States, and Canada, where sub-national jurisdictions share legal authority over water with their respective federal governments and with each other.

Box 7.1 The Tri-State Water Wars

The Tri-State Water Wars involving Georgia, Florida and Alabama reinforce the importance of effective transboundary water governance within a country. In 1990, Georgia sought additional water for the City of Atlanta from Lake Lanier, a reservoir on the Chattahoochee River in the upstream part of the basin. Negotiations over equitable apportionment of the watercourses that Georgia shared with Alabama and Florida failed, and thus the parties turned to the courts. On January 12, 2009, the Supreme Court ruled against Georgia. As a result, an agreement between Georgia and the US Army Corps of Engineers to take additional water out of Lake Lanier to supply Atlanta was declared illegal. After almost two decades of acrimony and uncertainty, the parties have had to turn again to negotiation to resolve the dispute.

Sources: DeButts (2009); Draper (2006); Jordan and Wolf (2006)

The need for cooperative management of transboundary water resources is high in Canada, a country with a vast territory that covers almost 10 million km^2, and is divided into 10 provinces and three territories. Given that approximately seven percent of the world's renewable freshwater resources are found within Canada's land area (Environment Canada 2006), it is not surprising that thousands of water bodies are shared by Canada's provinces and territories.

Governance of Canada's water resources is complex. The Canadian constitution assigns specific authority to the federal government and the provinces (Saunders and Wenig 2006). Water bodies that fall solely within provinces fall primarily within the constitutional authority of provinces. The federal government's authority relates to specific concerns identified in the Constitution, notably national parks, First Nations reserves, and other federal lands; fish and fish habitat; navigable waters; and waters that flow across provincial/territorial boundaries and the international boundary between Canada and the United States. Many other actors also play important roles in governance. Under the authority of provincial statutes, municipalities have important water-related responsibilities. In northern Canada, the roles of the territories in governance for water depend on whether or not devolution processes have been completed. In the Northwest Territories and Nunavut, the federal government is responsible for water except where Aboriginal governments have authority under self-government agreements. In contrast, in

Yukon responsibility for water management was transferred to that territory's government in 2003. Finally, as Phare (2009) notes, due to the entrenchment of Aboriginal rights in the Constitution, land claims and self-government agreements and treaties, and ongoing affirmation of Aboriginal rights by the Supreme Court of Canada, Aboriginal peoples in Canada have unique rights, both as governments and as individual rights-holders, to be active participants in water-related decision-making.

Pressure on Canada's water resources is increasing due to industrial development, urban growth, and climate change (Kreutzwiser and de Loë 2010). As a result, the need for effective shared management of water resources is growing. Examples of successful inter-jurisdictional cooperation over shared water resources in Canada exist. For instance, the 1969 Master Agreement on Apportionment established a framework for apportioning transboundary water resources among the federal government and the three prairie provinces of Alberta, Saskatchewan, and Manitoba (Oborne 2005). The equitable approach to sharing transboundary water resources established by this Agreement continues to this day.

A major basin in which shared governance for water is becoming essential is the Mackenzie River Basin (MRB) in northern Canada. This crucial basin is shared by three provinces (British Columbia, Alberta, and Saskatchewan) and by two territories (the Yukon and Northwest Territories), and falls within the area covered by treaties and land claim agreements that have been negotiated with Canada's Aboriginal peoples. The MRB is under pressure from industrial development, but the majority has not yet been despoiled. Governments have committed themselves to a cooperative approach – but the form of that cooperation has yet to be determined. Thus, there is still time to establish an effective transboundary water governance regime for the MRB that can address current and future threats and challenges.

This chapter outlines a rationale and vision for transboundary water governance in the MRB. A central argument in the chapter is that a limited, narrow form of transboundary cooperation focused simply on apportionment of available flows in the basin will not be sufficient to meet current and future challenges. Instead, reflecting constitutional obligations and the differing policies in each jurisdiction, transboundary water governance should be based on emerging international norms and best practices that call for deeper cooperation and a more comprehensive perspective. In the next section, a brief overview of the MRB's physical and socio-economic setting is provided. Key norms and benchmarks for transboundary water governance are then discussed. These provide the basis for the broad outline of a vision for transboundary water governance in the MRB that is presented at the end of the chapter.

Mackenzie River Basin

The Mackenzie River Basin (Figure 7.1) is an incredibly complex social-ecological system. Understanding the prospects for transboundary water governance in this system requires consideration of the basin's hydrology, ecology, population, and economy, along with the characteristics of key elements of the governance system, including constitutional, treaty and land claim obligations. This section provides a brief overview of considerations that are particularly relevant for transboundary water governance in the MRB.

Hydrology, ecology, population, and economy

With an area of approximately 1.8 million km^2, the MRB drains roughly 20 percent of Canada's land area. At 4,241 km, it contains Canada's longest river system (MRBB 2003). The basin is shared by the provinces of Alberta, Saskatchewan, and British Columbia (BC), and by two territories: the Yukon and Northwest (NWT) Territories. A small portion of the basin is found within Nunavut (Figure 7.1); nonetheless, Nunavut is not normally treated as a basin jurisdiction. Importantly, the basin also includes the traditional territories, treaty areas, and land claim settlement regions of Aboriginal peoples: First Nations, Métis, and Inuvialuit.

Figure 7.1 Map of the Mackenzie River Basin, Canada

The headwaters of the basin are found in the Peace and Athabasca rivers, which originate in BC and Alberta, respectively (Figure 7.1). These rivers flow into the ecologically critical Peace-Athabasca Delta, a Ramsar wetland of international importance that is located in Alberta. Flows in this delta are complex. When water levels in Lake Athabasca are lower than the Peace River, water flows into the Delta and Lake Athabasca. More commonly, high water levels on Lake Athabasca cause flows through Delta channels to meet the Peace River and then flow north in the Slave River into the NWT, which drains into Great Slave Lake.

The Mackenzie River itself runs north from Great Slave Lake, and is joined by the Liard, Great Bear, and Peel rivers before emptying into the Beaufort Sea (Figure 7.1). The various sub-basins that comprise the MRB create distinct settings for transboundary water governance. For example, even though the Slave sub-basin is a critical part of the larger Mackenzie River Basin, concerns relating to water quality and quantity on the Slave River are relevant primarily to Alberta, as the upstream jurisdiction, and to the Northwest Territories, as the downstream jurisdiction.

The basin is sparsely populated. Its total population in 2001 was estimated to be 397,000 people, with the majority residing in the Alberta portion, in communities such as Fort McMurray, Peace River, and Hinton (MRBB 2003). The lands and waters of this basin are extremely important to Aboriginal peoples, who comprised 15 percent of the total population in 2001. Where population density is the lowest – in the northern parts of the basin – the proportion of the population that is Aboriginal tends to be highest. To illustrate, the region along the Mackenzie River from Great Slave Lake to the Mackenzie Delta is home to approximately 7,800 people in 13 communities, 70 percent of whom are Aboriginal (MRBB 2003).

The basin's current and potential future economic significance for Canada is enormous. However, economic considerations must be considered alongside the fact that the basin contains some of the last remaining expanses of nearly pristine wilderness on the continent, and has globally important forests, tundra and wetland ecosystems that provide habitat for a host of species. For instance, breeding and staging areas for millions of migratory birds such as geese and tundra swans are located within the MRB (Nature Canada 2008). The Peace-Athabasca Delta on Lake Athabasca is one the most important waterfowl nesting and staging areas in North America; up to 400,000 birds are known to use the Delta in the spring, and more than one million in the autumn (Schindler *et al.* 2007). The basin's other major delta – the Mackenzie Delta on the Beaufort Sea – supports important wildlife species (including muskrat, beaver, moose, mink, lynx, beluga whales), fish species such as whitefish, inconnu and arctic char, and numerous bird species (MRBB 2003). Alongside their ecological significance, the fish and wildlife of the basin are a critical source of food for a significant portion of the basin's people (GNWT 2010b).

Fossil fuel developments and hydroelectric power generation are especially important economic activities that have implications for transboundary water governance in the basin. Oil and gas development is already extensive in the basin, primarily in the Alberta and BC portions, and much more is expected in the future. For example, a proposal to develop the vast natural gas reserves that are found in the Mackenzie Delta is currently being evaluated. This will require the development of a pipeline along the Mackenzie, which will also facilitate development of gas resources in NWT (GNWT 2007). Perhaps the most significant current fossil energy development at this time is the oil sands in Alberta, near the City of Fort McMurray (Figure 7.1). An estimated 300 billion barrels of recoverable fossil energy is found in these deposits (MRBB 2003). Development is proceeding rapidly. At the end of 2009, four surface mines and 87 in situ projects were in operation, with three additional mines approved or under development. In 2008, these projects were producing 1.3 million barrels a day. Production of 3 million barrels a day is expected by 2018, with 2030 production levels reaching 5 million barrels a day by 2030 (Government of Alberta 2010; Holroyd and Simieritsch 2009).

The economic benefits of oil sands development to Alberta and Canada are enormous, but they are matched by their environmental and social impacts. Bitumen is extracted through two different processes: surface mining and in situ developments involving, for example, the injection of steam that melts the bitumen and allows it to flow (known as steam-assisted gravity drainage). The magnitude and scale of oil sands developments is enormous. As of 2008, 530 km^2 of boreal landscape has been disturbed; tailing ponds alone cover 130 km^2 (Kelly *et al.* 2010). Environmental impacts associated with oil sands projects include emissions of greenhouse gasses, particulates, metals and polycyclic aromatic compounds (PACs); impacts on water quality and quantity; and loss of habitat due to land clearing for mine pits, roads, well sites, and pipelines (Holroyd and Simieritsch 2009; Kelly *et al.* 2009). Concerns exist regarding the effects of oil sands development on the health of downstream communities, particularly those where people consume water, fish, and wildlife from the Athabasca River watershed. Aboriginal peoples maintaining traditional lifestyles are at particular risk in this context. For example, Kelly *et al.* (2010) demonstrated that 13 elements considered priority pollutants under the United States Environmental Protection Agency's Clean Water Act were released via air and water to the Athabasca River and its watershed. An earlier study by these authors measured levels of PACs in snowpack within 50 km of oil sands upgraders, and in water downstream of new oil sands development (Kelly *et al.* 2009). These findings, the authors suggest, is cause for serious concern because of the impacts of these substances on fish, wildlife, and human health.

Hydroelectric power generation is important to the provinces of BC and AB, and to the NWT. Approximately 30 percent of BC Hydro's generating capacity is created by two stations located on the Peace River that are supplied by the Bennett Dam (Figure 7.1; MRBB 2003). Seasonal patterns of stream flow on the Peace River have been changed by this development, and the ecology of the Peace-Athabasca Delta has been affected (Prowse and Conly 2000). The BC government currently is planning the development of another project on the Peace River: the "Site C" project, downstream of the Bennett Dam. This project is expected to generate a further 900 MW of capacity (see www.bchydro.com); further changes to the ecology of the Peace-Athabasca Delta may be expected. Additional major hydroelectric power generation projects also are being considered in the basin by industries and governments. For example, TransCanada Corporation has proposed a $5 billion dam project on the Slave River, just south of the Alberta–NWT boundary, which would generate an estimated 1,200 to 1,300 MW of power (Calgary Herald 2008). The NWT government also views hydroelectric power development as an important part of the territories' energy future. Small-scale projects will be used to provide the energy needs of communities, while larger projects may supply industries such as diamond mines. In its analysis, the government identified 11,520 MW of undeveloped potential, including an estimated 10,450 MW of potential hydroelectric power on the main stem of the Mackenzie (GNWT 2007).

Pressure on the basin's water resources and ecosystems, and on the people who depend on them, is increasing due to the economic developments discussed above. However, climate change is another important stressor in the basin. Studies have identified changes in meteorological and hydrological parameters that appear to relate to observed changes in climate (Abdul Aziz and Burn 2006; Schindler and Donahue 2006). For instance, changes in annual precipitation between 1950 and 1998 have been observed in the basin, with the impacts most pronounced in the northern portion. The Athabasca Glacier has lost half its volume and has retreated by more than 1.5 km during the last 125 years. If the patterns identified to date continue into the future, significant effects on aquatic and terrestrial ecosystems are anticipated (MRBB 2003).

By themselves, anticipated changes in the basin's climate and hydrology warrant serious concern. However, their significance is magnified substantially when they are considered alongside the impacts of human developments on both water quality and quantity. For example, stream flow and water quality in the Athabasca River will be affected not only by climate change, but also by increased water withdrawals for oil sands development (Bruce 2006; MRBB 2003). Similarly, the impacts of additional hydroelectric power developments on the Peace-Athabasca Delta will be magnified by impacts of climate change (Prowse and Conly 2000). A more comprehensive, basin-wide perspective that takes account of the cumulative effects of development clearly is needed to address these interacting sources of change.

Governance

The term "water governance," as used in this chapter, refers to the ways in which societies make decisions and take actions that affect water. Considerations that are important in the context of water governance include the organizations and people involved, the roles they play, the relationships among the various actors, and the formal and informal institutions that facilitate decision-making. The biophysical and socio-economic setting within which governance occurs also is an important concern.

Water governance in the MRB is extremely complex. Key actors include the three provincial governments, which are responsible for water allocation, land-use planning, and energy development; the federal government, whose mandate is triggered in cases where water crosses interprovincial boundaries, and has constitutional responsibilities for Aboriginal peoples in the territories and for water in Nunavut and Northwest Territories; the MRBB, created by the 1997 Mackenzie River Basin Transboundary Waters Master Agreement; territorial governments, which fulfill some or all (in the case of Yukon) of the water-related functions of provinces; Aboriginal governments in parts of the basin where land claims agreements have been negotiated (e.g., the Gwich'in Tribal Council, for the Gwich'in Settlement Area); Aboriginal peoples, because of their Aboriginal and treaty rights; industry; citizens; and, increasingly, civil society groups such as the World Wildlife Fund (WWF) that have taken an interest in the basin (e.g., WWF 2005; WWF-Canada 2009).

Within each level of government, certain agencies and organizations have specific roles. For example, Aboriginal Affairs and Northern Development Canada (AANDC) is the agency primarily responsible for fulfilling the federal government's responsibilities in NWT and Nunavut, but Environment Canada and Health Canada also have lesser but still important responsibilities relating to water. In the Northwest Territories, the Department of Environment and Natural Resources coordinates GNWT involvement in water management. The five Water Boards (Mackenzie Valley Land and Water Board; Sahtu Land and Water Board; Gwich'in Land and Water Board; Wek'èezhìı Land and Water Board; and NWT Water Board) have specific responsibilities relating to water allocation and water quality management.

Laws and policies relating to water that have been created by the various governments are key elements of the governance system. For example, in Alberta, water is allocated under a provincial statute, the Water Act. In NWT, water boards issue licenses for water use under the Northwest Territories Waters Act and the Mackenzie Valley Resource Management Act. Basin governments also have created policy frameworks. Examples include BC's Living Water Smart (British Columbia Ministry of Environment 2008), Alberta's Water for Life (Alberta Environment 2008), and NWT's Northern Voices, Northern Waters stewardship strategy (GNWT 2010a), which is the product of close cooperation between the Government of the Northwest Territories (GNWT), Aboriginal partners, and Indian and Northern Affairs Canada (now AANDC; Box 7.2). Despite its critical role in NWT, the federal government does not currently have a comprehensive national policy framework for water. Importantly, however, the federal government has endorsed the NWT's water strategy.

The MRB is an integrated, hydrologic system, yet water governance is fragmented along jurisdictional and agency lines. Recognizing this concern, and accepting that a cooperative approach to transboundary water governance is needed, Canada, British Columbia, Alberta, Saskatchewan, Yukon, and the Northwest Territories negotiated the 1997 Mackenzie River Basin Transboundary Waters Master Agreement (MRBTWMA). The Agreement is a concrete step

Box 7.2 Northern Voices, Northern Waters: NWT Water Stewardship Strategy

Following a lengthy process involving visioning and detailed public consultation, the Government of the Northwest Territories, along with its Aboriginal partners and the federal government released Northern Voices, Northern Waters: NWT Water Stewardship Strategy in May 2010. The strategy is grounded in an overall vision that mirrors those contained in similar documents: "The waters of the Northwest Territories will remain clean, abundant and productive for all time." However, the strategy is distinctive for a number of important reasons:

- It is built upon a genuine commitment to shared governance with the territory's Aboriginal peoples. This is reflected in a commitment to engagement rather than simply consultation, the prominence given to Aboriginal traditional knowledge, and, the simple fact that implementation of the strategy so clearly depends upon Aboriginal partners. It clearly defines key concepts such as "ecosystem health" and includes tangible and measurable goals and objectives. Roles and responsibilities are clearly identified, and the foundation for collaborative, multi-level governance of water in NWT is established.
- It recognizes the importance of water to the territory as an economic good and foundation of economic prosperity, while at the same time accepting its significance for the environment and its cultural and spiritual importance to Aboriginal peoples.
- The importance of integrating decisions regarding water with related concerns such as land use planning and economic development, is clearly established.

Importantly, the strategy also emphasizes the extent to which NWT's water resources are vulnerable to decisions made in upstream jurisdictions; thus, it supports the need for effective transboundary water governance in the MRB.

towards the goal of a more coordinated approach that recognizes basin-wide concerns. It commits its signatories to a set of principles, including managing water resources "in a manner consistent with the maintenance of the ecological integrity of the aquatic ecosystem" (Government of Canada *et al.* 1997). The Agreement reflects many of the contemporary norms of international transboundary water governance that are discussed in the next section. For instance, the principle of equity is reflected in commitments to manage the use of the basin's water resources in a sustainable manner for present and future generations, and to not cause unreasonable harm to the integrity of aquatic ecosystems in other jurisdictions (Government of Canada *et al.* 1997).

The MRBTWMA does not undermine the jurisdiction of the signatories. For example, Alberta's ability to develop its natural resources and to allocate water resources within its territory under the Water Act is not affected because it signed the Agreement. Nonetheless, the parties have recognized the need for a coordinated approach to implementation of agreed-upon principles and goals. Therefore, the Agreement created the MRBB. Members of the MRBB include up to three representatives of Canada, and one each of the three provinces and two territories. Additionally, the agreement provides for a total of five board members who represent Aboriginal organizations in BC, Alberta, Saskatchewan, Yukon, and the Northwest Territories. Importantly, the MRBB is not a regulatory or licensing body, and it has no legal or policy basis for regulating resources in the jurisdictions of its members. Instead, the MRBB provides a forum for communication, coordinated action, information exchange and other activities that contribute to a basin-wide orientation (MRBB 2003).

In the context of this chapter, a critical function of the Agreement is the provision of mechanisms for the negotiation of "Bilateral Water Management Agreements" among the parties. As noted previously in the case of the Slave River watershed, the interests of the various basin jurisdictions are stronger in some sub-basins than in others. Thus, the Agreement permits negotiation of bilateral agreements for specific transboundary water resources. These should be consistent with the principles established in the Agreement. To date, only one bilateral agreement has been negotiated (between the Northwest Territories and the Yukon). Memoranda of Understanding that establish the frameworks for detailed negotiations have been signed between BC and Alberta, and between Alberta and Northwest Territories.

Recognizing the need for more progress in negotiating bilateral agreements, the MRBB recently published a guidance document that outlines a detailed implementation plan, including the sequence in which agreements should be negotiated (MRBB 2009). While this document clarifies next steps, considerable uncertainty remains regarding the scope and scale of these agreements, and, more importantly, the extent to which the overall principles for transboundary water governance outlined in the Agreement can be implemented. For instance, bilateral water management agreements negotiated under the MRBTWMA could be little more than apportionment arrangements that divide the flow of key transboundary watercourses. However, these agreements also could provide the foundation for shared or collaborative governance of the MRB according to accepted international principles and best practices.

Experiences from around the world demonstrate overwhelmingly that parties are significantly better off when they pursue collaborative approaches to transboundary water governance rather than acting independently, or in conflict with each other. In the MRB, for example, collaboration could result in better data bases for decision making, improved monitoring regimes, enhanced cooperation on mutually beneficial developments, better environmental quality, and reduced conflict. The increased certainty that is likely to result from cooperative management and robust institutions for shared governance should be a significant incentive to parties adopting a truly collaborative approach. Of course, whether or not these benefits can be achieved depends on the extent to which the parties commit to a broader vision of governance in the basin. In the next section, the building blocks for such a vision are outlined.

Principles and benchmarks for transboundary water governance

Transboundary basins are incredibly complex social-ecological systems. Hence, even countries with histories of antipathy have found that cooperation typically is needed to maximize their respective environmental, economic, and social interests (van der Zaag and Vaz 2003; Wolf *et al.* 2005). Specific outcomes of cooperative approaches evident from experiences around the world typically include the following (Draper 2006; Giordano and Wolf 2003; Uitto and Duda 2002; Wolf *et al.* 2005):

- greater likelihood of adequate amounts of water, of appropriate quality, for human and environmental needs;
- sharing of the risks of scarcity;
- reduced uncertainty;
- opportunities for identifying mutual interests and resolving conflicts (thereby permitting new options and solutions to emerge);
- strengthened trust and confidence through collaboration;
- higher probability that decisions made jointly will be accepted by the parties involved; and
- increased cooperation on other cross-border concerns.

The case for a cooperative approach to the management of transboundary water resources primarily reflects experiences with international watercourses. However, as suggested in the introduction to this chapter, these benefits are equally relevant at the sub-national scale. While the UN Water Convention clearly has been designed to guide nation states, its core principles (e.g., equitable and reasonable utilization of water by parties sharing the resource, not causing harm to other jurisdictions, cooperating with other jurisdictions to achieve optimal outcomes) can provide a basis for cooperation in basins located within one country but shared by sub-national jurisdictions.

Initiatives such as the UN Water Convention provide a foundation of basic principles for cooperation. However, every shared watercourse is unique. Thus, how these broad principles are implemented depends on local context. Not surprisingly, therefore, the UN Water Convention is silent on several specific issues that are considered critical in the contemporary water governance literature. To illustrate, the Convention does not address the roles of parties other than national governments. This is of course critical within countries, where citizens, local governments, industry, Aboriginal governments and others are (or should be) key participants in water governance.

In this section, five benchmarks for effective transboundary water governance are presented:

- integration;
- ecosystem protection;
- public involvement;
- collaborative, multi-level governance; and
- adaptability and flexibility.

These are drawn from the contemporary water and environmental governance literatures. Importantly, this literature is grounded strongly in actual practice. Thus, the benchmarks are not merely theoretical notions. Instead, they are strongly reflective of successful practices in transboundary water governance around the world. Other benchmarks certainly can be added to the list. However, the ones presented here are especially relevant in the context of transboundary water governance (in general) and the Mackenzie River Basin (in particular).

Integration

Water connects human activities over time and space because actions in one part of a watershed or aquifer will be felt in others. Thus, integration has emerged as a key benchmark for effective water governance in shared basins. Decisions and actions regarding the following should be made in an integrated fashion that addresses jurisdictional and administrative boundaries: surface water and groundwater interactions; land use planning and water management; human and environmental water needs; water quality and water quantity; and economic development and water management (Bjornlund 2003; Carter *et al.* 2005; Falkenmark 2003; Giordano and Wolf 2003; Murray *et al.* 2003; Phillips *et al.* 2008).

Ecosystem protection

Earlier agreements relating to transboundary water resources have focused primarily on concerns such as navigation, flood control and apportionment (Giordano and Wolf 2003). In contrast, contemporary agreements increasingly emphasize improving or maintaining environmental conditions (Tarlock and Wouters 2007). Concerns pertinent to ecosystem protection include improving or maintaining flows to protect fish and fish habitat (Dyson *et al.* 2003; Richter *et al.* 2003; Sengo *et al.* 2005); sustaining or improving riparian habitat (Brouwer *et al.* 2003); and achieving water quality objectives for ecosystem needs (Shmueli 1999). Aquatic ecosystems have specific needs in terms of the timing, volume, temperature and quality of flows (Dyson *et al.* 2003). Thus, despite the fact that a concern for integration captures some issues pertinent to ecosystem protection, transboundary water governance arrangements should pay particular attention to the kinds of concerns outlined above.

Public involvement

The need for, and desirability of, public involvement in water governance has emerged as a central concern in the contemporary literature (Affeltranger and Otte 2003; Bruch 2004; Bruch *et al.* 2005; Dellapenna 2007; Dyson *et al.* 2003). It is difficult to imagine implementing a goal such as equitable sharing of water resources without providing appropriate opportunities for the people who are affected to be involved, for instance, people who live in communities downstream of major water takings. The water management literature offers a host of additional reasons for public involvement. For example, water management is inherently a political activity (Swatuk 2005; Warner *et al.* 2008). Thus, effective public involvement is needed to reduce the potential for conflicts and to increase the likelihood of successful policy implementation. At the same time, the literature recognizes the limited capacity of the state, on its own, to manage systems as complex as transboundary watersheds (Draper 2006; Karkkainen 2005). Reflecting these concerns, modern agreements for transboundary water management increasingly include provisions for public involvement (Draper 2006; Muys *et al.* 2007).

Collaborative, multi-level governance

In many countries around the world, water governance increasingly is characterized by a sharing or distribution of authority and responsibility beyond the state. Terms such as "collaborative" and "multi-level" governance often are used to describe this more complex environment (Armitage 2008; Imperial 2005). The trend toward collaborative and multi-level water governance has many causes, including practical limitations on the ability of the state to deal with complex social-ecological systems, and a belief that sharing responsibility and power beyond the state can better reflect local circumstances and needs (de Loë *et al.* 2009). Transboundary water governance based on a desire to achieve basin-wide objectives is a setting where collaborative and multi-level governance are particularly important (Matthews and St Germain 2007). This reflects the fact that no one actor has the power and authority to manage a system that is shared by many actors.

Adaptability and flexibility

Daily, seasonal, and annual changes in precipitation, streamflow, lake levels, and other characteristics of the water cycle are a normal feature of water management (Cech 2003; McDonald and Kay 1988). Unfortunately, due to anticipated changes to the global climate, water managers can no longer assume that future climatic variability will be consistent with observed variability (Milly *et al.* 2008). Hence, they have to deal with increased complexity and uncertainty – likely at levels much higher than have previously been experienced (Draper and Kundell 2008; Kashyap 2004). Adding to this challenge is the fact that climate change is only one source of uncertainty. Others include changed demands for water due to population growth and economic development; new actors with different interests, goals and expectations; and new knowledge resulting from scientific advances (Kistin and Ashton 2008; McCaffrey 2003; Milich and Varady 1998; Swatuk and Wirkus 2009). Together, these considerations emphasize the critical importance of designing water management systems – such as arrangements for transboundary water governance – with flexibility and adaptability in mind. For example, provisions for apportionment of shared streamflow should permit responding to circumstances that were not conceived of when rules were drafted, and should accommodate changes in flows, demands and other key considerations such as the needs of the environment (Fischhendler 2004; McCaffrey 2003; van der Zaag and Vaz 2003).

Transboundary water governance in the Mackenzie River Basin

A wealth of experience with transboundary water governance exists around the world. Attention continues to be focused primarily on international transboundary water courses. However, recognition of the importance of effective transboundary governance within countries has grown in recent years, as witnessed by the publication of general guidelines (e.g., Draper 2006) and model compacts for interstate water governance (e.g., Muys *et al.* 2007). These specific guidelines and principles reflect a desire in the United States to avoid the costly legal disputes that emerge from situations such as the one currently faced by Georgia, Alabama, and Florida (Box 7.1). Canada, with its shared jurisdiction over internal transboundary basins, is by no means immune to these concerns.

This section outlines in broad strokes a vision for transboundary water governance in the Mackenzie River Basin. A basic premise in this section is that a limited form of transboundary cooperation focused narrowly on concerns such as apportionment of available flows in the basin will not be sufficient to meet the current and future challenges outlined previously, and would be a significant missed opportunity for all the parties. Instead, transboundary water governance in the MRB should be based on the principles and benchmarks discussed in the previous section so that the concerns identified in Box 7.3 can be addressed in a more holistic fashion. The discussion is organized around the major principles and benchmarks outlined in the previous section.

The need for transboundary water governance based on internationally accepted standards of equity is critical in the MRB in part because of the significant power imbalance that exists. The Northwest Territories – as the principal downstream jurisdiction – had a 2009 population of 43,400 people, whereas Alberta and BC, the principal upstream jurisdictions, had 2009 populations of 3,687,700 and 4,455,200 people, respectively (Statistics Canada 2010). The disparity in population size alone assures BC and Alberta a significant advantage over the Yukon and NWT in financial and technical resources. Equity also is a critical concern in the basin because of its Aboriginal population. Aboriginal

Box 7.3 Contextual factors relevant to transboundary water governance in the MRB

- Hydrological and climatological conditions in the basin (e.g., annual and inter-annual flow patterns in shared rivers and streams, groundwater-surface water interactions, water quality, drought frequency and magnitude, flood risk).
- Federal, provincial and territorial jurisdictions and responsibilities; traditional, treaty and legal rights of Aboriginal peoples.
- Institutions for water governance in the basin, including water allocation systems in each basin jurisdiction, and existing arrangements for transboundary water governance.
- History of cooperation between and among the basin jurisdictions (federal government, provinces, territories, and Aboriginal peoples), and their willingness to collaborate.
- Current and potential ability to regulate surface water flows using reservoirs.
- Financial, social and technical capacity of key actors who will be involved in transboundary water governance (e.g., hydrological modeling capabilities, level of organization, capacity and interest among citizens and non-government organizations).
- Availability and quality of data and information needed for purposes such as understanding the impacts of developments, monitoring cumulative effects, and forecasting of future conditions (socio-economic, hydrological).
- Existing and future pressure on water resources and ecosystems from industrial development, communities and climate change.
- Water needed to ensure aquatic environmental conditions (existing and desired).

peoples in Canada have historically been affected negatively by large water developments (Phare 2009; Quinn 1991). Current and future industrial developments have affected, and unquestionably will affect, the Aboriginal peoples who have made the MRB their home for millennia. Given that their territories do not fall neatly within provincial/territorial boundaries, their concerns and rights should be acknowledged and respected in a basin-wide approach to transboundary water governance.

A commitment to equity in transboundary water governance does not necessarily have negative implications for existing rights holders within basin jurisdictions (Muys *et al.* 2007). This is a critical point because the jurisdictions sharing the basin clearly are concerned about protecting their autonomy. This concern is demonstrated by the character of the 1997 MRBTWMA, and the fact that the MRBB it creates was explicitly not given legal or policy powers to regulate resources in the jurisdictions of its members. Adopting a basin-wide approach to water governance in the MRB does not require that Alberta, BC, and the other jurisdictions that share the basin must abandon their own policy frameworks or legal systems for water management, or that holders of existing water rights in those jurisdictions will lose those rights. Instead, a commitment to equity simply recognizes that the parties sharing a basin should not cause harm to each other. This principle already is contained in the MRBTWMA, which states that the parties are committed to "The right of each to use or manage the use of the Water Resources within its jurisdiction provided such use does not unreasonably harm the Ecological Integrity of the Aquatic Ecosystem in any other jurisdiction" (Government of Canada *et al.* 1997).

Integration is essential in any basin-wide approach to transboundary water governance. Sharing of transboundary surface water flows is a key concern in the MRBTWMA. This concern is particularly important in the Athabasca sub-basin in the context of withdrawals associated with oil sands development, and in several other basins in the context of the impacts of current and future hydro-electric power developments. However, integration – or at least coordination – of decision making is also needed in the context of interrelationships among water quality and water quantity; land development and water flows and quality; and energy policies and water policies. In some transboundary contexts, it also may be important to consider groundwater-surface water interactions. Focusing on the cumulative effects associated with water use and development – an approach advocated by several basin jurisdictions – is an appropriate vehicle for identifying and addressing relevant concerns. Integration of sub-agreements is also an important concern. As discussed previously, the MRBTWMA permits the signatories to negotiate separate bilateral agreements. Respecting the principle of integration, these individual agreements should be developed within a larger organizing framework that establishes common principles and expectations (whether the MRBTWMA or something else).

Building on the objective of integration, transboundary water governance in the MRB should make protection of aquatic ecosystems a basic requirement. The basin contains nationally and internationally significant water-dependent ecosystems that have not yet been entirely despoiled. With development pressure increasing throughout the entire basin, it is essential that mechanisms for transboundary water governance pay special attention to environmental water needs. Experiences from around the world demonstrate clearly that the needs of the environment cannot be met effectively once water resources have been committed overwhelmingly to human purposes (de Loë 2009). Thus, defining environmental water needs (quantity, quality, timing, etc.) and then protecting them through specific mechanisms in bi-lateral agreements is necessary.

The question of environmental water needs also reinforces the need for a basin-wide perspective. For example, many of the considerations that influence the quality, volume, and timing of flow at the various boundaries in the basin will be shaped by decisions not directly subject to bi-lateral agreements that are made by basin jurisdictions. The most prominent example is licensing and permitting decisions made in relation to oil sands development. These decisions will be made based on relevant Alberta and federal laws. However, a basin-wide vision of some kind is essential so that these decisions take appropriate account of downstream environmental impacts. At the same time, only a basin-wide monitoring regime can provide the basis for identifying and taking account of cumulative effects of decisions that influence environmental conditions in the basin as a whole.

Given the Mackenzie River Basin's enormous size and relatively low population density, and in light of its diverse Aboriginal peoples, effective public involvement in transboundary water governance should be a priority. It is difficult to imagine anyone defining a vision for water governance in the MRB without providing extensive public consultation and involvement opportunities; the process used to develop the NWT's water strategy sets a precedent (Box 7.2). Similarly, successful implementation of a broader vision for transboundary water governance (i.e., one that goes far beyond simply measuring flows at boundaries and dividing them according to a formula) will require the support and active involvement of people who live in the basin's communities and on the land. Experiences from around the world (de Loë 2009) demonstrate that public engagement at the scale envisioned necessitates not only commitment on the part of the basin jurisdictions but also a champion. To date the MRBB has not demonstrated that it has the capacity or legitimacy to play this role. However, the Board already exists and has a complementary mandate under the MRBTWMA. Therefore, empowering the Board to undertake basin-wide public engagement is a logical option.

The basin is shared by three provinces and two territories, Aboriginal governments, and the federal government. Therefore, a basin-wide approach to governance will necessarily be collaborative and multi-level. Numerous examples around the world demonstrate that collaborative, multi-level governance of shared basins is feasible, and that this approach does not necessarily impinge upon the sovereignty of the various participants. Bodies for deliberation rather than joint decision-making (of which the MRBB is an example) are used in many shared basins. Stronger models also exist. For example, the Murray–Darling Basin Authority (MDBA) in Australia is responsible for planning the integrated management of this critical basin (see www.mdba.gov.au); the Authority has legally defined decision-making authority for transboundary water governance in the Murray-Darling Basin. Another model is found in the River Basin Commission that is central to the Model Transboundary Water Compact proposed by the Utton Transboundary Resources Center at the University of New Mexico School of Law (Muys *et al.* 2007).

These examples demonstrate that proven options for a collaborative approach to governance of shared basins exist. Historically the basin jurisdictions clearly have been unwilling to constrain the scope of their own decision-making powers. This is reflected in their unwillingness to empower the MRBB to play a role beyond being a forum for deliberation. However, this may simply reflect the fact that Canada does not have a strong history of internal shared governance for water across provincial/territorial boundaries (as opposed to cooperation on apportionment). Thus, clarifying palatable options for a more collaborative approach to basin-wide governance should be a priority in the context of the ongoing transboundary negotiations. If the current agreement and MRBB is not the right mechanism, then another one should be sought.

In the context of the Mackenzie River Basin, a key governance challenge relates to the role of Aboriginal peoples. In the NWT and Yukon portions of the basin, Aboriginal governments exist under land claims agreements (e.g., the Gwich'in Tribal Council, for the Gwich'in Settlement Area). In the portions of the basin that fall within provinces, different arrangements exist. For instance, Treaty 8 covers the portion of northern Alberta that falls within the MRB, along with part of the southern NWT. In light of their rights to be involved in decision making due to treaties, land claims and their traditional Aboriginal rights as enshrined in section 35 of the Canadian Constitution, Aboriginal peoples must be involved in governance in the basin, rather than simply consulted as members of the general public. This is not simply a moral argument. The legal landscape relating to water and Aboriginal peoples in Canada is changing (Phare 2009). Failing to acknowledge this fact, and thus failing to view Aboriginal peoples as partners in the governance of the MRB, would be a source of considerable uncertainty and even conflict. This situation is not unique to Canada. For instance, the Utton Model Transboundary Water Compact contains specific provisions for involving tribal governments in the governance of shared basins in the United States (Muys *et al.* 2007). The role that Aboriginal governments play in the NWT's Water Stewardship Strategy (Box 7.2) is distinctive in Canada. Unfortunately, NWT's experiences provide both a model and a caution regarding the enormous challenges associated with transitioning to collaborative governance with Aboriginal people.

Finally, given the lack of high-quality data for decision making in many parts of the basin, the enormous uncertainty that exists regarding the cumulative effects of existing and future industrial developments, the water needs of the environment, and the impacts of climate change on water resources and ecosystems, it is critical that flexibility and adaptability be established as design principles for transboundary water governance in the MRB. For example, it would be entirely inappropriate in the bilateral negotiations that are currently underway for the parties to establish inflexible, volume-based allocations of water. Instead, in considering rules for sharing transboundary flows, mechanisms should be established that permit responding to unforeseen circumstances. This approach is well developed in other countries (e.g., under the Murray–Darling Basin Agreement, provisions exist for flexible apportionment among states based on water resource conditions, special provisions exist for dealing with droughts and low flows, and procedures exist for regular plan revision and amendment; de Loë 2009).

Conclusions and policy implications

The aim in this chapter was to outline a rationale and vision for transboundary water governance in Canada's Mackenzie River Basin. This precious transboundary resource is under pressure from industrial development, and under threat from climate change. Large-scale industrial developments already have left their mark, and in some parts of the basin have created significant negative ecological changes and environmental impacts. Nonetheless, it is not too late for the parties involved in the management and governance in the basin to commit themselves to a truly cooperative, basin wide approach to governance. The benefits of such an approach are numerous, and include a stronger shared knowledge base, reduced uncertainty for industry, and healthier aquatic ecosystems, to name a few.

Challenges certainly exist. These include the low population of the basin relative to its large size, limitations on the capacities of key actors to implement decisions (especially in the territories), and the rapid pace and scale of energy development. Clarifying the role of Aboriginal peoples in the governance of the basin as a whole also is a distinct challenge not faced by many other transboundary basins. Despite these challenges, the vision articulated in this chapter is within reach. A vast foundation of experience exists around the world for dealing with the challenges of transboundary water governance, as do concrete models. Achieving the kind of transboundary water governance advocated in this chapter certainly is a mammoth task. However, those favoring this approach can take heart from the fact that in basins around the world where the challenges are even more profound, people committed to cooperation in shared basins have found ways to govern them successfully. At the same time, addressing the challenges faced in the MRB – and achieving the vision articulated in this chapter, especially in terms of the roles of Aboriginal peoples – could offer a model for the rest of the world.

Acknowledgements

Major insights relating to principles and best practices for transboundary water governance were developed for a report prepared for International Red Rivers Board, International Joint Commission (de Loë 2009). Thanks are due to colleagues who commented on an earlier draft of the chapter, including David Livingstone, staff from the Government of the Northwest Territories, and Liana Moraru. Marie Puddister (Department of Geography, University of Guelph), who prepared Figure 7.1. Thanks are also due to Bob Sandford and Henry Vaux, on behalf of the Rosenberg International Forum on Water Policy, who offered helpful comments and feedback as the chapter was developed. Finally, Becky Swainson provided background research and support for the preparation of this chapter. Responsibility for any errors, and for the opinions expressed in this chapter, rests with the author.

References

Abdul Aziz, O. I. and Burn, D. H. (2006) "Trends and Variability in the Hydrological Regime of the Mackenzie River Basin." *Journal of Hydrology* 319: 282–94.

Affeltranger, B. and Otte, A. (2003) "Shared Freshwater Resources: Management or Governance?" In A. Turton, P. Ashton, and E. Cloete (eds), *Transboundary Rivers, Sovereignty and Development: Hydropolitical Drivers in the Okavango River Basin*, 251–74. Pretoria: African Water Issues Research Unit, Centre for International Political Studies, University of Pretoria.

Alberta Environment (2008) *Water for Life: A Renewal*. Edmonton, Alberta: Alberta Environment.

Armitage, D. R. (2008) "Governance and the commons in a multi-level world." *International Journal of the Commons* 2(1): 7–32.

Bjornlund, H. (2003) "Efficient Water Market Mechanisms to Cope with Water Scarcity." *Water Resources Development* 19(4): 553–67.

British Columbia Ministry of Environment (2008) *Living Water Smart: British Columbia's Water Plan*. Victoria, BC: British Columbia Ministry of Environment.

Brouwer, R., Georgiou, S., and Turner, R. K. (2003) "Integrated Assessment and Sustainable Water and Wetland Management: A Review of Concepts and Methods." *Integrated Assessment* 4(3): 172–84.

Bruce, J. P. (2006) "Oil and Water – Will they Mix in a Changing Climate? The Athabasca River Story." In T. Tin (ed.), *Implications of a 2°C Global Temperature Rise on Canada's Water Resources*, pp. 12–35. Toronto, ON: World Wildlife Fund Canada.

Bruch, C. E. (2004) "New Tools for Governing International Watercourses." *Global Environmental Change Part A* 14(Supplement 1): 15–23.

Bruch, C., Jansky, L. Nakayama, M., and Salewicz, K. A. (eds) (2005) *Public Participation in the Governance of International Freshwater Resources*. Tokyo: United Nations University Press.

Calgary Herald (2008) "Energy Giant Eyes $5B Hydro Project." *Calgary Herald* (March 20). Available at www.canada.com/calgaryherald/news/calgarybusiness/story.html?id=c207bfed-c861-430f-aa4d-9ff8c2aab4b2.

Carter, N., Kreutzwiser, R. D., and de Loë, R. C. (2005) "Closing the Circle: Linking Land Use Planning and Water Management at the Local Level." *Land Use Policy* 22(2): 115–27.

Cech, T. V. (2003) *Principles of Water Resources: History, Development, Management and Policy*, 2nd edition. Hoboken, NJ: John Wiley.

de Loë, R. C. (2009) *Sharing the Waters of the Red River Basin: A Review of Options for Transboundary Water Governance*. Prepared for International Red Rivers Board, International Joint Commission. Guelph, ON: Rob de Loë Consulting Services.

de Loë, R. C., Armitage, D., Plummer, R., Davidson, S., and Moraru, L. (2009) *From Government to Governance: A State-of-the-Art Review of Environmental Governance, Final Report*. Prepared for Alberta Environment, Environmental Stewardship, Environmental Relations, Solicitation Number 2009/ES-001. Guelph, ON: Rob de Loë Consulting Services.

DeButts, J. (2009) "Supreme Court Denies Georgia Petition in Water War with Alabama." Available at www.bizjournals.com/birmingham/stories/2009/01/12/daily4.html.

Dellapenna, J. W. (2007) "Transboundary Water Sharing and the Need for Public Management." *Journal of Water Resources Planning and Management* 5(1): 397–404.

Draper, S. E. (2006) *Sharing Water in Times of Scarcity: Guidelines and Procedures in the Development of Effective Agreements to Share Water Across Political Boundaries*. Reston, VA: American Society of Civil Engineers.

Draper, S. E. and Kundell, J. E. (2008) "Impact of Climate Change on Transboundary

Water Sharing." *Journal of Water Resources Planning and Management* 133(5): 405–15.

Dyson, M., Bergkamp, G. and Scanlon, J. (2003) *Flow: The Essentials of Environmental Flows*. Gland: IUCN.

Environment Canada (2006) *A Primer on Freshwater*. Ottawa, ON: Environment Canada.

Falkenmark, M. (2003) "Freshwater as Shared between Society and Ecosystems: From Divided Approaches to Integrated Challenges." *Philosophical Transactions of the Royal Society B* 358: 2037–49.

Fischhendler, I. (2004) "Legal and Institutional Adaptation to Climate Uncertainty: A Study of International Rivers." *Water Policy* 6(4): 281–302.

Food and Agriculture Organization of the United Nations (1984) *Systematic Index of International Water Resources Treaties, Declarations, Acts and Cases, by Basin. Volume II.* Legislative Study 34. Rome: Food and Agriculture Organization of the United Nations.

Giordano, M. A. and Wolf, A. T. (2003) "Sharing Waters: Post-Rio International Water Management." *Natural Resources Forum* 27(2): 163–71.

GNWT (2007) *Energy for the Future: An Energy Plan for the Northwest Territories*. Yellowknife, NWT: Government of the Northwest Territories.

—— (2010a) *Northern Voices, Northern Waters: NWT Water Stewardship Strategy*. Yellowknife, NWT: Environment and Natural Resources.

—— (2010b) *State of the Environment Report*. Available at www.enr.gov.nt.ca/_live/pages/wpPages/soe_conservation_sustainable_use.aspx#3.

Government of Alberta (2010) *Investing in Our Future: Responding to the Rapid Growth of Oil Sands Development*. Available at www.alberta.ca/home/395.cfm.

Government of Canada, Government of British Columbia, Government of Alberta, Government of Saskatchewan, Government of the Yukon, and Government of the Northwest Territories (1997) *Mackenzie River Basin Transboundary Waters Master Agreement*. Available at www.mrbb.ca/information/31/index.html.

Grey, D. and Sadoff, C. (2003) "Beyond the River: The Benefits of Cooperation on International Rivers." *Water Science and Technology* 47(6): 91–6.

Holroyd, P. and Simieritsch, T. (2009) *The Water That Binds Us: Transboundary Implications of Oil Sands Development*. Drayton Valley, AB: The Pembina Institute.

Imperial, M. T. (2005) "Using Collaboration as a Governance Strategy: Lessons from Six Watershed Management Programs." *Administration and Society* 37(3): 281–320.

Jordan, J. L. and Wolf, A. T. (eds) (2006) *Interstate Water Allocation in Alabama, Florida and Georgia: New Issues, New Methods, New Models*. Gainesville, FL: University Press of Florida.

Karkkainen, B. (2005) "Transboundary Ecosystem Governance: Beyond Sovereignty?" In C. Bruch *et al.* (eds), *Public Participation in the Governance of International Freshwater Resources*, pp. 73–87. Tokyo: United Nations University Press.

Kashyap, A. (2004) "Water Governance: Learning by Developing Adaptive Capacity to Incorporate Climate Variability and Change." *Water Science and Technology* 49(7): 141–6.

Kelly, E. N., Short, J. W., Schindler, D. W., Hodson, P. D., Ma, M., Kwan, A. K., and Fortin, B. L. (2009) "Oil Sands Development Contributes Polycyclic Aromatic Compounds to the Athabasca River and its Tributaries." *Proceedings of the National Academy of Science* 106(52): 22,346–22,351.

Kelly, E. N., Schindler, D. W., Hodson, P. V., Short, J. W., Radmanovich, R., and Nielsen, C. C. (2010) "Oil Sands Development Contributes Elements Toxic at Low

Concentrations to the Athabasca River and its Tributaries." *Proceedings of the National Academy of Science* 107(37): 16,178–16,183.

Kistin, E. J. and Ashton, P. J. (2008) "Adapting to Change in Transboundary Rivers: An Analysis of Treaty Flexibility on the Orange-Senqu River Basin." *International Journal of Water Resources Development* 24(3): 385–400.

Kreutzwiser, R. and de Loë, R. (2010) "Water Security: Current and Emerging Challenges." In B. Mitchell (ed.), *Resource and Environmental Management in Canada: Addressing Conflict and Uncertainty*, 4th edn, 207–37. Toronto, ON: Oxford University Press.

Loures, F., Rieu-Clarke, A. and Vercambre, M. (2008) *Everything You Need to Know About the UN Watercourses Convention*. Gland: World Wildlife Fund.

Matthews, O. P. and St Germain, D. (2007) "Boundaries and Transboundary Water Conflicts." *Journal of Water Resources Planning and Management* 5(1): 386–96.

McCaffrey, S. C. (2003) "The Need for Flexibility in Freshwater Treaty Regimes." *Natural Resources Forum* 27(2): 156–62.

McCaffrey, S. (2008) "Convention on the Law of the Non-Navigational Uses of International Watercourses, New York, May 21, 1997." Available at http://legal.un.org/avl/ha/clnuiw/clnuiw.html.

McDonald, A. T. and Kay, D. (1988) *Water Resources: Issues and Strategies*. Harlow: Longman Scientific & Technical.

Milich, L. and Varady, R. G. (1998) "Managing Transboundary Resources: Lessons from River-Basin Accords." *Environment* 40(8): 10–15, 35–41.

Milly, P. C. D., Betancourt, J., Falkenmark, M., Lettenmaier, D., and Stouffer, R. J. (2008) "Stationarity is Dead: Whither Water Management." *Science* 319(5863): 573–4.

MRBB (2003) *Highlights of the Mackenzie River Basin Board's State of the Aquatic Ecosystem Report*. Fort Smith, NWT: Mackenzie River Basin Board.

—— (2009) *Bilateral Water Management Agreements Guidance Document*. Fort Smith, NWT: Mackenzie River Basin Board.

Murray, B. R., Zeppel, M. J. B., Hose, G. C., and Eamus, D. (2003) "Groundwater-Dependent Ecosystems in Australia: It's More than Just Water for Rivers." *Ecological Management and Restoration* 4(2): 110–13.

Muys, J. C., Sherk, G. W., and O'Leary, M. C. (2007) "Utton Transboundary Resources Center Model Interstate Water Compact." *Natural Resources Journal* 47(1): 17–115.

Nature Canada (2008) *Protect Canada's Last Wild River: Mackenzie River Important Bird Areas*. Ottawa, ON: Nature Canada.

Oborne, B. (2005) *Interprovincial Case Study: The Prairie Provinces Water Board Analysis of Water Strategies for the Prairie Watershed Region*. Working draft. Prepared as input to the Prairie Water Policy Symposium – a project of the International Institute for Sustainable Development. Available at www.iisd.org/pdf/2005/pwps_case_inter_prov.pdf.

Phare, M. A. (2009) *Denying the Source: The Crisis of First Nations Water Rights*. Victoria, BC: Rocky Mountain Books.

Phillips, D. J. H., Allan, D. J. A., Clausen, S., Granit, J., Jägerskog, A., Kistin, E., Patrick, M., and Turton, A. (2008) *The TWO Analysis: Introducing a Methodology for the Transboundary Waters Opportunity Analysis*. Report Number 23. Stockholm: Stockholm International Water Institute.

Prowse, T. D. and Conly, F. M. (2000) "Multiple-Hydrologic Stressors of a Northern Delta Ecosystem." *Journal of Aquatic Ecosystem Stress and Recovery* 8: 17–26.

Quinn, F. (1991) "As Long as the Rivers Run: The Impacts of Corporate Water

Development on Native Communities in Canada." *The Canadian Journal of Native Studies* 11(1): 137–54.

Richter, B. D., Mathews, R., and Wigington, R. (2003) "Ecologically Sustainable Water Management: Managing River Flows for Ecological Integrity." *Ecological Applications* 13(1): 206–24.

Saunders, J. O. and Wenig, M. (2006) "Whose Water? Canadian Water Management and the Challenges of Jurisdictional Fragmentation." In K. Bakker (ed.), *Eau Canada: The Future of Canada's Water*, pp. 119–41. Vancouver: University of British Columbia Press.

Schindler, D. W. and Donahue, W. F. (2006) "An Impending Water Crisis in Canada's Western Prairie Provinces." *Proceedings of the National Academy of Science* 103(19): 7,210–7,216.

Schindler, D. W., Donahue, W. F., and Thompson, J. P. (2007) "Future Water Flows and Human Withdrawals in the Athabasca River," In D. J. Davidson and A. Hurley (eds), *Running out of Steam? Oil Sands Development and Water Use in the Athabasca River Watershed: Science and Market based Solutions*, pp. 1–39. Toronto, ON: University of Toronto, Munk Centre for International Studies and University of Alberta, Environmental Research and Studies Centre.

Sengo, D. J., Kachapila, A., van der Zaag, P., Mul, M., and Nkomo, S. (2005) "Valuing Environmental Water Pulses into the Incomati Estuary: Key to Achieving Equitable and Sustainable Utilisation of Transboundary Waters." *Physics and Chemistry of the Earth* 30(11–16; Special Issue): 648–57.

Shmueli, D. F. (1999) "Water Quality in International River Basins." *Political Geography* 18(4): 437–76.

Statistics Canada (2010) "Population by Year, by Province and Territory." Available at www40.statcan.gc.ca/l01/cst01/demo02a-eng.htm.

Swatuk, L. A. (2005) "Political Challenges to Implementing IWRM in Southern Africa." *Physics and Chemistry of the Earth* 30: 872–80.

Swatuk, L. A. and Wirkus, L. (eds) (2009) *Transboundary Water Governance in Southern Africa: Examining Underexplored Dimensions*. Baden-Baden: Nomos Verlagsgesellschaft.

Tarlock, A. D. and Wouters, P. (2007) "Are Shared Benefits of International Waters an Equitable Apportionment?" *Colorado Journal of International Environmental Policy* 18(3): 523–36.

Uitto, J. I. and Duda, A. M. (2002) "Management of Transboundary Water Resources: Lessons from International Cooperation for Conflict Prevention." *The Geographical Journal* 168(4): 365–78.

van der Zaag, P. and Vaz, A. C. (2003) "Sharing the Incomati Waters: Cooperation and Competition in the Balance." *Water Policy* 5: 349–68.

Warner, J., Philippus, W., and Bolding, A. (2008) "Going with the Flow: River Basins as the Natural Units for Water Management?" *Water Policy* 10(2): 121–38.

Wolf, A. T., Kramer, A., Carius, A., and Dabelko, G. D. (2005) "Managing Water Conflict and Cooperation." In E Assadourian *et al.* (ed.), *State of the World 2005: Redefining Global Security*, pp. 80–95. Washington, DC: WorldWatch Institute.

WWF (2005) *Implications of a 2°C Global Temperature Rise on Canada's Water Resources, Athabasca River and Oil Sands Development, Great Lakes and Hydropower Production*. Gland: World Wildlife Fund.

WWF-Canada (2009) *Rivers at Risk: Environmental Flows and Canada's Freshwater Future*. Toronto, ON: WWF-Canada.

8 The unintentional and intentional recharge of aquifers in the Tula and the Mexico Valleys

The megalopolis needs mega solutions?

Blanca Jiménez Cisneros

Introduction

A significant proportion of the wastewater produced in Mexico is used for the irrigation of agricultural land located in arid and semiarid areas. In 1995, 102 m^3 per second of wastewater was used to irrigate 257,000 ha over the whole country. One example of this situation is the Tula Valley, where the wastewater produced by the 21 million inhabitants of Mexico City is used for agricultural irrigation. Due to the type of soil and the amount of water used for crops, the local aquifers are being recharged. Groundwater supplies new springs and wells, and is used as a water source for 500,000 inhabitants. In addition, the recharge of the non-saturated soil has formed a new aquifer (recharging the non-saturated zone) that is being considered as a possible new water source for Mexico City, due to its water quality and quantity characteristics. The chapter describes how this situation came about and discusses ways to properly manage this "new water source," taking into consideration the different needs of both regions. The reuse of this wastewater will link the needs and interests of both groups of people.

Mexico City water use

Mexico City was founded by the Aztecs in 1325 and was named Tenochtitlan. When the Spanish arrived, in 1519, Tenochtitlan was a megacity with an area of 15 km^2 and 200,000 inhabitants, at least 10 and 20 times greater than the populations of Paris and London, respectively, at that time. Tenochtitlan was built in a natural closed basin with five main lakes. The city was located on an island connected to the land by four streets. Due to urban expansion and the fear of urban flooding felt by the Spanish and then subsequent governments, the valley was artificially dried by sending wastewater, lake water, and excess pluvial precipitation to the Tula Valley. Today only two small fragments of the original lakes remain within the metropolitan area. Mexico City currently has 21 million inhabitants and a surface area of 8,084 km^2 (808.4 ha) for a population density of 2,598 inhabitants per km^2, and is responsible for 21 percent of the GDP (gross domestic product) of the country (Jiménez 2008a). Mexico City has expanded into the so-called "metropolitan area" that includes the Federal District (DF), and

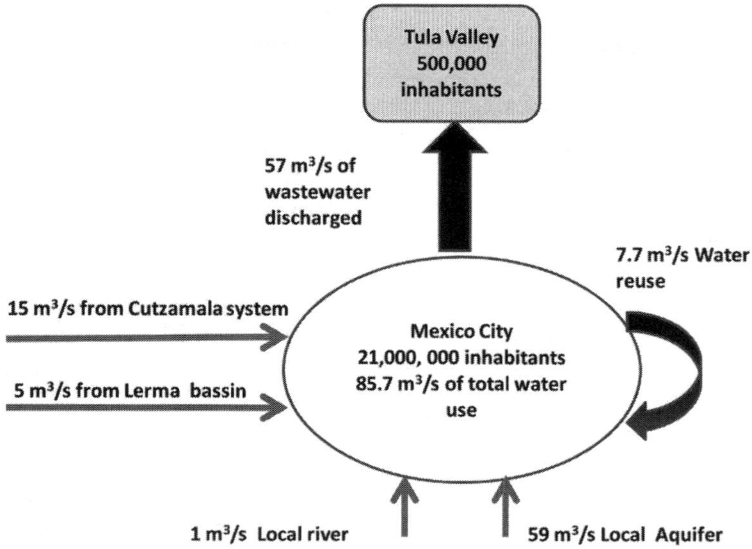

Figure 8.1 Water supply and discharge for Mexico City

also 37 municipalities of the State of Mexico. Each of these political entities manage water independently, but coordinate the disposal of their wastewater via the same infrastructure and to the same site. The intense economic activity of Mexico City combined with a huge population living in a city located at high altitude (2,220 meters asl) has created a complex water problem, related not only to supply but also to wastewater disposal.

Water sources and use

The Mexico City Valley has a mean annual temperature of 15°C, and a pluvial precipitation of 700 mm per year, varying from 600 mm in the north to 1,500 mm in the south. The rainy season is well defined; it extends from May to October and is characterized by intense showers lasting for short periods during the day. One single storm may produce 10–15 percent of the mean annual pluvial precipitation. As a consequence, in the Mexico Valley there are few perennial rivers, with the majority carrying water only during the rainy season (Jiménez 2009).

As Mexico City grew, water sources other than the local springs needed to be exploited. In 1847 – when the population was 0.5 million people – local groundwater began to be extracted from artesian wells 105 m deep. By the year 1857, there were 168 wells. Later, in 1942, when the population reached 2 million, water had to be imported from the Lerma Lake, 300 m above Mexico City and 100 km away, in the State of Mexico. In 1951 the Lerma groundwater began to be exploited, since the lake was almost depleted. Finally, when the population reached 7 million in 1975, surface water was imported from the Cutzamala basin, 130 km away and 1,100 m below Mexico City (Figure 8.2). The transfer of water from the Lerma and Cutzamala basins, located west of Mexico City, caused negative environmental and social impacts. The population of Lerma used to depend on sustainable fisheries, but due to over-extraction of groundwater to supply Mexico City, the Lerma Lake began to disappear and the local inhabitants had to become farmers to subsist. Furthermore, local inhabitants stopped using surface water to supply themselves, and instead began to extract their own water from deep wells. The Chapala Lake (the main lake in Mexico, located in the Lerma-Chapala Basin that was partly fed by the Lerma River) experienced a 5 m reduction in its level, compared to its maximum historical level. To reduce groundwater overexploitation in the Valley of Mexico basin, the flow to Mexico City has been reduced from the original 7 m^3 per second to only 3 m^3 per second. The transference of water from the Cutzamala basin has also reduced, from its original value of 20 m^3 per second to 15 m^3 per second since 2008 (and in drier periods even less). This can be attributed to a decrease in the amount of water stored in the Cutzamala dam system, due to a reduction in precipitation caused by the El Niño Southern Oscillation (ENSO). The reduced availability of water in the whole Cutzamala dam system has also reduced the amount of water available for power generation, and led to the loss of a large area of irrigated agricultural land

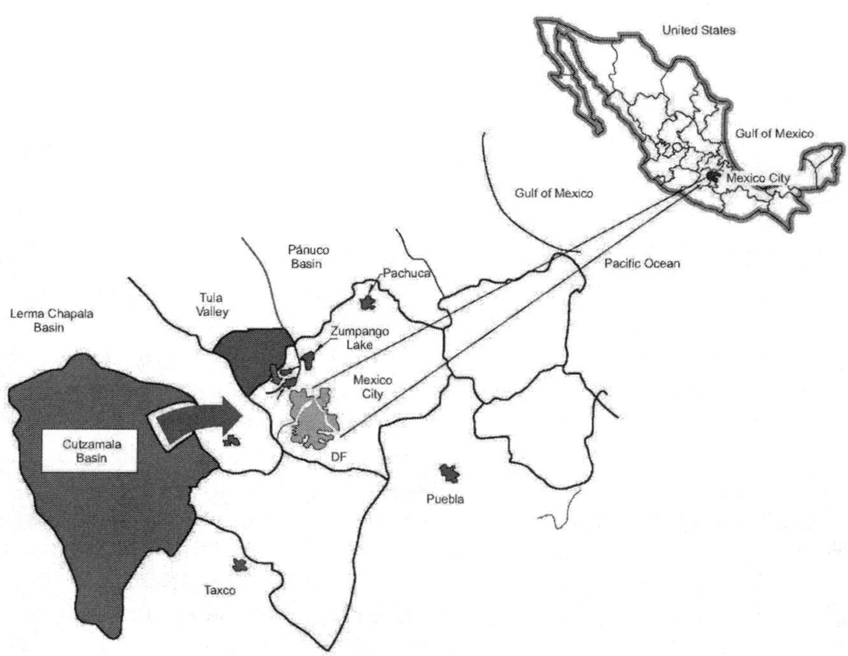

Figure 8.2 External water sources for Mexico City

(Jiménez 2009). Faced by this situation, the federal government made plans to incorporate additional sources of water into the Cutzamala system, but construction of the project was halted due to social pressure. The internationally renowned "Mazahuan Women's Movement to Defend Water" was created to stop the process. The roots of this movement lie in the fact that even though the Cutzamala system has been providing water to Mexico City for many years, the people of the region lack basic water services.

At the present time, Mexico City uses 85.7 m^3 per second of water (Figure 8.1); 57 percent of this is supplied through public mains, 34 percent is pumped by farmers and some industries directly from the local aquifer, and the remaining 9 percent is treated wastewater used for lawn irrigation, industrial cooling, landscape irrigation, fountains, car washing and the filling of lakes and canals for recreational and environmental use.

First-use water (78 m^3 per second) comes from:

- 1,965 wells that pump 59 m^3 per second from the local aquifer;
- a local river located in the southern part of the city (1 m^3 per second);
- the Lerma aquifer (3 m^3 per second); and
- the Cutzamala dam system (15 m^3 per second).

The last two sources are located in other basins. Water is used mostly for municipal purposes (74 percent), followed by fresh water irrigation (16 percent), self-supplied industries (2 percent) and for non-drinking water reuse (1 percent). Agriculture is practiced over 40,000 ha of the valley to produce flowers and vegetables that are sold in the city.

Municipal use

Water supply services have 89 percent coverage for the population within DF, and a lower and varied percentage in the municipalities of the State of Mexico. The service is provided through a water network but also through the use of water tanks. Poor families not connected to the network receive a limited amount of water twice a week at no cost, but they have to carry it considerable distances themselves from water tanks or distribution fountains to their homes. These distances may be small when compared to rural areas but they are still significant on the urban scale. Richer people not connected to the water network buy water from the local government at a rate of 8 m^3 (a water tanker) every two months for US$6.2. However, if they need more water or the supply quota has been met, they buy water on the black market at a price of around US$70 per 8 m^3. In DF alone, the number of people not connected to the network is around 1.15 million. No reliable data are available for the population of the municipalities of the State of Mexico, but it is estimated another 1.2 million people live there. Prior its distribution, groundwater is treated with chlorine and water from surface sources (Cutzamala and a local river) is treated through coagulation-flocculation, sedimentation, and chlorination.

The amount of water supplied to the city represents a daily per capita water use of 255 L. However, 40 percent of water is lost through leaks, so people actually receive an average of 153 L each per day, a value that falls within the 150–170 L per person per day range recommended by WHO (1995) for urban areas. In fact, the actual use of water varies according to social class. The upper classes, representing 5 percent of the population, use more than four times the amount used by members of the lower classes connected to the network, but 30–50 times more than people receiving water via tankers.

In general, in Mexico, tap water is considered unsafe to drink. Data from isolated academic studies show that drinking water prepared from groundwater contains nitrates and organochloride compounds at concentrations higher than US EPA drinking water standards of 200 μg per litre (USEPA 2004), especially during the dry season (Mazari-Hiriart *et al.* 1999). These same authors reported the presence of total coliforms, fecal coliforms, fecal Streptococcus, and pathogenic bacteria in water from wells before but also after chlorination. They isolated 84 microorganisms of nine genera all associated with human fecal pollution. One of these was *Helicobacter pylori*, a bacterium associated with gastric ulcers and cancer (Mazari-Hiriart *et al.* 2002). In addition, it has been shown that water quality deteriorates during distribution (Jiménez 2009). The water network operates at low pressure due to insufficient and intermittent water supply across the city. To ensure access to water throughout the day, people must use individual storage tanks (called *tinacos*). In low-pressure pipelines and through the use of water tanks, water quality deteriorates further. Official information is considered unreliable and insufficient. The best source of public information is the DF local government, but this relates only to the bacterial (types of bacteria unspecified) and free residual chlorine content at the exit of chlorination systems for only some sites within the network. The Ministry of Health of the federal government, tasked with assessing the quality of drinking water, occasionally provides data. As an example, the institution COFEPRIS reported in 2009 that the water distributed to the Federal District through the network fulfilled the level of free chlorine set by the norm in 94 percent of the 19 samples taken for the whole city, and that 7.5 percent of the total population was at bacteriological risk. This population was concentrated in only three of the 16 neighborhoods in DF, in an area to the south of the city where natural aquifer recharge occurs due to the volcanic soil. In this area, sewerage services are not provided or sanitation facilities consist of latrines (Durán *et al.* 2010).

Official information concerning the chemical characteristics of drinking water is even less readily available. In 1994, it was reported that only 64 percent of the drinking water from the Federal District fulfilled the required physicochemical parameters. These parameters were color, alkalinity, hardness, total solids, iron, manganese, ammonia, and organic nitrogen (although nitrate concentration is more commonly used to assess the quality of groundwater, this was not reported). The neighborhoods with these problems are the same as those mentioned previously located to the south of the city, and others located to the southwest, where ancient landfills used to be in operation.

Regardless of the quantity and quality of information available, most families do not drink tap water directly. In order to ensure the quality of drinking water, people either buy bottled water, boil water, add chemical disinfectants or buy their own potabilization systems (filtration with ozone or UV light, or filters with colloidal silver). The cost of these systems at least doubles the price of tap water (Jiménez 2009). A family of four earning four times the minimum wage spends 6–10 percent of its income on bottled water or potabilizing tap water at home.

The need for alternative water supply options

It is estimated that in order to continuously supply water to Mexico City's entire population through the network, there is a need for 1–2 m^3 per second of water; to provide 240 L per person per day to the entire population, an additional 5 m^3 per second are needed. To prevent overexploitation and inject water to control soil subsidence, at least 15 m^3 per second of additional water are required. Therefore in total 22 m^3 per second of water are needed (Jiménez 2009). Where to take it from has become a major concern for the different local and also federal governments. Under the present scenario, the Mexico Valley aquifer is being overexploited by at least 117 percent of the natural recharge and is creating an increasingly significant soil subsidence problem. In fact, the 7 m of subsidence that occurred in 1957 was the root of the decision to import water from other basins. Following this, wells located in the central part of the city were closed. Nevertheless, to cope with the water demand of a still-growing population, new wells were opened in the southern and northern part of the city, where it was thought they would have a much smaller effect on subsidence (Santoyo *et al.* 2005). However, the continuous extraction of water from new wells coupled with urban growth in the area of natural recharge are still causing soil subsidence, which progresses at different rates over the city. This causes what is referred to as "differential sinking," with rates as high as 40 cm a year, resulting in different negative impacts, such as the loss of drainage capacity from the sewerage system (which used to work entirely by gravity). To recover the original capacity of 40 m^3 per second one of the sewer drains (the Gran Canal), which was reduced to only 15 m^3 per second due to the loss of slope (Figure 8.3), a pumping station was built in 2008 to raise wastewater 30 m, at a cost of US$30,000. Before this pumping system began operation, the wastewater that could not be conveyed by the Gran Canal needed to be transported through the Deep Drainage System. This was critical as the drainage system operated for nearly 12 years without maintenance, and 400 km^2 of the city was at risk of flooding with 1.2 m of wastewater, affecting at least 4 million people (Domínguez-Mora *et al.* 2005). Maintenance of the Deep Drainage System was finally performed in 2009 at a cost of around US$19 million. In addition, the construction of an additional deep sewer had to be initialized at a cost of US$1 billion.

A total of 20–30 floods occur in Mexico City per year with a mixture of pluvial and wastewater (SACM 2006). The investment needed to recover wastewater drainage capacity in the Gran Canal alone is US$305 million (Jiménez 2009).

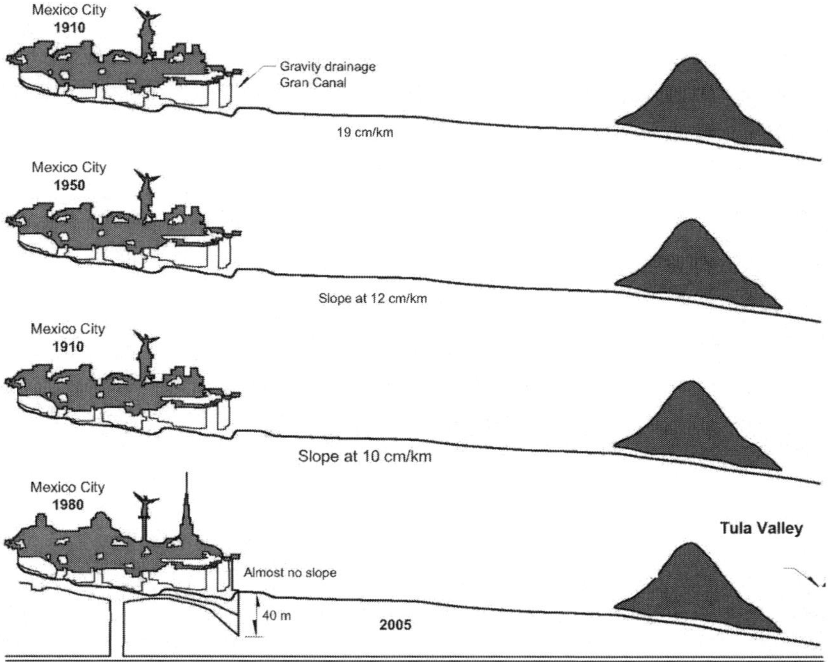

Figure 8.3 Change in the slope of the drainage system because of soil subsidence

Despite all of these efforts, floods of wastewater in the city are still frequent. Some of them have had severe effects. For example, in February 2010, 4,000 houses and 485 schools were flooded in several municipalities in the State of Mexico. One sewer broke apart, resulting in a 60 m long hole. This caused the level of wastewater to rise by up to 1.70 m. Several low-income families lost all of their property, and it cost the government US$2.5 million to repair the hydraulic infrastructure and to partially pay damages. In July 2010 new floods occurred. More recently, in 2011, three floods affected more than 1 million poor people with levels of up to 1 m of wastewater. Many of these people lost all of their already few belongings.

Serious structural problems in buildings. As soil sinks differentially, buildings are affected. Considering the historic buildings (for which a survey has been performed), 46 have been identified as severely damaged (Santoyo *et al.* 2005). Due to its historic value, Mexico City Cathedral is being repaired. It is estimated that in the last 50 years, differential sinking has led to an 87 cm difference between the level of the apse and the western bell tower, partly due to water over-exploitation. The total investment required to redress the situation was US$32.5 million in 2000 (Santoyo and Ovando-Shelley 2002).

Differential sinking put stress on water mains, sewers, oil pipelines and tanks that are located below ground. For the water supply network, this is one of the main causes of leaks. Losses of around 37–40 percent of water are experienced within the system, representing a total water loss of 23 m^3 per second, or in economic terms US$56 million (considering the lowest municipal water tariff for the city of 1 peso per m^3, or US$0.08 per m^3). No data on the effects on the sewer, oil pipelines, and tanks are reported.

Due to soil subsidence, the metro rails need to be leveled each year, and in some parts accumulated changes are compromising its operation. In addition to soil subsidence, groundwater overexploitation is causing groundwater quality to deteriorate. Different research studies (Jiménez 2009) show that the TSS content has increased from 1,000 to 20,000 mg per litre, the sodium content from 50–100 to 600–800 per litre, the ammoniacal nitrogen content from 0–0.03 to 6–9 per litre, and the iron content from < 0.1 to 3–6 per litre. The sources of these pollutants are different; in some cases it is the intrusion of water from the saline aquitard above the groundwater, in others it is the intrusion of leachates from landfills or wastewater from sewers.

What are the future water supply options?

As discussed previously, at least 22 m^3 per second of water is needed to redress the situation. Part of this volume could come, and actually is coming, from a leakage control program. Controlling leaks does not affect groundwater recharge, as most of the city lies on an impervious clay layer above the aquifer, and therefore water leaks collect in the deep drainage system. However, considering its cost (US$1.5 million to sectorize and control pressure in the water network, plus US$500,000 per year to repair and change deteriorated pipelines), another source of water is needed. Furthermore, as the time required to complete this program is very long (around 50 years) there is a need to either transfer water from other basins (far from Mexico City) or to implement a program to reuse water for human consumption.

Table 8.1 compares the cost of different alternatives, including water reuse. The cheapest option, importing water from Temascaltepec (part of the Cutzamala system), is not viable due to opposition by local people. The Amacuzac and the Tecolutla options require the pumping of water from 1,700 and 1,266 m below the level of Mexico City respectively, and hence their feasibility is tightly linked to the future price of energy. As a result, Mexico City is seriously considering the reclamation of its own wastewater for human consumption. Among the options to reclaim wastewater, one directly uses the wastewater produced and treated at the Mexico Valley, and another considers its use after treatment in the Mexico Valley and its utilization for agricultural irrigation and groundwater infiltration in the Tula Valley. The latter is considered the safest option and will be thus discussed in more detail in the next section.

Table 8.1 Cost of future water supply options for Mexico City

Projects	*Difference in altitude (m)*	*USD/m³*
Amacuzac	1,700	2.36
Tecolutla	1,266	2.13
Temascaltepec	1,570	0.75
Tula	300	0.72
Potabilization *in situ* of the wastewater	0	1.00
Potabilization *in situ*, reinjection and extraction for water supply	0	1.30

Source: adapted from Jiménez (2009)

Mexico City's wastewater

The sewerage coverage for the population of DF is 94 percent, but decreases to 85 percent as mean value for the municipalities of the State of Mexico. As mentioned previously, part of the wastewater produced in Mexico City (7.7 m^3 per second) is collected and treated in local wastewater treatment plants to be reused in the city. The remainder, 57 m^3 per second, is transported away from the Mexico Valley.

In the metropolitan area, there are at least 91 wastewater treatment plants, 27 operated by the DF government, 44 by private companies or different federal institutions (Ex-Texcoco Lake Commission, the Federal Electricity Commission and the army), and 20 by different municipalities of the State of Mexico (Merino 2000). The total amount of wastewater treated in public facilities is 7.7 m^3 per second and all is reused. Reuse began in 1956 for landscape irrigation. At the present time, reused water is used to fill recreational lakes and canals (54 percent), to irrigate agricultural land and green areas over a total area of 6,500 ha (31 percent), industrial cooling (8 percent), car and street washing (5 percent), and to recharge the local aquifer (2 percent). There is no data on the total amount of wastewater treated privately, but it is known that all of it is reused for lawn irrigation or cooling. Considering that 100 percent of the treated wastewater is reused, equivalent to 12 percent of the wastewater produced, Mexico City is among the world's most intensive reusers of wastewater.[1] One of the biggest public reuse projects is the Ex-Texcoco Lake project. Within this, a plant has been used to treat 0.6 m^3 per second of wastewater since the 1980s, to produce water originally intended for agricultural irrigation and to restore part of one of the original lakes of the valley. The project consists of an activated sludge treatment plant, followed by maturation ponds that produce water to feed a 1,380 ha artificial lake. Treated wastewater is successfully used to refill the lake, creating an environment in which a wide variety of birds from Canada and the United States live during the winter. Recovering part of the Texcoco Lake was also very important to control the dust storms of which the city frequently suffered that were formed during late winter by the wind carrying fine dust from the ancient lake bed. Unfortunately, the high evaporation rate of the region that concentrates salts in water, and the leaching of salts from the extremely saline soil at the bottom of the lake both act to increase the salinity of the treated water, rendering it unusable for agricultural irrigation.

Disposal of Mexico City's wastewater

Mexico City's wastewater has been sent to the Tula Valley since 1789, where it has been used for agricultural irrigation since 1896. The use of wastewater quickly became a source of livelihoods as it enabled agriculture and, furthermore, allowed crops to be produced all year round instead of being limited by rainfall only. Realizing these advantages, the farmers requested the government to implement an irrigation system, and construction began in 1920. The inauguration of this irrigation district by the government was an informal recognition of the legality, or at least the tolerance, of the use of non-treated wastewater to irrigate. Later, in 1955, the farmers requested the concession of Mexico City's wastewater from the president. This was subsequently granted for 26 m^3 per second – at that time the total flow rate of wastewater to be disposed of (Jiménez 2008b, 2009). At the present time, the irrigation infrastructure is still owned by the government, in contrast to the rest of the country where the entire infrastructure has been transferred to farmers. It comprises nine dams (three containing freshwater and six wastewater), three rivers, and 858 km of water distribution or irrigation canals. The irrigated area is around 95,000 ha. The region, colloquially known as the Mezquital Valley, has been considered since 1989 the largest area continuously irrigated with wastewater in the world (Figure 8.4). The Mezquital Valley is located in the Tula Valley in the State of Hidalgo, 100 km north of Mexico City. It has a population of 500,000, distributed over 4,100 km^2 and 294 localities. The altitude of the Valley varies from 2,100 m in its southern part, closest to Mexico City, to 1,700 m in the northern part (Jiménez 2008a, 2008b). The climate is semi-arid, with a mean annual temperature of 17°C, annual rainfall of 527 mm, and evapotranspiration of 1,750 mm. The economy is based mainly on agriculture.

The agricultural soils, in general, were low in organic matter content and needed to be supplied with water and nutrients to become productive (Siebe 1998). This was provided by applying non-treated wastewater. Corn and alfalfa for use as fodder are the main crops (60–80 percent of the area), followed by oats, barley, wheat and some vegetables (chili, Italian zucchini and beetroot; Siebe 1994). A large proportion of the produce is sold in Mexico City markets, but it is also used locally. The wastewater nutrient content has improved crop yields between 67 and 150 percent for corn, barley, tomato, oatmeal, alfalfa, chili, and wheat, depending on the type of crop, when compared with produce irrigated with clean water. The reliability of wastewater all year round means that two to three crops per year can be raised instead of just one (Jiménez 2008b). For this reason, land with access to wastewater is rented at US$455 per hectare per year instead of the US$183 per hectare per year charged in areas using rainwater only. Certainly the most visible impact is the boom in the local economy. The

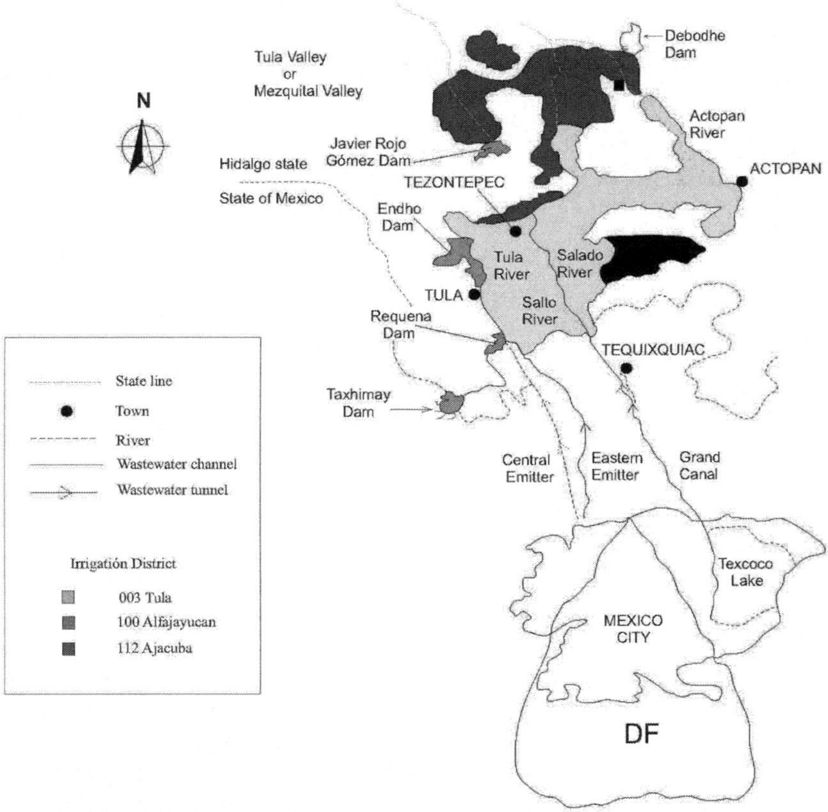

Figure 8.4 Mexico City's wastewater disposal drainage system and the main components of the irrigation system in the Tula Valley

Source: Jiménez (2008a)

Mezquital Valley was once a region so poor that the government considered moving the indigenous people to other sites because their land was not able to produce food. Nowadays the situation has radically changed, and it is one of the most productive irrigation districts. Even though these positive impacts are recognized, others, which are negative, have occurred. The two most important ones concern health effects provoked by the use of wastewater and the recharge of the aquifer with it. With respect to the former, Cifuentes *et al.* (1992) showed that diarrheal diseases caused by helminths (worms) have increased 16-fold in children under 14 years of age. Severe helminthioses are a cause of undernourishment that results in decreased physical and mental development (10–15 cm in height and 10–20 IQ points; Moore *et al.* 2001; Berkman *et al.* 2002). As mentioned previously, the second impact concerns the incidental recharge of the aquifer with the wastewater used to irrigate. This is a consequence of the transportation and storage of wastewater in unlined channels and dams, but is also due to the irrigation method (flood and furrow) and the excess of water applied to control salinity in soil. The recharge of the aquifer with wastewater has been reported since 1975, when Payne and Latorre estimated that 90-100 percent of the aquifer recharge volume in Tula Valley was formed by Mexico City's wastewater. In 1997, the recharge rate was estimated by the British Geological Survey and the National Water Commission (BGS-CNA 1998) to be at least 25 m^3 per second for only one of the irrigation districts located within the Tula Valley. This flow represents 13 times the amount produced through natural recharge (Jiménez and Chavez 2004). Within the Tula Valley, a large part of the high ground is composed of volcanic rock of varying age and composition, and calcareous sediments (BGS-CNA 1998). From the hydrogeological point of view, studies of this region show the presence of three overlapping aquifers. The upper or first aquifer is a shallow non-confined system of variable depth. It is recharged by surface infiltration and lateral groundwater contributions. Transmissivities range between 0.0001 and 0.001 m^2 per second. Most of the water supplies in this system come from springs. The lower or second aquifer is located in the basaltic zone with some volcanic ash and lava intervals. Transmissivities are 0.01 m^2 per second or higher, therefore it is more productive than the upper aquifer. The third aquifer is located within Cretaceous limestone; and on some occasions it behaves as a water-table aquifer.

The intense recharge of the groundwater with non-treated wastewater for more than 110 years has considerably raised the groundwater level. Between 1938 and 1990, the groundwater level rose 15–30 m, and dozens of new springs were formed with flows varying from 0.1 to 0.6 m^3 per second. In some areas, the emerging water has even caused water logging, growth of hydrophilic vegetation and loss of large volumes of water due to evapotranspiration. As a result of being fed by additional groundwater, the Tula River flow increased from 1.6 m^3 per second to more than 12.7 m^3 per second between 1945 and 1995. All of these new sources are used as supply by the 500,000 inhabitants and for several economic activities. A total of 6 m^3 per second is used for agricultural irrigation (38 percent), industry (33 percent), human consumption (17 percent), and other uses (12 percent). Water is extracted from 283 springs and wells. Prior to distribution to households, water is only chlorinated (Jiménez and Chavez 2004). In 1938, the change in the water quality of wells began to be noticed. When, in 1995, it was officially acknowledged (although not publicly) that infiltrating wastewater was the origin, several studies were begun to assess water quality (Jiménez 2008a, 2008b). Up to now, five different assessments have been performed, utilizing local and internationally certified laboratories. All of these studies have highlighted the same water quality problems but have also shown the improvement of the quality from the wastewater used to irrigate to the water infiltrated into the aquifer. The quality of the water found in the aquifer is so improved that it is considered similar to that of any other used water source. Table 8.2, which presents data from several monitoring studies comprising at least 30 sampling points, shows that problems are related mainly to a dissolved salt content greater than 1,000 mg per litre, fecal coliforms, and in some cases nitrates and fluorides. These

Table 8.2 Number of sites that did not meet the Mexican drinking water standards. In total 34 sampling sites were considered in three monitoring campaigns covering the dry and wet season, with analysis performed in triplicate

Parameter	*Sites not complying with drinking water standards*		*Mexican drinking water standard*
	Number %	*Volume %*	
Dissolved solids	64	95	1,000 mg/L
Sodium	38	73	200 mg/L
Fecal coliforms	42	25	0 MPN/100 mL
Nitrates	31	12	10 mgN/L
Chlorides	24	10	250 mg/L
Hardness	31	9	500 mg$CaCO_3$/L
Sulfates	18	2	400 mgSO_4/L
Fluorides	18	1	1.5 mgF/L
No problem	13	5	

Source: adapted from Jiménez and Chavez (2004)

pollutants originate from wastewater, as has been demonstrated by the BGS-CNA 1998 study. The analysis performed covered 288 parameters in total, including different types of pathogens, pesticides, organic compounds, and toxicity tests, and showed that the water fulfilled the requirements of a regular source of water, or that at least the pollutants it contained were also found in water sources used as supply. More recent studies targeting emerging compounds showed that although these compounds are contained in Mexico City's wastewater, their presence in the Tula Valley aquifers and springs is in most cases undetectable, and for the others the content is very low and restricted to a small number of sites (e.g., carbamazepine; for other pollutants consult Gibson *et al.* 2007; Durán-Álvarez *et al.* 2009; Durán *et al.* 2010).

Health effects due to the water supply in the Tula Valley

As local people have been drinking water from the new water sources for many years, a risk assessment was performed. According to health experts (Cifuentes *et al.* 2002), the main short-term risks associated with the use of non-conventional water sources relate to the presence of *Vibrio cholerae* NO-01 and other pathogens. According to Downs *et al.* (2002), health risks are possible at sites where the fecal coliform content is above 2,000 MPN per 100 mL. To date, health risks appear to be reasonably controlled by chlorine addition as no massive outbreaks have been reported in the region. In contrast, high nitrate and nitrite values (up to 29 mg N per litre), exceeding the Mexican drinking water norm 3–4-fold, are a concern. However, no methemoglobinemia in infants has been reported. This concurs with a recent publication prepared on behalf of the World Health Organization by Fewtrell (2004) highlighting the fact that although it is assumed in WHO guidelines that a high nitrate content in drinking water may cause methemoglobinemia in infants, it now appears that nitrates may be only one of a number of co-factors that play a sometimes complex role in causing the disease. Moreover, nitrates have been removed from the WHO drinking water guidelines since 2011. Research studies to quantitatively assess health risks from recently detected organic compounds have not yet been performed. However, from the point of view of policy makers, they should be removed from water if used as supply for Mexico City.

Will the people of Mexico City be drinking the Tula Valley groundwater?

As discussed previously, aquifer recharge with wastewater used to irrigate occurs at a rate of at least 25 m^3 per second. During storage, transportation and the use of this water to irrigate, it is cleaned by different physical, chemical, and biological mechanisms, producing water with a quality at least equal to many groundwater sources used for Mexico City (Downs *et al.* 2002). The use of this water by the local population, even if it poses some ethical questions, is also proof that water can be safely used. Nevertheless, the presence of emerging pollutants in some of the sources of the Tula Valley is a concern that deserves independent analysis, as the government decides whether this water should be used as supply for Mexico City, and even for the Tula Valley. For this reason several assessment studies and pilot plant tests using membrane treatment processes are ongoing, so far with promising results. In order for this option to be sustainable, three requisites need to be met:

1. Independently of the present natural treatment given by the agricultural soil to Mexico City's wastewater, it is necessary to treat it in order to fulfill the norms, control the health risks created by the use of the wastewater to irrigate but also to maintain the soils' pollution-removing capacity, which in some places seems to have already been exceeded (Jiménez 2008b).
2. A detailed project needs to be developed in order to assess the social viability of installing several wells to extract a total of 6 m^3 per second, in an area where land is considered to be shared and communal property. In addition, the cost of transporting water back to the city 100 km away and with a difference in height of 150 m needs to be considered in terms of future energy prices.
3. Political negotiations are needed. Although by law, groundwater belongs to the nation, Hidalgo's population considers that groundwater is "theirs" and that Mexico City should pay for it and for the environmental service of having it cleaned.

In addition, the project to reuse water in Mexico City once it has been used for irrigation in the Tula Valley has a number of advantages. The first is that it allows the Tula Valley to continue using the water for their needs. Conversely, if on-site reuse of Mexico City wastewater is selected then almost no water will be available for Tula. The second benefit is that the extraction of groundwater helps to control the salinization and flooding problems observed in the lower agricultural fields of the Tula Valley due to the rise in the groundwater level.[2] The third, relating to Mexico City itself, is that the potabilization process for wastewater cleaned by the soil is cheaper when compared to treating a secondary effluent to drinking quality on-site.

Lessons learned

From this example there are several lessons to be learned. Perhaps the most important is that you can never predict when you will be downstream of your own effluent, moreover you can never predict if you are going to need it. In the future, water reuse for human consumption may be the case for several (or at least some) populations located in arid and semiarid regions, especially if care is not taken to put precautions in place to limit local population growth. In the case of Mexico City, the lesson to be learned should be that population growth may have a limit in terms of water availability. The city was at its limit in hydraulic terms when it reached a population of around 8 million. Although some researchers pointed this out, the city still grew by another 12 million inhabitants. Currently, the city is still growing and there are no plans to control it. Other lessons learned are:

- A megalopolis needs special forms of government in order to be able to manage the related problems in their entirety, notably those related to water.
- Unusual situations provide excellent opportunities to provide innovative solutions and to move toward truly integrated management of water.
- The so-called "inefficient" use of water by agriculture is in fact not an inefficient use. Water is just being transported to another compartment of the environment where it can be used once again, sometimes to produce even better quality water.

There is a need to set up an ethics committee to evaluate the way in which human effects are being studied and interpreted by politicians and private companies. This committee should also analyze the cases in which cities are using the environment in other regions' environment to depollute their water. This could include the adoption of ecosystem service payments.

Options to better manage water in the Mexico Valley

Due to the complexity of the problem there is no single solution, but rather a whole set. These include:

- *The creation of a metropolitan water authority*. In order to integrally manage water sources in the valley it is important to have a unique water authority with a sufficient budget and the capacity to make decisions. Interestingly, a metropolitan commission to manage air pollution for the metropolitan area of Mexico City was easily and quickly put in place, and its actions have significantly reduced air pollution within the city. A similar plan for water has experienced a number of barriers since many different interests are involved.

- *The creation of an integrated water management program*. This should consider surface and groundwater, local and external sources, and the quantity, quality and the uses of water over the short, medium and long term. This program needs to be accepted by society in order to ensure its implementation independently of the political parties that govern each of the municipalities of the metropolitan area.
- *Exchange of reclaimed water* with the groundwater used for agricultural irrigation within Mexico Valley. This is a program planned from the technical perspective. However, social and economic aspects still need to be included to allow its successful implementation.
- *Education*. People must be educated in the efficient use water in order to protect and preserve its quality. The target audience for such educational programs is not only society in general, but also specific groups of society that have not been previously exposed to the idea. A good example is government workers. In many public offices high consumption toilets are still used and leaks from washrooms are often uncontrolled.
- *Economic tools*. In Mexico the price of water is highly subsidized. To redress this situation, the Federal District has recently raised water tariffs, but since the use of water is low given its scarcity, elasticity of the water tariff is almost nonexistent, and therefore the use of tariffs as mechanisms to reduce water demand is largely useless.
- *Public campaigns to save water*. The present governments (of both the Federal District and the State of Mexico) invest a significant proportion of their budget in media campaigns to encourage society to save water. However, as discussed above, the amount of water that most of the population is actually receiving and using would be classified under the category of efficient use of water for urban areas. Therefore instead of investing money on these types of campaigns, greater investment should be made in leakage control programs.
- *Rainwater harvesting*. Mexico City receives significant pluvial precipitation at an average rate of 12 m^3 per second. Rainwater is partly responsible for the urban flooding problem. Rainwater harvesting could be part of the solution for people living in the southern part of the city. Here, rainfall is heaviest, and the area is sufficient to collect and store water to reduce costs. It is estimated that using pluvial water as source of water costs around US$10 per m^3, which can only be afforded by wealthier people. For the reclamation of pluvial water to be used as part of the water supply, it is estimated that due to the lack of places to store water in such a densely populated city, at the most, 1 m^3 per second could obtained in this way.

- *Industrial reuse*. Even though industrial activity in Mexico is low (most registered companies are corporate offices, with their production sites in other parts of the country), the capacity to increase the industrial reuse of water is limited to around 1 m^3 per second. For this to be effective the cost of reusing industrial water needs to be increased to match the treatment and distribution cost of reused wastewater.

Conclusions

The main conclusion with regard to Mexico City is that there is a need to create a Metropolitan Water Authority with the participation of the different political regions, sectors and levels of government (federal, regional, and local). This should be organized to manage water in an integrated way. To be effective, this water authority needs to have the capacity to take all decisions related to the management of water, have the possibility to change land use policy, to assist in the whole planning for the city, and have a sufficient budget to allow its operation. The main task of the water authority would be to elaborate a short- and long-term Integrated Water Resources Management Program, which should consider not only technical aspects but also social and economic ones. This program should involve views of society and include activities such as land use management, soil subsidence control, stopping and even reversing the population growth of Mexico City, protection of groundwater quality, leakage control, aggressive reuse and recycling programs, innovative and comprehensive educational programs, the search for alternative tools other than economic ones to manage water, rainwater harvesting, and implementation of professional and public participation programs (Jiménez 2008a). Mexico City is undoubtedly experiencing a very challenging situation concerning its water supply and wastewater disposal system, which may have no precedents in other parts of the world. Nevertheless, it is highly likely that at least some of the problems discussed are already being experienced elsewhere, hence the need to create awareness of the importance of managing urban water in an integrated manner, particularly in megacities.

It is evident that infiltration through the soil of the Tula Valley is acting as an unintentional soil aquifer treatment system that efficiently remediates Mexico City's wastewater. While the origin of the groundwater in the Tula Valley is not creating evident problems to local inhabitants, it is certainly a source of great concern, especially as it is not known how long the soil's treatment capacity will last. For this reason studies need to be carried out to determine the fate of pollutants and to quantify their behavior in soil, especially that treated with wastewater. The process selected for the Atotonilco wastewater treatment plant (planned to be operating in 2012) will produce treated water with a low organic matter content, which risks mobilizing heavy metals and organic pollutants accumulated in the Tula soil over many years, polluting the groundwater. In addition, further guidance and education has to be given to farmers in order to assist them to control soil salinity problems where they arise.

Finally, independently of Mexico City's decision, the government of the State of Hidalgo should be reviewing the potabilization process applied in the area (chlorination), or as proposed by other researchers, extracting water from parts of the aquifers where wastewater has little or no effect.

Notes

1 This does not take into account that 100 percent of the non-treated wastewater is also reused, as will be presented later in the chapter.

2 The rise in the water table is actually causing a loss of 0.95 m^3 per second of water through evaporation.

References

Berkman, D. S., Lescano, A., Gilman, R., Lopez, S. and Black, M. (2002) "Effects of Stunting, Diarrheal Disease, and Parasitic Infection during Infancy on Cognition in Late Childhood: A Follow-Up Study." *The Lancet* 359: 564–71.

BGS-CNA (1998) *Effects of Wastewater Reuse on Groundwater in the Mezquital Valley, Hidalgo State, Mexico*. Technical report WC/98/42. Nottingham: BGS.

Cifuentes, E., Blumenthal, U., Ruiz-Palacios, G. and Beneth, S. (1992) "Health Impact Evaluation of Wastewater in Mexico." *Public Health Revue* 19: 243–50.

Cifuentes, E., Suárez, L., Solano, M. and Santos, R. (2002) "Diarrheal Diseases in Children from Water Reclamation Site, Mexico City." *Environmental Health Perspectives* 110(10): 619–24.

Domínguez-Mora, R., Jiménez-Cisneros, B., Carrizosa-Elizondo, E. and Cisneros-Iturbe, L. (2005) *Water Supply and Flood Control in the Mexico Valley*. No. 06-cd-03-10-0274-1-05, project 5341. Mexico City: Engineering Institute, National Autonomous University of Mexico [in Spanish].

Downs, T., Cifuentes, E., Ruth, E. and Suffet, I. (2002) "Effectiveness of Natural Treatment in a Wastewater Irrigation District of the Mexico City Region: A Synoptic Field Survey." *Water Environment Research* 72(1): 4–21.

Durán, J., Mendez, J. and Jiménez, B (2010) "The Quality of Water in Mexico." In B. Jiménez, M. L. Torregrosa, and L.Aboites (eds), *The Water in Mexico*, 259–90. Mexico City: Mexican Academy of Sciences and CONAGUA.

Durán-Álvarez, J. C., Becerril, E., Castro, V., Jiménez, B. and Gibson, R. (2009) "The Analysis of a Group of Acidic Pharmaceuticals, Carbamazepine, and Potential Endocrine Disrupting Compounds in Wastewater Irrigated Soils by Gas Chromatography–Mass Spectrometry." *Talanta* 78(3): 1159–66.

Fewtrell, L. (2004) "Drinking-Water Nitrate and Methemoglobinemia: Global Burden of Disease: A Discussion, *Environmental Health Perspectives* 112(14): 1371–4.

Gibson, R., Becerril, E., Silva, V. and Jiménez, B. (2007) "Determination of Acidic Pharmaceuticals and Potential Endocrine Disrupting Compounds in Wastewaters and Spring Waters by Selective Elution and Analysis by Gas Chromatography–Mass Spectrometry." *Journal of Chromatography A* 1169(1–2): 31–9.

Jiménez, B. (2008a) "Wastewater Risks in the Urban Water Cycle." In B. Jiménez and J. Rose (eds), *Urban Water Security: Managing Risks*. London: CRC Press.

—— (2008b) "Unplanned Reuse of Wastewater for Human Consumption: The Tula Valley, Mexico." In B. Jiménez and T. Asano (eds), *Water Reuse: An International Survey of*

Current Practice, Issues and Needs, pp. 414–33. London: IWA Publishing.

—— (2009) "Risks and Integrated Management of the Urban Water Cycle in Megacities of the Developing World: Mexico City." In J. Feyen, K. Shannon, and M. Neville (eds), *Water and Urban Development Paradigms*, pp. 387–96. London: CRC Press.

Jiménez, B. and Chávez, A. (2004) "Quality Assessment of an Aquifer Recharged with Wastewater for its Potential Use as Drinking Source: El Mezquital Valley Case." *Water Science and Technology* 50(2): 20, 269–73.

Mazari-Hiriart, M., Torres Beristain, B. Velázquez, E., Calva, J. and Pillai, S. (1999) "Bacterial and Viral Indicators of Fecal Pollution in Mexico City's Southern Aquifer." *Journal of Environmental Science Health* A34(9): 1715–35.

Mazari-Hiriart, M., López-Vidal, Y., Ponce de León, S., Calva-Mercado, J. J. and Rojo-Callejas, F. (2002) "Significance of Water Quality Indicators: A Case Study in Mexico City." In *Proceedings of the International Conference: Water and Wastewater, Perspectives of Developing Countries*, Indian Institute of Technology Delhi–International Water Association. New Delhi, India, December 11–13, 2002, pp. 407–16.

Merino, H. (2000) *The Hydraulic System of Mexico City in Mexico City Towards the Second Millennium*. G. Garza (ed.). Mexico City: Federal District Government and the El Colegio de México [in Spanish].

Moore, S., Lima, A., Conaway, M., Soares, A. and Guerrant, R. (2001) "Early Childhood Diarrhea and Helminthiases Associated with Long-Term Linear Growth Faltering." *International Journal of Epidemiology* 30: 1457–64.

SACM (2006) *Water and Politics*. Proceedings of the International Tlalocan Festival, Mexico City Water Works, Mexico City, March 10–15.

Santoyo, E. and Ovando-Shelley, E. (2002) *Underexcavation at the Tower of Pisa and at Mexico City's Metropolitan Cathedral*. Proceedings of International Workshop, ISSMGE Technical Committee TC36, Foundation Engineering in Difficult, Soft Soil Conditions, Mexico City. CD edition. [in Spanish].

Santoyo, E., Ovando, E., Mooser, F. and León, E. (2005) *Geotechnical Syntheses of the Mexico Valley Basin*. TGC, Geotecnia, S.A. de C.V. México[in Spanish].

Siebe, C. (1994) "Heavy Metal Accumulation in Soils from the Irrigation District 03, in Tula, Hidalgo Irrigated with Wastewater." *International Magazine of Environmental Pollution* 10: 15–21 [in Spanish].

—— (1998) "Nutrient Inputs to Soils and their Uptake by Alfalfa through Long-Term Irrigation with Untreated Sewage Effluent in Mexico," *Soil Use and Management* 14: 1119–22.

USEPA (2004) *Guidelines for Water Reuse*. EPA/625/R-04/108. Washington, DC: USAID.

WHO (1995) *WHO Drinking Water Quality Criteria*, 2nd edn. Geneva: World Health Organization.

Part V

Indigenous cultures and rights

9 Water conflicts and human rights in indigenous territories of Latin America

Patricia Ávila-García

Introduction

Water conflicts may arise through the confrontation of two or more cosmogonies and social perceptions of water's value. Examples exist from the Colonial period in Mexico: while for indigenous people lakes were a source of multiple material and spiritual assets, for the Spaniards lakes were a source of disease from the stagnant and foul-smelling waters; a conception that instigated the strategy of desiccating the lakes, which in the valley of Mexico was achieved by draining the lakes' water to another watershed basin (Musset 1992; Espinosa 1996).

In the present, the contrast in values is reflected in the rupture between institutions and social agreements, such as *usos y costumbres* (customary uses or consuetudinary law) in the management of water at the community level: the major part of Latin American states ignore the water rights of indigenous peoples and introduce modalities going from supporting individual rights to the public and private management of water (Stavenhagen 1990; Boelens 2009). An interesting exception is Bolivia, where during the last decade the indigenous movement was able to attain legal repercussions: consuetudinary law was recognized by the state, which has direct implications on communitarian management of water in indigenous territories (Perreault 2008).

However, the conflict is more deeply rooted in perceptions of communities that, on one hand, water should be a common good, and on the other, the perceptions of the state that promote the revaluation of water as an economic good that should have a market value and a price. In that sense, disassociating or even omitting the existence of the social and cultural dimensions of water is a way of endangering both the basis of contemporaneous civilization and the indigenous regions in which there is a culture of sustainable use and management of water. In addition, it is a way of generating water conflicts and attacking collective rights and forms of management in indigenous territories that since ancient times have supported a sustainable appropriation of water (Ávila 1996; Vargas 2006).

At present, water conflicts have been intensified by the processes of accumulation by dispossession and of neoliberalization of nature (Harvey 2004; Castree 2008), which in the case of water are expressed in the dispossession and privatization of collective property and in the commodification of water that prioritizes the economic value over other forms of value (Bakker 2007). In that sense, the role of the state has been crucial in the rise of the neoliberal project, including promoting legal and institutional changes that give certainty to private investments to unlawful acts, such as land and water dispossessions and violation of human rights of indigenous peoples. This role of the state explains the emergence of greater conflicts and the need for alternate instances of environmental justice as in the case of the Latin American Water Tribunal (Bogantes 2007; Ávila 2008).

Water rights in indigenous territories

Throughout history, water has had deep, mythical-poetical, and sociocultural meaning and value associated with cosmogony and with the perception of the world and nature (Blattner and Ingram 2001; León-Portilla 1992; Ilich 1993). This has resulted in cultural ways of managing water within an integrated water-land-forest matrix, and in social recognition of water as a collective good or a *common* (Robert 2002).

The relevance of the recognition of the value of water in its amplest sense is based on its being the key factor for understanding the past and present existence of the water cultures that have been founded on the principles of social and environmental sustainability (Ávila 1996; Palerm 1972; Rojas 1985). Historically, water has been a common good that is socially regulated in order to guarantee a more equitable access to it; and since it is not being dissociated from the territorial water–land–forest matrix, its appropriation was based on an integrative logic and on the profound knowledge of the cycles of nature (Espinosa 1996; Robert 2002).

For Mesoamerican and Andean peoples alike, water was a gift from the gods with which they would live and by which they would be strengthened (León-Portilla 1992; Estermann 2006). The availability of water in the territory contributed to the birth of communities and people that settled following the water-forest pattern along valleys, hills, and mountains in which springs and rivers were born. Conservation and adequate management of water, land, and forests enables life itself and the development of communities, as in the case of the Mesoamerican and South American hydraulic societies (Palerm 1972; Rojas 1985; Gelles 2000; Mazadiego *et al.* 2009).

Indigenous peoples created rights, regulations and collective practices about water, in order to guarantee its adequate use and appropriation (León-Portilla 1992; Robert 1994; Ávila 1996; Boelens 2009). As stated by Robert (2002), "In history, water has been the great maker of communities. Always people from diverse origins learned to share the same fountains and to coexist beside the same rivers and, by the act of concluding agreements, set the bases of a community." In this framework, water was considered to be a common good contributing to reinforce the territorial links of belonging and identity.

Social organization and the water rights: water as a collective good

At the present time, indigenous peoples from Latin America represent a mosaic of cultures adapted to different ecosystems and having diverse forms of social organization and territory appropriation modalities. Instead of integrating a homogeneous cultural entity, indigenous peoples in the region go from small groups, isolated from national society, to communities that are integrated to national economies (Stavenhagen 1988).

According to Del Popolo and Oyarce (2005) and to UNICEF (2012), an estimated number of more than 500 indigenous groups with about 30 million inhabitants represent 6 percent of the total population of the region. Their distribution is variable according to country: Mexico, Bolivia, Guatemala, Peru, and Colombia concentrate most of the indigenous population on the continent, although Bolivia has the largest relative proportion of indigenous population. Brazil concentrates the largest number of indigenous groups but at a low demographic density.

In general terms, it can be assumed that indigenous peoples share some elements, such as collective property modalities and customary uses. Their identity is associated with communitarian appropriation of territory, given that they have a special relationship with land (Stavenhagen 1988). In the case of the Andean region, according to Gentes (2002), the essential elements of the subsistence strategy of indigenous peoples are collective property and kinship. The advantage of having a common property system is that water resources represent an indivisible good that requires an integrated management of the catchment, and that access, use, and management of these resources becomes socially controlled and regulated. The regulation of water resources in indigenous territories is carried out by means of rules that are largely structured within concrete practices, beliefs, and sociocultural values.

Customary uses become local regulation systems, in many cases based upon the consuetudinary or ancestral law of indigenous peoples that was established before the formation of nation-states – in the case of Latin America, corresponding to the pre-Hispanic period (Stavenhagen 1990). As a result of this social organization, accumulation of goods by families is limited in favor of communitarian reciprocity. Conversely, the autonomy of indigenous peoples with respect to the state power guarantees access to natural resources present in the territory, and establishes that the appropriation of water should be based on kinship and cooperation (Gentes 2002).

However, as argued by Boelens *et al.* (2006) in a scenario of growing scarcity and competition for water resources, the water rights become essential in the struggle of indigenous peoples for defending their territory. Control of water resources is both a source of power and of conflicts, because it is strategic for productive, social and cultural activities, and for the identity building of indigenous peoples (Gelles 2000; Budds 2004). The notion of water as a common good is sustained upon a social organization and collective activities that implicate cooperation instead of competition in order to survive. It also assures water rights in adverse environmental conditions, such as in arid and mountainous zones.

These collective actions are expressed as a sort of reciprocity that sustains and reproduces both the water resources management systems and the households that depend on its use (Boelens 2009).

Water rights are thus related to access to water and its infrastructure, namely to: the rules and collective obligations regarding the resources management, the legitimacy of the communitarian authority for establishing and enforcing rules and rights, and the discourses and policies for the regulation of the resource. In other words, the right to water is more than a relation between access and use or between subject and object – it is a social and power relation that involves having control over decision-making and management (Boelens 2009; Budds 2004, 2010; Swyngedouw 2004; Perreault 2008).

Boelens *et al.* (2006) state that the indigenous regulatory frameworks have proven to be flexible and dynamic, given that they have nourished themselves with the various formal legislations implemented since the Colonial period and until the present. Throughout that historical process, indigenous peoples' legislation has been intercalated with the norms, procedures, and organization forms of the official legislation in a sort of pragmatism that ensures their survival. Interlegality, understood as the intersection of several legal orders within a society (Urteaga 2001), has been essential for the definition of water rights, for it is the result of the coexistence of the state's and the local regulations underlain by a structure of power and domination.

Hence, legal pluralism (multiple legal systems within one geographical area) is a part of indigenous peoples' strategies for the defense of their interests and for the management of conflicts within their territories. The reason is that there is a social, cultural, and legal diversity inside indigenous peoples' territories that coexists with the centralism involved in the regulations, procedures, and the definition and assignment of the water rights as a dominium belonging exclusively to the state. Overall, the result is a creative response of indigenous peoples for resisting the dissolutive influence of the state's legislation, which is hegemonic.

Formal and consuetudinary law of water: coexistence, integration and exclusion

The state faces legal pluralism following incorporation and recognition of indigenous peoples' rights. Incorporation, which is the predominant approach, aims at assimilation and subjugation of indigenous regulations to the state's legal framework. Recognition, instead, proposes the respect for consuetudinary law and for autonomy of indigenous peoples, but becomes inoperative due to the rigidity of the state's legislation that excludes the recognition of a pluralistic and democratic perspective. This provides the grounds for the questioning of multiculturalism as a means for the administration by the state of the differences, in terms of market demands and following a neoliberal project, without giving consideration to policies proposed by contemporaneous indigenous movements for the acknowledgment of identity and regarding natural resources. Briefly stated, multiculturalism excludes indigenous peoples' demands that tend to disturb the state's power, but includes whatever is compliant to it or that serves a function towards the state's specific objectives or projects in the territory (Boelens *et al.* 2006).

The right to have control of the territory is among the central claims of indigenous peoples, because land tenure does not provide the rights over underground resources, water, wetlands, and biodiversity. Underground natural resources are recognized as being a property of the state or nation, and their appropriation is made by means of land expropriation by cause of public interest or through concessions and licenses to private owners. Such scenario of legal defenselessness in indigenous territories has cultural, environmental, and economic implications, given that rights become limited by the state's actions or by the presence of private actors seeking, under market logic, to gain benefic ownership over natural resources (Gentes 2002; Budds 2004; Boelens 2009; Bakker 2007; Romero Toledo *et al.* 2009).

About 20 years ago, most Latin American countries lacked in their political constitutions an explicit recognition of indigenous peoples' existence and of their most elemental rights to control their territory and natural resources, such as water (Stavenhagen 1988). This is explained by exclusion policies of national states, which since the Colonial times held a racist and discriminatory posture toward indigenous peoples. Such strategy made possible land and water dispossession and hence, accumulation by dispossession, because indigenous peoples' rights were formally inexistent.

The subscription of international treaties, such as Convention 169 of the International Labor Organization in 1989, several countries in the region made a commitment to recognize and respect the rights of indigenous peoples and tribal rights. During the decade of 1990 advances were made at a constitutional level in countries such as Peru, Colombia, Brazil, Bolivia, Ecuador, and Mexico, among others. This implied that national states recognized legal equality of indigenous peoples through an integration policy that limited customary norms and common rights to align them with formal state laws. In other words, integration was based on considering indigenous peoples as equal to the rest of the society, their individual rights being assured (Boelens *et al.* 2007).

Legal pluralism as a mechanism for the coexistence of state law and consuetudinary law has been only recently recognized in countries in which social movements of ethnic origin had national repercussions that permeated the states' power structure, such as in Bolivia and Ecuador (Perreault 2008; Boelens *et al.* 2007) – their political constitutions becoming the most advanced in the continent in terms of indigenous rights.

It is pertinent to mention that in the case of Mexico, legal pluralism was denied, despite a social movement in 1994, which while not reaching a national coverage achieved an international presence. Constitutional reforms in indigenous matters made in 2001 did not include the demands made by the Zapatista movement, nor the San Andres Agreements in the sense of greater autonomy of indigenous territories and the recognition of consuetudinary law (Korsbaek and Vivanco 2005). However, for the first time, indigenous peoples were recognized as a part of the nation but without a clear implication regarding the collective right to the control of indigenous territory.

Otherwise, with the exception of Bolivia, constitutional reforms regarding indigenous rights have had a minimal or null impact over water legislation in most Latin American countries. These reforms omit or only partially include the existence of indigenous peoples and their communitarian rights for water, which represents the hegemony of state law over customary norms (Stavenhagen 1990; Gentes 2002; Boelens 2009).

Recent water policies and their impact on indigenous territories

During the 1980s and 1990s, Latin American states made structural reforms to promote an economic model based on the free market, with dominant participation of the private sector in strategic areas of the economy and ensuring legal certitude of private property of natural resources, such as land and water. To give sustenance to the implemented national public policies, changes were made to the legal and institutional frameworks. The neoliberal model impacted on indigenous peoples by favoring in their territories mining operations led by transnational companies; the production of export crops demanding large amounts of water, such as vegetables and fruits; the building of communication and hydraulic infrastructure for facilitation of commodities mobilization and the exploitation of natural resources; the exportation of water from watersheds or the artificial deviation of water courses in order to supply water to urban centers; and the development of tourism in areas having ecological and cultural relevance, which implies the privatization of land and water (Gentes 2002, 2009; Boelens 2009; Bakker 2007; Budds 2004, 2010; Perreault 2008).

The defense of territory and natural resources became central demands of the indigenous movement. The lack of acknowledgment of indigenous territories by the state and the fragmentation of rights linked to land and water favored pillage and dispossession in the absence of an inclusive normativity. This is due to the indigenous conception of territory as including all associated natural resources such as land, water, wetlands, forests, and grasslands; in contrast, the legal conception of land disarticulates these elements in different land tenure regimes and in licenses given to individuals.

The implications of these legal reforms in the territories of several indigenous peoples have led to fragmentation and to the private ownership (by non-local people) of common goods that are part of the land-water-forest sociocultural matrix. In the case of water, management topics were reduced to the logic of cost-benefit, economic efficiency, and maximum profit, while omitting social forms of organization, communitarian legal frameworks, and sociocultural strategies for the appropriation of a common good (Ávila 2007). As a result, the culture of indigenous peoples based on the common management of water is threatened: "when the state and the agents of neoliberal development attempt to alter the forms of collective management that conjugates the material, political and cultural sustenance, they attempt against the most intimate fibers of the social organization" (Boelens *et al.* 2006: 417).

In that sense, Gentes (2009) criticizes the new water policies in the region as being a neoclassical interpretation of economics, given that they aim at the satisfaction of the demands of dominant, economically productive sectors, and are based on the recognition of a single law and the obligation to register all rights to water. Under these assumptions, it is pretended to achieve a higher economic efficiency and an adequate framework for the rights to ownership of water – rights that could be traded in title markets.

For example, Chile was the first country in Latin America to adopt a neoliberal program and to make changes to the legislation about water in order to create private rights for controlling both the resource and the markets for the corresponding transactions, uses and locations (Bauer 2004; Budds 2004, 2009). Mexico also made important legal reforms in relation with land tenure and water, which enabled the possibility of private ownership of social property, such as *ejidos* and communities, making it available to land markets. Regarding water, concessions and allocations were given for beneficial ownership, and restrains for free marketing in water markets were released (Wilder 2006, 2010; Whiteford and Melville 2002).

In summary, neoliberal reforms made in water issues in both countries gave more certainty to individual rights and the creation of a water market (Chilean Water Code of 1981 and Mexican National Water Law of 1989). These trends further hampered the possibility of applying integration policies and the coexistence of collective rights to water in indigenous territories by the mere fact that such rights became unrecognized. This gave place to processes of water rights dispossession:

> Communities are dispossessed through destruction of collective rights over resources. Recognition of private property rights has allowed rapid incorporation of land and water into the market system. Thus, the deployment of secular, rational, universally applicable irrigation models, supported nowadays by water management privatization ideologies, is a powerful means by which contemporary nation-states and private-interest sectors extend their control.
>
> (Boelens *et al.* 2007: 104)

In the case of Mexico, the indigenous issue is simply absent from National Water Law, despite recent reforms, and social property of land, and the recently assigned water rights have trended toward privatization (Ávila 2007). In the case of Chile, the Chilean Water Code of 1981 contributed to the privatization of water rights in indigenous territories – a fact that generated tensions and conflicts with the Mapuche people to the extent that the reforms to the Code in 2005 had to include some elements providing greater social equity in the assignation of individual rights (Bauer 2004; Gentes 2009).

Specifically, the balance made by Gentes (2009) of the social impact of the

Water Code of Chile shows that the market of water rights model is not flexible when assigning rights (collective or communitarian) and benefits private interests, giving priority to accumulation and allocation of ownership rights of water resources by economically and culturally dominant agents. In other words, it stimulates monopoly practices in ownership rights of water that are assigned to a few interested parties. The author also analyzes the environmental impact of the Waters Code of Chile, concluding that the law is weak in terms of environmental, recreational and ecological uses in the basins, because the rights to ownership of water were almost totally given to private users.

Bolivia is an exception to these trends toward the commodification of water in Latin America. Due to conflicts arising from the privatization of water in Cochabamba during the year 2000, an opposing social movement was generated with deep roots in rural and indigenous territories. The movement was able to stop advancement of a transnational corporation over urban management and to derogate the 2009 law, giving legitimacy to such an initiative (Kruze 2005; Assies 2001). Likewise, years later this social movement had influence on the contents of an irrigation law enforced in 2004 – known as Law 2878 of Promotion and Support to the Irrigation Sector for Agricultural, Animal Husbandry, and Forestry Production – as well as in the rules of the same law enforced in 2008. The innovation of these legal instruments is that they are supported by a decentralized institutional framework, including social participation in decision-making and ensuring water use rights through an authorized registry (Perreault 2008).

Law 2878 forbids the transfer of rights and the creation of water markets, giving priority to communal over individual rights. The registrations are granted to local families or indigenous communities and were meant for ensuring access to water for domestic use or for traditional agriculture. The normative principle applied is consuetudinary law for the management of irrigation water. These legal and institutional reforms arose from ethnic movements and the struggles against privatization and, in particular, from the defense of regent organizations of the inclusion in the law of existing customary norms (Perreault 2008; Asamblea Constituyente 2008).

Another interesting case is that of Ecuador where, since 2010, the indigenous movement has opposed the project of the new water law, because the proposal only recognizes the state's authority and disregards the existence of a multinational authority regarding water. Until today, the law has not been approved under such terms, which demonstrates the opposing power exerted by social movements despite the central pressure of the state showing legal and political contradictions.

The human right to water as an international-level defense strategy of indigenous peoples

Facing a scenario of state crisis and of constant violations of essential rights in indigenous peoples' territories, a number of water conflicts have arisen in Latin America that demonstrate the limitations of institutional and legal procedures at the national level to guarantee their solution. The human right to water has turned into a new defense strategy of indigenous peoples at the international level, and from formal (United Nations, World Water Forum) or non-formal (ethical tribunals, media, networks of non-governmental organizations) instances. As such, it is a political demand of indigenous peoples in international spaces having a binding or moral sanction character and aimed at committing states to respect human rights in their territories, including that to water.

According to Langford and Khalfan (2007), the approach of water as a human right is based on legal and normative principles having universal validity that should lead to:

- governments giving priority access to water, above all, of the poorest and more vulnerable sectors of the population;
- the assumption of water supply as a right rather than as an act of charity or as a commodity;
- water supply not generating discrimination because of socioeconomic status, culture, race or gender, religious belief, political affiliation or ideology;
- the consultation and participation of society in decision-making process, in particular regarding issues related to access, supply, and conservation of water; and
- national governments, the international community, and the private sector becoming responsible for guaranteeing access to water.

From an inclusive perspective, the human right to water is considered to be a guarantee for reaching an adequate living standard, given that water is essential for the survival of the population. However, in order to achieve total enforcement and respect of human rights to water, other human rights are equally guaranteed, such as the rights to health, housing, and nourishment; the rights to human life and dignity; the right to be free from racial discrimination; the right to participate; the right to personal and communitarian integrity; and the right to development (UNDP 2006; CESCR 2002).

The right to water has been recognized by a number of countries through a series of international treaties, declarations, and other measures. Important referents are articles 11 and 12 of the International Covenant for Economic, Social and Cultural Rights (ICESCR), a multilateral treaty signed in 1976 and ratified by nearly 200 countries, which addresses water issues. In order to make advances and to provide more content to the ICESCR, the United Nations Organization appointed a Committee on Economic, Social and Cultural Rights (CESCR) with the support of the state parties. In the year 2002, the CESCR issued the General Comment No. 15, confirming the right to water: "Water is a limited natural resource and a public good fundamental for life and health. The human right to water is indispensable for leading a life in human dignity. It is a prerequisite for the realization of other human rights" (CESCR 2002). The comment states that water must be treated as a social and cultural good rather than as an economic commodity and that the exercise of the right to water must be sustainable so that future generations can enjoy it.

Despite the reluctance of countries such as the United States of America, Australia, and Saudi Arabia to raise water to the category of human right, the General Comment No. 15 was accepted in the year 2003 by nearly 70 countries. In the case of the Latin American region, Uruguay was the first country to approve in a 2004 referendum the adoption of water as a human right, and the constitution was reformed (Langford and Khalfan 2007). Later on, Venezuela, Bolivia, Ecuador, Brazil, Nicaragua, and Mexico included the notion of water as a human right in their constitutions or legislation.

As a result of political lobbying of several countries and civil actions in defense of water as a human right, on July of 2010 the General Assembly of the United Nations declared access to clean water and sanitation as a human right. The text proposed by Bolivia and backed by other 33 United Nations state members received 122 votes in favor, and zero votes against, while 41 countries abstained from voting. The main points of the resolution were:

> 1. *Declares* the right to safe and clean drinking water and sanitation as a human right that is essential for the full enjoyment of life and all human rights. 2. *Calls upon* states and international organizations to provide financial resources, capacity-building and technology transfer, through international assistance and cooperation, in particular, to developing countries, in order to scale-up efforts to provide.
>
> (UN 2010)

The resolution underlines the responsibility of states of promoting and protecting all human rights with the same commitment, given these are interwoven with the right to water.

The legal–institutional framework in some Latin American countries and the recognition of indigenous peoples' rights and of water as human right

In this section, a comparison is made between the legal–institutional frameworks of three North, Central, and South American countries that are characterized by the presence of indigenous populations: Mexico (10 percent of total population), Guatemala (41 percent) and Bolivia (55 percent). The idea is to show the advances made by these countries in the recognition of water as a human right and in the inclusion of indigenous people rights in their constitutions and legislation. Under that perspective, it is possible to observe to what degree both international agreements and national legislation are being complied with or violated in terms of water and human rights of indigenous peoples (Boelens *et al.* 2006).

Regarding international agreements about indigenous peoples' rights, the three countries signed the Indigenous and Tribal Peoples Convention 169 of the International Labour Organization (ILO) in 1989, and ratified it in 1990 and 1991. Among the basic concepts of the Convention 169 are the respect and participation of indigenous and tribal peoples and the recognition of their culture and religion, social and economic organization, and own identity. In that sense, when applying the Convention 169, the state parties must make a consultation with indigenous peoples potentially affected by any public policy or project and to establish mechanisms for their participation in decision-making processes. It also states that indigenous and tribal peoples should have the right to define their own priorities for development in terms of maintaining their life style, beliefs institutions, and spiritual wellbeing, the lands they inhabit or otherwise use, and the right to control, as much as possible, their own economic, social and cultural development. In other words, indigenous and tribal peoples should participate in the formulation, application, and evaluation of any national and regional development plan or program that is susceptible of causing a direct impact on them.

In addition, Convention 169 underlines the importance of recognizing in national legislations the customary tribunals and laws of the indigenous and tribal peoples, in terms of the special relation with the lands and territories they occupy, in particular, the collective aspects in that relation; their rights to natural resources (such as water) present in their territories, and to their participation in land utilization, administration and conservation; and the relevance of their permanence in their territories, or when their relocation is deemed necessary by an exceptional reason, that such relocation must always be agreed upon by the peoples, and made freely and with full understanding of the situation.

These three countries share being signatories of the ICESCR. Mexico signed and ratified the ICESCR in 1981 and, since then, the multilateral treaty became a binding norm to the Mexican legal system that is hierarchically placed below the constitution but above federal and state laws and presidential decrees. The significance of the signing of the ICESCR is the voluntary assumption of the obligation to progressively use the maximal amount of available resources, and observe and respect the rights it contains.

Most countries that signed the ICESCR (including Mexico, Guatemala, and Bolivia) approved the General Comment No. 15 of the CESCR, relating to the right to water in 2003, implying these states are committed with the international community to make the right to water to become real (CESCR 2002). However, the compliance of governments to such international agreements in many cases is not expressed in modifications to the national legal systems or in the implementation of policies, programs, and strategies for guaranteeing the human right to water. The consequence is that many states are in a situation of constant violation of the law.

In the case of Mexico, article 2 of the Political Constitution of the United States of Mexico states that the country is a multicultural nation, but no recognition is given to customary laws and indigenous peoples' forms of social and political organization; however, principles that are linked to the autonomous control and management of their territories and the natural resources (such as water) are present in them. The above matter is the essence of the social conflict that took place during the 1990s between the Zapatista National Liberation Army and the Mexican State – a conflict that remains unsolved.

The lack of recognition of indigenous peoples as stakeholders playing a central role in the control and management of water is expressed in the National Water Law. In it, indigenous peoples are inexistent, and no recognition is given to their water rights and to their social and communitarian organization (Ávila 2007). Such a legal void is one of the main causes of water conflicts in the country, given that there is no respect for the diversity of forms of regulation and management of water present in indigenous peoples' territories, forms that preceded the present notion of legal systems from a state's perspective (Boelens *et al.* 2006; Gentes 2009). Several examples exist in Mexico, such as the affectation of water rights of the Yaqui people in order to supply water to urban populations and industries in Hermosillo, and the dispossessions of land and water from the Raramuri people to favor transnational touristic projects in the Sierra Tarahumara.

The constitutional recognition of water as a human right was absent until January 2012. Constitutional article 4 was reformed,[1] which undoubtedly represents an advance. However, more changes need to be made to the National Water Law, and more economic resources need to be allocated in order to warrant its enforcement. It must be said that it is precisely the rural population, and particularly that from the indigenous areas, the one having a larger deficit in water supply and infrastructure. For example, the Raramuri and Mazahua peoples display critical levels of access to water: 78 percent and 75 percent, respectively, of their households lack water supply (Ávila 2007). Therefore, the constitutional recognition of water as a human right must be translated into a public policy strategy leading to an increase in coverage of the country's drinking water supply.

In the case of Guatemala, no advances have been made in legal terms toward the recognition of water as a human right. However, the country signed in 2009 the parallel declaration of human rights to water during the Fifth World Water Forum, a proposal of countries such as Bolivia. However, no advances have been made in national legislative terms by the government of Guatemala for the recognition of the rights of indigenous peoples to control their territories and natural resources. While in March of 2009 several indigenous peoples' organizations submitted to the Guatemala Republic Congress, a project of a General Law of Indigenous Peoples Rights, the legislative body did not consider the initiative. Despite that, in June 2010 the United Nations rapporteur of indigenous peoples' rights made a recommendation to the Guatemalan congress regarding the importance of making legal advances in the observance of the Indigenous Peoples' Consultation Law in the events of development or investment projects in their territories (as a part of the Convention 169 relating to the right to consultation). Currently, the indigenous issue remains to be stalled at the legislative level, and there is no interest or political willingness of the state, despite that at the level of international treaties it assumed the commitment of recognizing the rights of indigenous peoples.

In Bolivia, before the arrival of Evo Morales to the presidency, the case was similar to those of Mexico and Guatemala. In fact, between 1999 and 2000, a conflict due to the opposition to privatization of water in Cochabamba led to the emergence of a mobilization of indigenous peoples and subsistence farmers, a social movement that became a key factor of the reforms later made in Bolivia

(Assies 2001; Perreault 2008). The presidency of Evo Morales is remarkable for the recognition of the human right to water in articles 20 and 373 of the new Constitution of October 2008.[2]

Likewise, the constitution establishes in its Article 374 the role of the state as the responsible agent of water resources (which must include social participation) and of guaranteeing the population's access to water. Also, it establishes the recognition and respect of uses and customs of indigenous peoples and of their institutions and forms of social organization in relation to water.[3]

The Constitution of Bolivia also has an advanced vision about the recognition of the rights of indigenous peoples, which seems to be non-existent in the cases of Mexico and Guatemala. These include a quota of indigenous parliamentary representatives; the right of indigenous peoples for autonomy and self-government, together with the official recognition of their territorial limits and institutions; and the exclusive property of the forest resources present in their communities (Asamblea Constituyente 2008). While legal advances have been made in Bolivia in terms of recognition of rights of indigenous peoples and in human rights, the main challenge lies in its application through public policies and actions throughout the country. The evaluation of legal changes in Bolivia is yet a pending task, given the recentness of the new constitution.

The violations of human rights to water in indigenous peoples' territories in Latin America

In the presence of the constant violation by states of human and indigenous peoples' rights, the scenario of social conflict for water is intense and complex in the Latin American region. These circumstances have been worsened by structural reforms that have led to a decreased role of states, which are expressed through more flexible legal and normative frameworks that favor the ascension of the private sector to a prominent role, and in increased incentives for private investments in strategic areas such as energy, water, mining, and urbanization.

Many of the conflicts occurring at present fall within such a category and are not necessarily the result of a water crisis (the available water within a region is less than the region's demand). Rather, they are an expression of omissions and direct actions of the state and of other actors or economic stakeholders that have made vulnerable the essential rights of the poorest and marginal sectors of the population: the indigenous peoples.

Therefore, in the last 15 years, a variety of conflicts over water in the indigenous regions of Latin America have emerged, which demonstrate a tension, due to the modification of rights (both recognized and unrecognized) to control over territory and the management of natural resources, as well as negative social and environmental impacts associated with public and private investments undertaken to favor the dominant economic model and the urbanization process.

Among the socio-environmental conflicts connected with water access are those associated with the expansion of mining in indigenous regions of North, Central, and South America (the Huichol, Raramuri, Nahua, and Mixtec peoples in Mexico, Maya peoples in Guatemala, and Andean peoples in Peru); the privatization of water in Bolivia (indigenous peoples of Los Altos and Cochabamba regions); the construction of hydroelectric dams in Brazil (the Amazonian Kayapo peoples), Brazil-Bolivia (the Karitana, Karipuna, Oro Bom, Cassupá, Salamai, Katawixi, Uru-eu-Wau-Wau peoples), Chile (Mapuche Pehuenche peoples), Ecuador (Afro-Ecuadorean peoples), and Panama (the Naso and Ngöbe peoples); the construction of highways in Bolivia (Moxeño, Yuracaré and Chimán peoples); the supply of water from one watershed to another for urbanization purposes in Mexico (the Mazahua, Nahua, and Yaqui peoples) and Peru (peoples of the Huancavelica region); and the expansion of tourist projects in Mexico (the Raramuri, Maya, Purépecha, and Nahua peoples).

As examples of such situation in the Latin American region, two conflicts for water are analyzed here:

- in Mexico, the conflict of the Mazahua people for the defense of water, as an expression of the tensions between rural and urban areas due to the building of large hydraulic infrastructure in indigenous peoples' territories; and
- in Guatemala, the conflict of the Maya people due to the social and environmental negative impact of recent mining projects in their territory and in their water resources in particular.

Mexico: the conflict of the Mazahua people for the defense of water

According to the census of 2010, the indigenous population in Mexico included about 10 million people, representing nearly 9 percent of the total population of the country; a figure that may vary according to the criteria applied (Boege 2008; INEGI 2010). Because of their social exclusion, indigenous peoples live in situations of high poverty and vulnerability: 73 percent of their municipalities have very high or high indexes of marginality (INEGI 2010). Income levels are among the lowest in the country because their main activity is subsistence farming. In addition, their access to public infrastructure and services is unequal. For example, the percentage of houses having water and electrical services is below the national average and localities with a higher number of indigenous population have limited access to water: 42 percent of houses lack piped water supply (Ávila 2007).

One of the reasons for the deficient supply of water to indigenous peoples' regions, predominantly in rural settlements, is the nearly non-existent public investment in water supply and sanitation. This was made evident in a study of five indigenous regions in Mexico (Ávila 2007) showing deficiencies in access to piped water supply: 78 percent of houses lack the service in the Tarahumara area; 75 percent in the Mazahua area; 41 percent in the Purépecha area; 32 percent in the Mixteca area; and 39 percent in the Nahua area. In addition, these communities suffer from a lack of regularity in the water supply (two or three times per week during a few hours), the inaccessibility of supply sources (springs are up to

10 km away), and the low quality of the water being consumed (pollution of superficial and groundwater supplies).

The amount of public investment aimed at solving problems of access to water in indigenous regions is so reduced that the Mexican government will have difficulties in reaching the Millennium Development Goals. For example, during 2004, the per capita federal aid for drinking water supply and water sanitation was of US$7.7 million in the Tarahumara area, while these values in the Mazahua area were US$5.0 million; in the Nahuaarea, US$1.7 million; in the Purépecha area, US$0.9 million; and in the Mixteca area, US$0.2 million (Ávila 2007). These budgets make clear that the indigenous regions are not a priority for the Mexican government, and there will continue to be an increase in the occurrence of problems of access to adequate quantity and quality of water. Despite that, in the year 2003 the federal government of Mexico obtained loans from the Inter-American Development Bank (BID) in order to be able to achieve the Millennium Development Goals; however, the problem is that the funds were applied to satisfy an urbanization model that privileges public investment in large cities concentrating on population and economic activities. This assignment pattern of public resources enhances the contrast between rural and urban areas (Ávila 2007).

Similarly, social inequity in indigenous regions of Mexico and the subordination of rural areas to urban areas in terms of projects involving the extraction of strategic natural resources from their territories (water, forest products, minerals), have been an important cause of the appearance of social conflicts.

The importance of the region where the Mazahua people are located is that it provides a third of the water consumed in the Metropolitan Area of Mexico City – that is, 15 cubic meters per second. During the decades of the 1980s and 1990s, a complex system of water supply that implied the transference of water from one watershed to another was constructed (dams, canals, tunnels, treatment plants, and pump systems) with a length of around 300 km and a change in elevation of 1,100 meters. To do that it was necessary to redirect water from the neighboring Lerma and Balsas basins (water that was used by people since Prehispanic times for human consumption and for agriculture, gathering, and fishing) to the Valley of Mexico (Perló and González 2005).

The problem is that the hydraulic works of the Cutzamala System were constructed without considering the interests of the local population (peasants and indigenous people), thereby affecting their rights related to control of their territory and natural resources (water). All of this was undertaken with federal public funds to favor the urban-industrial expansion of Mexico City in the state of Mexico and the Federal District (Perló and González 2005). The city's interests were put before those of the country and, consequently, the indigenous peoples' rights were affected.

The argument of the Mexican government for justifying the expropriation of the Mazahua land and the transfer of water for promoting urban and industrial development in the center of the country was that these actions were a matter of national interest, as stated in the country's political constitution. The indigenous owners most often were never compensated for the land, and no investment programs were applied to compensate for the benefits received by the city. In that sense, there was no compensation for the environmental services provided by the Mazahua territory; the method followed was land expropriation and predation of water resources (Ávila 2007).

The social and environmental costs of the Cutzamala System were very high for the Mazahua people: the transfer to the valley of Mexico of a significant volume of water narrowed their possibilities of development without satisfying their basic needs (access to water and food production). The reduction in water volume affected lacustrine and riparian ecosystems, and a number of marshland areas and rivers became dry. In addition, the polluted discharge from the water purification plant "Los Berros," forming part of the Cutzamala System, was poured untreated in a stream used by several Mazahua settlements. Fish and plants died due to the high concentration of toxic substances, and the stream never again served as a fountain of life and food to the population (Ávila 2007; Tirel 2006).

The case of the "Mazahua Womens' Movement for the Defense of Water" is a clear example of the tensions rising between the state and the indigenous peoples. Conflict for water was raised in the year 2004 when the Mazahua people publicly questioned the authoritarian and asymmetrical way in which water resources from the region had been extracted (Tirel 2006). Among their main claims was the application of a "Plan for Sustainable Development" in the region as a compensation for the damages caused by the transfer of water to Mexico City and for the limitations for an autonomous local development; that is, for compensating the ecological debt with the Mazahua people accumulated since the construction of the Cutzamala System (Ávila 2007).

During 2004, the collective actions of the Mazahua women included social mobilization (marches, demonstrations, sit-ins, hunger strikes) and "symbolic" takeovers of hydraulic installations and buildings of the Cutzamala System. Their proposal went beyond access and management of water by its interconnection to the management of forests and of the territory (Ávila 2007). For that reason, integrated measures were proposed spanning both productive projects (forestry, crop diversification for self-consumption and commercialization, development of organic agriculture, establishment of domestic and collective greenhouses, tank building for aquaculture, and husbandry of small livestock) and communitarian projects (water supply and improvement of its quality, building of distribution tanks, sewage, dry latrines, and paving, among others).

In response to the indigenous peoples' mobilizations and political pressure, the National Water Commission (CNA by its Spanish acronym) and the government of the state of Mexico acted to satisfy part of the demands. By the end of 2004, a convention was signed between the government ministry and the Mazahua movement to aid the realization of several social projects with a character of "Band-Aid measures," such as the building of piped water distribution and sewage networks and of dry latrines. The problem is that several Mazahua communities were either excluded or partially covered because of political divergence between groups and due to the strategy of the state to weaken and fragment the social movement (Ávila 2007).

Since the main demands remained unanswered, collective actions continued and by the middle of 2005 a long "water strike" was held by the Mazahua organization in front of the central quarter of the CNA. Results were null, given that the dialog was not reestablished and public resources were not distributed in a more equitable way. Later on, an internal excision of the movement gave rise to "the Mazahua Front for Water," of which its main leaders showed an attitude of "aperture" to the federal government, which caused their favoring in the reception of aid and public investments, which undoubtedly exacerbated the social tensions in the region.

However, despite their exclusion from economic aid from the state, since 2006 the Mazahua Womens' Movement developed several self-managed projects in the region, including organic agriculture in experimental plots in which vegetables were grown and tanks were built for storage of rainfall water. The innovation in this social movement was that its perspective was not centered on the actions of the state but instead gave impulse to a self-managed regional development based on principles, such as integrated management of the territory and its natural resources, the strengthening and diversification of agriculture for food production and for improving the diet and nutritional level of the population, and the conservation and protection of sources of water and their forests in order to guarantee quality and quantity of water for present and future Mazahua. In short, the Mazahua social movement displayed a view of the sustainable development of the region that was not limited to partial or disarticulated demands (such as short term "Band-Aid" measures) and transcended the actions of the state (Ávila 2007).

The responsive and even anti-state position of the movement lead in the year 2007 to selective repression, and one of the leaders was incarcerated with the argument that he had committed crimes in the state of Mexico in 1999 (equated kidnapping against two employees of the CNA), which responded to his opposition to the implementation of the fourth stage of the Cutzamala System that attempted to transfer more water to Mexico City from the state of Guerrero. Four months later, he was freed after demonstrating his innocence. However, this event is symptomatic of the new actions of the Mexican state in front of social movements: the hardening and selective repression of the main leaders, and the violation of human rights as in the cases of Atenco, Oaxaca, and Guerrero. This is coincident with the trend in Latin America: the criminalization of social protest, such as in Peru, Colombia, Brazil, and Chile, among other countries.

Guatemala: the resistance of Maya people to mining projects

Guatemala had nearly four decades of civil war that ended with the signing of the peace agreements in 1996. Because of the instability and violence generated during those years the social lags were made more acute, above all, in regions with a predominant indigenous population. The economy of Guatemala is one of the smallest in Latin America as is seen in the low levels of social welfare: 3

million inhabitants lack a water supply (representing nearly 25 percent of the total population) and 6 million (nearly 50 percent) have no water sanitization. These values become even more dramatic in the rural areas where 40 percent of the population lacks water supply and 74 percent have no sanitization.

After the end of the military dictatorship the new state proposed legislative and institutional changes to promote a model of development that would reactivate the economy and stimulate private investment in strategic areas. One of these areas was mining. Legal reforms were made to attract investment; for example, the former mining law stated that mining companies must pay the government 6 percent of their earnings, and the new law lowered that payment to only 1 percent. Also, financial support was obtained from supranational organisms, such as the World Bank for building social and transportation infrastructure in indigenous territories. Remarkable among these are the financing of educational and sanitary infrastructure in the San Marcos region (US$30 million) and the loan of the Guatemalan government to finance the building of the San Marcos-Tacaná highway that would provide access to the zones having mining potential (Castagnino 2006).

Once the conditions for the expansion of mining were created, an open sky mine named "Marlin" was projected and located in Maya territory, precisely in the San Marcos region where the above-mentioned investments were made. The strategy of the state was to favor the interests of the foreign investors over those of the Maya people, given that no information was given to the population about the existence of gold deposits, and the population was not consulted about the mining project planned for their territory.

The procedure was to cover the basic institutional requirements for the mine "Marlin" to be made real: the environmental impact manifestation was approved, minimizing the effects on ecosystems and the population's health that would derive from open sky exploitation and from the use of cyanide and large amounts of water for lixiviation of the mineral – practices considered to have a large negative environmental impact, and which are prohibited in many countries.

Once the mine was in operation, the risks for spills of contaminated muds due to an earthquake (geologic faults of high seismicity risk cross the region) or to inadequate management would be increased and could potentially affect the rivers and aquifers in the region. Also, the operation of the mine would increase the competition for industrial and human use of water because the process of gold extraction requires large volumes of water.

The mining company in charge of the prospecting in a region in Guatemala that was until then unexplored was Glamis Gold Ltd., based in Reno, Nevada (US), and whose actions were traded in the stock markets of New York and Toronto. The company was able to obtain all the permits from the state and even obtained a loan from a filial of the World Bank to execute the project. The entrance of the company into the region was stealthy; the land where the mine was to be located was acquired from its indigenous owners at very low prices and without informing them about the existence of gold, and the mining project had no diffusion at the local and regional levels (Castagnino 2006).

The conflict was originated when the transit of vehicles transporting equipment and heavy machinery on the new San Marcos highway awakened the suspicions of the population of some project or development being implemented in the region without their knowledge. The tension peaked when heavy machinery was retained in a Maya locality to demand an explanation from the government or from the private sector about the project being built. In response, without giving signs of social and political sensitivity, the state sent 1,500 soldiers to the area, generating confrontations with the population that resulted in one indigenous inhabitant's death and several being wounded (Castagnino 2006). Despite the civil resistance, the mining project was realized a few months later, and the gold deposits began to be exploited in the year 2005. The state's arguments were that the project was strategic for national development and a source of employment and social wellbeing for the local population.

Months later, the population first noticed the negative effects of the mine: the landscape was transformed after the explosions made to extract the mineral destroyed the hills and forests that were part of the indigenous territory. Many small houses close to the mine started suffering structural damage (wall fractures at 45 degrees); the traditional sources of water diminished their availability because of the exploitation of aquifers for supplying the mine; the inappropriate management of muds led to their mixing with natural water currents that became contaminated (Castagnino 2006; TLA 2006). The population began to present dermatologic afflictions and health problems. A recent study made at the University of Michigan found that the concentration of heavy metals in the blood of people living close to the mine was higher than that of people living at a distance of 20 km from the mine. The problem is that the continued exposure to the pollutants may lead in a short time to exceeding the permissible levels set by the international legislation and the health of the population is at risk because of the mining activities in the region.

The movement opposing the mine was able to establish links with more ample sectors of the Guatemalan society and even called the attention of the international community. Among the activities of civil defense was the claim to the Inter-American Human Rights Commission (CIDH by its Spanish acronym) of the Organization of American States. Also, a demand was raised against the Guatemalan government for violation of indigenous peoples' rights and for not respecting the ILO Convention 169 or the ICECR of the United Nations, which among other things claims there must be a previous consultation to the population about projects planned to be built in their territory.

In reply to these petitions, the United Nations human rights rapporteurs exhorted the Guatemalan government to take into account the public opinion about the permanence and expansion in their territory of the Marlin mine (CRG 2010). Also, in May 2010, the CIDH submitted a recommendation to the government as an interim measure for the population of 18 indigenous communities:

> (1) Stop mining activity in the Marlin project, and take measures to prevent pollution. (2) Take measures for decontamination of the sources of water

> supplying the inhabitants of both municipalities. (3) Provide medical attention to the population that could have been affected by the pollution from mining. (4) Adopt measures to guarantee the life and physical integrity of inhabitants of communities. (5) Plan protection measures with the participation of the population.
>
> (Siglo.21 2010)

Under this scenario of conflict that has surpassed the local boundary, it becomes clear that the Guatemalan government must review its political strategy and equilibrate economic and social interests in decision-making about the Marlin mine, because if no response is given to the exhort of the CIDH, the case may pass to the court of the Inter-American Human Rights Commission, due to its binding character.

However, in December 2011, the CIDH modified the precautionary measures it granted 18 months earlier: the petitions were suppressed for the suspension of operations in the Marlin mine, the decontamination of water sources and the attention of health problems. The CIDH asked the government of Guatemala to adopt measures for assuring that the sources of water used by communities have an adequate quality for domestic use and for irrigation. The Center for International Environmental Law (CIEL) and Mining Watch Canada expressed their deep concern for the political pressure exerted over the CIDH, the main organization in the American continent for the protection of human rights, to change the precautionary measures (Ramazzini 2012).

Regarding the right to consultation of indigenous peoples whenever a project exists that may affect their territory, stated in Covenant 196 of the International Labour Organization, more than one million people participated in 58 communitarian consultations to solve a "No" to mining exploration and exploitation in Guatemala. In response to social participation, the government sent a law initiative to the congress to regulate the processes of communitarian consultation. The Council of Western Peoples appealed and, finally, on December 2011, they obtained a favorable sentence that recognized that indigenous peoples must be consulted before an administrative and legal measure is taken within their territory, and that the decision of communities must be respected, thus validating their common rights (Ramazzini 2012).

The ethical tribunals as alternative spaces of environmental justice and defense of human rights

In the same measure as the states omit their social responsibilities, violate international agreements to guarantee the rights of indigenous peoples, the human right to water, and favor of private over collective interests, will the importance of civil monitoring and social mobilization be ever more necessary. This also implies the appearance of alternative spaces of environmental justice, such as the ethical tribunals to face the scenario of immunity and violation of the law by the state and its institutions. Under these premises, the Latin American Water

Tribunal was created in the year 2000 as an international, autonomous and independent instance of environmental justice, in order to aid the solution of conflicts related to water in the region. It is based on principles of coexistence, respect to human dignity, solidarity among peoples, and sacredness of living forms and environmental responsibility. Its role is essentially didactic and of conscience given that it attempts to achieve a political and social consensus to transform ethical-environmental values and a change in the dominant paradigms (Ávila 2008; Bogantes 2007).

A conscience tribunal is based on the strength of moral condemn and civil mobilization for the defense of the fundamental right of Latin Americans to have water available to them in adequate quantity and quality. The people have a right, over corporate and state powers, to the use and protection of their water systems for present and future generations. Society must make a conscience decision about the importance of managing water with social and environmental sustainability and a vigilant attitude toward public or private projects that actually or potentially affect the hydric systems in Latin America (Bogantes 2007).

Until today, the tribunal has held sessions on six occasions and has analyzed 53 cases of water conflicts in several Latin American countries. The public sessions offer a chance for people to expose their demands and present evidence beyond the traditional legal proof. The members of the tribunal jury analyze each case, based on a file compiled by the contradicting part, and the arguments are exposed in a public audience. A constant in all cases is the violation of human rights by the state or other actors (transnational mining companies, private companies that supply water, etc.), as well as the helplessness of the population in a judicial system acting partially and setting aside the essential rights of the population (Ávila 2008).

Among cases analyzed by the tribunal jury are the privatization of water in Los Altos, Bolivia, the case of the Marlin mine in Guatemala, and the case of water transfer and affectation of the Mazahua people in Mexico. For the present assay, a summary is made of the latter two cases with their corresponding sentences.

First, the Guatemalan case was analyzed as a Central American block, including El Salvador, Honduras, Nicaragua, and Costa Rica, to denounce the presence of open-pit mining, which attempts against human rights, in particular, that to water. In the sentence general precisions were emitted for each country. The resolution for the case of the Merlin mine follows (Latin American Water Tribunal 2006):

1 A moral censorship was made to the government of Guatemala and, in particular to its President for allowing the presence of mining activities conveying a high health risk to the population and harmful to the ecosystems, with the goal of favoring particular interests and transnational enterprises in detriment of the Guatemalan population.
2 To morally censor the government of Guatemala for overlooking its obligation of consultation of the indigenous population affected by mining activities and omitting the results of consultations independently made that oppose to such activities.

3 To morally censor the Ministry of Environment and Natural Resources for not assuming the responsibility of talking care of and assuring supply of water to the population in appropriate quality and quantity, by means of allowing the deterioration of supply sources through use and pollution by the mining industry.
4 To exhort the Congress of Guatemala to review the Mining Law or emitting a new law that assures the sovereignty, the defense of human rights and the patrimony of the people of Guatemala.
5 To exhort the government of Guatemala to respect the dispositions of the international treaties they have promised to honor and that are above the Constitution.

The case of Mazahua Movement for the Defense of Water and Human Rights is examined in Box 9.1, in which a 2006 resolution recognized the importance of water as a human right, the role of the state as a warrantor of that right, and the need to respect the right of indigenous peoples to control their territory (Box 9.1). The recommendation points out that the infrastructure for water transfer to Mexico City directly affect the Mazahua population, in terms of their essential rights (water, food, development, culture) and that there are important omissions of the state, in terms of recognition to human and indigenous peoples rights. For those reasons, it is resolved that the transfer of water is not a solution for the water supply problems of Mexico City, because it affects the essential rights of the Mazahua people to control their territory and natural resources and because it attempts against their culture.

Box 9.1 Latin American Water Tribunal: Case Transfer of water from the region of the Cutzamala System to the Valley of Mexico basin (Mexican United States)

Actors of the contradiction: Mazahua Movement for the Defense of Water and Human Rights
In opposition to: Regional Management of Waters of the Valley of Mexico
Federal Commission of Electricity (Spanish abbreviation: CFE)
Ministry of Environment and Natural Resources (Spanish abbreviation: SEMARNAT)
National Commission of Water (Spanish abbreviation: CNA)

Recitals

1 The recognition of the universal human right to water in adequate quantity and quality as a fundamental human right, whose full exercise must be protected by the States.

2 The guarantee to all human beings of each and every basic public service, in particular of drinking water in adequate quantity and quality involves the premise of respect to human dignity and the exercise of citizenship.
3 The transfer of water through the importation of water from other aquifers by means of reservoirs and other infrastructures causes damage to originating populations in relation to their culture, land tenure and subsistence means.
4 The non-recognition of the responsible authorities of the right of indigenous people to develop according to their customary uses, culture and ways of living.
5 The omission of authorities of complying their obligations to give a response to the needs and demands of the Mazahua People and of communities affected by the hydraulic projects.

In view of the facts and recitals that precede, the Jury of the Latin American Water Tribunal *resolves*:

> To declare that the transfer of water to Mexico City from other basins is not viable as a solution to solve the problems of supply in that it violates the rights of the Mazahua People to the control of their territory and natural resources and attempts against their culture.

Recommendations

1 That the fourth stage of the Cutzamala System be cancelled.
2 That the Mazahua region be compensated for the benefits received by the water supply to Mexico City and for the socio-environmental deterioration caused.
3 That a drinking water program be implemented to contribute to solve the supply problems in communities.
4 That the implicated authorities provide financial support to local initiatives in the execution of the Sustainable Integrated Plan for the region of the Cutzamala System with the objective of benefiting all the Mazahua population.
5 That the ecological flow of the rivers Malacatepec, Tiloxtoc and Tingambato are guaranteed and that a limit is set to exploitation of wells in the Lerma System in order to recover the aquifers.
6 That, wherever possible, the land expropriated and not used by the project is restituted to their legitimate owners, *ejidos* and communities, and compensation be given for other damages caused.
7 That the emission of muds and polluting substances from the purification plant of "Los Berros" be controlled in order to comply with environmental norms and the degree of pollution of superficial water currents is diminished.

8 That water treatment plants are built for the control of wastewaters directly discharged to bodies of water.
9 That the archaeological sites are protected and the expansion of the agricultural frontier be stopped in forest areas with the objective of protecting zones of high hydrological and ecological importance.

Source: TLA (2006)

As a recommendation, the tribunal appointed the state to stop the expansion of the water transfer project (Stage IV, Temazcaltepec) that would cause affectation to more localities and indigenous regions in the states of Mexico and Guerrero; that a compensation program is applied through public investment to the Mazahua region in exchange for the environmental services it provides Mexico City; to implement actions to solve the deficit in water supply in the Mazahua region and guarantees their essential rights to an adequate access to the service; and that it gives impulse to initiatives toward the conservation of water and other natural resources (forests, soils) that lead to a sustainable development of the region.

Conclusion and policy implications

Water has played a primordial role in the pattern of human settlement, productive strategies and development of indigenous peoples of Latin America. The sociocultural value of water is expressed through the various worldviews, myths, perceptions, and archetypes connecting the indigenous peoples with a sacred and divine origin. For Mesoamerican and Andean cultures, water was a gift from the gods that must be cared for and earned through rituals and practices of use and appropriation that were supported on a relation of respect and integration with nature.

Water rights arose in a sociocultural and ecological context that provided belongingness to a territory: the notion of water as a collective good and the respect for social agreements for its management were the normative basis of the uses and customs of indigenous peoples. At the same time it was an adaptation mechanism for the ecological settings with difficult climatic conditions and water scarcity (such as in the Andes and in the arid zones in Mexico). Until the present, there are indigenous regions in Latin America in which worldviews and sociocultural strategies persist, and in which for centuries a culture of sustainable management of water has been generated and adapted, having as its principle the collective rights and the communitarian management of the territory with its associated natural resources.

Historically, the coexistence of different standards for valuing water have been a focus of tension, as it occurred with the indigenous and Spaniard perceptions of water during the Colonial period, or with the current monism of the state that only recognizes formal law and imposes it over other social rights and non-formal, preexistent regulations (consuetudinary law, customary uses).

However, in recent years, due to states' reforms and changes in the economic model that privilege private property and free market, sociocultural valuing of water has tended to be replaced or even annulated by an economic valuing. In other words, during the neoliberal period, water has tended to lose its integrating sense to become a commodity having an economic value and a price, a trend that finds support in legal and institutional reforms made by the state regarding access, appropriation, and management of the resource.

Resistances and disputes for the defense of water as a common good with a regulated access and a free and collective beneficial ownership have occurred in Latin America. The problem is that the channels for negotiation and management of the conflict have closed as a result of the new legislation and water policies that have directly affected the rights of indigenous people. The clearest expression of these has been the privatization of water rights and land in their territories.

It is in this context that the notion of water as a human right has been, at the international level, a new strategy for the defense of indigenous peoples to face the attacks of the state or its alliance with the private sector in order to implement modernization projects and foreign investments in their territories. The defense of water rights by indigenous peoples has expanded their margin of action and alliance with other actors because it is included as a human right. This has in addition implied the defense of legal plurality in spaces of alternative justice, such as the Latin American Water Tribunal that aims to have incidence in the resolution of water conflicts in the region.

Recommendations

In conclusion, we end this chapter with the following recommendations:

- Going beyond the economic vision of water resources and to revalue its social and cultural importance for the indigenous people, as well as the role played by communitarian institutions and forms of social organization in the sustainable management of water resources.
- Rethinking novel schemes of water management in the indigenous territories that do not necessarily entail its privatization or the state's control, such as co-management and decentralized management.
- Recognizing the water rights of the indigenous peoples as a form of legal pluralism or coexistence of state laws with the consuetudinary right (uses and customs), which would avoid the development of social conflicts in its territories.
- Linking legislation and national policy of international commitments about human rights and indigenous rights, so the Latin American states stop being in a constant violation of legality. For that, it is also required that the international cooperation guarantees the fulfillment of such commitments, as in the case of the Millennium Development Goals (for example, regarding access to water).

Acknowledgements

Special thanks to the National Autonomous University of Mexico for the support for this research received from PAPIIT 2012-IN301712, "Water Security and Social-Environmental Conflicts in Mexico: The Challenge Of Global Change" project.

Notes

1 "Every person has the right to access, disposition and sanitation of water for human consumption and domestic use in a sufficient, sanitary, accessible and feasible manner. The State will guarantee that right and the law will define the basis, aids and modalities for the access and the equitative and sustainable use of water resources, establishing the participation of the Federation, the federated entities and the municipalities, as well as the participation of the citizenship for the achieving of the above-said means" (Estados Unidos Mexicanos 2012: 6).

2 "Article 20. I. All persons have the right of universal and equitable access to basic services of drinking water, sewage...II. The State in all its levels is responsible for the provision of basic services through public, mixed, cooperative or communitarian [entities]...The provision of services must respond to the criteria of universality, responsibility, accessibility, continuity, quality, efficiency, efficacy, equitable fares and needed coverage, with social participation and control. III. The access to water and sewage are human rights, not an object of concession nor privatization and are subjected to a licensing and registers regime, according to the law" (Asamblea Constituyente 2008).

3 "Article 374. I. The State will protect and guarantee the priority of the use of water for life. It is the duty of the State to manage, regulate, protect and plan the adequate and sustainable use of water resources, with social participation, guaranteeing the access to water to all its inhabitants. The law will establish the conditions and limitations of all uses. II. The State will recognize and respect the uses and customs of communities, its local authorities and those of the originating indigenous sustenance farmer organizations about the right, administration and sustainable management of water..." (Asamblea Constituyente 2008).

References

Asamblea Constituyente (2008) *Nueva Constitución Política del Estado de Bolivia*. Bolivia: P Asamblea Constituyente.

Assies, W. (2001) "David vs. Goliat en Cochabamba: los derechos del agua, el neoliberalismo y la renovación de la propuesta social en Bolivia." *T'inkazos: Revista Boliviana de Ciencias Sociales* 8: 106–34.

Ávila, P. (1996) *Escasez de agua en una región indígena de Michoacán*. Mexico: El Colegio de Michoacán.

—— (2007) *El manejo del agua en territorios indígenas en México*. Serie del Agua en México, vol. 4. Mexico: Departamento de México y Colombia, Región de Latinoamérica y el Caribe, Banco Mundial.

—— (2008) "Déficits legislativos y gestión dialogada de conflictos hídricos en América Latina: la experiencia del Tribunal Latinoamericano del Agua." In Fundación Seminario de investigación para la paz-Gobierno de Aragón, *El agua, derecho humano y raíz de conflictos*, Serie estudios para la paz 22. Zaragoza: Colección Actas 71.

Bakker, K. (2007) "Commodity: Alter-Globalization, Anti-Privatization and the Human Right to Water in the Global South." *Antipode* 39 (3): 430–55.

Bauer, C. J. (2004) *Canto de sirenas: El derecho de aguas chileno como modelo para reformas internacionales*, Bilbao: Bakeaz/Fundación Nueva Cultura del Agua.

Blattner, J. and Ingram, H. M. (eds) (2001) *Reflections on Water: New Approaches to Tranboundary Conflict and Cooperation*. Cambridge, MA: MIT Press.

Boege, E. (2008) *El patrimonio biocultural de los pueblos indígenas de México*. Mexico: Instituto Nacional de Antropología e Historia and Comisión Nacional para el Desarrollo de los Pueblos Indígenas.

Boelens, R. (2009) "Aguas diversas. Derechos de agua y pluralidad legal en las comunidades andinas." *Anuario de Estudios Americanos* 66(2): 23–55.

Boelens, R., Getches, D., and Guevara, A. (2006) *Agua y derecho: políticas hídricas, derechos consuetudinarios e identidades locales*. Lima: WALIR-Universidad de Waginen/Instituto de Estudios Peruanos.

Boelens, R., Bustamante, R. and de Vos, H. (2007) "Legal Pluralism and the Politics of Inclusion: Recognition and Contestation of Local Water Rights in the Andes." In B. van Koppen, M. Giordano, and J. Butterworth (eds), *Community-Based Water Law and Water Resource Management* 96 *Reform in Developing Countries*. Wallingford: CAB International.

Bogantes, J. (2007) "Tribunales éticos: un acercamiento filosófico y práctico a la justicia ambiental." in S. Esch *et al*, *La gota de la vida: hacia una gestión democrática y sustentable del agua*. Mexico: Fundacion Boll.

Budds, J. (2004) "Power, Nature and Neoliberalism: The Political Ecology of Water in Chile." *Journal of Tropical Geography* 25(3): 322–42.

—— (2009) "The 1981 Water Code: The Impacts of Private Tradable Water Rights on Peasant and Indigenous Communities in Northern Chile." In W. L. Alexander (ed.), *Lost in the Long Transition: Struggles for Social Justice in Neoliberal Chile*. Lanham, MD: Lexington Books.

—— (2010) "Las relaciones sociales de poder y la producción de paisajes hídricos." In H. Vélez *et al.*, *Justicia Hídrica*. Bogotá: CENSAT-Agua Viva.

Castagnino, V. (2006) *Minería de metales y derechos humanos en Guatemala: La mina Marlin en San Marcos*. London: Peace Brigades International.

Castree, N. (2008) "Neoliberalising Nature: Processes, Effects, and Evaluations." *Environment and Planning A* 40: 153–73.

CESCR (2002) *General Comment No. 15: The Right to Water*. Articles 11 and 12 of the International Covenant on Economic, Social and Cultural Rights. Geneva: United Nations Committee on Economic, Social and Cultural Rights.

CRG (2010) "Commission of Indigenous Peoples Meets United Nations Rapporteur, Guatemala." June 16. Commission of the Republic of Guatemala. See www.congreso.gob.gt/gt/ver_noticia.asp?id=10723.

Del Popolo, F. and Oyarce, A. M. (2005) "Población indígena de América Latina: perfil sociodemográfico en el marco de la CIPD y de las Metas del Milenio." In *Seminario Internacional Pueblos indígenas y afrodescendientes de América Latina y el Caribe: relevancia y pertinencia de la información sociodemográfica para políticas y programas*. Santiago de Chile: CEPAL.

Espinosa, G. (1996) *El embrujo del lago: el sistema lacustre de la cuenca de México en la cosmovisión mexica*. Mexico: UNAM-IIH-IIA.

Estados Unidos Mexicanos (2012) *Constitución Política de los EUM*. Diario Oficial de la Federación, February 9. Available at www.diputados.gob.mx/LeyesBiblio/pdf/1.pdf.

Estermann, J. (2006) *Filosofía Andina: Sabiduría indígena para un mundo nuevo*. La Paz: Instituto Superior Ecuménico Andino de Teología.

Gelles, P. (2000) *Water and Power in Highland Peru*. New Brunswick, NJ: Rutgers University Press.

Gentes, I. (2002) *Agua, poder y conflicto étnico*. Santiago: CEPAL.

—— (2009) "Las aguas transadas. Hacia una evaluación del impacto social y ambiental del mercado de derechos de agua en Chile." In S. Vargas *et al.* (eds), *La gestión de los recursos hídricos: realidades y perspectivas*, vol. 2. Mexico: IMTA.

Harvey, D. (2004) *El nuevo imperialismo*. Madrid: Ediciones Akal.

Ilich, I. (1993) *El H_2O y las aguas del olvido*. Mexico: Joaquín Mortiz.

INEGI (2010) *Principales resultados del censo de población y vivienda 2010*. Mexico: Instituto Nacional de Geografía e Informática.

Korsbaek, L. and Vivanco, F. (2005) "La sociedad plural y el pluralismo jurídico, un acercamiento desde la antropología del derecho." In J. E. Ordóñez Cifuentes (coord.), *Pluralismo jurídico y pueblos indígenas: XIII Jornadas Lascasianas Internacionales*. Mexico: Instituto de Investigaciones Jurídicas.

Kruze, T. (2005) "Capítulo IV: La Guerra del Agua en Cochabamba, Bolivia: terrenos complejos, convergencias nuevas." In E. de la Garza (coord.), *Sindicatos y nuevos movimientos sociales en América Latina*. Buenos Aires: CLACSO.

Langford, M. and Khalfan, A. (2007) "Introducción al agua como derecho humano." In S. Esch *et al.*, *La gota de la vida: hacia una gestión democrática y sustentable del agua*. Mexico: Fundacion Boll.

Latin American Water Tribunal (2006) "Verdict of the Regional Public Hearing, Case of Expansion of Mining Concessions and Activities in Central American Territories." March 25. Available at www.tragua.com/audiencias/2006/veredictos_2006/CasoCentroamerica.pdf.

León-Portilla, M. (1992) "El agua: universo de significaciones y realidades en Mesoamérica." *Ciencias* (October 28).

Mazadiego, L. F., Puche, O. and Hervás, M. (2009) "Water and Inca Cosmogony: Myths, Geology and Engineering in the Peruvian Andes." *Geology and Religion* 310: 17–24.

Musset, A. (1992) *El agua en el Valle de México: siglos XVI–XVIII*. Mexico: Pórtico de la Ciudad-CEMCA.

Palerm, A. (1972) *Agricultura y Sociedad en Mesoamérica*. Mexico: Sepsetentas.

Perló, M. and González, A. (2005) *Guerra por el agua en el valle de México?: estudio sobre las relaciones hidráulicas entre el Distrito Federal y el Estado de México*. Mexico: UNAM-Fundación Friedrich Ebert.

Perreault, T. (2008) "Custom and Contradiction: Rural Water Governance and the Politics of Usos y Costumbres in Bolivia's Irrigators' Movement." *Annals of the Association of American Geographers* 98(4): 834–54.

Ramazzini, Á. (2012) "Guatemala: Los problemas creados por la mina Marlín." *Prensa Indígena* (February 27). Available at www.prensaindigena.org.mx/?q=content/guatemala-los-problemas-creados-por-la-mina-marl%C3%ADn.

Robert, J. (1994) *Water is a Commons*. Mexico: Habitat International Coalition.

—— (2002) "Las aguas arquetípicas y la globalización del desvalor." In P. Ávila (coord.), *Agua, cultura y sociedad en México*. Mexico: El Colegio de Michoacán/ Instituto Mexicano de Tecnología del Agua.

Rojas, T. (1985) *La cosecha de agua en la cuenca de México*. Cuadernos de la Casa Chata no. 116. Mexico: CIESAS.

Romero Toledo, H., Romero Aravena, H., and Toledo Olivares, X. (2009) "Agua, Poder y

Discursos: Conflictos Socio-territoriales por la construcción de centrales hidroeléctricas en la Patagonia Chilena." *Anuario de Estudios Americanos* 66(2): 81–103.
Siglo.21 (2010) "La CIDH solicita frenar explotación en Marlin." *Diario Siglo.21*, Guatemala (May 22). Available at www.s21.com.gt/nacionales/2010/05/22/cidh-solicita-frenar-explotacion-en-marlin.
Stavenhagen, R. (1988) *Derecho indígena y derechos humanos en América Latina*. Mexico: Instituto Interamericano de Derechos Humanos, El Colegio de México.
—— (1990) *Entre la ley y la costumbre: el derecho consuetudinario indígena en América Latina*. Mexico: Instituto Interamericano de Derechos Humanos, Instituto Indigenista Interamericano.
Swyngedouw, E. (2004) *Social Power and the Urbanization of Water: Flows of Power*. Oxford: Oxford University Press.
Tirel, M. (2006) "Mazahuas y guerrerenses, unidos en defensa de los ríos." *La Jornada Ecológica* (September 25). Available at www.jornada.unam.mx/2006/09/25/eco-d.html.
TLA (2006) *Expediente de casos en controversia de la primer sesión internacional*. Mexico: Tribunal Latinoamericano del Agua.
UN (2010) *Declaration the Human Right to Water and Sanitation*. July 26. New York: United Nations.
UNDP (2006) *Beyond Scarcity: Power, Poverty and the Global Water Crisis*. Human Development Report 2006. New York: United Nations Development Programme.
UNICEF (2012) *Los pueblos indígenas en América Latina*. Available at www.unicef.org/lac/pueblos_indigenas.pdf.
Urteaga, P. (2001) "Interculturalidad, interlegalidad y derechos humanos." Presentation at Curso Internacional, "Constitución y Derechos Humanos." Iquitos: Defensoría del Pueblo and la Facultad de Derecho de la Universidad Nacional de la Amazonía Peruana.
Vargas, R. (2006) *La cultura del agua: lecciones de la América Indígena*. Montevideo: UNESCO/Programa Hidrológico Internacional.
Whiteford, S. and Melville, R. (eds) (2002) *Protecting a Sacred Gift: Water and Social Change in Mexico*. San Diego, CA: Center for US–Mexican Studies at the University of California.
Wilder, M. (2006) "Paradoxes of Decentralization: Water Reform and Social Implications in Mexico." *World Development* 34(11): 1977–95.
—— (2010) "Water Governance in Mexico: Political and Economic Apertures and a Shifting State-Citizen Relationship." *Ecology and Society* 15(2): 22.

10 Northern voices, northern waters

Traditional knowledge and water policy development in the Northwest Territories

J. Michael Miltenberger

Within the context of the critical need to protect and manage global water resources in a manner that preserves water quality, quantity, and flow for future generations, this chapter explores the state of traditional knowledge in northern Canada. It then considers in some detail the challenges associated with use and application of traditional knowledge, and the opportunities for its enhanced use and application to inform environmental management and decision-making in the north generally, and water management specifically.

Acceptance not only of the credibility of traditional knowledge, but also of its relevance and importance to environmental management, is increasing around the world; and its compilation and codification is an evolving field. This chapter examines the barriers to the use and application of traditional knowledge, and proposes that, for a number of reasons, the time is right for considerable progress to be made in this area.

Finally, the chapter proposes a way forward and makes practical recommendations for future actions by governments, indigenous groups, academic institutions, and resource developers, using current policy initiatives by the Government of the Northwest Territories (GNWT) as a focal point.

Note that the term "indigenous knowledge" is in common usage throughout much of the world. In the Northwest Territories, the term "traditional knowledge" is more commonly used, but can generally be understood to be synonymous with "indigenous knowledge." For convenience, this chapter will use the term "traditional knowledge."

Introduction

The Northwest Territories (NWT) of Canada covers 13 percent of Canada's land mass, an area of 1,346,106 square kilometers, which is larger than Great Britain, Northern Ireland, France, and Germany combined. The NWT is a geographically remote area with, until recently, largely undisturbed landscapes and habitats. The NWT is home to huge water bodies, and its pristine and extensive water sources are one of the most valued features of the territory's natural capital. Twelve percent of the surface of the NWT is fresh water. This includes the Mackenzie River, which is the largest river in Canada and whose watershed is among the world's 10 largest. The 1.8 million square kilometer river basin encompasses one-fifth of the entire area of Canada. The NWT is home to Great Slave Lake and Great Bear Lake, Canada's fourth and fifth largest lakes. In addition to these well-known water bodies, the NWT landscape includes a multitude of lakes, rivers, streams, ponds, and many deltas – extensive wetlands that are critical for migratory waterfowl, and widespread permafrost.

The NWT has a population of approximately 43,000 people, of whom half are of Aboriginal descent. The territory has a population density of 0.03 persons per square kilometer, while Canada has a corresponding density of 3.5 (2006 census). By way of comparison, Argentina's population density is 14.9 persons per square kilometer.

Aboriginal cultures are known to have inhabited the area for thousands of years, relying on the land and its resources to provide for food, clothing, water and all the necessities of life, leading to a detailed knowledge of the land, animal behavior, seasonal and climatic changes and ecological relationships. Aboriginal people in the NWT today maintain strong ties to their traditional way of life and cultural traditions, even as they adopt and embrace modern technology and lifestyles.

The lives of the peoples of the NWT are inexorably linked to the NWT's waterways. Rivers and lakes have provided traditional transportation routes, and are imbued with deep cultural and spiritual significance. The fish and wildlife that have been the source of food, clothing, tools and other necessities, as well as the vegetation that provides food, medicine, and shelter, all rely on the water to grow and flourish. More recently, the water systems of the NWT have continued to play a critical role in the evolution of the northern economy. Barges bring much-needed fuel and supplies to northern communities with no road access. Hydroelectric developments supply much of the NWT's electricity. Resource extraction industries rely on ice roads across frozen water bodies to haul supplies and equipment to remote mine sites. And the NWT's pristine wilderness and world-class fishing and boating opportunities are a strong draw for tourists.

Management of land and water in the NWT

Aboriginal rights to the continued use and ownership of certain lands in the NWT are established through a constitutionally-based legal framework, beginning with the signing of treaties by the government of Canada with the Dene in 1900 and 1921. Among other provisions, the treaties contain a promise that Aboriginal people will be permitted to continue their traditional activities of hunting, trapping, and fishing in perpetuity. More recently, the legal and constitutional basis for governing in the NWT has changed dramatically. In 1982 the Canadian Charter of Rights and Freedoms entrenched a combination of Aboriginal rights to resources and Aboriginal treaty rights in s. 35 of the Constitution Act. Canadian courts have recognized Aboriginal rights, and federal government policy has established processes in which those legally recognized rights are negotiated through land claims agreements.

The completion of these agreements has resulted in a complex but progressive governance framework in the NWT, with jurisdiction split among Canada, the Government of the Northwest Territories and Aboriginal governments. The regulatory framework that governs the management of renewable and non-renewable resources is not static, but evolving as each land claims or self-government agreement is finalized and implemented. It involves numerous agencies that work within a common legislative framework.

The Government of Canada retains lead authority for environmental assessment, issuing land use permits and water licenses. This authority is exercised through the Mackenzie Valley Land and Water Board, which has jurisdiction in areas where land claims are not settled, and which also ensures consistency of regulation and policy across the territory and deals with transboundary issues. Co-management boards provide a forum in which the Aboriginal governments can exercise shared jurisdiction with Canada for land and water regulation within their claims areas, and with the territorial government for management of wildlife and forestry. Five other federal departments exercise some measure of jurisdiction over water. Within the GNWT, the Department of Environment and Natural Resources has legislated authority for environmental protection, including safeguarding the sustainability of water resources. Three other departments play an active role in ensuring the quality of drinking water.

In addition to legal responsibilities established through legislation, the Government of Canada also has a constitutionally based fiduciary obligation established through land claims agreements, which call for waters "to remain substantially unaltered as to the quality, quantity and rate of flow."

As the second largest river basin in North America, the Mackenzie River Basin supports many diverse and sensitive ecosystems, and stretches across the legal jurisdiction of three Canadian provinces and two territories. In 1997, a Transboundary Waters Master Agreement was signed among the governments of Canada, Saskatchewan, Alberta, British Columbia, the NWT, and Yukon. The parties agreed to a series of principles to guide their actions in carrying out their legislative responsibilities in the Mackenzie River Basin. A 13-member Mackenzie River Basin Board was established as a result of the agreement, with representatives from the federal, provincial, and territorial signatory governments, and Aboriginal groups in each jurisdiction. However, the board has no regulatory authority, and no legal or policy basis to regulate water resources. The board can provide information to regulatory processes, but with few resources and no real commitment from member jurisdictions it has not played an effective role.

Northern Voices, Northern Waters: The NWT Water Stewardship Strategy

Northerners have long understood that maintaining the quality of northern water systems is essential to maintaining a way of life. Water quality has a direct impact on the daily lives of individuals and the health of communities. Water is increasingly recognized as an economic resource, given the key role that it plays in energy production, manufacturing, and the agricultural sector. As southern jurisdictions begin to face challenges with the quantity and quality of local water sources, they will turn to northern Canada to tap into the vast reserves of northern lakes and rivers.

Northern Canada's water systems are not immune to the impact of industrial and agricultural use elsewhere in North America. Water flows in the Mackenzie River Basin have been affected by upstream hydroelectric developments and a host of other developments – especially oil sands in Northern Alberta. Industrial toxins such as mercury have been found in the flesh of Mackenzie River fish. Climate change, whether anthropogenic or otherwise, appears to be affecting the Peace and Athabasca rivers, as higher temperatures and reduced precipitation rates combine to result in reduced flows and the associated cumulative impacts. Residents of communities along the Mackenzie River particularly have expressed concerns repeatedly over the past 20 years, to regulatory agencies and government departments, about deteriorating water quality, as evidenced by numerous indicators; including among others the taste and appearance of the water, flow levels, health and quality of fish, changing vegetation, and aquatic habitat productivity.

The massive development of the northern Alberta oil sands uses enormous quantities of water to extract oil from the sandy soil. The water then contains a highly toxic mix of hydrocarbons and other chemicals, and has to be disposed of as waste material. This process poses two threats to the Mackenzie River Basin – a direct impact on river flow levels as countless millions of cubic meters of water are diverted to the oil sands project, and a potential long-term impact on surface and groundwater quality. The Province of British Columbia has just announced plans to conduct an environmental assessment for a proposed massive hydroelectric project on the Peace River, which could also have a direct impact on water levels in the Mackenzie River Basin if it proceeds.

Concerns about threats to the quality and quantity of NWT waters led the Government of the Northwest Territories (GNWT) to undertake a collaborative, multi-stakeholder process to develop a strategy to begin the daunting task of safeguarding northern waters. *Northern Voices, Northern Waters: NWT Water Stewardship Strategy*, which was made public in May 2010, is the result of three years of collaborative effort between the GNWT and the Government of Canada, working in collaboration with Aboriginal governments, northern land and water boards, and organizations from across the territory (GNWT and Government of Canada 2010; hereafter, "the strategy"). The strategy outlines a series of goals designed to ensure the continued quality of waters not only in the NWT, but also in adjacent jurisdictions that flow into or through the NWT. It aims to ensure that aquatic ecosystems are healthy and diverse, and that residents of the NWT can rely on safe and plentiful supplies of water for drinking and to support traditional cultural activities. It outlines a broad-ranging and ambitious set of tasks to accomplish these goals, ranging from increased research and monitoring, to development of a system of community-based monitoring on NWT waterways, to strengthened transboundary water agreement negotiations with neighboring jurisdictions.

Of most significance to the discussion in this chapter is the emphasis in the strategy on the recognition and use of traditional knowledge through each aspect of managing water resources. Aboriginal governments, organizations and users of traditional knowledge were involved in the development of the strategy, recognition of traditional knowledge is a guiding principle of the strategy, and the use and application of traditional knowledge in protecting northern waters is a key feature.

Traditional knowledge

The concept of "indigenous knowledge" or "traditional knowledge" is a relatively recent area of exploration in the scientific, academic, and regulatory arenas. Indigenous cultures throughout the world have lived in a close and interdependent relationship with their natural environment over centuries, and have relied on an intimate knowledge and understanding of the natural environment to survive. Their traditional knowledge is based on historical continuity in resource use, within a prescribed geographical area, and generally in a non-industrial society.

It is important to note that there is a wealth of locally acquired knowledge among populations of people, irrespective of cultural or ethnic orientation, who live in close contact with the land, through agriculture, fishing, or other land-based activities, and who have accumulated a lifetime of observation and experience of a particular environment. Their knowledge is equally valid and has been demonstrated to play an important role in environmental management and decision-making. What distinguishes traditional knowledge is the accumulation of knowledge over many generations, leading to a broad and deep understanding of baseline conditions and patterns over time in a particular area.

Much energy has been expended in the literature on debating the most appropriate term, and definition, for the concept. Some take exception to the term "traditional," concerned that it may imply knowledge that is archaic and out-of-date rather than of use in contemporary society. Some take exception to the use of the term "indigenous," feeling that it excludes important local knowledge that is not embedded in the language and culture of a specific group. A generally accepted definition of traditional knowledge in Canada is "a cumulative body of knowledge, practice and belief, evolving by adaptive processes and handed down through generations by cultural transmission, about the relationship of living beings (including humans) with one another and their environment" (Berkes 1999).

Because traditional knowledge covers such a broad range of concepts, some have argued that it is more accurate and appropriate to use the term "traditional environmental knowledge" when discussing knowledge related to ecosystems, that is, to the subject matter that might be studied in the biological, environmental and earth sciences. The discussion in this chapter will focus primarily on this narrower construct.

Traditional knowledge is made up of a logical system of organized knowledge, based on empirical data that draws on observations over time, and historically has been codified and transmitted through oral narrative. The acquisition of traditional knowledge is not an activity distinct from everyday life – knowledge is experiential in nature. Stories told by elders recount their personal experiences, or those of their ancestors, while incorporating important information both about environmental elements and processes, and the underlying values or world view that informs their interpretations of changes in the environment.

In northern Canada, there is an important concept underlying all traditional knowledge, which is a broad definition of what in English might be known as "the environment." Aboriginal people do not distinguish between human beings and the rest of the natural environment, while western science has historically perceived the natural environment to be separate and distinct from humans. All Dene languages have a term that refers to the entire ecosystem as understood by Aboriginal people, including the land and natural features, water and water systems, vegetation, wildlife populations and their behavior, the climate, the wind, and the human inhabitants.

Although traditional knowledge flows from and deals with a very broad concept of the natural environment, categories of knowledge can be identified (Usher 2000). Traditional knowledge related to the natural environment includes factual, rational knowledge that is based on empirical observations by individuals, also drawn from experiences of numerous individuals over a long time, as expressed through shared experience, stories, and teachings. It also includes knowledge about a specific indigenous group's historic and contemporary use of the environment, including harvest patterns, methods and yields, patterns of land use, travel routes, and changes over time in response to changing environmental conditions. A third category of information can be described as culturally based value statements about how people use the land, including rules about respecting the land and animals, when and how to harvest, how to prepare and dispose of harvesting products, and other social mores.

These categories are presented only for the purpose of providing an overview. These are not distinctions that are generally made by indigenous people, and underlying all these categories is an inherent cosmology, or knowledge system, which is inextricably linked to culture.

What is of particular significance for environmental management is that this knowledge constitutes a comprehensive baseline of information accumulated over generations, which can provide a reference point for monitoring changes; and includes a detailed and subtle understanding of the interrelations within a natural system that can be used to interpret changes.

Comparing and contrasting traditional knowledge to western science

Much effort has been put toward identifying the differences and similarities between traditional knowledge related to the environment and western scientific knowledge. Some key distinctions noted by various authors include:

- western science knowledge is acquired through experimentation and field research, while traditional knowledge is acquired through daily interaction with people and the environment;

- western science is compiled and transmitted through written records, traditional knowledge is through oral narrative;
- western science is derived from testing of hypotheses, and is rooted in the scientific method, while traditional knowledge is based on examples and anecdotal information.

A more complex distinction has been made about how the two types of knowledge are understood. Many propose that western science is understood in a secular context, and is distinct from the belief systems of western culture; while traditional knowledge has a spiritual dimension, and is linked to cosmology and cultural values. Other distinctions have been drawn, describing western science as "intellectual" while traditional knowledge is "spiritual," or asserting that western science is not practical while traditional knowledge has practical application. Such comparisons are somewhat subjective, rooted in the world view and values of the observer, and do little to inform the important discussion about the role that traditional knowledge can play in environmental management and protection.

Perhaps more useful than attempting a black-and-white contrast of western scientific and traditional knowledge is to consider how the two fields are perceived. Barnaby and Emery (2008) suggest that practitioners of western science may regard traditional knowledge with skepticism due to several factors, including distrust of non-scientific data (i.e., data that are not derived through accepted scientific methods), uncertainty about the accuracy of data and repeatability of derived relationships asserted through traditional knowledge, and dismissal of non-familiar indicators of change in biological systems. Similarly, traditional knowledge practitioners may be equally skeptical about the results of western scientific exploration as it relates to their geographic areas of expertise, based on distrust of the findings of scientists who have no direct relationship to the field of study, distrust of a sampling approach that may be seen as incomplete, and distrust of data that is accumulated over a short period of time as opposed to generations.

More recently, observations in the literature have dismissed the contrasts outlined above as artificial distinctions. In northern Canada, anthropologists and geographers including Harvey Feit, Fikret Berkes, Peter Usher, and Milton Freeman have spent decades studying harvesting practices of Aboriginal peoples, and concluded that traditional knowledge is used not only to ensure success in harvesting, but also to make resource management decisions. Hunters monitor population trends and changing conditions, and can detail those trends over many years. They monitor indicators that are similar to those used by biologists, for example for moose and caribou they observe the size of groups, frequency of calving, frequency of twinning, trends in survival rates of young, and changes in age or sex composition of populations. They are aware of fish migration routes and spawning areas, and they understand when wildlife populations are most vulnerable. More importantly, this knowledge has been put into practice to ensure the integrity of ecosystems through adaptive management practices. Adaptive management is practiced both through the establishment of harvesting rules to protect species integrity, such as proscription on harvesting pregnant cows, and through responses to changes in population health and trends, for example, ceasing harvesting activities in a specified area for a period of time to allow a population to re-establish.

Traditional harvesting management practices, whether applied to hunting, fishing or forest management, share many characteristics with those of contemporary ecological science. They focus on ecosystem processes, health, and resilience, and they recognize discrete natural geographical units (e.g., watersheds), and they consider ecosystem components such as plants, animals, and humans within these geographical units to be interlinked. Modern resource management practices increasingly recognize that it is not possible to manage only one discrete category of resource in an environment (e.g., timber) without paying attention to the broader environmental arena. It is now generally understood that ecosystems must be viewed as integrated and holistic entities, whose parts do not function independently but must be understood as a complex and interrelated system. Thus, there is a convergence between science and traditional knowledge, and the boundaries between the two knowledge systems may be less rigid than was once thought.

This convergence may be most evident with regard to the biological sciences, particularly applied wildlife biology and wildlife management, which tend to be less experimental and more observation-based than what is commonly known as "pure science." Wildlife biology and traditional knowledge both rely on some elements of quantitative analysis and knowledge gained through experiment, combined with extensive observation and intuitive reasoning.

Just 30 years ago, the concept of traditional knowledge was relatively unknown to western academics outside the realm of anthropology. Today, traditional knowledge is a widely recognized and accepted concept in Canada, and its importance and contribution has been acknowledged in policy and legislation at several levels – although there remain substantial challenges to effectively delivering on these commitments, as discussed later in this chapter.

Bridging the gap between traditional knowledge and modern management systems

Recognizing the credibility of traditional knowledge, however, is just the first step toward seeing it established as a fully contributing field of endeavor. The Alaska Native Science Commission (no date) notes that traditional knowledge is more than the sum of its parts:

> The richness and complexity of local knowledge systems derive principally from the fact that they incorporate, and are often the resolution of, two very different world views. A researcher cannot separate out any one aspect or component of Native knowledge (e.g. traditional ecological knowledge) to the exclusion of any other without misinterpreting it as Natives see and understand it. This is why Natives want control over how their knowledge is collected, interpreted and used.

Fenge and Funston (2009) note that indigenous peoples experience frustration in being asked by scientists and policy-makers to quantify and articulate concepts that might not fit easily into scientific or policy templates, and to record their traditional knowledge into user-friendly compendia. The contextual nature of traditional knowledge, and the nature of its transmittal through oral narrative, makes it difficult to separate discrete pieces of information specific to a species, a plant or an area from the broader context within which it is understood.

Scientists, policy-makers, regulators and resource developers also experience frustration about "where to go to find (traditional knowledge); how to know it when they see it and how to use it given their adherence to the scientific method which relies on searchable data bases, peer-reviewed reports, experimentation and episodic field-work" (Fenge and Funston 2009).

The use of traditional knowledge to inform or enhance scientific knowledge has often focused on attempts to integrate or combine the two streams of knowledge. There is a perception by Aboriginal groups that this generally results in the western science perspective dominating, and there is a concern that regulatory and management decision-makers will take traditional knowledge out of context and use it to justify policy or licensing decisions. This concern has a political dimension as well, linked to the desire of Aboriginal peoples to have control over regulatory and environmental decision-making on their traditional lands.

The potential for traditional knowledge to contribute to environmental management

Although documentation of traditional knowledge and development of appropriate research methods are still at the early stages, it is generally accepted that there is substantial potential for it to inform environmental management processes. Areas in which such knowledge may inform environmental assessments include hydrology and hydrogeology, soil conditions and terrain, air quality, vegetation (abundance, diversity, health), wildlife (abundance, health, nesting or denning areas, migration patterns), and fisheries (spawning grounds, abundance, health, overwintering areas). Additional information that may be obtained from traditional knowledge informants relates to issues such as cumulative effects, long-term ecosystem effects and trends, mitigation recommendations, and monitoring approaches. The Mackenzie Valley Environmental Impact Review Board's *Guidelines for Incorporating Traditional Knowledge into Environmental Impact Assessment* process state that "if properly documented, it can add an important historical perspective and understanding of the variability and extent of biophysical, social and cultural phenomena; and traditional knowledge holders are often able to identify links between seemingly unrelated components of the environment" (MVEIRB 2005).

There are numerous examples that illustrate how traditional knowledge has been used to inform decision-making, or has been demonstrated to have the potential to do so, in some of the above areas.

- In 1982, a proposal was made by Northern Transportation Company to blast and dredge the Mackenzie River just upstream from the community of Fort Good Hope, close to the Ramparts rapids section of the river, since low water levels were impeding the passage of heavily loaded barges. Concerns were expressed by the community, because local harvesters were aware that this area was a critical spawning ground for several fish species, including whitefish and inconnu. Community concerns resulted in a delay of the proposed activity. Although at the time, the Department of Fisheries and Oceans could not confirm the community's concerns, subsequent migration studies conducted by government field staff did confirm the location of spawning grounds in the Ramparts (DeLancey 1984).
- Biologists have worked with Inuit informants in the Belcher Islands to document information on marine birds. Eider ducks overwinter in the Belcher Islands, feeding in areas of permanent open water. In the mid-1990s, Inuit elders reported a decline in the eider population. Biologists and local informants conducted an aerial survey and confirmed a substantial decline since the last survey in the late 1980s. Inuit elders stated that unusually extensive sea ice had occurred in the winter of 1991–1992, leading to mass starvation of the ducks. Gilchrist *et al.* (2005) write that the cause of the changes in sea ice was a volcanic eruption in the southern hemisphere, which lowered circumpolar temperatures that winter. He notes that locals did not know the cause, but detected both changes in sea ice and its impact on the eider population. If Inuit elders had not flagged the issue, "this dramatic population decline would have gone undetected by western science."

Traditional knowledge in northern Canada

Interest in traditional knowledge of northern Canada has been strong among Canadian social scientists for some time. The Government of the Northwest Territories was the first jurisdiction in Canada to officially recognize the role of traditional knowledge and attempt to prescribe its application within a broader governing system through the approval of the Traditional Knowledge Policy in the late 1980s. This policy represents an early attempt to define traditional knowledge, and to promote its use by committing that the government will "incorporate traditional knowledge into government decisions and actions where appropriate." The policy assigns responsibility to all departments to identify areas in which traditional knowledge may be relevant, and places particular importance on the role that traditional knowledge can play in "environmental management actions and decisions."

More recently, recognition of traditional knowledge has been formalized in legislation or policy in a number of instances, including the following:

- The Canadian Environmental Assessment Act (federal legislation) states that, "Community knowledge and aboriginal traditional knowledge may be considered in conducting an environmental assessment" (16.1).

- The Mackenzie Valley Resource Management Act (federal legislation) provides for the use of "scientific data, traditional knowledge and other pertinent information" for the purpose of monitoring environmental impacts.
- Comprehensive land claims and self-government agreements include references to traditional knowledge. For example, the Tlicho Land Claims and Self-government Agreement signed in 2003 specifically directs that the Tlicho Government and co-management agencies established under the Agreement "shall take steps to acquire and use traditional knowledge as well as other types of scientific information and expert opinion" when exercising their powers in the areas of wildlife management, forest and plant management, and land and water licensing.
- The NWT Protected Areas Strategy, a joint initiative of the GNWT and the Government of Canada, promotes "a balanced approach to land use decisions by incorporating the best available traditional, ecological, cultural and economic knowledge."

The Government of Nunavut has incorporated the concept of Inuit Qaujimatunqangit (IQ) as a guiding principle for all government operations. IQ can roughly be translated as "Inuit knowledge," although it is a broad-based term that encompasses all aspects of Inuit traditional culture including values, worldview, language, social organization, knowledge, life skills, perceptions and expectations (Wenzel 2004).

Along with increased recognition and formal acknowledgement of the role of traditional knowledge has also come skepticism. As noted above, scientists may question the validity of traditional knowledge because it is viewed as less credible, or less defensible, than knowledge gained through "pure science" (i.e., the scientific method). Some scientists dismiss it as anecdotal and too rooted in unscientific values and beliefs, while others who accept the validity of traditional knowledge are unclear as to how it can be verified, and thus uncertain about its application to decision-making processes.

There is a legitimate basis to some of these concerns. Just as western science can reach conclusions that are later disproved, traditional observations and explanations may lack completeness or accuracy. Traditional knowledge is by its very nature linked to a specific geographical area, which makes it difficult to extrapolate to a broader context. Dowsley and Wenzel (2008) have documented an example in which harvesters in two Inuit communities observed that polar bear populations were increasing, an observation that was contrary to the assertions of polar bear biologists that populations are decreasing and likely endangered due to climate change. In actual fact, the harvesters' observations were correct within the limited context of their knowledge, as it was subsequently determined that bears were congregating in specific areas adjacent to those two communities due to changing climactic conditions, even though overall populations were declining.

Some skepticism may also be rooted in the broader politics that surround discussions of traditional knowledge, as the need to find ways to apply traditional knowledge to environmental management and decision-making is often linked to the broader discussion of Aboriginal rights and the demand by Aboriginal people for control over their traditional lands and resources.

There is a considerable amount of activity with regard to traditional knowledge in northern Canada today. Aboriginal groups are working actively to document, translate, and codify their traditional knowledge. This activity is stimulated in part by an awareness that much knowledge lies with the elders, and a sense of urgency to document as much as possible while they are still alive. It is often linked to related initiatives to preserve and enhance Aboriginal language use, and to ensure that language and traditions are transmitted to youth both through the formal school system and through traditional means of education. Another impetus for traditional knowledge work is the need to respond to proposals for development on Aboriginal traditional lands, specifically through the land and water use licensing process. And as the cumulative impacts of increased industrial development are perceived, traditional knowledge is seen as an important contributor to impacts monitoring.

Traditional knowledge studies

Several comprehensive projects have been undertaken in the NWT to document traditional knowledge. Some of this research has been funded through the West Kitikmeot/Slave Study Society, a partnership of Aboriginal and environmental organizations, government and industry that was established to conduct research to develop an information base against which to examine the effects of development in the Slave Geological Province, a geographical area that includes parts of the NWT and Nunavut. The WKSSS has funded several baseline traditional knowledge studies over the last decade.

The Lutselk'e Dene Band undertook traditional ecological knowledge research, and established an extensive traditional monitoring program that used culturally appropriate methods to gather data about environmental indicators that were identified as important in the initial research. The list of indicators monitored was chosen to illuminate the population health, dynamics and resilience of animals, plants, and people, and to detect changes occurring in natural cycles and patterns. Information was gathered through standardized questions posed to elders and harvesters through personal interviews, both individually and during collective community land-based activities. Information was organized and stored in a traditional knowledge database, and presented back to elders for verification. The intent of the program was to compile baseline data, and to establish a mechanism for on-going monitoring of environmental trends.

The Dogrib Treaty Council 11 (the forerunner to the Tlicho Government) received funding to document Tlicho knowledge about caribou habitat and caribou migration patterns over time, as well as the relationships between the Tlicho and the caribou. Tlicho elders were concerned about the potential impacts of diamond mines on caribou habitat, and worried that the development of mines would disrupt caribou migration patterns and distribution. The purpose of the study was in part to establish baseline data that would support on-going monitoring of cumulative impacts of development. Using participatory action research methods, the study involved interviews with elders both in their communities and on the land, language terminology development, and archival research on caribou migrations, mining activity and forest fire activity. Stemming from this work were recommendations for a permanent Tlicho knowledge research and monitoring program, which would continue to compile historical baseline data while at the same time adding to the baseline through contemporary observations. A key emphasis of the Tlicho elders was the need to establish multi-generational knowledge transfer processes that involve elders, active harvesters, young adults and youth, working and learning on the land together. In this way, it is felt that knowledge will be passed on in a culturally appropriate manner that ensures it is contextualized.

These studies, and others, faced similar challenges in that they were effectively starting from scratch with regard to the development of appropriate research methodologies, the need to establish accepted terminology and ensure accurate translation, the need to develop Aboriginal residents as researchers, and the need to develop databases capable of storing and retrieving the very specialized information resulting from the research.

Regulatory processes

Pursuant to the requirement in the Mackenzie Valley Resource Management Act that traditional knowledge be considered in environmental impact assessment, the MVEIRB established the guidelines referred to earlier in this chapter (MVEIRB 2005). These generic guidelines, the first of their kind to be developed in Canada, provide background information and advice for developers about traditional knowledge, including an explanation of how traditional knowledge can add value to the environmental impact assessment process, how to work with Aboriginal communities to ensure their policies and protocols are respected, and issues surrounding confidentiality of knowledge.

Community-based monitoring

There is an increasing interest in the potential for using the knowledge and expertise of Aboriginal community residents for environmental monitoring. The first effort to train community monitors was sponsored by the Dene Nation in association with the development of the Norman Wells oil pipeline to Zama, Alberta in the mid-1980s. Since then, several Aboriginal organizations have taken steps toward setting up community monitoring programs. The Inuvialuit Joint Secretariat has implemented a training course for community environmental monitors in partnership with the federal government's Department of Indian and Northern Affairs.

In 2000, an Environmental Monitoring Advisory Board for the Diavik Diamond Mine was created as a result of an agreement among the governments of Canada and the NWT, Diavik Diamond Mines Inc., and several Aboriginal groups. The board's mandate creates a formal, multi-party structure to monitor all aspects of the project, including environmental impacts, and includes references to traditional knowledge as one means to achieve the mandate.

It would not be possible in the space allotted to give a complete overview of current program and policy activity related to traditional knowledge in the NWT, but these examples provide a sense of the scope and significance of the work that is being undertaken.

Current application of traditional knowledge to water policy and management

Examples provided above illustrate the extent to which traditional knowledge can inform environmental and resource management decision-making. Another example from Canada in the Province of Manitoba speaks more directly to the field of water management. Traverse and Baydack (2005) have compared traditional knowledge perspectives about the impacts of the Fairford Dam on Lake St Martin and the Aboriginal communities surrounding the lake, and concluded that subtle environmental changes caused by the construction of the dam could not be detected by statistically based parameters and analysis, but were easily discerned by Aboriginal residents. Hydrological analysis revealed that increases in water levels in Lake St. Martin were not statistically significant. However, water levels in the lake fluctuate as the dam is opened and closed, leading to constant flooding, which has caused damage to the land adjacent to the lake. Aboriginal residents have noted that there are fewer fish, and the fish have a "grassy" taste that they ascribe to the changing vegetation as a result of cyclical flooding. Wildlife numbers have also declined, as has the taste and quality of meat, and there are fewer birds. Edible and medicinal plants that previously grew around the lake have been replaced by bulrushes in marshy areas. The authors concluded that Aboriginal observers have been able to discern changes that were not identified by western science based on detection-limit methodologies and instrumentation – changes that although not deemed statistically significant have a perceptible and demonstrable impact.

Failing *et al.* (2007) describe a structured decision-making process introduced by the British Columbia government to re-examine water allocation at major hydroelectric sites, and how the involvement of multiple stakeholders brought together in decision-making forums to collectively address the systematic treatment of fact-based and value-based knowledge claims results in collective recommendations for action. They provide an example in which the input of Aboriginal participants was critical in developing an effective model for major factors limiting fish populations, through their identification of the need to include tributary spawning success as a performance measure in the decision model. Moreover, the dialogue process itself facilitates an enhanced mutual understanding of the substantive issues and interests – which contributes to a more robust level of understanding of the primary and secondary impacts.

NWT Aboriginal peoples have been outspoken in expressing observations about changes to water level and appearance, water quality, the taste of water, and the health and quality of fish, for many years. They are keen observers of variations over time and continue to monitor and compare contemporary observations with historical trends. Elders throughout the Mackenzie River Valley can comment knowledgeably on the impacts of the construction of the Bennett Dam in British Columbia on Mackenzie River water levels, and associated changes in travel, harvesting and fishing habits. A community harvest study in Fort Good Hope identified decreasing fish catches in the mid-1980s. Some NWT communities have changed their drinking water source due to concerns about algal growth, turbidity, and changes in water taste. More recently, changes to water systems as a result of climate change have become part of the dialogue between harvesters, communities, Aboriginal groups, and government.

The examples above demonstrate that there is an opportunity for western scientists and Aboriginal people to work together to identify appropriate and accurate indicators of ecosystem health, to ensure that monitoring is robust and comprehensive, and targets the right indicators. From a simple efficiency perspective, engaging harvesters and other users of the land as part of the monitoring network can yield significant increases in field observations and sampling and ultimately reduce operational costs, or support more comprehensive and effective monitoring within current resources.

The potential for use and application of traditional knowledge

The exploration of traditional knowledge and its potential applications is a relatively recent field, and one in which research and publication has burgeoned over the past 20 years. Although skepticism about the validity and utility of such knowledge still exists to varying degrees in the scientific community and elsewhere, the degree of acceptance and credibility among both scientists and policy-makers is much greater than was the case 10 or 20 years ago. The most persuasive arguments for the efficacy of working with the two types of knowledge come from those who have actually undertaken fieldwork and analysis in genuine partnership with traditional knowledge holders.

Concomitant with gradually increased acceptance is the developing awareness that the distinctions between traditional knowledge and western science may not, in fact, be as great as was once generally perceived to be the case. The emphasis on the interconnectedness of ecosystems that is characteristic of traditional knowledge is consistent with the concepts and principles of sustainable development. Rather than being distinct from western science, there is an emerging consensus that traditional knowledge and western science are complementary. The strengths of traditional knowledge to expand the store of data accumulated through scientific study and resource management methods can be attributed to several characteristics of this approach:

- The traditional approach generates hypotheses, which can be tested by western science research methods, as with the eider duck example cited above.

- Traditional observers may consider different indicators than those selected by western scientists – for example, a fish species that is valued as traditional food may not be selected as an indicator species by western science, and the identification of these indicators may provide an important insight into monitoring approaches.
- Traditional observers are interested in deviations from the norm, and therefore may focus on outlier events that might be discounted by western science methods – for example, concerns were raised by Dene harvesters in Fort Good Hope in the 1980s about diseased livers in burbot but testing did not lead to any conclusive evidence of a widespread problem. The limits of detection methodologies and instrumentation are contributing factors in excluding what are viewed as qualitative observations.
- Traditional observers take into consideration subtle changes that may not be deemed statistically significant and may nonetheless be important, as with the Lake St Martin example outlined above.

Further, the depth and richness of traditional knowledge may surpass what is observed by western scientists. Basso (1972) studied the rules of Dene from Tulita for travelling on ice, and determined that harvesters utilized a complex model that specifies the conditions under which ice is safe to traverse, based on a set of categories. He identified 13 terms that can be translated loosely as "thin ice," but each term incorporates information on a set of eight sub-conditions – state of the ice (solid, melting or cracked); presence or absence of sub-surface water or surface water; texture; thickness; clarity; color; and cracking features. Thus, for example, one Dene term that might be translated as "thin ice" actually transmits a level of detail (e.g., a condition in which ice is solid, has no air pockets, no overflow, is less than one-inch thick, and is transparent).

These strengths of traditional knowledge have led to considerable discussion in the literature about the potential for it to serve as an "early-warning" system in environmental management and monitoring. Bringing together information from two streams of knowledge – western scientific and traditional – can strengthen observations and conclusions that can only be of benefit to environmental managers and decision-makers. Some authors have noted that traditional knowledge is especially relevant to the field of cumulative effects assessment and management, precisely because of the holistic and integrated nature of the field. Other features of traditional knowledge that directly support cumulative effects assessment and management include the ability to define pre-development baseline information for use in later impact assessment monitoring of effects, the ability to discern relationships among species and between biological and non-biological systems, and the ability to describe subtle variations in many naturally occurring events from year to year. The indicators identified by traditional observers are often similar or identical to the "valued ecosystem components" identified through the environmental impact assessment process.

But in spite of widespread recognition of the potential, the extent to which traditional knowledge has systematically been incorporated into environmental management and decision-making, and the degree to which opportunities have been formalized to ensure an effective role, are limited. Proponents of traditional knowledge note that it often plays a secondary role to western science; that knowledge which cannot be categorized according to the "who," "what," "where," and "when" criteria of western science is often undervalued or ignored; that traditional knowledge is only deemed credible when it compares favorably with observations and explanations generated by scientific means or bolsters existing scientific evidence; and that it is often dismissed as anecdotal or personal opinion (Barnaby *et al.* 2003; Ellis 2005). An examination of why this state of affairs exists can support recommendations for change.

Challenges to the use and application of traditional knowledge

There are a number of barriers to the effective utilization of traditional knowledge. These stem both from the inherent nature of traditional knowledge and the need to develop realistic and appropriate expectations for its application, and from challenges that are attributable to the emerging nature of the discipline in a modern context.

Nature of information

Although traditional knowledge can provide a robust, multi-layered and diverse stream of richly contextualized information, its application can be constrained by the geographical boundaries of the individual or collective knowledge holders. Local-level observations are not always relevant or accurate to discussions at a larger geographical scale.

Data provided through traditional observation may be viewed as insufficiently rigorous in terms of methods and documentation. Although knowledge is held and shared collectively, there is also a highly individual component in many circumstances that may lead to questions about the integrity of the information, particularly when the information provided by two or more knowledge holders does not agree. This can lead to an assumption by individuals more comfortable with the methods of western science that traditional knowledge is vague, speculative and value-laden. Traditional knowledge claims may therefore be subjected to greater scrutiny than those of western science, which can be accepted uncritically without recognition of the inherent degree of uncertainty that exists that many scientific assertions, or the fact that western scientists also often disagree. Not every Aboriginal person is a traditional knowledge expert, but there is no established credentialing process to help determine levels of expertise.

In the field of water resources management, where methods are engineering focused and tend to rely on verifiable measures that are deemed "precise," there may be even less openness to accepting the credibility and utility of traditional knowledge information than in fields such as biology. In the NWT, with its spatial expanse of over 1.3 million square kilometers, the lack of consistent and comprehensive baseline data on many areas relating to water resources management means there is a limited basis for comparative analysis, which might shed light on the accuracy of traditional observations.

Emerging field of practice

The effort to document and codify traditional knowledge in such a way that it can be used to inform modern environmental management and decision-making is a relatively recent field of endeavor, and as such faces many challenges – both methodological and normative.

One of the greatest strengths of traditional knowledge lies in its nature as a body of observation that has been accumulated over time, which when properly documented can provide badly needed baseline data about a variety of topics – wildlife migration patterns and population trends, weather patterns, impacts of forest fires and other environmental disasters, water levels and flows, and cumulative impacts of development. To date, however, efforts to incorporate traditional knowledge, particularly in environmental impact assessment processes, have tended to be project-specific, and have been constrained by the lack of thoroughly documented baseline observations. There is also a need for standardized development of geo-databases to permit storage and retrieval of knowledge.

Another drawback is the lack of generally accepted research methods for eliciting, documenting, and storing traditional knowledge; and there are no common standards for collection and use of data. There is a tremendous amount of work occurring in Canada and internationally in this regard, and the continued sharing of best practices will mitigate this to some extent. However, the very fact that traditional knowledge is so deeply rooted in cultural and linguistic context means that methods that are appropriate in one cultural and linguistic context may well not work in a different setting.

The perception of traditional knowledge as anecdotal, or as personal opinion rather than scientific fact, may impede its incorporation in regulatory decision-making processes that deal with highly technical engineering issues (e.g., construction of pipelines, bridges or highways).

Related to this is a concern that the full depth and complexity of traditional knowledge held by elders will be lost as younger generations spend less time learning from their elders on the land, and lose their fluency in Aboriginal languages. Traditional knowledge programs and projects are often integrally linked to language preservation and revitalization for this reason.

Another constraint exists with regard to language and the need for translation of traditional knowledge for incorporation in assessment and decision-making processes that are conducted in the dominant language (generally English). English often cannot accommodate or reflect the richly textured layers of detail that is understood and described in Aboriginal languages. To bridge this gap will require considerable investment of time and resources in the development of terminology that is understandable and acceptable in the Aboriginal linguistic context and translatable into English.

Data derived from traditional knowledge research cannot be divorced from the context in which it has been accumulated and transmitted, which means that complicated issues may need to be clarified or addressed in order to accurately understand and appreciate the import. This may require dealing with sensitive issues, such as topics that are considered taboo or only appropriate for discussion with certain categories of people, even within Aboriginal communities.

Related to this is the difficulty of bringing together the insights gleaned from two different ways of understanding the world into a meaningful, cohesive whole. Even for those who are open to the prospect, it is not always easy to relate findings from one knowledge system to another without affecting the integrity of either.

There is also a political dimension to this issue that cannot be ignored. In some instances, Aboriginal groups feel that traditional knowledge is being appropriated by western institutions for their own purposes, and are reluctant to see it shared except for situations in which they retain full control. At the other end of the spectrum, traditional knowledge representations may sometimes be accepted uncritically by those who are afraid of giving offense by questioning the legitimacy or validity of knowledge claims.

Although there have been numerous projects undertaken in the NWT over the past 20 years, the knowledge gathered by these projects is inconsistent, incomplete, and often not in a format that can be shared, compared and contrasted. In some cases, lack of continuity in funding and personnel has led to the loss of project results. There is limited capacity or resources to aggregate study results into broader baseline summaries, for example, or to bring together the results of community-based monitoring projects to provide insights into broad trends.

Finally, and perhaps of most importance, is the fact that the infrastructure for effective, adequate traditional knowledge work does not yet exist. Traditional knowledge efforts are constrained by limited and inconsistent funding. There are few established funding sources or long-term funding programs in Canada dedicated solely to this purpose, which results in lack of continuity in research and personnel. Training and capacity is also an issue. For effective documentation and codification of traditional knowledge, highly trained cultural interpreters are needed who can work with equal comfort in two arenas – that of environmental managers and that of elders.

The lack of infrastructure creates a Catch-22 effect: traditional knowledge cannot establish its credibility without the appropriate funding support, but funding support will be difficult to justify if the credibility of the knowledge to be gained is not recognized.

In summary, the emerging field of traditional knowledge faces a number of challenges before it can take its place as a respected and fully participating contributor to environmental management and decision-making. These can be summarized as follows:

- the need to establish credibility and overcome resistance by the scientific community;
- the need to establish traditional knowledge as relevant and credible in regulatory processes;

- the need to establish and document generally accepted research methods, while recognizing the need for flexibility to adapt to cultural requirements;
- the need to develop effective mechanisms for storing and retrieving information;
- the need to develop a cadre of trained and competent researchers;
- the need to develop terminology in Aboriginal languages and English that is capable of translating the complex and multi-dimensional aspects of traditional observations and conclusions;
- the need to address sensitive issues like ownership, control and intellectual property rights collaboratively and constructively;
- the need to identify dedicated, adequate funding sources to support this work; and
- the need to overcome the fragmentation of traditional knowledge research and findings.

Finding a way forward

The discipline of traditional knowledge is positioned to move into a new era of credibility and increasing utility. In spite of the methodological challenges, work over the past 30 years has resulted in the gradual emergence of effective and accepted research methods. There continues to be increased acceptance of the credibility, the reliability, and the utility of traditional knowledge as it pertains to environmental management and decision-making. The implementation of land claims and self-government agreements have not only given Aboriginal groups greater control political control and the resources to determine research needs and priorities, but they have also resulted in co-management bodies that are more open to using traditional knowledge as a matter of course.

In a time of increased public concern over the need for environmental sustainability, and in the face of environmental pressures like climate change and the Deepwater Horizon oil spill, there is renewed interest in finding ways of adaptive management that allow humans to benefit from the earth's resources without doing irreparable damage.

The importance of traditional knowledge for water management and policy in northern Canada

Nowhere is the need to find sustainable ways of using resources more urgent than as it relates to the need to manage valuable water resources – the NWT's greatest natural capital. In the NWT as elsewhere, water resources need to be managed, protected and preserved to ensure the future health of the environment and the well-being of northern populations. But equally important is the socio-economic dimension. Water represents the largest stock of natural capital in the NWT, and a hugely important future economic resource. Jurisdictions such as Alberta will increasingly look to the north as their own water resources are depleted through a combination of changing climate patterns and industrial use.

The Aboriginal subsistence economy, while limited in terms of its gross domestic product quantum, continues to play a vital socio-cultural role in the northern economy, and its continued viability is seen by Aboriginal people as critical to the health, well-being, and sustainability of their communities.

Tourism is also a significant contributor to NWT economic activity. Like the traditional economy, tourism does not generate large revenues, but provides a sustainable economic activity for northern communities that is dependent on a healthy environment and the continued quality and quantity of NWT water sources.

Investments in protecting NWT waters are thus investments in the future economic prosperity of the NWT. But the challenges are huge. There is a critical shortage of baseline data to support environmental impact assessment and on-going monitoring. This issue is not new – it was flagged in the mid-1980s by the Mackenzie Environmental Monitoring Program – but resources have never been made available to implement a scientific monitoring system that adequately addresses the immensity and complexity of the Mackenzie River Basin system. The need for on-going monitoring becomes increasingly critical in the face of enhanced industrial development upstream.

Attention to impacts on water resources is arguably the single biggest determinant of workload, cost driver, and review process time requirements in the NWT impact assessment process. Water resources governance and management activities comprise a significant proportion of total workload for staff, decision-makers, and interveners. There is a perceived lack of efficacy in this area, in large part due to the insufficient capacity of the regulatory and management system.

The traditional knowledge of NWT Aboriginal people is an invaluable resource that can be drawn upon to strengthen and enhance not only the environmental impact assessment process, but the existing monitoring regime, for NWT water resources. The geographic positioning of Aboriginal communities in the NWT provides a network of potential monitoring nodes strategically positioned to encompass critical components of the Mackenzie River basin drainage system. Many Aboriginal people maintain land-based lifestyles, and continue to monitor and analyze environmental trends as they have always done. They have the expertise, they are on the spot, and they have the political desire to play a management role.

But the knowledge and skills of Aboriginal people should not be seen simply as a resource to help improve existing monitoring processes. The unique strengths of traditional knowledge as outlined above can be brought to the task. Identifying indicators that are meaningful in a traditional knowledge context; tracking subtle changes (i.e., those below current detection and significance limits) that may not be captured through hydrological studies or may not be deemed statistically significant; identifying system-wide changes and interpreting this information through the knowledge base that has developed over centuries; all will position Aboriginal monitors to contribute a range of knowledge that is now absent from existing monitoring approaches.

What is needed

The potential is huge, but it cannot be realized without a concerted effort involving Aboriginal governments and organizations, federal and territorial government departments, co-management boards, regulatory agencies and academia. It will require sustained and broad-based political will, and commensurate resources, over an extended time period, to move forward. With reference to the constraints and challenges outlined above, an approach for success would include all of the elements outlined below.

1. Stakeholders must work collaboratively to establish realistic and meaningful expectations for the role the traditional knowledge can play in environmental management and decision-making. This will include understanding and accepting the differences between traditional knowledge and western science while honoring the similarities. It will include an acceptance that traditional knowledge claims, like scientific claims, must be analytically rigorous and defensible, and subject to challenge. And it will include the establishment of standards of practice, to address the issues such as the fact that not every Aboriginal person is a qualified traditional knowledge practitioner, just as not every non-Aboriginal person is a qualified scientist. Aboriginal communities will play a lead role in defining standards and expectations that will guide appointments to co-management boards, selection of researchers, etc.
2. Stakeholders must work collaboratively to identify sensitive issues such as confidentiality and intellectual property rights, and develop solutions.
3. Government agencies and Aboriginal governments and organizations must work in partnership to establish robust, on-going monitoring programs – not only to provide input to existing monitoring programs but as parallel processes that can contribute insights and data.
4. Stakeholders must work collaboratively to establish mechanisms to bring together two streams of knowledge – traditional and scientific – in a manner that acknowledges the uniqueness of each but finds a way to weave their insights into a cohesive whole. This should happen at a project-specific level during the course of environmental assessments.
5. A broader forum or process needs to be established to provide a means by which traditional knowledge findings from specific Aboriginal groups can be brought together to inform regional, territorial, and interjurisdictional or transboundary discussions that deal with larger geographical areas – for example, caribou migration issues, or managing at a watershed scale.
6. Protocols should be established to ensure the appropriate use of traditional knowledge at all stages of environmental decision-making.
7. Resources will be required for programs to enable all of the following:
    - compilation of historical and existing baseline data;
    - ongoing community-based monitoring to contribute to baseline data;
    - development of database systems;
    - training of researchers; and

- development of linguistic terminology.

8 Standards should be developed for geo-database programs to ensure that data can be compared, consolidated, and contrasted among regions/jurisdictions.

9 Mechanisms should be developed to enable best practices, research methods and evaluation approaches of traditional knowledge programs.

To be successful, all of this work will require truly collaborative processes, based on partnership and a common vision; and it must be recognized that Aboriginal groups will only be interested in collaboration to the extent that they are not asked to give up control over the process or the results. This is why the GNWT made every effort to involve Aboriginal stakeholders in the development of the NWT Water Stewardship Strategy – and this strategy identifies some initial steps towards responding to the actions outlined above.

Based on the results of the GNWT's consultations, the strategy emphasizes the importance of finding ways to utilize traditional knowledge. It proposes to achieve this by completing an inventory of all traditional knowledge protocols already completed in the NWT by Aboriginal, territorial and federal governments, communities and regions. This would be an important first step toward the necessary sharing of best practices. The strategy also proposes to support the development of traditional knowledge protocols where needed, which will help to put all Aboriginal groups and regions in the NWT on more even footing. It recognizes the need to develop management decision models that identify appropriate ways to apply traditional, local, and scientific knowledge to management decisions through a collaborative process.

At a more local level, the strategy commits to support the development of community capacity through effective community-based monitoring programs. It proposes a pilot study for community water source protection that links aquatic ecosystem indicator development and community-based monitoring. This could be an important first step toward establishing a broader system of community monitoring nodes. In order to make such programs effective and relevant, the strategy recognizes the need for research in a number of areas, including receiving water standards, thresholds and carrying capacity, sensitivity of northern aquatic species to toxins produced by industrial activities, water quality and quantity, and the effects of climate change on ecosystems.

These commitments in the NWT Water Stewardship Strategy represent a first step toward finding effective mechanisms to use traditional knowledge to strengthen and support the water management system in the NWT. The GNWT looks forward to continuing its work with all other stakeholders to advance the state of traditional knowledge use and application in northern Canada.

References

Barnaby, J. and Emery, A. (2008) *Report of Traditional Knowledge Project*. Toronto: Nuclear Waste Management Organization.

Barnaby, J., Emery, A. and Legat, A. (2003) *Needs Assessment Study to Identify the*

Knowledge and Skills Required to Fully Utilize the Strengths of Traditional Knowledge and Western Science in the Management of Northern Resources. Final report submitted to Indian and Northern Affairs Canada. Unpublished document.

Basso, K. H. (1972) "Ice and Travel among the Fort Norman Slave: Folk Taxonomies and Cultural Rules." *Language and Society* 1: 31–49.

Berkes, F. (1999) *Sacred Ecology: Traditional Ecological Knowledge and Resource Management.* Philadelphia, PA: Taylor & Francis.

DeLancey, D. (1984) "Research in Northern and Remote Areas – the Native Experience." *Lectures in Community Medicine* 4: 5–11.

Dowsley, M. and Wenzel, G. (2008) "The Time of Most Polar Bears: A Co-management Conflict in Nunavut." *Arctic* 621(2): 177–89.

Ellis, S. C. (2005) "Meaningful Consideration? A Review of Traditional Knowledge in Environmental Decision Making." *Arctic* 58(1): 66–77.

Failing, L., Gregory, R. and Harstone, M. (2007) "Integrating Science and Local Knowledge in Environmental Risk Management: A Decision-Focused Approach." *Ecological Economics* 64(1): 47–60.

Fenge, T. and Funston, B. W. (2009) Arctic Governance: Traditional Knowledge of Arctic Indigenous Peoples from an International Policy Perspective. Arctic Governance Project. Available at www.arcticgovernance.org/arctic-governance-traditional-knowledge-of-arctic-indigenous-peoples-from-an-international-policy-perspective.4667262-142902.html (accessed 5 March 2014).

Gilchrist, G., Mallory, M. and Merkel, F. (2005) "Can Local Ecological Knowledge Contribute to Wildlife Management?" *Ecology and Society* 10(1): 20.

GNWT and Government of Canada (2010) *Northern Voices, Northern Waters: NWT Water Stewardship Strategy*. Yellowknife, NWT: Government of the Northwest Territories.

MVEIRB (2005) *Guidelines for Incorporating Traditional Knowledge in Environmental Impact Assessment*. Yellowknife, NWT: Mackenzie Valley Environmental Impact Review Board.

Traverse, M. and Baydack, R. (2005) "Observing Subtleties: Traditional Knowledge and Optimal Water Management of Lake St. Martin." *Ethnobotany Research and Applications*: 3: 51–6.

Usher, P. J. (2000) "Traditional Ecological Knowledge in Environmental Assessment and Management." *Arctic:* 53(2): 183–93.

Wenzel, G. W. (2004) "Inuit Qaujimajatuqangit and Inuit Cultural Ecology." *Arctic Anthropology:* 41(2): 238–50.

Part VI

Institutional innovations

Learning from Asia

11 Water governance

Institutional response as an adaptation to water scarcity

R. Maria Saleth

Introduction

The global water sector underwent revolutionary changes during the twentieth century. Human water use increased, at least, by six-fold while the human population increased only by three-fold (Cosgrove and Rijsberman 2000). Added to the demographic growth is also the fact that the world has become more urban than rural since 2007 (United Nations 2005), causing water pollution and damaging aquatic ecosystems and reducing, thereby, the usable freshwater in many countries. The symptoms of water scarcity are already evident in 80 countries with 40 percent of global population. Eighteen of these countries, located mostly in the Middle East and North Africa, are actually drawing either close to or more than their renewable supply limits (Falkenmark and Lindh 1993; Gleick 1993). Already, 55 countries are not in a position to meet even the basic water needs of their growing population. What is notable is the fact that the share of global population facing the predicament of water scarcity and conflict is projected to increase from 44 to 75 percent by 2025 (Postel 1999: 138–40).

Although water scarcity is usually viewed in physical terms as a widening gap between water demand and supply, in reality it is much more than a hydrological phenomenon in view of its economic and institutional causes and ecological and health consequences. The increasing gap between water demand and supply creates economic incentives and political compulsions to constantly adapt the institutional arrangements governing water development, allocation, use, and management. As a result, the physical changes in the water sector have induced concurrent and continuous changes in water institutional arrangements in almost all countries around the world. These institutional changes were not sudden but occurred more as an evolutionary process and essentially as an adaptive response to the economic, social, political, and ecological costs engendered by increasing water scarcity and water conflicts in different contexts. Unfortunately, the institutional adaptation to water scarcity has been rather slow, uneven, and lagged far behind the real institutional requirements across countries. Consequently, the institutional arrangements observed in the water sector of most countries remain inappropriate and ineffective in solving their water problems. It is in view of this institutional gap that the prevailing water crisis in most countries is viewed essentially as a "crisis of governance" (GWP 2000; Saleth and Dinar 2004).

The overall objective of this chapter is to delineate the existing forms or typologies of water institutional arrangements observed across countries, evaluate them for their relative effectiveness, and identify the institutional arrangements that will be more appropriate for different conditions. Treating different water institutional arrangements as different forms of water governance and using the available literature on the subject, this chapter aims to:

- identify the broad typologies of water governance;
- apply an analytical framework for characterizing different forms of water governance in terms of their key institutional features and operational environments;
- describe the governance typologies relevant for urban water supply and agricultural water provision;
- evaluate the relative effectiveness of different governance typologies;
- discuss the roles of institutional principles and transaction cost theory that govern the process of institutional response and adaptation towards appropriate water governance; and
- conclude with a discussion on the governance configurations appropriate for the conditions of the Americas.

The chapter is organized, more or less, in line with the listed set of objectives. As to its approach and scope, the chapter relies on analytical approaches and anecdotal evidence from a few countries and focuses mainly on the agricultural and urban water sub-sectors, which together share most of the water used in many countries.

Typologies of water institutional arrangements

From an analytical perspective, water institutions are defined as the configurations of different legal, policy, and organizational elements involved in water development, allocation, ownership, use, and management (Bromley 1989; Ostrom 1990; Saleth and Dinar 2004). Such institutional configurations differ considerably in terms of their sectoral coverage, resource focus, and unit of analysis. For instance, the institutional arrangements governing the agricultural sector are different from those governing urban water sectors. Likewise, the institutional arrangements related to water quantity are different from those related to water quality. Similar distinctions also exist between the institutional arrangements governing groundwater and those dealing with surface water. Water institutional arrangements also differ in terms of their scale of coverage and unit of analysis, such as watershed, aquifer, river basin, region, country, and transboundary (Ostrom 1990; Huitema and Bressers 2007; Tropp 2007). Despite their contextual variations, water institutional arrangements do have strong lateral and hierarchical linkages across contexts due to inter-sectoral, inter-source, and inter-regional water dependence.

Much more important than the contextual variations in water institutional arrangements are their typologies in terms of the underlying ownership pattern, functional form, and decision structure. These institutional typologies are useful to distinguish institutional arrangements found in different contexts and also to evaluate them for their relative effectiveness and performance. For instance, in terms of the property rights or ownership, water institutional arrangements can be characterized as open access, common property, state property, and private property (Ostrom 1990; Bromley 1992). Similarly, from a functional perspective of water provision and water allocation, water institutional arrangements are also characterized as state or bureaucratic, community-based and user-oriented, and market-centric (Meinzen-Dick and Mendoza 1996; Dinar *et al.* 1997). One can also add here another institutional typology based on private water companies operating both in urban and agricultural sectors. Water institutional arrangements are also distinguished as centralized vs. decentralized, public vs. private, single actor vs. multiple actors or stakeholders, top-down vs. bottom-up, and bureaucratic vs. market-centric. In terms of decision structure, water institutional arrangements are also characterized as hierarchical, poly-centric, and distributed (Kooiman 1993; Keohane and Ostrom 1995; Ostrom *et al.* 1999). Based on these considerations, one can identify six distinct institutional typologies: open access, state, community, user, private, and market-centric arrangements.

The ownership, function, and decision system-based typologies of water institutional arrangements noted above are overly simplistic. This is because they subsume the wide variations that exist both in their structural features and operational environments. These variations are important because they have a major bearing on the relative performance of different institutional typologies. For instance, the open-access system under water-abundant conditions will have differential performance as compared to the same under water-scarce conditions. Likewise, the performance of the state-based arrangements found in developed countries differ from the same found in developing countries, due to differences not only in information, technology, and enforcement but also in the scale of operation, resource conditions, political factors, and general social and economic intuitions. Similarly, the private provision of urban water supply subsumes varying arrangements, such as service or management contract, lease, concession, and complete transfer. The fact of diversity and the role of exogenous factors are also equally applicable to both user and market-based institutional arrangements. Market-based arrangements vary both within and across countries in terms of the nature of property rights (riparian rights, appropriative rights, water permits, or water quotas) and the conditions for their issue and use. Similarly, in terms of their organizational features and rule structures, the user and community-based arrangements also vary both within and across countries. The variations in the feature and performance of the institutional typologies are obviously due to country-specific differences in physical, cultural, socio-economic, historical, institutional, and technological factors.

Water governance forms: structure and environment

The diversity in the features of institutional typologies and the role of non-institutional and external factors in institutional performance suggest two key points: (a) the six institutional typologies noted above represent only the discrete points within the long continuum ranging between complete open access system to a full-fledged market-centric arrangement; and (b) for evaluating the effectiveness and performance of different institutional typologies, it is necessary to look both at their structural features and also their external environment as characterized by demographic, resource, economic, social, institutional, political, and cultural factors. In order to demonstrate the role of internal institutional features and external influence of both institutional and non-institutional factors, it is instructive to view different water institutional typologies as different forms of water governance. For this purpose, the analytical framework developed by Saleth and Dinar (2004) is useful. Before the application of the analytical framework, let us first define water governance and show its relation with water institutional arrangements.

The concept of water governance has different but closely related definitions (GWP 2000; Rogers and Hall 2003; Franks 2004; Tropp 2007). The GWP (2000), for instance, defines water governance as the range of political, social, economic, and administrative systems that are in place to develop, allocate, and manage water resources at different levels. According to Rogers and Hall (2003), water governance "encompasses laws, regulations, and institutions but it also relates to government policies and actions, to domestic activities, and to networks of influence, including international market forces, the private sector, and civil society. These, in turn, are affected by the political systems within which they function." From an institutional economics perspective, this definition distinguishes clearly the two analytical dimensions of governance (i.e., governance framework or environment and governance structure; North 1990; Saleth and Dinar 2004). The governance structure is defined by institutional components covering water-related legal, policy, and organizational aspects whereas the governance framework captures the physical, technical, economic, social, and political setting within which the governance structure operates. These two analytical dimensions are presented in Figures 11.1 and 11.2, respectively.

Figure 11.1 depicts the water governance environment within a simplified setting. The governance environment covers the elements of the general governance system in the country, including the constitution and political arrangements, technological status, resource potential, development stage, and demographic conditions. Figure 11.1 shows clearly how the water governance structure is embedded within the water governance environment. The water governance structure operates within the governance environment defined not only by the exogenous factors but also by the general governance system of the sector, region, or the country itself. Thus, the relationship between water institution and water sector performance is influenced not only by factors that are both internal and external to the water sector but also by factors endogenous to the water governance structure itself. A change in any of these factors can, therefore, affect the performance of water institutional arrangements, irrespective of their typologies. The importance of the role of the institutional and non-institutional elements defining the governance environment also suggests that water scarcity

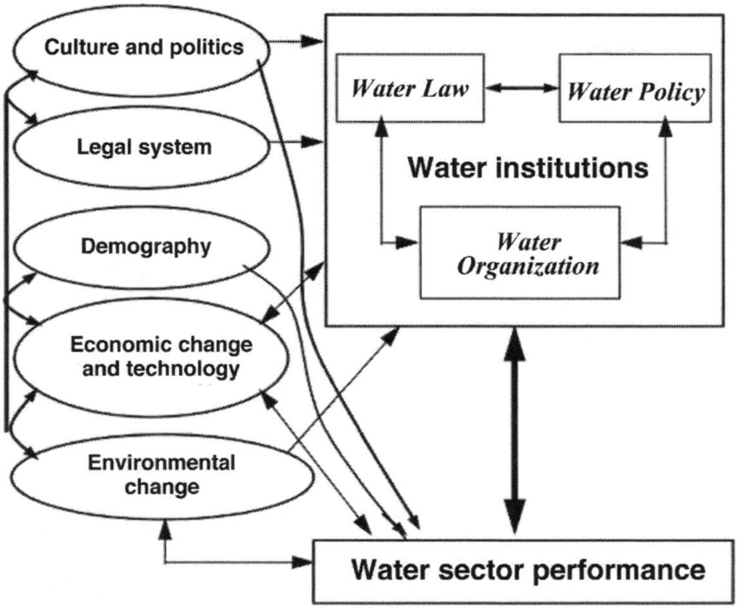

Figure 11.1 The water governance environment
Source: Saleth and Dinar (2004)

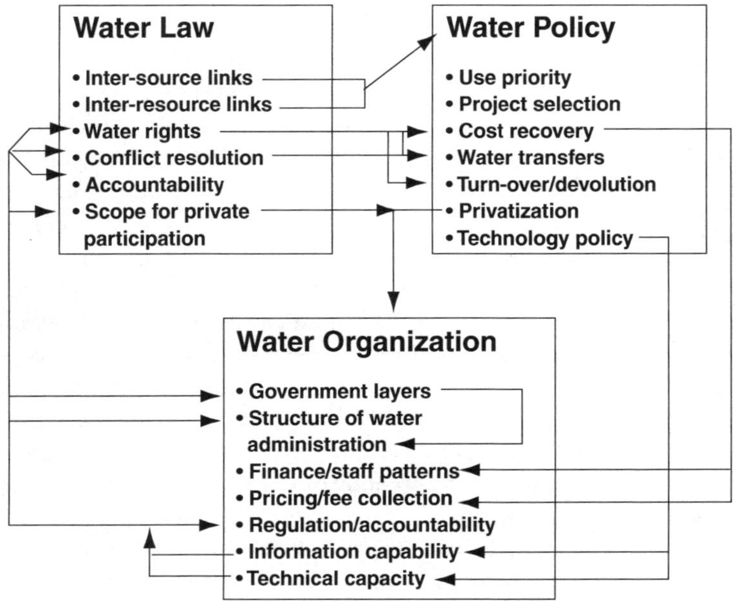

Figure 11.2 Water governance structure
Source: Saleth and Dinar (2004)

is only one among many factors that determine institutional change, performance, and adaptation.

While the water governance environment captures the influence of factors external to water institution, water governance structure captures the effects of internal institutional features. As a result, the water governance structure constitutes the institutional setting within which the water sector operates. It covers essentially the water-related legal, policy and organizational elements. To see these elements, one can follow an unbundling exercise. Initially, water governance structure is unbundled to identify its three main components (i.e., water law, water policy, and water organization). Then, each of these components is unbundled further to identify the key institutional aspects as shown in Figure 11.2. The main analytical advantage of this exercise is that it is possible to trace the structural and functional linkages evident both within and across the institutional components. These institutional linkages are very important determinants of performance in the sense that the stronger the linkages within and among institutional components, the more effective the water governance structure will be.

The analytical framework depicted in Figures 11.1 and 11.2 deal with water governance at the macro or national level. Similar framework can also be specialized for specific contexts such as water sub-sector, water source, and spatial scale. The water governance arrangements in these specific contexts have unique characteristics and are not independent but hierarchically or laterally linked for the obvious reason of inter-sectoral, inter-source, and inter-regional water dependence. In view of this fact, different governance typologies, though distinct, operate more in a complementary than in a competitive manner. In this sense, the institutional typologies can be alternative in specific contexts and are compatible with each other in the larger context of water governance.

As we apply the analytical framework specified in Figures 11.1 and 11.2, we can identify a wide variety of governance forms even within the same institutional typology, depending on the nature and feature of the underlying institutional elements shown in Figure 11.2. In this sense, the range of governance forms will include not only the six discrete institutional typologies (i.e., open access, state, community, user, private, and market-centric) but also all the institutional variants that are intermediate to all six typologies. Since the institutional configurations in each of these governance forms are different, they will have differential performance even within the same governance environment. For instance, given the typical governance environment in developing countries, a bureaucratic state-based system will perform better than an anarchic open-access system. Similarly, user, community, and market-based systems will perform relatively well as compared to the open-access and state-based systems. The same governance form can have a differential performance when there are changes in the configuration of exogenous factors defining the governance environment. For instance, market system, though more efficient than other governance forms, will have better performance under water-scarcity conditions as compared to the same under water-surplus conditions. This is also true when there are changes in other factors defining the governance environment such as technology, economic development, and general institutional health.

Existing water governance typologies

Although we can identify a wide variety of governance forms, each varying in their institutional details and operational environments, for analytical convenience and simplicity we will use only the six governance forms identified above. Since they are easier to characterize in specific context, we will evaluate the existing governance typologies by water sub-sectors.

Governance typologies in the urban water sector

Broadly speaking, seven governance forms are observed in urban water sectors. These governance forms and their relationship with each other are depicted in Figure 11.3, and the institutional features of some of these forms are presented in Table 11.1. As can be seen, these governance forms are distinct in terms of asset ownership, decision making, risk allocation, and economic incentives (Menard 2009). The seven governance typologies or forms can be grouped into three governance categories: state provision, public–private partnership, and private provision. State provision includes both the state-based governance arrangements involving agencies such as public bureaus, municipalities, and other local government bodies, as well as the governance arrangement involving autonomous public corporations run on commercial principles.

Although converting a public water utility into a corporatization provides autonomy and incentives to operate on commercial lines, such an attempt avoids neither the public ownership of assets nor the political interferences, which are rampant in developing countries (Menard and Saleth 2010). Between the two extremes of state and private provision lie the four forms of public and private partnership in water service delivery. The category of public–private partnership involves different combinations of public and private sector roles in the provision, management, and regulation of urban water supply. This category includes the four governance forms involving management contract, service contract, lease, and concession. In this governance category, as we move from the left to the right, the role of the private sector is increasing in the operation of water supply systems while that of the public sector is declining to confine mostly to regulatory or facilitative functions.

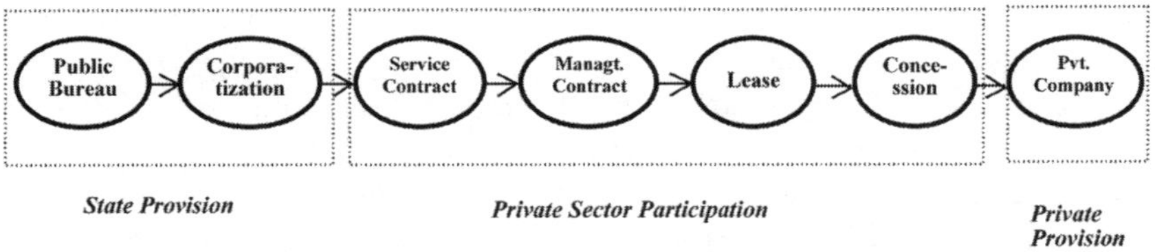

Figure 11.3 Institutional typologies in urban water supply
Source: Menard (2009)

Table 11.1 Institutional features of some urban water governance forms

Particulars	*Public corporation*	*Management contract*	*Lease contract*	*Privatization*
Property rights	Public	Public	Infrastructure: Public Equipment: Private	Private
Autonomy of decision rights	Partial (political control in last resort)	Limited; strategic decisions remain in public hands	Extended, but also dependent on decisions of public authorities	In theory: total In practice: highly regulated
Risk sharing	None: public	None: public	Very limited for lessee	Total (but can be limited by contractual clauses)
Incentives	Weak	Weak (cost plus system)	Intermediate	Strong
Mode of regulation	Command-and-control	Combination of public bureau and contract	Through contracts	Regulatory agency or competition laws
Political interferences	Significant	Significant	Mostly on strategic decisions (through control over major investments)	In principle: none In practice: through regulator

Source: Menard and Saleth (2010)

While the service contract allows private participation in the delivery of specific services (e.g., fee collection and system maintenance), the management contract allows the private sector to operate the water supply system for a management fee. Under the lease contract, the private operator gets the full responsibility for management and maintenance and gets the profit while the government has the responsibility for the asset and investment. In the arrangement involving concessions, the state transfers the entire responsibility to the private operator usually under certain conditions stipulated by the public authorities related especially to the expected level of investment and permitted range of water rates. The concession has a variety of forms such as build–operate–own, build–operate–transfer, build–own–operate–transfer, and so on. Under full privatization, the private operator has complete control and full responsibility for the development, operation, and management of the system.

Besides the seven forms of urban water governance noted in Figure 11.1, one can also add two other forms, which are becoming important due to the limitations of both the public and private arrangements in delivering urban water services. One is the arrangement involving the role of local entrepreneurs and small independent water providers. They are common in Latin America, Africa, and Asia. Their importance can be judged by the fact that they serve about 25 percent of the urban population in Latin America and 50 percent of the same in Africa (Davilla and Whiteford 2009). The other form involves the role of urban water cooperatives such as those operating in the Municipality of Morenos, Buenos Aires, and Argentina (Moccia 2007).

Corporatization of public water utilities is observed particularly in Latin America and Australia. Public–private partnership has been tried in a number of countries in the 1990s, essentially through management or lease contracts (Gassner *et al.* 2009). Full privatization has been tried with varying degrees of success in Australia, the United Kingdom, the United States, and Chile. Based on a review of 977 urban water utilities in 71 developing countries during 1973–2005, Gassner *et al.* (2009) concluded that while 85 percent of these utilities were state or state-owned enterprises, only the remaining 15 percent were under different forms of public–private partnership. Notably, more than 67 percent of the utilities under public–private partnership were concentrated in the Latin American and Caribbean regions. The market share of the utilities under the public–private partnership in the developing and emerging countries has increased from about 1 percent in 1997 to 7 percent in 2007. During 1990–2002, the number of people being covered by some sort of privatization has increased from 51 to 300 million (Palaniappan 2004). The number of utilities under public–private partnership has reached the peak at the end of the 1990s, followed by an abrupt decline, except for a brief upward trend during 2003–2005, followed, again, by a declining trend (Marin 2009: 24).

Water governance forms in the agricultural sector

All six of the governance typologies that we have identified (i.e., open access, state, community, user, market, and private) are relevant for the agricultural sector. While considering these forms of governance across countries and regions, it is useful to keep in mind the following two key points related to their spatial and structural relationships. First, since the agricultural sector is spatially vast and physically diverse across countries and regions, all six forms of governance can co-exist to fit different agronomic, socio-economic, and regional needs. Second, although some governance forms can be alternative (e.g., state or private and bureaucratic or market-based) in specific contexts, from a general perspective, they can be complementary in the sense that even within a centralized and bureaucratic system, community, user, and market-based water allocation can operate without much difficulty.

There is a rich body of knowledge on the nature and features of water governance arrangements in the agricultural sector in a wide variety of countries around the world (Maass and Anderson 1978; Ostrom 1990; Keohane and Ostrom 1995; Ostrom *et al.* 1999; Saleth and Dinar 2000, 2004). Broadly speaking, state or bureaucratic allocation and management of surface water is common in most of the countries in Asia and Africa, including India and China. Regarding groundwater irrigation, most countries lack any formal or systematic governance arrangements, leading to anarchic conditions in groundwater withdrawal and use. Although a formal and legally specified water rights system is absent, under a de facto system of rights operating within an open-access regime, groundwater markets have emerged in several countries such as India, Pakistan, China, Bangladesh, Indonesia, and Jordan (Shah 1993; Saleth 1994; Mainzen-Dick and Mendoza 1996; Dinar *et al.* 1997). Reviews of groundwater markets in India, for instance, suggest that they are quite effective in promoting efficiency in water use and equity in the access to water by small farmers, but lead also to aquifer depletion and inter-generational inequity (Saleth 1994; Palanisami 2009).

Market-oriented governance forms are common in the allocation of agricultural water in the western states of the United States, especially, California, Colorado, and New Mexico, and countries such as Australia, Chile, Mexico, and Spain (Colby and Bush 1987; Rosegrant and Schleyer 1994; Rosegrant and Binswanger 1994; Dinar *et al.* 1997; Garrido 1997). They are supported by a formally specified and volumetrically defined water rights system for both surface water and groundwater and by an efficient water-measuring and conveying infrastructure. Notably, in these cases, the state plays major roles in the spheres of regulation, enforcement, and monitoring of water rights. The state also plays a facilitative role by providing information and sharing conveyance facilities for water exchanges. The community-based forms of water governance exist in countries such as India, Nepal, and Bangladesh as well as in many countries in Africa. They confine mainly to surface water, especially in the context of small streams and other water bodies in fragile regions.

Although the state-centered arrangement is the dominant form of agricultural water governance in the canal regions of most developing countries, there have been significant changes thanks to the increasing role of user organizations in water allocation and management, especially at the outlet level. With the implementation of the irrigation management transfer program since the 1970s, many water user associations were created in countries such as Bangladesh, Columbia, India, Indonesia, Mexico, Pakistan, the Philippines, and Turkey (Vermillion 1997). These user-based governance forms, which are operating at the local level within the overall state-based governance, deal with such functions as fee collection, system maintenance, water allocation, and conflict resolution. In contrast to mere water management transfer, the entire irrigation systems, including their ownership, operation, and management were also transferred to user groups or irrigation companies in Argentina, Australia, and New Zealand.

As to the private form of agricultural water governance, there are numerous examples such as the irrigation and ditch companies and irrigation mutual companies operating in the southwestern United States and in the Murray, Coleambally, and Murrumbidgee irrigation areas located in the New South Wales and Victoria states in Australia (Colby and Bush 1987; Lynne and Saarinen 1993; Meinzen-Dick and Mendoza 1996; Saleth and Dinar 2004). A new form of governance arrangement has also emerged in India, which involves the formation of irrigation water development corporations, such as the Krishna Water Corporation created by Karnataka in 1994 and the Krishna Valley Development Corporation floated by Maharashtra in 1996. As these corporations obtained their funds through redeemable long-term "water bonds" assuring a rate of return up to 17 percent, they have incentives for achieving financial viability, accountability, and efficiency (Saleth 2004).

Relative effectiveness of governance typologies

How do we evaluate the relative effectiveness and performance of different governance typologies? This evaluation can be done using both a rigorous approach involving statistical analysis as well as a simple approach involving descriptive analysis. Both approaches rely on a combination of qualitative (subjective) and quantitative (objective) information on some of the key institutional and performance features of water governance. However, the rigorous approach uses one or more variables to capture each of the micro and structural features of water governance, whereas the descriptive approach uses a set of indicators to capture the macro and functional features of water governance. The effectiveness of each institutional aspect of water governance (i.e., the legal, policy, and organizational elements specified in Figure 11.2) can be evaluated more closely using one or more variables to capture its status and effectiveness. The overall effectiveness and performance of water governance can be evaluated based on the results for individual institutional elements. This rigorous and variable-based approach is particularly effective for the evaluation of water governance arrangements in comparative and cross-country contexts (Saleth and Dinar 2004).

Although the rigorous approach is more realistic, it is information-wise much more demanding, requiring special surveys to capture the institutional assessment by a select set of stakeholders. It is also less appealing for evaluating the relative effectiveness of governance forms within a given regional or sub-sector contexts, where they are complementary rather than alternatives. In this context, the descriptive approach based on indicators capturing the overall macro and functional features of water governance are easier to develop and apply. As a result, we rely here on the indicators suggested by Rogers and Hall (2003) for the evaluation of the relative effectiveness of different governance typologies. These indicators are:

- transparency;
- accountability;
- participatory;
- communicative;
- integrative;
- efficiency;
- incentive-compatibility;
- sustainability; and
- equity.

We can also add the criteria of feasibility and replicability given the physical, socio-economic, political, and technical conditions present across countries (Menard and Saleth 2010). Although some of these indicators can be assessed quantitatively in a specific context (e.g., efficiency and equity), others can be evaluated largely from a qualitative perspective and descriptive context.

As we apply these indicators for evaluating the governance typologies observed in the urban water sector, we find that the governance form involving state bodies fails on most counts. Although the governance form involving the publicly owned but autonomous corporation is conducive for efficiency, transparency, and accountability, it has a fundamental incentive problem, especially when there is excessive political interference. As to the relative performance of governance forms involving private sector participation, the evidences are mixed (Marin 2009; Davilla and Whiteford 2009). Based on the results of their empirical study, Gassner *et al.* (2009: 4–5) conclude that there has been some gains in staff productivity and mixed gains in efficiency but no gains in investment levels and no significant changes in price levels. Similarly, based on a review of 27 econometric studies covering hundreds of water utilities, Perard (2009) concludes that only eight of these studies have shown private operators to be more efficient than public operators. Three studies have shown the public entities to be more efficient. But, the remaining 16 studies found that there was no substantial difference in efficiency. The governance form involving independent water providers, who serve mostly the excluded groups and poorly served peri-urban areas, promotes equity and accountability. The mixed performance of the urban water governance forms actually provides evidence for the critical role that the governance environment plays in determining their relative performance.

Turning to the agricultural sector, a state-based centralized system is more efficient, equitable, and environmentally conducive than the open-access regime, because the former reduces the anarchy in resource use, enhances the access by poor groups, and ensures ecological water needs. But, when compared to decentralized arrangements such as the user-based or market-oriented system, a centralized system cannot be considered effective because it fails to meet the desirable features of efficiency, accountability, transparency, and participation (Rosegrant and Binswanger 1994; Meinzen-Dick and Mendoza 1996; Dinar *et al.* 1997). More importantly, the state-based governance arrangements, especially in developing countries, also lead to rent-seeking and corruption (Wade 1982; Repetto 1986). The market-based system, although efficient, transparent, and participatory, may not be able to meet the equity and sustainability criteria (Brown and Ingram 1987; Dinar *et al.* 1997). Similarly, decentralized arrangements, including market, user, and community-based arrangements, are effective in terms of transparency, participation, and equity (Dinar *et al.* 1997; Vermillion 1997). But, for achieving the goals of the integrated water resource management, decentralized systems may not be effective, unless they are functioning within an overall framework of centralized coordination. Although community-based governance arrangements promote equity, participation, and sustainability, they are difficult to upscale or replicate in view of their context-specificity.

Institutional response, adaptation, and appropriate governance

The appropriateness of a governance typology or a configuration of governance typologies depends on the application context, water-related functions, supportive conditions (technology, infrastructure, and information) and sector, region, and country-specific requirements. For instance, the governance typology involving water markets is difficult to introduce in contexts with no formal water rights system and suitable water infrastructure. Similarly, market and user-based arrangements can be efficient in performing the allocation function, but state-based institutional arrangements are necessary to perform the regulatory and enforcement functions. This means that the identification of appropriate governance form(s) requires a demarcation of different water-related activities such as planning, allocation, use, management, and regulation. While governance forms with centralized features are required for planning and regulation as well as for protecting poor groups and environment, market or user-based mechanisms are ideal for water allocation.

The governance form(s) appropriate for a given context emerge as an adaptive response to the changing physical, economic, and institutional requirements of water sector. Such an institutional adaptation takes the form of either an autonomous institutional evolution or induced institutional changes through purposive reforms. These adaptive processes of institutional evolution and change are governed by two major factors. One relates to the role of a few institutional principles and the other relates to the role of the institutional transaction cost theory. Institutional principles such as path dependency and structural and spatial embeddedness play a major role in the evolution and development of an appropriate governance arrangement (Ostrom 1990; Saleth and Dinar 2004). They limit the governance options that are feasible for a given context. For instance, in the case of most developing countries in Asia and Africa, the introduction of full-fledged water markets is difficult because of the constraint imposed by the absence of both the formal water rights and the technical and organizational conditions necessary to underpin water market operation. In this case, water markets are path-dependent and structurally embedded with the water rights system, enabling technical conditions, and enforcement and monitoring mechanisms.

Another institutional principle affecting institutional adaptation and governance choice relates to the nature of the process of institutional change itself. Institutions change only slowly and gradually over a long evolutionary process (North 1990). In this sense, the development of an appropriate institutional typology or configuration is not a single-step activity but involves a constant and consistent process of institutional reforms undertaken over a period of five to 10 years, depending on resource availability, existing institutional potential, and political economy context (Saleth and Dinar 2006). While the path dependency ensures that change once happened cannot be reverted back, the "scale economies" in institutional change, and "increasing returns" in institutional performance ensure that institutional change becomes self-sustaining once a critical minimum level of change has been initiated (North 1990: 95, 100). This means that the evolution and development of an appropriate governance arrangement is closely linked with the process of institutional reform and change.

The nature and intensity of water institutional reforms, which are needed for creating an appropriate governance typology or configuration, depend on the real and monetary costs of transacting the institutional reforms. These costs, known as the "institutional transaction costs," cover not only the economic and financial costs but also the social and political costs of undertaking the reforms. The institutional transaction cost theory basically compares these transaction costs of creating a given governance typology with the opportunity costs that actually captures the social losses associated with an inappropriate governance typology. When the opportunity costs are more than the transaction costs, there is an economic justification for institutional change and adaptation. Otherwise, the prevalent governance typology is optimal from the perspective of the institutional transaction cost theory. For instance, in the case of many developing countries having a vast and diverse agricultural sector with millions of small farmers, the transaction costs (including the social and political risks) of developing a water rights system and market-based governance typology may very well outweigh their opportunity costs, especially in the reckoning of political leaders.

Fortunately, the transaction and opportunity costs are not static but change due to the influence of various factors implicit in Figures 11.1 and 11.2. The factors that affect the opportunity costs are mostly endogenous to the water sector such as water scarcity, use inefficiency, water conflicts, financial crisis, drought/flood problems, and water-quality issues. But, the transaction cost is influenced not only by the exogenous factors such as political reforms, macro-economic crises, social issues, water agreements, and donor pressures but also by the internal institutional features related to water governance structure itself. For instance, the political and economic reforms can reduce the transaction costs of water institutional reforms because the later form only a small part of the former. Similarly, the transaction costs are also reduced by institutional factors such as path dependency, scale economies, and institutional synergy (Saleth and Dinar 2004). For instance, the prior existence of institutional elements such as water rights and user organizations makes it easy for water markets to emerge. This means that the costs of undertaking subsequent institutional reforms tend to decline as the reform reaches higher and higher stages (Saleth and Dinar 2006).

Due to their influence on either the opportunity or transaction costs, the endogenous and exogenous factors play a major role in triggering water institutional reforms, thereby paving the way for the process of institutional change and adaptation. The relative importance of these factors in the recent reform initiatives observed in six countries is shown in Table 11.2. Although water scarcity and conflicts remain the underlying force for reforms in all cases, there is variation in the immediate factor(s) that trigger the reforms across the countries. For instance, in Australia, the reform trigger came from salinity, drought, and macroeconomic reforms. In Mexico and Sri Lanka, the macro economic crisis of the

Table 11.2 Relative roles of factors behind water governance reforms

Particulars	*Australia*	*Chile*	*Morocco*	*Namibia*	*South Africa*	*Sri Lanka*
Water scarcity/conflicts	**	*	**	**	**	*
Financial crisis	*	**	**	***	*	***
Draughts/salinity	***	–	***	*	**	–
Macro-economic reforms	***	**	***	–	–	***
Political reforms	–	***	–	***	***	*
Social issues	*	–	*	**	**	–
Donor pressures	–	*	**	*	–	***
Internal/External agreements	***	–	–	*	*	–
Institutional synergy/pressures	**	***	*	*	*	*

Note: The number of asterisks signifies the relative importance of the factors in the context of each country. A dash means that the aspect in question is not applicable or not evaluated.

Source: Saleth and Dinar (2005)

1980s was the dominant trigger for water institutional reforms. In Chile and South Africa, dramatic political change provided the necessary trigger for water institutional reforms. In Morocco, physical scarcity of water due to a near-exhaustion of freshwater was the main trigger. The water institutional reforms in Namibia were part of the economic and political reorganization of the country following its independence in 1990.

Despite the political difficulties, institutional change and adaptation have occurred in many countries both due to the natural process of institutional evolution as well as due to the purposive reforms undertaken by the state. The institutional change and reform processes have improved the appropriateness of their water governance arrangements in many contexts. Specific reforms observed across countries include the creation of basin organizations, promotion of user organizations, and decentralization to promote stakeholder participation, privatization of urban and agricultural irrigation water supplies, establishment of water rights system, promotion of inter and intra-sectoral water markets, reorientation of water prices, and implementation of water-quality regulations (Saleth and Dinar 2000, 2006).

The general thrust of institutional change and adaptation is indeed positive from a long-term historical perspective. But, they are far from adequate for creating the governance arrangements that are required for meeting the current and future realities of the water sector in many countries. From an overall perspective, some countries (e.g., Australia and Chile as well as regions like California and Colorado in the United States) already have a relatively more effective water governance configuration. Others (e.g., Spain, Mexico, Chile, South Africa, Brazil, and China) are moving quickly to develop the institutional potential needed for effective governance, whereas the remaining countries (e.g., India, Pakistan, Sri Lanka, Indonesia) have a long way to go in creating more appropriate water governance arrangements (Saleth and Dinar 2004). The occurrence of reforms and the difference in their extent and speed observed across countries can be explained in terms of the factors related to the institutional principles (path dependency and the structural and spatial embeddedness) and the transaction cost theory that we have discussed at the start of this section.

Concluding remarks and policy implications

There is no particular governance typology that is appropriate to all contexts. Some governance typologies are relatively more effective than their counterparts in particular contexts and in achieving specific goals. Some are good for efficiency while others are good for equity. Similarly, for some functions such as planning and regulation, centralized forms may be better on scale-economic and technical considerations. But, for other functions such as allocation of day-to-day management, decentralized and market or negotiation-based arrangements are better in terms of their flexibility. From a general perspective, however, the different governance forms remain complementary to each other as they often operate side-by-side or hierarchically. As a result, cooperative relationships among various governance forms, representing complementary logics and functions, will provide a more durable solution (Blatter and Ingram 2000). In this sense, rather than being dogmatic, it is more realistic to look for a more appropriate mix or configuration of governance forms that can fit well with the governance environment as characterized by varying economic, resource, technical, and institutional conditions prevailing across sources, sectors, regions, or countries.

As to the appropriate governance forms for the Americas, the answer depends on how different the water challenges facing the countries in this region are, as compared to other countries in the rest of the world. In many respects, the countries in the Americas face, more or less, the same set of water problems as found elsewhere in the world. However, there are also a few but very important distinctions.

First, the American continent, taken as a whole, is blessed with a relatively abundant water supply condition. But, there are vast regional variations in water supply and demand. For instance, the regions such as the western parts of the United States, the northeastern region in Brazil, northern Mexico, the coastal region of Peru, and southern parts of Chile face severe water scarcity as water demand far exceeds the available supply.

Second, the demographic pressure on water resources is relatively lower as compared to other continents. But, the population concentration due to urbanization is more intense in the Americas, especially in South America, as urban areas account for more than 75 percent of the total population. As a result, with the exception of few regions, the water sector is oriented more towards the urban, industrial, and mining sectors than the agricultural sector.

Third, with the exception of Australia and a few countries in Europe, most countries in the American continent have a relatively more mature water institutional arrangement with a relatively advanced water law and policy framework and water management organizations.

Fourth, similarly, they also display a relatively stronger orientation towards the private sector (in urban water supply) and market-based allocation (in agricultural sector). But, the state also plays a more constructive role both in water planning and regulation as well as in facilitating more decentralized institutional arrangements such as irrigation districts, river basin organizations, and institutional framework for stakeholder participation.

Fifth, unlike countries such as India and China, groundwater use in the Americas is not that widespread but confined only to a few regions such as the Ogallala aquifer in the United States.

Finally, unlike many countries in Asia, the Middle East, and North Africa, where water quantity is the dominant problem, the countries in the Americas have an equal focus on both water quantity and water quality.

Despite these distinguishing features of the water sector in the Americas, the main characteristics of the institutional arrangements appropriate for this region remain, more or less, the same as those appropriate for most countries in the world. Considering the diversity of economic and resource conditions present in the Americas, no single governance form can be advocated as "the solution." Multiple and poly-centric governance forms are needed to meet different regional and sectoral requirements. Indeed, such a governance configuration has actually evolved in this region over time. For instance, in most of the water-scarce but agriculturally advanced regions, market and user-based governance forms have already emerged. Notably, these governance forms are operating within the general framework of state-based regulatory and enforcement arrangements. In California, for instance, 80 percent of inter-regional water transfers within the state were facilitated by the state-managed water conveyance networks. The state has not only promoted water banks to manage inter-year variations in water supply but also entered into the water market as a key player for buying water for meeting environmental needs.

Water markets have also emerged in countries such as Canada, Chile, Brazil, and Mexico. Basin organizations, watershed committees, and irrigation districts have also been developed to institutionalize stakeholder participation in water allocation and management decisions. In countries such as Mexico and Columbia, irrigation management has been transferred to user associations. In urban water supply, Latin America and the Caribbean regions account for 67 percent of the total public–private partnership arrangements observed at the global level. Corporatization of urban water supply entities and provision of autonomy to municipal and local water supply units have enhanced the user coverage, service quality, and financial performance. Despite the general tendency towards market, private, and user-based governance forms, in the areas of water resource planning and development as well as environmental and water quality protection, the state and the state-based organizations continue to play a dominant role. Thus, the actual situation in the water sector of the countries in the Americas can be characterized as a multiple and poly-centric water governance system. But, just as the present governance configuration is the outcome of historical evolution, the future configuration will also evolve as an adaptive response to water scarcity and other economic and institutional requirements. However, judging by the trend observed so far, the optimal governance configuration for the countries in the Americas will become more and more oriented towards market, user, and private sector-based governance forms as compared to their counterparts in the rest of the world.

References

Blatter, J. and Ingram, H. M. (2000) "States, Markets and Beyond: Governance of Transboundary Water Resources." *Natural Resources Journal* 40: 439–52.

Bromley, D. W. (1989) *Economic Interests and Institutions: The Conceptual Foundations of Public Policy*. New York: Basil Blackwell.

—— (1992) *Making the Commons Work*. San Francisco, CA: Institute for Contemporary Studies.

Brown, F. L. and Ingram, H. M. (1987) *Water and Poverty in the Southwest*. Tucson, AZ: Arizona University Press.

Colby, B. G. and Bush, D. B. (1987) *Water Markets in Theory and Practice*. Boulder, CO: Westview Press.

Cosgrove, W. J. and Rijsberman, F. R. (2000) *World Water Vision: Making Water Everybody's Business*. London: Earthscan.

Davilla, A. and Whiteford, A. (2009) "Water, Water, Everywhere?: Legal Structures for Contracting and Privatization of Public Water Resources." *Missouri Environmental Law and Policy Review* 15(1): 49–65.

Dinar, A., Rosegrant, M. and Meinzen-Dick, R. (1997) *Water Allocation Mechanisms: Principles and Examples*. World Bank Policy Research Working Paper 1779. Washington, DC: World Bank.

Falkenmark, M. and Lindh, G. (1993) "Water and Economic Development." In P. H. Gleick (ed.), *Water in Crisis: A Guide to the World's Fresh Water Resources*, pp. 80–91. New York: Oxford University Press.

Franks, T. (2004) *Water Governance: What is the Consensus?* Paper prepared for the ESRC-funded seminar on The Water Consensus: Identifying the Gaps, Bradford Centre for International Development, Bradford University, November 18–19. Available at www.bradford.ac.uk/acad/des/seminar/water/seminar1/papers/Franks_Water_Governance_04_11_15.pdf (accessed May 7, 2010).

Garrido, A. (1997) "A Mathematical Programming Model Applied to the Study of Water Markets within the Agricultural Sector." Paper presented at the 8th European Agricultural Economists Association Congress, Edinburgh, UK.

Gassner, K., Popov, A. and Pushak, N. (2009) *Does Private Sector Participation Improve Performance in Electricity and Water Distribution?* Washington, DC: World Bank.

Gleick, P. H. (1993) "Water in the Twenty-First Century." In P. H. Gleick (ed.), *Water in Crisis: A Guide to the World's Fresh Water Resources*, 105–14. New York: Oxford University Press.

GWP (2000) *Towards Water Security: A Framework for Action*. Stockholm: Global Water Partnership.

Huitema, D. and Bressers, H. (2007) *Scaling Governance: The Case of the Implementation of the European Water Framework Directive in the Netherlands*. Available at www2.bren.ucsb.edu/~idgec/papers/David_Huitema.pdf (accessed May 7, 2010).

Keohane, R. and Ostrom, E. (eds) (1995) *Local Commons and Global Interdependence: Heterogeneity and Co-operation in Two Domains*. New York: Sage Publications.

Kooiman, J. (ed.) (1993) *Modern Governance: New Government–Society Interactions*. New York: Sage Publications.

Lynne, G. D. and Saarinen, P. (1993) "Melding Private and Public Interests in Water Rights." *Journal of Agriculture and Applied Economics* 25: 69–83.

Maass, A. and Anderson, R. L. (1978) *. . . and the Desert Shall Rejoice*. Cambridge, MA: MIT Press.

Marin, P. (2009) *Public–Private Partnerships for Urban Water Utilities: A Review of Experiences in Developing Countries*. Washington, DC: World Bank.

Meinzen-Dick, R. and Mendoza, M. (1996), "Alternative Water Allocation Mechanisms: Indian and International Experiences." *Economic and Political Weekly* 31(13): A25–A30.

Menard, C. (2009) "Why to Reform Infrastructures and with What Institutional Arrangements? The Case of Public–Private Partnerships in Water Supply." In R. Kunneke, J. Groenewegen, and J. F. Auger (eds), *The Governance of Network Industry*. Cheltenham: Edward Elgar Publishing.

Menard, C. and Saleth, R. M. (2010) "The Effectiveness of Alternative Water Governance Arrangements." Background paper prepared for the: *Greening the World Economy* report. Geneva: United Nation Environment Programme.

Moccia, S. (2007) *Beyond the Public–Private Binary: Cooperatives as Alternative Water Governance Models*. MA Thesis, Faculty of Geography, University of British Columbia, Vancouver, Canada. Available at http://hdl.handle.net/2429/284 (accessed May 7, 2010).

North, D. C. (1990) *Institutions, Institutional Change, and Economic Performance*. Cambridge: Cambridge University Press.

Ostrom, E. (1990) *Governing the Commons: The Evolution of Institutions for Collective Action*. Cambridge: Cambridge University Press.

Ostrom, E., Burger, C. J., Field, B., Norgaard, R. B., and Policansky, D. (1999) "Revisiting the Commons: Local Lessons, Global Challenges." *Science* 284(5412): 278–82.

Palaniappan, M. (2004) "Water Privatization Principles and Practices." In P. H. Gleick (ed.), *The World's Water: The Biennial Report on Fresh Water Resources*. Washington, DC: Island Press.

Palanisami, K. (2009) "Water Markets as a Demand Management Option: Potentials, Problems, and Prospects." In R. M. Saleth (ed.), *Promoting Irrigation Demand Management in India: Potentials, Problems, and Prospects*. Colombo: International Water Management Institute.

Perard, E. (2009) "Water Privatization: An Analysis of the Choice between Public and Private Water Supply." Ph.D. thesis, Institut de Sciences Politiques, Paris.

Postel, S. L. (1999) *Pillars of Sand: Can the Irrigation Miracle Last?* New York: W. W. Norton.

Repetto, R. (1986) *Skimming the Water: Rent-Seeking and the Performance of Public Irrigation Systems*. Research report no. 4. Washington, DC: World Resources Institute.

Rogers, P. and Hall, A. W. (2003) *Effective Water Governance*. Global Water Partnership TEC Paper no. 7. Stockholm: Elanders Novum.

Rosegrant, M. W. and Binswanger, H. P. (1994) "Markets for Tradable Rights: Potential for Efficiency and Developing Country Water Allocation." *World Development* 22(11): 1613–25.

Rosegrant, M. W. and Schleyer, R. G. (1994) *Tradable Water Rights: Experiences in Reforming Water Allocation Policy*. Arlington, VA: United States Agency for International Development.

Saleth, R. M. (1994) "Groundwater Markets in India: A Legal and Institutional Perspective." *The Indian Economic Review* 29(2): 157–76.

—— (2004) *Strategic Analysis of Water Institutions: An Application of a New Paradigm for India*. Research Report 97. Colombo: International Water Management Institute.

Saleth, R. M. and Dinar, A. (2000) "Institutional Changes in Global Water Sector: Trends, Patterns, and Implications." *Water Policy* 2(3): 175–99.

—— (2004) *The Institutional Economics of Water: A Cross-Country Analysis of Institutions and performance*, Cheltenham: Edward Elgar Publishing.

—— (2005) "Water Institutional Reforms: Theory and Practice." *Water Policy* 7(1): 1–16.

—— (2006) "Water Institutional Reforms in Developing Countries: Insights, Evidences, and Case Studies." In R. Lopez and M. Toman (eds), *Economic Development and Environmental Sustainability: New Policy Options*. New York: Oxford University Press.

Shah, T. (1993) *Groundwater Market and Irrigation Development*. Bombay: Oxford University Press.

Tropp, H. (2007) "Water Governance: Trends and Needs for New Capacity Development." *Water Policy* 9(Supplement 2): 19–30.

United Nations (2005) *World Urbanization Prospects: The 2005 Revision*. New York: Population Division, Department of Economic and Social Affairs, United Nations.

Vermillion, D. (1997) *Impact of Irrigation Management Transfer: A Review of Evidences*. Research Report no. 11. Colombo: International Water Management Institute.

Wade, R. (1982) "The System of Political and Administrative Corruption: Canal Irrigation in South India." *Journal of Developing Studies* 18(3): 278–328.

12 Innovations in agricultural groundwater management

Examples from India

Tushaar Shah

Groundwater and global agriculture

Rapid growth in groundwater use is a central aspect of the world's water story, especially since 1950. Shallow wells and muscle-driven lifting devices have been in vogue in many parts of the world for the millennia. In British India (which included today's India, Pakistan, and Bangladesh), wells accounted for more than 30 percent of irrigated land even in 1903 when only 14 percent of cropped area was irrigated (HMSO 1905). With the rise of the tubewell and pump technology, groundwater use soared to previously unthinkable levels after 1950. In Spain, groundwater use increased from 2 km^3 per year to 6 km^3 during 1960–2000 before it stabilized (Martinez Cortina and Hernandez-Mora 2003). In the United States, groundwater share in irrigation has increased, from 23 percent in 1950 to 42 percent in 2000 (Hutson *et al.* 2004). In the Indian sub-continent, groundwater use soared from around 10–20 km^3 before 1950 to 240–260 km^3 today. Data on groundwater use are scarce; however, Figure 12.1 attempts to backcast the probable trajectories of growth in groundwater use in selected countries. In the United States, Spain, Mexico, and north African countries like Morocco and Tunisia, total groundwater use peaked during the 1980s, or thereabouts. In south Asia and the North China Plains, the upward trend began during the 1970s and is still continuing. A third wave of growth in groundwater use is likely in the making in many regions of Africa and in some south and southeast Asian countries such as Vietnam and Sri Lanka.

Clearly, until 50 years ago, groundwater's role in agriculture was insignificant in much of today's developing world. But today, the situation is vastly different. Table 12.1 provides a recent global estimate of irrigated areas in different parts of the world and the share of groundwater in irrigated areas. This shows that more than one-third of the world's irrigated areas of 303 million hectares is served by groundwater. The Food and Agriculture Organization of the United Nations (FAO) estimates are based on figures provided by governments of member states. In South Asia, it is common knowledge that groundwater-irrigated areas are seriously underestimated, and surface-irrigated areas are seriously over-estimated. The same situation occurs in China, another major groundwater irrigating country, where estimates of groundwater-irrigated areas are being

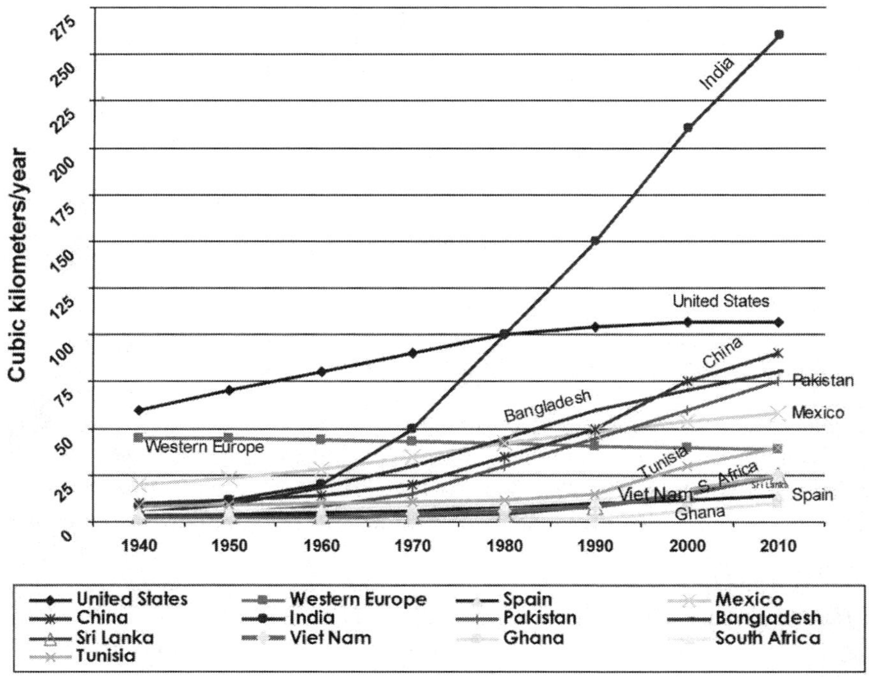

Figure 12.1 Growth in groundwater use in selected countries

Source: author's estimate

Table 12.1 Part of total area equipped for irrigation by groundwater

Continent regions	*Area equipped for irrigation*		
	Total (*thousand ha*)	*Groundwater* (*thousand ha*)	*Gw as % of total (% of the word groundwater irrigated area) (%)*
World	300,895	112,936	37.5 (100%)
Africa	13,576	2,506	18.5 (2.3%)
Americas	48,904	21,548	44.1 (19.3%)
Asia	211,796	80,582	38.0 (70.8%)
Europe	22,652	7,350	32.4 (6.6%)
Oceania	3,967	950	23.9 (0.8%)

Source: Shah (2014)

constantly revised upwards (Shah 2009). As more research results become available, it is becoming clear that in much of Africa, too, informal groundwater irrigation in the private sector is booming while many public irrigation systems are stagnant (Giordano 2006). In actual terms, groundwater is likely even more important in global agriculture today than FAO numbers suggest.

Structure of the global groundwater economy

While groundwater use in agriculture is growing around the world, the drivers of this growth are different in different parts with different implications on resource productivity and governance regimes. For a long time, water scientists believed that groundwater irrigation would intensify only in arid or semi-arid areas of the world, such as California which, except for a shortage of rainfall and surface water, are otherwise ideal for agriculture. But booming groundwater irrigation in humid Bangladesh and eastern India questions this argument. Many scientists also thought that intensive groundwater irrigation would sustain only in alluvial aquifers that are constantly recharged by floods (e.g., Ganga basin) or canal irrigation (e.g., Indus Basin Irrigation System) and not in hard rock aquifers with low storage and yield. But rapid expansion of groundwater irrigation hard rock peninsular India defies this hypothesis. Henry Vaux has argued that "sustained depletion of groundwater aquifers is self-terminating" because rising pumping costs would make groundwater use unsustainable. However, such depletion has been sustained in South Asia and Mexico by farmers organizing into powerful political-interest groups to extract power subsidies for groundwater pumping (Shah 2009). All in all, groundwater irrigation dynamic varies around the world in keeping with the changing socio-ecological context.

Four broad types of global groundwater socio-ecologies can be identified around the world as in Table 12.2: arid agrarian systems, industrial agricultural systems, groundwater-supported extensive pastoralism, and smallholder intensive farming systems. These differ from one another in their overall climatic, hydrologic, and demographic parameters, their land-use patterns, their organization of agriculture, and the relative importance of irrigated and rain-fed farming. Also different are the drivers of expansion in groundwater irrigation in these areas and the nature and level of these societies' stake in their groundwater-irrigated agriculture.

In the mostly arid countries of the Middle East and north Africa (MENA), water scarcity is the key driver of groundwater irrigation. The challenge here is of striking the balance between present versus future use and irrigation versus urban uses of what is mostly non-renewable fossil groundwater. Even industrialized countries – such as Spain, Italy, the United States and Australia – groundwater in some areas suffer from depletion as well as pollution from agriculture, but it supports high-value export agriculture. These countries bring together vast financial and scientific resources to agricultural groundwater management; as a result, it is here that much of today's scientific and institutional knowledge base for groundwater management has evolved and has been tested.

Table 12.2 Global typology of groundwater use in agriculture and animal husbandry

System	*Arid agrarianism*	*Industrial agriculture*	*Smallholder intensive farming*	*Extensive pastoralism*
Region	Middle East and North Africa[a]	US, Australia, Spain, Italy, Mexico	Monsoon Asia[b]	West and sub-Saharan Africa
Groundwater-irrigated area	< 6 million ha	15 million ha	> 100 million ha	> 500 million ha of grazing land
Climate	Arid	Semiarid	Semiarid to humid; monsoon	Arid to semiarid
Water resources per person	Very small	Good to very good	Moderate to good	Moderate to good
Population pressure on agricultural land	Low to medium	Low to very low	High to very high	Low, with high pressure on grazing areas
Percentage of geographic area under cultivation	1–5%	5–50%	40–60%	5–8%
Percentage of cultivated areas under irrigation	30–90%	2–15%	40–70%	> 5%
Percentage of irrigated areas under groundwater irrigation	40–90%	5–20%	10–60%	< 1%
Percentage of geographic area under groundwater irrigation	0.12–4.0%	0.001–1.5%	1.6–25.0%	< 0.001%[c]
Organization of agriculture	Medium size, market-based	Industrial, export-oriented farming	Smallholder farming and intensive diversification	Small-scale pastoralism, smallholder farming
Driver of groundwater irrigation	Lack of alternative irrigation	Wealth-creating agriculture	Land-augmenting, labor-absorbing agriculture	Stock watering
Groundwater contribution to national economy	Low: < 2–3% of GDP	Low: less than 0.5% of GDP	Moderate: 5–20% of GDP	Moderate: 5–20% of GDP
Groundwater contribution to national welfare	Low to moderate	Low to very low	40–50% of rural population, 40–80% of food supply	High for extensive pastoralism, domestic water supply, and smallholder agriculture

Table 12.2 continued

System	*Arid agrarianism*	*Industrial agriculture*	*Smallholder intensive farming*	*Extensive pastoralism*
Groundwater contribution to poverty reduction	Moderate	Very low	Very high	Central to pastoral livelihoods
Gross output supported by groundwater (US$)	$6–8 billion	$100–120 billion	$250–300 billion	$2–3 billion

Notes: [a]Iran, Iraq, Libya, Tunisia, Morocco, Turkey, Algeria, Egypt.
[b]India, Pakistan, Nepal, Bangladesh, North China, Afghanistan.
[c]Groundwater-supported grazing areas for stock watering are about 17% of total area (Giordano 2006).

Source: FAO Aquastat Global Map of Irrigated Areas (www.fao.org/ag/agl/aglw/aquastat/irrigationmap/index.stm)

In Sub-Saharan Africa and Latin America agricultural groundwater use is small not only in absolute terms but also in relation to available (known) potential. However, groundwater is becoming increasingly significant for supporting smallholder agriculture and the livestock economy that supports millions of poor people in Sub-Saharan Africa. In none of these three regions, however, is the groundwater dynamic as complex and overwhelming as in smallholder intensive farming system of Monsoon Asia. Explosive growth in agricultural groundwater use in South Asia and China is driven less by water scarcity and more by land scarcity, making it imperative for smallholders to intensify their land use to protect their livelihoods. India, Pakistan, Bangladesh, Nepal, and China likely account for more than 70 percent of global annual groundwater diversion of around 1,000 cubic km; and it is here that some of the worst consequences of groundwater overdraft are visible in large and growing pockets. The rise of water-scavenging atomistic irrigation by millions of private tubewell owners defines the resource management challenge here. True, supply-side factors, such as government subsidies for pumps and electricity, helped promote intensive groundwater irrigation, but the primary driver is the rise in population pressure on farmland, which has made intensive diversification a precondition for smallholder subsistence – something unlikely ever to occur in the other three socio-ecologies.

In all the four groundwater socio-ecologies, a variety of environmental and economic externalities associated with groundwater intensification are observed in some pockets. In the Smallholder Intensive Farming Systems, however, these externalities are a norm rather than exception and encompass vast areas. The most common is depletion of alluvial as well as hard rock aquifers signified by secular decline in groundwater levels. This in turn gives rise to soaring pumping costs, increasing investments required in installing new tubewells, interference among wells, and so on. Also evident on a large scale are other symptoms: drying up of wetlands, declining low-flows in rivers and streams, secondary salinization and increase in the concentration of geogenic contaminants such as fluoride, arsenic and nitrates in groundwater which is the main source of drinking water supplies. Flourosis and arsenicosis are considered major public health risks in large areas of South Asia and China. All these externalities have put into bold relief urgent need to put into place a groundwater governance regime that minimizes ill-effects while sustaining the massive poverty-reduction benefits that the groundwater boom has produced in Asia.

Groundwater governance discourse worldwide is a product of the growing threat of water scarcity, which has made the transition from resource development to resource management mode critical. In this transition, groundwater – an invisible, fungible resource – has proven to be particularly difficult, and although the western United States, Spain, Mexico, and other countries offer lessons about attempts to craft groundwater governance regimes, nowhere are the outcomes fully satisfactory. However, as the groundwater question becomes more pressing, South Asian policymakers must understand what has been tried elsewhere and ask what has (or has not) worked and why (or why not). To this end, the following sections briefly review the experience with five major groundwater governance instruments, each of which seeks to directly influence the actions and behavior of users.

Instruments of groundwater governance

Administrative regulation

Governments in many countries, notably Oman, Iran, Saudi Arabia, Israel, and countries in South Asia have often used laws and administrative regulation to control agricultural groundwater draft. These have worked when the state is strong – even authoritarian – and the number of groundwater users is small, as in Oman. However, almost everywhere else, administrative regulation of agricultural groundwater use has been generally poor because of lack of three essential needs: popular support, political will, and enforcement capacity.

Economic instruments

Using a price or a Pigovian tax is generally considered a superior method of influencing human behavior rather than using coercion or invoking eminent domain. In China, pricing has been important in managing urban groundwater demand. Pricing works best when it is easy to measure and monitor groundwater abstractions; that is, where abstractors are few and large. Where groundwater abstractors are small, numerous, and poor groundwater pricing becomes difficult to administer without awkward use of force. Jordan had to create a water police to install meters on deep tubewells and enforce pricing. As a result, while the principle of "scarcity pricing" is widely accepted, its actual practice has proved difficult in the developing world.

Tradable property rights

In the New World countries like the United States and Australia, secure property rights were essential to encourage settlers to make private investment in land and water development during eighteenth and nineteenth centuries. Groundwater governance in these countries is based on the premise that users *can* evolve regimes for self-governance of water resource with the state, providing an overarching regulatory and facilitative framework. The institution of tradable property rights in water is the basis for such self-governance. The experience of the United States has given birth to a growth industry for promoting tradable water rights as a one-stop solution problems of groundwater misgovernance. The ultimate result of creating tradable rights in groundwater, however, is by no means clear in the United States or elsewhere. The impact of introducing tradable water rights in Chile has been vigorously lauded as well as roundly criticized. As with pricing, with tradable property rights, too, there is no gainsaying the principle that these can result in superior allocation of scarce groundwater. The real problem is the transaction cost of enforcement, which rise in geometric progression with the number of users. Because transaction costs matter, groundwater institutions in the United States and Australia carefully exempt numerous *de minimis* users to reduce transaction cost of institutional management of groundwater to manageable levels. However, if India or China were to exempt *de minimis* users that are exempted say in Kansas, Nebraska, and Australia, more than 95 percent of groundwater users would fall through the sieve.

Community aquifer management

Mexico and Spain have adapted the United States' experience of tradable water rights and groundwater districts to promote groundwater management through farmers' organizations. Spain's 1985 water act made basin-level groundwater federations responsible for resource planning and management. Similarly, Mexico's 1992 Law of the Nation's Water created aquifer management councils, known as COTAS, for groundwater management. While the idea has great merit, the implementation of this mandate has proven to be difficult in Spain as well as Mexico. While Mexican COTAS have played a useful role in information generation and farmers' education, the effectiveness in managing groundwater overdraft has been poor.

Crowding out tubewells through supply augmentation

Instead of relying on demand-management, developing alternative water sources has been one of the most effective and time-tested approaches for easing agricultural pressure on stressed aquifers. In the Western United States, imported surface water supplied in lieu of groundwater pumping has been a central feature of groundwater governance for decades. The central Arizona approach is one example; but there are many other federally supported projects that import surface water to ease pressure on and/or recharge groundwater aquifers. Spain's much-proposed water transfer project from Ebro River, China's south-to-north water transfer project, and India's proposed project to link Himalayan with peninsular rivers are all inspired in part by groundwater depletion and stress. The fact that the supply side initiative is used more widely signifies the huge implementation difficulties in direct demand of groundwater management in developing countries.

Groundwater governance in smallholder intensive agriculture systems

Can a groundwater cess or a system of groundwater entitlements or a powerful groundwater law restore order in South Asia's irrigation economy? In theory, yes. The problem is how to make any or all of these actually work on the ground, given the atomistic nature of the subcontinent's irrigation economy. In Mexico, Spain, and even the United States, according to their own researchers, practice has defeated the precept, even though their groundwater economies are much smaller and simpler than South Asia's. Consider the organization of groundwater economies of the six countries listed in Table 12.3, with India on one extreme and the United States on the other. Indian farmers withdraw around 230 billion m^3 of groundwater annually, more than twice as much as the US users do. But India has 100 times more independent diverters of groundwater. In addition more than half of all Indians – compared with less than 2 percent of Americans – will proactively oppose or frustrate any groundwater governance regime that hits their livelihoods. We know that transaction costs of groundwater regulation are determined less by the volume of groundwater used but more by the number of independent users involved in groundwater irrigation.

Table 12.3 Organization of groundwater irrigation economies of selected countries (c.2000)

Country	*Annual groundwater use (km^3)*	*Agricultural groundwater structures (million)*	*Average extraction/ structure (m^3/year)*	*Population dependent on groundwater irrigation (percentage)*	*Average annual farm income per farmworker (US$)*
India	210	17.5	12,000	55–60	~350
Pakistan	55	0.9	60,000	60–65	~400
China	105	4.5	23,000	22–25	~458
Iran	29	0.5	58,000	12–18	~2,200
Mexico	29	0.07	414,285	5–6	3,758
United States	100	0.2	500,000	<1–2	67,800

Source: Shah (2009)

The Murray–Darling basin in Australia is widely acclaimed worldwide as a water governance exemplar. Yet, governing groundwater has challenged Australian water managers; and the Australian Groundwater School at Adelaide says, "Groundwater will be the enduring gauge of this generation's intelligence in water and land management." Many south Asian water country policy makers are hopelessly attracted to the Murray–Darling model but overlook the differences between the Australian and South Asian groundwater economies. Just 5.5 percent of Australia's irrigated area depends on groundwater, compared with more than 60 percent in India and 90 percent in Bangladesh. The 285 to 300 km^3 of groundwater that south Asia withdraws every year to water crops is 50 times what Australia uses. But most importantly, south Asia has 20 million groundwater diverters – 5,000 times more people to whom groundwater governance must speak.

China is discovering the implementation challenge of demand management in a vast and atomistic groundwater economy. Just issuing water withdrawal permits to some 7.5 million tubewell owners is a logistical nightmare, let alone monitoring their withdrawals. Not surprisingly, Wang *et al.* (2007: 53), who recently surveyed 448 villages and 126 townships from 60 counties in Inner Mongolia, Hebei, Henan, Liaoning, Shaanxi, and Shanxi, found that:

> inside China's villages few regulations have had any effect . . . despite the nearly universal regulation that requires the use of a permit for drilling a well, less than 10 percent of the well owners surveyed obtained one before drilling. Only 5 percent of villages surveyed believed their drilling decisions needed to consider spacing decisions . . . Even more telling was that water extraction was not charged in any village; there were no physical limits put on well owners. In fact, it is safe to say that in most villages in China, groundwater resources are almost completely unregulated.

Groundwater management innovations in India

In many countries, especially in India, groundwater over-draft is in effect state-sanctioned. During 1935–1965, governments and international donors were concentrating all their efforts and resources to get reluctant farmers to irrigate with groundwater. Rural electrification investments were justified on the potential that groundwater be offered for agricultural growth. State governments established, and the World Bank funded, large public tubewell programs to provide subsidized groundwater irrigation to farmers. Eventually, when farmers began taking to groundwater irrigation in a big way around 1970, governments offered other incentives: liberal electricity connections, low electricity tariffs, subsidy on irrigation equipment. These seemed justified when the groundwater-led Green Revolution staved off the prospects of a famine. These also seemed justified because subsidized canal irrigation seemed like a huge fraud on rainfed areas; and subsidizing groundwater irrigation in rainfed areas had an equalizing impact of sorts. By mid-1980s, groundwater irrigation was pervasive and well-entrenched in most of India as were the subsidies that came with it. The most important of these was electricity subsidy. Until 1970, a subsidized tariff was collected on a volumetric basis from metered tubewell connections. But the electricity companies found the transaction costs of metering farm power supply too high compared to the amount to be collected. Therefore, most Indian state electricity companies switched from a metered tariff to a flat tariff linked to the horsepower of pumps during 1970s and 1980s. Around this time, politicians also figured out the political clout of groundwater irrigators and began to use farm power pricing and supply as a tool to galvanize them as a "vote-bank." Some chief ministers won elections by offering free power to farmers; others refused to raise flat power tariff for decades, fearing they would lose farmer support.

The original idea of moving from metered tariff to a flat tariff had some logic. The cost of metering millions of tubewells scattered in a vast countryside was high; the cost of reading meters, issuing bills, and recovering dues were high too. Moreover, metering created incentives to pilfer and to manipulate meters that raised the cost of meter maintenance. On the other hand, farmers' demand for power was derived from demand for water; they did not need power 24/7 like domestic and industrial consumers; they could meet their irrigation demand as long as they got a few hours of power supply every day. Rationing farm power supply and charging a break-even flat tariff therefore made sense. But the play of political gamesmanship transformed this sensible second-best scheme into a "degenerate system," which incentivized unfettered over-exploitation of groundwater but at the same time made public sector electricity companies bankrupt. In this sense, one can argue that the over-exploitation of groundwater in many parts of India remains state-sanctioned. Henry Vaux's contention that "groundwater overdraft is self-terminating" would be true in about 20 percent of India's land mass but for the farm power subsidy. Indeed, irrigated agrarian economies in some 100 of India's 650 districts would nearly close down overnight – and groundwater overdraft brought to a halt – if power subsidies were abolished. No politician would accept such a consequence.

Groundwater demand management

On demand-side groundwater management, then, the Indian track record is rather indifferent. The standard bureaucratic response has been to make laws with provisions to regulate new tubewells and the pumping of groundwater. But their enforcement has been abysmal; the sheer numbers of small-scale groundwater users makes even their identification a major logistical exercise, let alone their constant monitoring and regulation. Limited administrative and enforcement capacity is an issue; but even more important has been the reluctance of the government machinery, and actually its sympathy for farmers. Central Groundwater Board categorizes areas (blocks of around 100 villages) according to the state of their groundwater development from white (under-developed) to dark, critical, and over-exploited blocks where known groundwater resource has been fully or over-developed. In theory, new tubewells are banned in the latter areas; yet, come an election, and politicians relax the ban. Most collateral damage associated with groundwater over-development – declining low flows, drying up of wetlands, increasing energy costs, mobilization of harmful salts such as fluoride, etc. – are evident on large and growing tracts of India.

Non-governmental organizations (NGOs) have tried some interesting experiments at demand management. The most notable and widely publicized is Andhra Pradesh Farmer Management of Groundwater Program implemented over a dozen years ago with support from FAO. A recent World Bank report has held out the project as an exemplar in need of outscaling and replication. Basically, the project involved farmer communities in a program of groundwater education and monitoring using simple devices and methodologies. Groundwater data are publicly displayed in real time on Village Panchayat notice boards, and farmers are engaged in discussion on how best to arrange their cropping pattern decisions based on available groundwater. The project managers claim enhanced groundwater literacy and more enlightened decision-making, resulting in reduction in groundwater withdrawals in some 700 villages. The project has now run out of funding support and it is a moot question of how long will the activities sustain on their own.

Governments in India are often more concerned about the damage the groundwater economy is doing to the electricity industry than to the resource and the environment. As in Texas, when it comes to groundwater production, distribution and its externalities, the implicit assumption is "let the locals figure it among themselves." But some states have begun to act to cut the damaging power sector impacts of the groundwater economy. West Bengal's communist government has always championed the cause of farmers but has adopted the classical free-market approach to farm power pricing and supply. It has installed tamper-proof meters on all electrified tubewells, introduced remote meter readers, imposed a time-of-the-day power tariff, and cut farm power subsidies. It could do this for two reasons: it already charged very high flat power tariff that put tubewell owners at the mercy of their water buyers; second, less than 100,000 of its nearly 1 million shallow tubewells are electrified. The capacity of electric tubewell owners to put up political opposition is therefore limited. Early assessments show that this change has transformed West Bengal's groundwater markets from buyers' into sellers' markets. Tubewell owners are emerging as "water lords"; their clients, marginal farmers dependent upon buying water from them can no longer afford the price and instead lease their land to tubewell owners and become share croppers instead (Mukherji *et al.* 2010).

While West Bengal has followed the "best" solution to the energy-irrigation conundrum, Gujarat has chosen a "second best" path based on International Water Management Institute (IWMI) research recommendations. IWMI researchers pointed out that following the West Bengal solution in Gujarat would impose huge political costs because:

- 800,000 out of Gujarat's 1.1 million irrigation tubewells are electrified;
- most of these are pumping groundwater from depths at which diesel pumps would be unviable; and

- Gujarat's groundwater irrigators organize quickly and easily around power supply and pricing issues.

IWMI therefore suggested that groundwater draft as well as power subsidies can be curtailed by "intelligent rationing" of farm power supply. It argued that tubewell owners do not need 24/7 power supply; they would be happy if plenty of quality power was provided to them at times of peak irrigation need. This was not happening. The electricity company was rationing farm power by providing three-phase power for 8–12 hours and one- or two-phase power for the remainder of the day. The assumption was that since irrigation pumps need three-phase power to work, their operation would be restricted to hours of three-phase power. There were many problems with this arrangement, but two were critical. First, the power ration was imposed on non-farm users of heavy-duty equipment, including the cottage industry, hospitals, schools, and such other. Second, farmers used capacitors to run their pumps on two-phase power, thereby reducing the voltage for all downstream users. Thus, while the tubewell irrigators held to ransom the entire rural economy, the electricity company managers, frustrated with farm-consumers, treated them with poor-quality power supply with low-voltage and frequent trips. Everyone was unhappy in this arrangement.

In 2003, Gujarat initiated the Jyotigram Yojna ("lighted village") scheme under which it invested US$250 million to rewire the countryside such that all tubewells were separated from feeders supplying power to non-farm users (see Figure 12.2). With this, it became possible for the electricity company to impose an effective ration on farm power supply on all tubewell irrigators of Gujarat. A

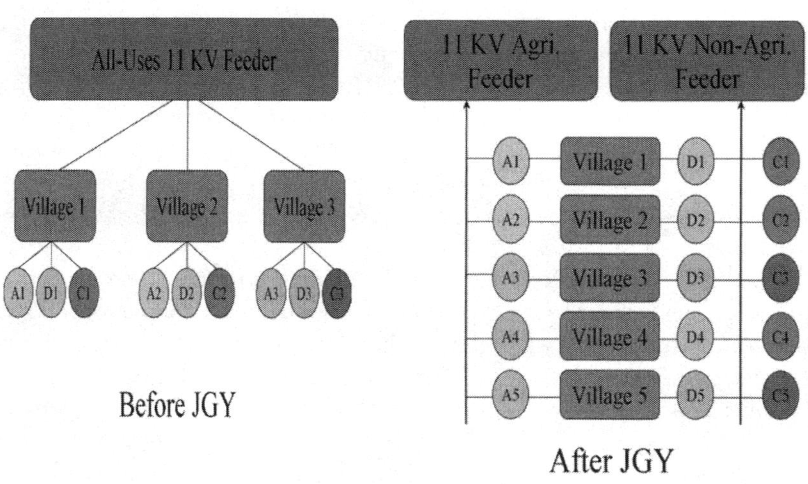

Figure 12.2 Electricity network (a) before and (b) after the Jyotigram Yojna scheme

2008 study showed that this helped to reduce farm power subsidies and groundwater withdrawal significantly (Shah *et al.* 2008). More importantly, it created a "switch-on-off" groundwater economy in which the government had effective leverage to control aggregate groundwater use. This worked both ways: in 2009 when the monsoon was delayed and farmers were getting edgy about completing sowing operations, the government persuaded industries to take a power cut to enhance farmers' power ration. In contrast, during good monsoons, when farmers' irrigation needs are minimal, the electricity company was able to reduce farm power rationing and groundwater draft. Gujarat's solution, though "second best" seems to have resolved major issues reasonably well. The 2008 study referred to earlier found that farmers were generally happy despite strict ration because, following IWMI recommendations, the electricity company now offered them full voltage power with minimal interruption along a schedule that was strictly adhered to.

Supply side groundwater management

Indian farmers, NGOs, and governments have been far more enthusiastic to augmenting the supply of groundwater resources rather than containing its demand and overdraft. This is understandable for several reasons: first, Indian agriculture has come to rely mostly on dynamic, shallow-circulating groundwater – unlike agriculture in, for example, Middle Eastern countries such as Saudi Arabia where the bulk of the groundwater withdrawn by farmers is fossil groundwater. Second, India's high labor availability increases the feasibility of farm and community level rainwater harvesting and management options that would be unattractive to farmers in a country like Australia. Third, the annual groundwater draft in India is just around 5 percent of the country's rainfall, while the natural recharge is 7–10 percent. If farmers can help nature improve its natural groundwater recharge performance, they can make a huge difference to the groundwater balance. Of course, these gross numbers conceal wide regional variations; parts of India in the west and south that get less rainfall withdraw far more groundwater than eastern parts that get most of the rainfall and use little groundwater. Yet, even dry areas of the country get every once in a while massive rainfall events that provide opportunity to recover a part of the accumulated groundwater deficit. Finally, and most importantly, nearly two-thirds of India is underlain by hard rock formations, which have little storage and low transmissivity. Hydro-geologists consider these poor in potential; but farmer communities that try harvesting rainwater and recharge aquifers in many hard rock areas find visible change in water levels in their wells and are able to augment their groundwater supply in times of need. These do not happen in rich alluvial aquifer areas, which have massive aquifer storage (as in Punjab, Haryana, western Rajasthan, and North Gujarat). Community-level groundwater recharge efforts have no visible impacts; and high transmissivity ensures that communities that recharge are able to retrieve very little of the water they put into their aquifers.

This has created a strange paradox in India's groundwater scene. Large pockets of arid alluvial aquifer areas – Punjab, western Uttar Pradesh, Haryana, western Rajasthan, and North Gujarat have excellent aquifers with large storage; yet these are the areas where farming communities depend on "competitive deepening" of their wells to chase declining groundwater levels. In many hard rock areas with intensive groundwater development for irrigation, farming communities have, over the past four decades, moved from unfettered private exploitation of groundwater to recognizing the shared nature of the aquifer space and thence to groundwater adaptive management of water resources at local watershed levels as outlined in Figure 12.3. Forty years ago, there was hardly any interest in groundwater recharge among farming communities that exploited the resource at will. Today, however, harvesting rainfall and using proximate water bodies – including tanks, streams, and canals – for groundwater recharge is becoming increasingly common. In southern India, where irrigation tanks were the mainstay of agriculture for millennia, it is now common for tank communities to seal the sluice gate and convert the irrigation tank into a recharge tank. This is also happening with government canals, which farmers find more useful for recharge than for direct irrigation. The Indian government runs a nation-wide watershed development program to improve soil moisture regime and make rainfed farming productive; however, farmers everywhere judge their efficacy by how much watershed treatment increases water levels in their wells.

By far the best results of farm power rationing combined with a community-based groundwater recharge program on sustainability of groundwater irrigation can be witnessed in Gujarat. Here, a mass movement for groundwater recharge was catalyzed by religious gurus and spiritual leaders after a debilitating drought in 1986–1988 in Saurashtra and Kutch, two of India's driest regions. Early successes fueled popular enthusiasm; voluntary labor was mobilized on a massive scale to modify open wells for recharge, and construct check dams and percolation ponds in thousands. Cement factories offered free cement; and diamond merchants hailing from the area threw in cash contributions. Soon, political leaders spotted a great opportunity to earn recognition and offered support to farmer communities to build community-scale recharge structures in massive numbers. The scheme performed best in the Saurashtra and Kachchh regions. However, for the state as a whole, by December 2008, nearly 500,000 recharge structures were created – 113,738 check dams, 55,917 bori bandhs (sand-bag dams), 240,199 farm ponds, besides 62,532 large and small check dams constructed under the oversight of the Water Resources Department of the Government of Gujarat (Pathak and Shah 2010) – all in a campaign mode.

There is a controversy raging among hydro-geologists about whether this runaway rainwater harvesting is creating much new water and value, mostly because the Saurashtra and Kutch hardrock aquifers have very limited storage. However, farmers in these drought-prone region swear by check-dams; and more than 20 years after the movement began, constructing new check dams has still not gone out of fashion. Other evidence suggests these are helping. Since 2000, when the government of India announced a target of 4 percent annual growth in agriculture while national achievement had barely crossed 2 percent per year,

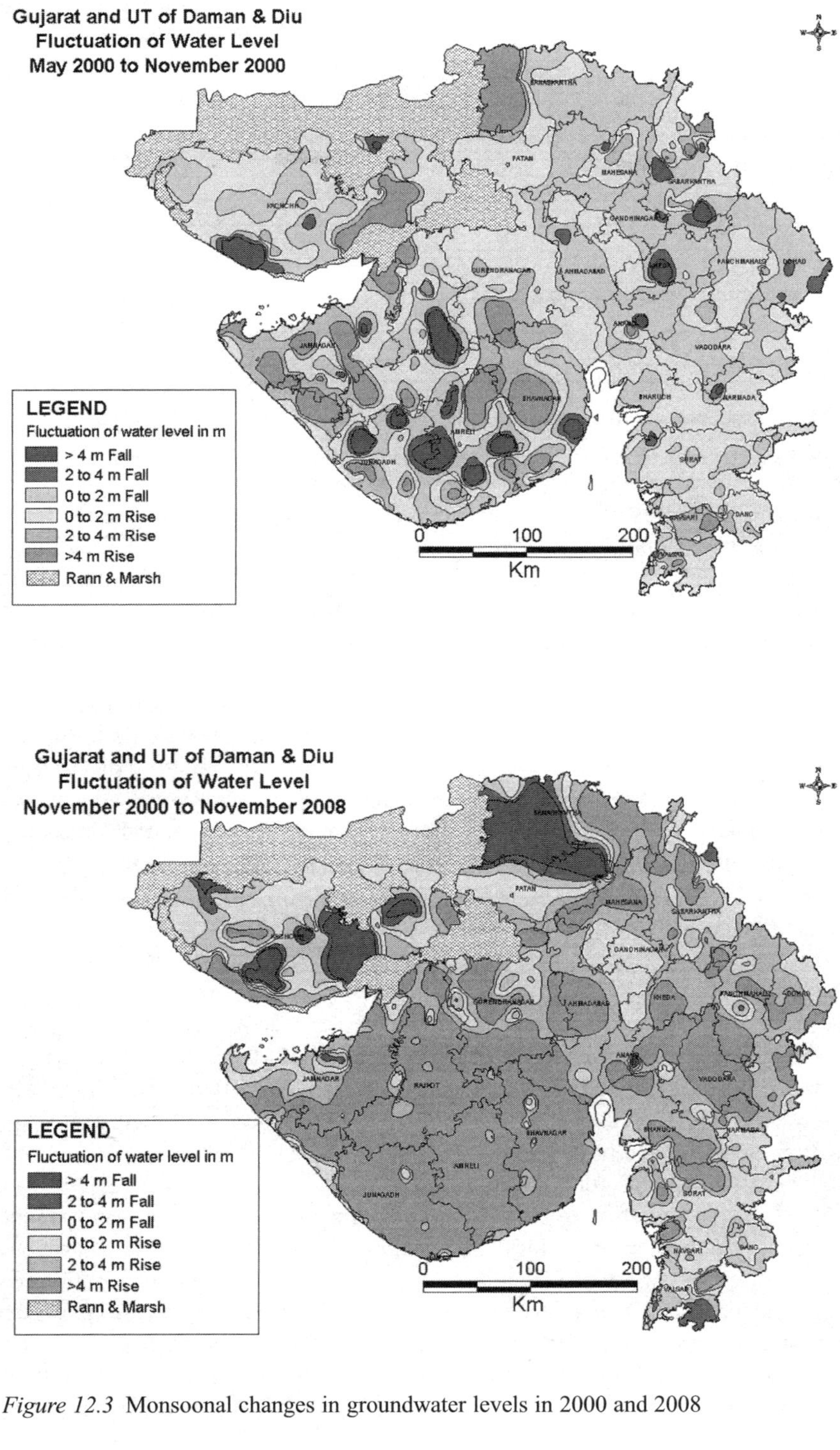

Figure 12.3 Monsoonal changes in groundwater levels in 2000 and 2008

Gujarat posted an agricultural growth rate of a miraculous 9.6 percent during 2000–2008 (Shah *et al.* 2009). This was made possible, among other things, by a 30 percent increase in groundwater-irrigated area. Despite this increased groundwater use in agriculture, Gujarat seems to be the only state in India where the groundwater regime is improving as shown in Figure 12.3. In 2000, large areas were experiencing declining groundwater levels from May through December when they should be rising. But in 2008, areas showing decline were much smaller. A succession of good monsoons helped; but what thousands of community-level recharge structures seem to do is to enhance the drought-resilience that a good rainfall season imparts to the agricultural economy of a region.

Conclusion and policy implications

This chapter covered three things: first, we outlined the shape and structure of the global groundwater irrigation economy; second, we explored the range of groundwater instruments that have been tried out in different parts of the world with varying degrees of success; and third, we specifically examined how India is coping with groundwater over-development issues. We noted that many approaches tried in the industrialized world have great appeal to policy makers in India. However, the structure of India's groundwater economy – with millions of small-scale groundwater users – makes the implementation of such approaches problematic. India's groundwater economy and its management challenges are huge and urgent; and India needs robust approaches that can work in large areas and on large numbers of people immediately. Contrasting approaches to the co-management of groundwater resources and farm power supply tried out in Gujarat and West Bengal offers a robust, quick-acting demand-management tool that has appeal in all regions where the groundwater economy depends on energy subsidies. In West Bengal, electricity price is used as the key tool for groundwater-demand management. In Gujarat, quantity restrictions on farm power supply are the key groundwater-demand management tool.

The Gujarat approach would work if groundwater overdraft is sustained by energy subsidies. In the America's, Mexico is one country in which the Gujarat approach to energy-irrigation nexus may have relevance. Groundwater irrigators in Mexico enjoy a significant power subsidy of around US$1,600 per hectare per year. It can be argued that farmers cannot have subsidized farm power supply in unlimited quantity. A case can be made to raise power prices to farmers or impose a ration on subsidized power supplies – both of which will encourage water use efficiency and curtain groundwater draft.

The Indian NGO effort to organize farmer communities for local management of groundwater in Andhra Pradesh has closely followed the Mexican experiment with Aquifer Management Committees (COTAs). In my assessment, both have merit and produced laudable outcomes by educating farmers on groundwater processes and creating an information base on aquifer characteristics. However, they have common limitations: first, COTAs of Mexico are unlikely to sustain without constant support from the Comisión Nacional de Agua (CAN); likewise, the sustainability of the Andhra Pradesh Farmer Management of Groundwater Project is open to questions now that FAO support has ended. In their regulatory effectiveness, both are slow in producing large-scale results. Finally, it is really doubtful whether on their own, small farmers of India would agree to reduce groundwater use to save it for future generation. When I asked a north Gujarat farmer why he is not saving water for future generations, he quipped, "so that *my* future generation will not need to be farmers."

India, at least hard rock India, will likely take to groundwater centric adaptive management of rainwater and surface water bodies in response to progressive intensification of groundwater irrigation. In tank commands and even command areas of major public canal systems, groundwater wells are fast becoming the prime source of irrigation water. This is because India's small farmers are intensifying their land use by taking two or three crops a year, which wells can support but surface sources cannot. As a result, new tanks/check dams are being dug and existing ones are being modified to enhance recharge. Many public irrigation systems generate more value by keeping the aquifers recharged than by directly irrigating crops. All in all, the groundwater boom is rewriting India's irrigation and water management rulebook.

India's groundwater situation is in many ways unique and different from what is obtained in the Middle East or in the Western and Southern United States and Mexico. Equally unique, therefore, are the responses that India is evolving. Attempts towards copycat transplantation of groundwater management lessons from the industrialized world (tradable property rights, water pricing, etc.) have come unstuck. By the same token, rationing a power supply to reduce groundwater draft may be hardly acceptable to California farmers. Likewise, Texas farmers may be enthusiastic about large-scale transformation of the geomorphology of their landscape to enhance infiltration of rainwater into their aquifers. The upshot of the discussion is that groundwater governance has more to do with people, social structure, and the nature of the state than with groundwater; and to be effective, groundwater governance strategies are best tailored to fit the socioecological specifics of a locale than blindly transplanted from totally different contexts.

References

Giordano, M. (2006) "Agricultural Groundwater Use and Rural Livelihoods in Sub-Saharan Africa: A First-Cut Assessment." *Hydrogeology Journal* 14(3): 310–18.

HMSO (1905) "Statistical Abstract Relating to British India from 1894–95 to 1903–04." Available at http://dsal.uchicago.edu/statistics/1894_excel (accessed March 5, 2014).

Hutson, S. S., Barber, N. L., Kenny, J. F., Linsey, K. S., Lumia, D. S. and Maupin, M. A. (2004) *Estimated Use of Water in the United States in 2000*. Circular 1268. Reston, VA: US Geological Survey. Available at http://pubs.usgs.gov/circ/2004/circ1268/pdf/circular1268.pdf (accessed March 5, 2014).

Martinez Cortina, L. and Hernandez-Mora, N. (2003) "The Role of Groundwater in Spain's Water Policy." *Water International* 28(3): 313–20.

Mukherji, A., Shah, T. and Verma, S. (2010) "Electricity Reforms and Their Impact on

Groundwater Use in States of Gujarat, West Bengal and Uttarakhand, India." In J. Lundqvist (ed.), *On the Water Front: Selections from the 2009 World Water Week in Stockholm*, pp. 100–7.Stockholm: Stockholm International Water Institute.

Pathak, M. and Shah, V. D. (2010) "Five Decades of Gujarat Agriculture: Some Reflections." In R. H. Dholakia and S. K. Dutta (eds), *High Growth Trajectory and Structural Changes in Gujarat Agriculture*, pp. 15–28. New Delhi: Macmillan India.

Shah, T. (2009) *Taming the Anarchy: Groundwater Governance in South Asia*. Washington DC: RFF Press.

Shah, T. (2014) *Groundwater Governance and Irrigated Agriculture: Global Challenges and Emerging Experience*. GWP Background Paper. Stockholm: Global Water Partnership (GWP).

Shah, T., Bhatt, S., Shah, R. K. and Talati, J. (2008) "Groundwater Governance through Electricity Supply Management: Assessing an Innovative Intervention in Gujarat, Western India." *Agricultural Water Management* 95(11): 1233–42

Shah, T., Gulati, A., Pullabhotla, H., Shreedhar, G. and Jain, R. C. (2009) "The Secret of Gujarat's Agrarian Miracle after 2000." *Economic and Political Weekly* 44(52): 45–55.

Wang, J., Huang, J., Blanke, A., Huang, Q. and Rozelle, S. (2007) "The Development, Challenges and Management of Groundwater in Rural China." In M. Giordano and K. G. Villholth (eds), *The Agricultural Groundwater Revolution: Opportunities and Threats to Development*, pp. 37–62. Wallingford: CAB International.

Part VII

Conclusions

13 Water and the Americas

Lessons for the world

Robert W. Sandford

Introduction

Familiar problems are growing more complicated

The message that emerged from the Seventh Biennial Rosenberg International Forum in Buenos Aires was not one of doom but one of caution and of some urgency with respect to how the Western Hemisphere might prepare and act to prevent further crisis with respect to fresh water supply and quality. It was made very clear at this forum that water scarcity is becoming a major issue throughout the Americas. The big problems are all well known from elsewhere in the world. These problems include rapid and expansive urbanization, unsustainable groundwater use; the failure to adequately address the issue of indigenous water rights; and matters related to environmental protection and growing tension over transboundary water issues. All of these problems are to some extent magnified by the realization that past climatic patterns are not likely to be a reliable guide to future climatic patterns.

There appeared to be consensus at the Rosenberg Forum that water policy must respond simultaneously to all these issues if we are to avoid a crisis of scarcity in many places in North, Central, and South America. As some of the places in Central and South America where water scarcity exists now or is likely to appear are politically unstable, this means that such crises may radiate outward to affect the rest of the hemisphere. But even in politically stable regions, the status quo may very well be disturbed first and most dramatically by the loss of stability in hydrological regimes.

Water for cities; water for agriculture

The theme that ultimately dominated the Seventh Biennial Rosenberg International Forum on Water Policy was the problem of rapid urbanization. Explosive urbanization is having unexpected effects on water supply, water quality and sanitation not just within affected municipalities but widely throughout the regions that surround them. We can expect sustained population in the next 40 years, 20 percent by 2030 in the Americas, during which, as participants at the forum pointed out, will express itself in part in increasingly rapid urbanization of our population.

Population growth and rapid urbanization are significant challenges everywhere, but particularly in the Americas. The proceedings of the Rosenberg International Forum on Water Policy in Buenos Aires made it clear that exalting growth for growth's sake can have huge impacts on the quality of life – not just in cities, but in the regions surrounding them. While a great deal of hope has been invested in demographic analyses that suggest a shift is occurring, which is projected to stabilize our global human population at somewhere around 9.4 billion, such projections do not offer much if any solace in the short term.

The preceding chapters of the Water for the Americas symposium make it clear that successful water management in any country demands not only full support from – but the leadership of – municipalities in the establishment, implementation, enforcement and ongoing evaluation of enlightened water management policies. It is very interesting to note that many of the now water-troubled cities in Latin America at one time considered themselves leaders in public supply of high-quality drinking water. It appears that in the 1950s and 1960s cities like Buenos Aires were doing much better than they are today in meeting domestic water supply and sanitation needs. It is instructive to examine what happened over the past 50 years with respect to the management of water in these large Latin American urban municipalities so as to determine the causes of decline in their capacity and reliability.

The first thing that history illustrates is that it is a huge mistake to consider the water available to any municipality as limitless. For a century in Buenos Aires, for example, everyone thought there was so much water that there was no need to conserve it. The public was entitled to use all it wanted for whatever purpose it liked. As a consequence citizens became accustomed to hosing down sidewalks and driveways every day; to elegant green landscaping; and to unlimited domestic use. Such use, in fact, was so widespread for so long it became such an entrenched cultural tradition that the citizens of Buenos Aires would later fight to use water as they please as a right not as a privilege.

The second thing that many major cities in the Western Hemisphere now regret is that they did not charge adequately for water. As water was free – or as close to it as governments could make it – no one thought water had value, which, in turn, amplified wasteful use. As water utilities could not recoup the cost of operation, maintenance, and replacement of their water supply systems, they had to rely on government subsidies when the system needed improvements or expansion. Such subsidies, however, were not forthcoming in times of economic decline, during periods of political instability or inaction, when governments were too far in debt or when government priorities were focused on other crises – which got to be more and more often.

In the midst of such decline, Latin American cities learned very quickly that if you don't supply water, somebody else will. Private water supply companies abound in the Western Hemisphere. They range from big multinationals supplying whole regions to unlicensed individual water vendors selling municipal water from tankers in slums. The cruel irony of poverty is that people living in unserved slums pay five to 10 times more for water than those on municipal service in the same city. If you live on a few dollars a day, that matters. Another irony that many cities in the Western Hemisphere have discovered is that you never know when you are going to be downstream of your own effluent. The use of contaminated wastewater for irrigation can, for example, contaminate groundwater later used for drinking as has happen in and around Mexico City. This is also the almost universal problem associated with contaminated agricultural run-off.

Agricultural run-off has become a serious problem throughout the Americas. Some 75 percent of all the lakes and streams in Latin America have been eutrophied as a result of nutrient loading and pesticide contamination from upstream agricultural areas. Now Buenos Aires has to track algal blooms in the delta of the La Plata River by satellite to know when it can withdraw the drinking water it supplies to most – but not all – of the city.

It is interesting to note that Buenos Aires privatized its water utility when the country changed its constitution in the mid-1990s. A decade later, however, they nationalized that same utility because it did not fulfill its promise to expand services to the millions of people in the city's growing slums and failed in its promise to build the city's proposed sewage treatment plant.

When examined closely, however, it is easy to see what went wrong. Though the private utility had the technical expertise to manage and improve the water distribution system in this city of 12 million, it could not overcome the cumulative difficulties Buenos Aires confronted as a result of decades of inadequate water governance.

These included the following problems. The organizational structure of the water utility was completely inadequate; by law, billing could not reflect actual costs; there were inadequate policies with respect to metering and accounting; the utility had limited ability to collect overdue accounts; and there were system leakages of 40 to 50 percent, depending upon district, and many people were stealing water. Without adequate income, there was no way the utility could act on the results of water-quality monitoring.

Since local government took back the utility, little has changed. If anything, things appear to be getting worse. Highly contaminated groundwater is now oozing to the surface in Buenos Aires eroding building foundations and destroying sewers and roads. People living in unserved slums now number in the millions. On top of all this, the non-stationary of hydrological regimes is making the future uncertain. Climate change has become a serious concern in parts of Latin America. Storms of an intensity that used to occur only once in a century are now hammering places like Buenos Aires every two to four years. Each of these major storms causes hundreds of millions of dollars in flood damage to already run-down water systems.

Cities throughout the Western Hemisphere are also learning that the growing impacts of major floods are often as much a function of transformations of upstream land-use and urbanization, characterized by the uncontrolled expansion of impervious areas and lagging drainage infrastructure as they are expressions of climate change. The maintenance of water-related infrastructure is a major challenge not just in Central and Latin American countries but also in North America throughout the hemisphere. Current water collection, storage and distribution systems were based on nineteenth- and twentieth-century hydrological patterns that in many cases no longer apply and are likely to apply even less in the future in terms of supply reliability, flood risk, health concerns, energy production needs, and aquatic ecosystem function requirements.

There simply isn't enough public money available to keep up with maintenance and expansion of water and sanitation services under current circumstances, let alone to meet the expanded needs many large Western Hemisphere cities will face in 2025.

So what can we learn from these examples? The first thing we learn is that through an unfortunate combination of social, cultural, economic, and environmental factors, it is possible – despite the best of intentions – to lose control of your water supply and distribution systems, which in turn can diminish the quality of life of otherwise prosperous cities. It all starts innocently enough with taking water supply for granted. The myth of limitless abundance is the greatest of all threats to water security, because it makes the populace consumers complacent about how much water they have and how it is managed on their behalf. It allows wasteful habits to become cultural traditions and then inalienable rights for which citizens will often fight bitterly against all common sense to maintain.

The chapters of this volume also demonstrate that even where there is enough for both cities and agriculture, there will not be enough water left for nature in many parts of the world to prevent biodiversity-based planetary life support function from being compromised. Counting on the problem taking care of itself somehow in 2050 is irresponsible. The crisis we hope to avoid in 2050 is already here and will only get worse in the next 40 years.

The challenges facing agriculture are enormous. In the coming decades agriculture will have to find ways to keep producing an adequate amount of healthful, nutritious food for an exploding global population in the face of disappearing fossil fuels and fossil water, declining biodiversity and a more unstable and unpredictable climate. Agriculture is going to have to increase food production dramatically with 50 percent less water and energy, while at the same time reducing its impact. The Green Revolution was largely a genetic revolution. But genetics alone will not address all the problems we face. Irrigation and other farm practices are going to have to change in the future so that we grow food in a way that ceases to cause eutrophication of surrounding streams and rivers and stops creating massive dead zones at the estuaries of our largest rivers.

Tempering provincial and national concerns and narrow self-interest is a chronic problem in the resolution of transboundary water issues throughout the Western Hemisphere. If we can learn anything from international example it is that water management has to go beyond primitive assertion of legal argument in support of parochial interests and supposed legal rights. There is also an urgent need to transcend self-interested competition for water. We have to stop trying to solve scarcity problems by pretending they are isolated supply and delivery issues confined to individual economic sectors as we are doing widely in North America.

Effective water policy should anticipate the combined needs of people, agriculture, and nature 15 years from now in 2025 and be building infrastructure and improving practices so as to anticipate those circumstances now. There is an equally urgent need for integrated resolution of major water issues at regional if not national scales. While it may seem improbable now, it is not inconceivable that cities may eventually pay rural people to provide ecological services we can't afford to provide ourselves or don't know how to reproduce except in nature.

To this end, federal governments may need to play a role like that of the United Nations in efforts to bring provincial, territorial, and other jurisdictions together in service of the common good with respect to water stewardship. It won't be easy, especially in countries like Canada where the federal government is not interested in that role. In many Western Hemisphere countries, industrial and agricultural demands for water are on a collision course with the demands of growing cities and nature's need for water. In many of these countries in it is the government itself that is the biggest obstacle to progressive change.

Our embattled institutions

It is the slowness of institutional adjustments to water scarcity that has made the global water crisis a crisis of governance more than a crisis of absolute water availability. We are not facing water scarcity so much as we are facing water governance scarcity. We learn from what is happening widely in the Western Hemisphere that the failure of governance with respect to water management is often a failure to assert existing authority. Our problem globally appears to be with follow-through. We have yet to arrive at a mechanism for evolving our governance structures fast enough to catch up with the problems we are creating for ourselves through population growth, destruction of biodiversity-based planetary life support function, and climate change.

We have to create effective policies and then act on them until they are implemented and enforced long enough to allow us to evaluate their success. A new focus on water – both as a basic human right and simultaneously as an economic driver – may allow us to reframe the social, economic, environmental, and political benefits of extending water and sanitation services to all. Such a focus could be an impetus for the resolution of uncharacterized and unaddressed indigenous water title and rights as well as equity between rural and urban peoples. But there are limits to the extent to which access to water can be both a human right and an economic good. Given the uncertainties of future water supply and quality, we shouldn't allow private interests to use political means at their disposal to translate a water-use privilege into permanent property rights.

Finally, the participants of the Seventh Rosenberg Forum made it clear that the disparity between North and South is less pronounced in the Western Hemisphere than it is between, say, Europe and Africa. The forum also observed that there have been some very promising developments in terms of transboundary water relations in the Americas. Bold new efforts to jointly manage a major international aquifer are underway on the La Plata River system in South America. The forum also noted that there are still places in North America, such as the Northwest Territories, where it may still be possible to get water governance right from the outset which, if achieved, would suggest hope for the future for all.

Transboundary water issues had a high profile at the forum. Transboundary considerations in two large river basins – one in the Northern Hemisphere and one in the Southern Hemisphere – were examined and compared. The comparison of international examples makes it very clear that cooperation is essential to the long-term success of transboundary relations. We have known for 20 years that no one actor should ever be allowed the power or authority to manage or unilaterally affect an entire transboundary system.

It was also made clear that broader principles must be incorporated into transboundary treaties if such agreements are to remain relevant in changing hydrological circumstances. These principles include integration of surface and groundwater interactions with land-use planning and water management, ecosystem protection, public involvement, collaborative multi-level governance, and the need for adaptability and flexibility in the management of shared waters. Examples from around the world also demonstrate that principles that work at the international level are also applicable at the sub-national level. Strengthened trust and confidence can only emerge through collaboration and public involvement at all levels of basin governance.

By way of these examples, the Rosenberg Forum on Water Policy once again affirmed that strong and persistent political leadership in combination with broad on-going collaboration can make real progress in water governance possible. We see that it is possible to build a durable bridge between science and public policy that will help us successfully address the global water crisis. To do so in time, however, we have to move – and move quickly – if we are to keep up with changes in the way water has begun to move through the global hydrological cycle.

Hydrologic stationarity and water in the Americas

Evidence presented at the Rosenberg International Forum on Water Policy in Buenos Aires also demonstrated that hydrologic stability can no longer be a pivotal assumption in water planning. Rather, it is now understood that what has been defined as non-stationarity – changes in climate from previous patterns – will be the rule for the future.

To appreciate what hydrologic stationarity means and the important role that stationarity plays in modern life, it is important to understand the central function that water plays in our planet's weather and climate system. What is happening is that increased temperatures are changing the way water moves through the global hydrological cycle. Precipitation and other climate patterns are now regularly moving outside the ranges we took as normal in the past.

What this means is that the statistics from the past related to how surface, subsurface and atmospheric water will act under a variety of given circumstances are no longer reliable. The problems this creates are manifold. The stationarity associated with those statistics – the notion that natural phenomena fluctuate within a fixed envelope of certainty – is the foundation of risk assessment in engineering upon which we depend for the construction of our buildings, roads, bridges and other infrastructure. Stationarity is also the foundation for determining insurance rates related to risks associated with the protection of our homes and property from fires, flood, tornadoes, and hurricanes. Stationarity is also the foundation of the reliable function of the natural ecosystem processes that provide a stable and resilient backdrop to human existence.

Past changes demonstrate that climate cycles have occurred regularly on time scales ranging from decades to centuries, and longer, and are most likely to have been caused by oceanic and atmospheric variability, and variability in solar intensity. Taken alone, the consequences of this variability for hydrologic cycles imply that climatic patterns are characterized by non-stationarity. It is clear, however, that while there have been periods of relative stability, there has never been a time in human history when the climate has not been changing to some extent.

Ours is not the first civilization to make the terrible mistake of assuming that the climate experienced over a few generations represented a reliable picture of the climatic circumstances that could be expected over the long term. By building our cities and our shared infrastructure to engineering standards based on climate observations of limited duration, and by developing our agriculture on the same limited climatic assumptions, we are repeating the fatal mistakes previous civilizations have made. We have built our civilization and then rapidly expanded it based upon false assumptions of climate stability. We have failed to fully acknowledge or anticipate either the natural or potential longer-term variability of our global climate.

For all intents and purposes, our basic reality as we knew it in the past has been altered. In a very real way something as fundamental as the gravity of our world has shifted. It is now realized that if we want to be able to predict the future with any kind of reliability, we need a completely new worldview – a new way of understanding the inter-connected, inter-dependent processes of nature, and a new way of relating to planetary systems upon which we depend to make our lives possible and meaningful.

We do not as yet have an adequate replacement for stationarity statistics. We have nothing at the moment that works as well as they once did in helping us feed ourselves, design and build our cities, and plan for the future. Nor have we committed enough resources to explore new ways of coming to terms with what has become a rapidly sliding scale of change in the fundamental conditions of human existence on this planet. Once again, climate change in itself is only one factor influencing the breakdown of modern stationarity. The central problem is not global warming per se, but its growing influence – in combination with other human activities – on hydro-climatic circumstances.

Non-stationarity demands sweeping changes in the way we think about water supply. Until we find a new way of substantiating appropriate action in the absence of stationarity, risks will become increasingly difficult to predict or to price.

To respond to hydrologic non-stationarity, investment is needed in monitoring; in the development of new mathematics-statistics to describe hydro-climatic parameters more accurately so that we can more completely characterize what is actually happening in nature; and in the development of new models that accurately represent our changing hydrology so that we can more successfully predict the frequency, intensity, and duration of extreme weather events such as droughts and floods.

Conclusion

The current water governance situation in the Western Hemisphere suggests that the global water crisis is not going away. The crisis continues to be exacerbated by a number of fundamental problems that appear to be worsening in many parts of the world, including the Western Hemisphere. These problems include relentless population growth and the attendant acceleration of urbanization; the incomplete status and already deteriorating condition of much of the world's water treatment and delivery infrastructure; the widespread and almost uncontrolled extent of groundwater overdraft in many important food-producing areas of the world and some urban areas; the increasingly damaging effects of modern agricultural practices on water quality; the effect of rural poverty on water supplies; unresolved issues related to Indigenous land title and water rights; and the widespread failure of governments to be able to address these matters in a timely and enduring way. All of these problems, unfortunately, are being compounded by the accelerating effects of climate change which, in many places, are occurring much more rapidly than anticipated.

Long before we have even come close to achieving the UN's Millennium Development Goals with respect to reliable water supply for all, we are confronted with the realization that much of the water infrastructure that we have put in place around the world is no longer adequate, and will be even less so in a climate-changed future. Population growth, rapid urbanization, and climate change are poised to overwhelm efforts to meet existing water supply and sanitation goals not only in Latin and Central America but in North America, as well.

We know that solutions exist, and we are employing many of them. Our global strategy makes sense. Extend coverage of potable water and sanitation to all. The goal must be to get water infrastructure in place for the poor – everywhere. We should then concentrate on improving its reliability for all. We must recognize the high economic, social, environmental, health, and political costs of failing to do so.

Index